Fatal Indifference

The G8, Africa and Global Health

Ronald Labonte, Ted Schrecker, David Sanders and Wilma Meeus

Research Assistance:
Jennifer Cushon
Renee Torgerson

UCT
PRESS

International Development Research Centre
Ottawa • Cairo • Dakar • Montevideo • Nairobi • New Delhi • Singapore

Fatal Indifference
© UCT Press and Authors, 2004

Jointly published by
The University of Cape Town Press
PO Box 24309, Lansdowne, 7779, South Africa
uct@juta.co.za/www.jutaacademic.co.za
ISBN 1-91971-384-0

and the
International Development Research Centre
PO Box 8500, Ottawa, ON Canada K1G 3H9
info@idrc.ca/www.idrc.ca
ISBN 1-55250-130-2

Project management: Liesbet van Wyk
Copy editing: FPP Productions
Proofreading: Andrew van der Spuy
Indexing: Marlene Burger
Cover design: Pumphaus Design Studio
DTP and design: Lebone Publishing Services
Printed and bound in the Republic of South Africa by CTP, Parow, Cape Town

Table of Contents

Dedication

To the memory of Eberhard Wenzel (1950–2001). A dedicated academic/activist with a keen analytical capacity and a huge sense of humour, Eberhard developed a website and hosted a listserv on globalization and health from his base at Griffiths University in Brisbane, Australia, that garnered a world-wide readership. His archived materials are still available at: http://www.ldb.org/.

Acknowledgements

Funding for the research undertaken for this book was provided by the International Development Research Centre of Canada (IDRC), Grant # 101241–002. All opinions expressed herein are those of the authors and do not necessarily reflect those of the grant funder.

Ronald Labonte also acknowledges his wife, Lisa Coy, for patience, when it was needed, impatience, when it was required, and enough love and wisdom to know the difference.

Royalties from the sale of this book will go to the Stephen Lewis Foundation, Easing the Pain of HIV/AIDS in Africa.

Table of Acronyms

AFRODAD	African Forum and Network on Debt and Development
C$	Canadian dollar
CAC	Codex Alimentarius Commission
CCIC	Canadian Council for International Cooperation
CCPA	Canadian Centre for Policy Alternatives
CDF	Comprehensive Development Framework
CELS	Centro de Estudios Legales y Sociales
CIDA	Canadian International Development Agency
CMH	Commission on Macroeconomics and Health
DAC	Development Assistance Committee
DALY	disability-adjusted life year
DRC	Democratic Republic of Congo
DSI	Double Standards Index
EC	European Commission
ECA	export credit agency
ECOSOC	Covenant Committee on Economic, Social and Cultural Rights.
EFA	Education for All (Dakar Framework)
EU	European Union
EURODAD	European Network on Debt and Development
FATF	Financial Action Task Force (against money laundering, OECD)
FCTC	Framework Convention on Tobacco Control
FDI	foreign direct investment
FSF	Financial Stability Forum
FTI	Fast Track Initiative (to meet Dakar EFA goals)
GATS	General Agreement on Trade in Services
GATT	General Agreement on Tariffs and Trade
GAVI	Global Alliance for Vaccines and Immunization
GFATM	Global Fund to Fight AIDS, Tuberculosis and Malaria
GFHR	Global Forum for Health Research
GNI	gross national income
GNP	gross national product
GPGs	global public goods
HIPC	heavily indebted poor country
ICFTU	International Confederation of Free Trade Unions
ICTs	information and communications technologies
IDA	International Development Association
IDG	International Development Goal
IEA	International Energy Agency
IFC	International Finance Corporation (World Bank)

IFI	international financial institution
ILO	International Labour Organization
IMF	International Monetary Fund
IMR	infant mortality rate
IP	intellectual property
IPCC	Intergovernmental Panel on Climate Change
IRIN	Integrated Regional Research Network
JIC	Joint Implementation Committee
JPPI	joint public and private initiatives
LDC	least developed country
MDBs	multilateral development banks
MDGs	Millennium Development Goals
MMR	maternal mortality ratio
NAFTA	North American Free Trade Association
NCCTs	Non-Compliant Countries and Territories
NEPAD	New Partnership for Africa's Development
NGO	non-governmental organization
NHS	National Health Service
ODA	official development assistance
OECD	Organization for Economic Cooperation and Development
OFC	offshore financial centre
PAHO	Pan American Health Organization
POP	persistent organic pollutant
PRSP	Poverty Reduction Strategy Paper
R&D	research and development
SAGIT	Cultural Industries Sectoral Advisory Group on International Trade
SAL	structural adjustment loan
SAP	structural adjustment program
SAPRIN	Structural Adjustment Participatory Review International Network
SPS	Agreement on Sanitary and Phytosanitary Measures
TB	tuberculosis
TBT	Agreement on Technical Barriers to Trade
TRIPS	Agreement on Trade-Related Intellectual Property Rights
UN	United Nations
UNCTAD	United Nations Conference on Trade and Development
UNDP	United Nations Development Programme
UNEP	United Nations Environment Programme
UNESCO	United Nations Educational, Scientific and Cultural Organization

UNFAO	United Nations Food and Agriculture Organization
UNICEF	United Nations Children's Fund
UNRISD	United Nations Research Institute for Social Development
UPE	universal primary education
US	United States
US$	United States dollar
USGAO	United States General Accounting Office
U5MR	under-five mortality rate
WCED	World Commission on Environment and Development
WHO	World Health Organization
WSSD	World Summit on Sustainable Development
WTO	World Trade Organization

A Note on Country Designation

We are aware of the linguistic problems difficulties in demarcating differences between countries. The categories of 'developed', 'developing' and 'least developed' have been criticized for their Western-based normative assumptions about what constitutes development. Similarly, designating countries as part of the 'First', 'Second', 'Third' and 'Fourth Worlds' has been challenged as hierarchical, and even the older divisions of 'North' and 'South', while still encountered, are not geographically accurate. The World Bank now organizes countries by per capita income levels ('high', 'upper middle', 'lower middle', 'low'). This usage is becoming increasingly common, but reduces differences to a single economic metric. There is no universally accepted or acceptable way of denoting country differences; therefore we adopt the usage most frequently encountered in the documents we reviewed, i.e. that of 'developed', 'developing' and 'least developed' countries.

Foreword

For most of the past century, the spread of mysterious, frightening diseases is something that has occurred mostly in poorer parts of the planet. Now that it is identified as primarily a 'Third World', especially African, condition, AIDS has briefly managed to make it to the highest level of political agendas, including the UN Security Council. But all in all, the G8 countries under scrutiny in this book have for decades lived as though immune to at least two of the biblical scourges – famine and pestilence.

Enter Severe Acute Respiratory Syndrome (SARS). As this book goes to press, SARS has suddenly put Canada on the same plane – in the eyes of much of the world – as rural China. SARS has brought home how completely we rely on the uninterrupted rhythm of our interdependent society – from family and cultural events, to transportation systems bringing us to work and tourists to us, to the smooth workings of a complex economy that is highly dependent on the goodwill and good commerce of other jurisdictions. And, of course, a public health system with enough trained people, enough resources, and enough built-in reserves to monitor, recognize, interpret and act on the blips on the epidemiological radar screen that signal a potential epidemic.

But SARS is clearly not just a medical problem. What SARS also highlights is the extent to which the health of the public – and, importantly, perceptions and actions half a world away – influence the health of the polity and the economy.

This is, then, an opportune time to reflect on some of the less obvious pathways and effects of globalization, and this book is an important contribution to such reflection. The authors pursue the logic of globalization in arguing that if we truly live in an interdependent world, then we will often have to look to policies and decisions in one place in order to understand effects in another. They argue further that if the G8 is in many ways a new seat of global governance, then the G8 should be assessed as a group. This book is, to our knowledge, the first attempt to bring together an analysis of G8 policies, commitments and actions related to the South in the major domains known to influence health: macroeconomic policy and debt; health-care and health systems; education; nutrition and agriculture; official development assistance; trade; and the environment. It evaluates each area from the perspective of public health, and presents data from each country as well as the G8 overall. In addition to providing a rigorous and well-referenced evidence base for policy makers, researchers and activists, it is also an innovative presentation of what is effectively a textbook on policy for global health.

But the book does not support a simple North-South division of labour, responsibility and blame. The project that led to this book was an intensive research collaboration between Canadian and South African scholars in the months leading up to the June 2002 G8 summit at Kananaskis, Canada. It was this South-North and South-South dialogue, focused on rigorous analysis and collegial debate on timely and important issues, that inspired the International Development Research Centre to support the study. The project sought to engage Canadian and African researchers, policy makers and activists in a discussion about G8 health commitments, as well as NEPAD, the New Partnership for Africa's Development. NEPAD was to be presented at Kananaskis as an African plan for Africa's development, but many African critics had pointed out that the drafts had been much more widely circulated among G8 leaders than among ordinary Africans. The sector strategies to implement NEPAD are still being developed; the 'NEPAD report card' is consequently much more preliminary than that on the G8. While NEPAD can be analyzed and monitored relative to its internal propositions, it is important to recognize that it is also 'globalized' – the underlying assumptions, proposed strategies and the document itself are very much a product of global discourses and dynamics. It is therefore not accidental that an analysis of NEPAD is integrated into a book about G8 promises.

Sadly, the authors conclude that the currently dominant vision of how economies and societies should function is not conducive to an early improvement in the dismal health situation of most of the world's population. Even on a simple count of 'promises kept versus promises broken,' G8 countries have a long way to go simply to fulfill explicit commitments made in official communiqués. On the NEPAD front, the authors see promising signs of a realistic and pro-poor health strategy under development. Whether the other sections of NEPAD and, more importantly, the political and economic climate in Africa and globally, are likely to allow its successful implementation is, in the authors' view, more doubtful. The principal challenge remains: how to put human health and well-being at the centre of development, rather than at the margins. This book provides an invaluable foundation for addressing this challenge. We hope that these researchers as well as other colleagues will continue the work begun here, notably through analyzing the dynamics and processes through which the documents under examination have been produced – and democratizing these dynamics.

Christina Zarowsky, MD, PhD
International Development Research Centre

Introduction

Estimated amount spent globally in 2003 on increased security against terrorism: US$551 billion (Equity International, 2003).[1]

For the US alone: US$57 billion (Equity International, 2003).

For Canada alone: US$7.5 billion (Equity International, 2003).[2]

Best estimate one-time cost of total debt relief required to meet development goals for all developing countries: US$600 billion (Hanlon, 2000).

High-end estimate of annual costs to meet the first seven of the Millenium Development Goals: US$70 billion (Devarajan *et al.*, 2002).

Total G7 development assistance, 2001: US$38 billion (OECD, 2003).

Total G7 development assistance to basic health, 2001: US$950 million (OECD, 2003).

In 1978, building on the 1948 Universal Declaration of Human Rights, a United Nations conference proposed the goal of health for all by the year 2000 (WHO, 1978). In 2003, only limited progress has been made toward that goal. Most notably, for much of the world's population, the ability to lead a healthy life is limited by the direct and indirect effects of poverty. Almost half the world's people live on an income of US$2 per day or less (World Bank, 2001b: 36–68), creating vulnerabilities that all too often magnify one another. Lack of access to health care is just one of these vulnerabilities. Among many consequences is the fact that communicable diseases continue to comprise a significant portion of the burden of disease in the developing world. At the same time, many people outside the industrialized world now face a double burden of disease, as they are exposed not only to communicable diseases associated with poverty and inadequate health-care infrastructure, but also to non-communicable diseases such as diabetes, and to industrial pollution, associated with rapid transitions to patterns of production and consumption more typical of the industrialized world (WHO, 1999; Sen & Bonita, 2000; Yach, 2001).

Ill health not only results from poverty, but also can limit the ability of individuals and entire societies to escape from poverty: '[G]iven limited assets, for the poor their body is often their only asset, and when the body is weakened through hunger, illness and accidents, an entire family can plunge into destitution' (Narayan, 2001: 15; see generally Narayan *et al.*, 2000). The contribution that interventions to improve population health can make to economic development was a central theme of the work of the World Health Organization (WHO) Commission on Macroeconomics and Health (CMH)

(CMH, 2001). Improved health, for example, may have accounted for as much as one third of the East Asian 'economic miracle' (Bloom & Williamson, 1998). Conversely, the impacts of HIV/AIDS and malaria provide especially dramatic, large-scale illustrations of the economic damage that can result from poor health (Haacker, 2002; Sachs & Malaney, 2002). Malaria is estimated to be slowing African economic growth by up to 1.3 per cent per year (Gallup & Sachs, 2000), while HIV/AIDS is substantially slowing income growth in Africa and could account for an annual loss equivalent to 2.6 per cent of gross domestic product (GDP) in many sub-Saharan African countries (Bonnel, 2000). As the CMH summarized, 'health status seems to explain an important part of the difference in economic growth rates [between developed and least developed countries] even after controlling for standard macroeconomic variables' (CMH, 2001: 24).

By way of the social disintegration and lost economic opportunities they create, high rates of disease are also linked to a decline in state capacity, and in extreme instances can lead to state failure, and national and regional conflict (Cornia & Court, 2001; Price-Smith, 2002). High income inequality and economic stagnation also underpin disease burden, state collapse and regional conflict (Nafziger & Auvinen, 2002). Protecting health, partly by direct intervention and partly by creating conditions in which it is possible to be healthy, is now a security issue for the world community, as well as a humanitarian or human rights issue and a key element of development policy. Unfortunately, as attested to by the data cited at the beginning of this Introduction, this is not currently how the world's wealthier governments allocate their resources for security.

Policy choices made in the rich countries that dominate the world economic and political order can affect the prospects for health half a world away. In 1987, the World Commission on Environment and Development (WCED) emphasized the two-way causal relations between poverty and environmental destruction, as well as the opportunities for the industrialized world to intervene positively – e.g. by resolving the debt crisis that was even then draining capital from the poor of the world to the rich. In the same year, a UN Children's Fund (UNICEF)-sponsored study indicated that a combination of global recession and the 'adjustment' policies adopted by national governments, often as preconditions for receiving assistance from the World Bank and the International Monetary Fund (IMF), had the effect of reducing such basic indicators of child welfare as nutrition, immunization levels and education. The study pointed out that such outcomes were neither universal nor inevitable, calling for 'adjustment with a human face', with a special focus on protecting the vulnerable (Cornia *et al.*, 1987; see also Stewart, 1991).[3]

Subsequently, 'globalization' became familiar as a way of describing a set of changes in the organization of production, trade policy and law, investment flows, and the diffusion of cultural commodities exemplified by the emergence of global brands. Globalization affects the determinants of health by changing exposures to health risks and the characteristics of health systems, and by affecting the structure of household, community and national economies. 'The asymmetric nature of international trade and financial relations is such that any change in performance in the industrialized countries is amplified in its effects on the developing economies' (Cornia, 1987: 16). As national economies are more exposed to global financial flows, economic crises of the kind that occurred in Mexico in 1994–95 and in South Asia in 1997–98 dramatically increase the number of people living in poverty. Relocation of 'dirty' industries or waste disposal operations to low-wage countries may increase exposure to hazardous pollutants (Burns, 1988; Puckett *et al.*, 2002). Privatization and cost recovery initiatives demanded by the international financial institutions (IFIs), primarily the World Bank and the IMF, as conditions of development assistance may raise the cost of access to health care or access to safe drinking water. The reorientation of national economies toward production for export in order to service foreign debt, often another condition of IFI loans or grants, may lead to diversion of agricultural resources from food production for domestic use to production of commodity crops for export (Mediterranean Commission on Sustainable Development, 2001; Costello *et al.*, 1994; Iannariello *et al.*, 2000; Murphy, 2000; Pinstrup-Andersen, 1987). It may also be another risk factor for domestic conflict. An analysis of civil wars between 1965 and 1999 found that countries in which a substantial share of national income was derived from the export of primary commodities, including agricultural crops, were more prone to conflict (Thorbecke & Charumilind, 2002: 1486; see also Collier (2000); and Collier and Hoeffler (2001) for detailed discussion of the primary studies on which this conclusion is based).

Why a Focus on the G8?

The G7 (or Group of Seven Nations) was formed in 1975, after the so-called oil crisis highlighted the increasing interconnectedness of the world's economies. The six countries originally included were France, the United States, Britain, Germany, Italy and Japan. Canada joined the 'summit seven' in 1976, and hosted the G7 summit in 1981; the European Community (now the European Union, or EU) joined in 1977, although the EU does not have the same status as national governments. Russia achieved partial membership in the group in 1998, and full membership as of 2003; thus the G7 have become the G8. The purpose of the G8 and their summits is described as threefold: providing collective management of the world economy; reconciling globalization tensions among

G8 members; and generating global political leadership 'where heads of state and government take cooperation further than their officials and ministers can' (Bayne, 2001: 23).

John Kirton, who heads the University of Toronto's research center on the operations of the G8 process (the G8 Research Group), believes the G8 grouping 'is emerging as an effective centre, and is prospectively the effective centre, of global governance' (Kirton, 1999: 46). Certainly, the G7 economies are collectively dominant in statistical terms, with their 11.5 per cent of the world's people accounting for 44.7 per cent of global economic activity and 46.5 per cent of its exports (IMF, 2002: Table A). Perhaps even more importantly, these countries dominate World Bank and IMF decision-making and also wield considerable power in the World Trade Organization (WTO), because the size of their markets provides them with formidable bargaining advantages *vis-à-vis* the countries of the developing world.

This claim to emergent global governance, backed by economic clout, has brought the G8 and their summits under increased scrutiny in recent years. Civil society groups concerned with the environmental and social costs of globalization criticize G8 leaders for managing the world economy for their own benefit, with police-protester interaction turning violent at the 2001 Genoa summit. Fiscally conservative commentators wonder whether summits provide value for money, especially given the extra security precautions now taken, which were estimated to push the hosting costs of the 2002 Kananaskis summit to between US$130 and US$200 million. Despite the G8's improving compliance record, others question the adequacy of its commitments, particularly on the environment (Bayne, 2001), and ask whether the neo-liberal economic policies the G8 continue to defend can succeed in reducing global poverty or reaching other International Development Goal (IDG) targets, which it endorses (Dallaire, 2001).

The Report Card Project

Against this background of increasing globalization and increased attention directed toward the G8 by globalization's civil society critics, we set out to prepare a 'report card' on how commitments made at the summits affect health and the determinants of health, with particular reference to countries outside the industrialized world that account for roughly five-sixths of the world's population. Our research explores (a) the extent to which G8 countries have lived up to summit commitments, and (b) the adequacy of those commitments when measured against the large and growing literature on globalization and health. A special sub-theme of our work is the effect of summit commitments and subsequent (in)actions on health and the determinants of health in sub-

Saharan Africa, one of the world's poorest regions and the current epicentre of the HIV/AIDS epidemic. In the lead-up to the 2002 summit, considerable attention was paid to the New Partnership for Africa's Development (NEPAD) proposal as a solution to the long-standing crisis of development in sub-Saharan Africa. The NEPAD document is a merger of two separately conceived plans, the Millennium Africa Recovery Plan (MAP), developed by South Africa, and the OMEGA plan, developed by the Senegalese Head of State. The OMEGA plan largely focused on infrastructural improvements, while MAP focused on economic policies aimed at sustainable development through stimulating economic growth on the continent. NEPAD was 'welcomed' in one of the documents emanating from the 2002 summit, the *G8 Africa Action Plan*.

Methodology

We confined our analysis to commitments made at the three summits that had taken place when our research began: Cologne (1999), Okinawa (2000) and Genoa (2001). In addition, we limited most of our analysis to the actions of the G7 countries, given Russia's newer membership and transitional situation. Indeed, despite Russia's geopolitical significance, recent deterioration in the health status of its population and its demonstrated vulnerability to the same conditionalities that affect 'developing countries' as conventionally defined (Cohen, 2000; Field *et al.*, 2000) suggest that Russia today may have as much in common with them as with its new G8 partners.[4]

At the start of the study, we confronted a fundamental choice. We could restrict our assessment of G8 performance to a few specific commitments, ideally involving dichotomous endpoints. This would resemble the methodological approach employed by the G8 Research Group at the University of Toronto (http://www.g8.utoronto.ca).[5] Alternatively, we could err on the side of inclusiveness, starting from an inventory of commitments, many of which are not readily amenable to quantitative assessment. We followed the latter course, for three reasons. Firstly, it is more appropriate to the complexity of the relations between social policy, economic policy and the determinants of population health, which we describe in more detail in Chapter 1. Secondly, fulfilling a commitment does not mean that the response is appropriate or adequate to the need. Thirdly, for purposes of assessing impacts on health, we are especially interested in the extent to which summit commitments are driven by prior allegiances to a particular conception of the relations among economic growth, poverty reduction and integration into the global economy, without specific attention to the consequences for population health. Our results constitute an interrogation of the way in which selected policy commitments made at the highest levels of G8 governments have promoted or undermined population health on a global scale, and an agenda for future research on how the leaders chosen by the world's economically most fortunate define and fulfil their obligations to the rest of humanity.

We began our inquiry with key texts associated with the past three summits, primarily the formal statements issued at the start of and during the summits. These texts are not the results of brainstorming sessions during the summits; rather, they are carefully crafted and negotiated by officials of participating governments well in advance of the events themselves. Three individuals, each familiar with population health determinants, read these texts and independently identified statements with population health significance, using 13 subject matter headings. Under these 13 headings, summit commitments were then classified into one (or, sometimes, more) of three columns in a matrix:

1. Commitments that could be assessed in quantitative or dichotomous terms (e.g. expenditure figures, actions taken or not); this most closely mirrors the approach taken by the G8 Research Group.
2. Commitments about which data exist, but where assessment would be primarily qualitative or narrative (e.g. commitments using language such as 'improve' or 'increase').
3. Commitments reflecting a pre-existing position on appropriate social and economic policies (e.g. the presumption that integrating developing countries into the global economy represents the only appropriate development strategy).

Inter-rater agreement, though not tested statistically, was high, and consensus was reached on a matrix of commitments and categorizations (see Appendix 1). Many commitments spanned more than one column; some also related to more than one subject matter heading. Potential indicators for compliance with summit commitments were next identified, using secondary data sets regarded as valid and reliable (from such sources as the World Bank, UN agencies, and the Organization for Economic Cooperation and Development (OECD)), as well as an extensive body of research by non-governmental organizations (NGOs). We conclude each of our chapter analyses of these commitments with a table in which the G8, as a group, is assessed on whether it achieved its explicit or specific and implicit or generic commitments; and on whether these commitments were adequate to the need. We include in these tables brief comments summarizing the chapter's findings, noting important individual country differences where they exist. While the G8 should be judged as a group, if its claim to global leadership is to be taken seriously, there are important disagreements between and differences among the individual member nations.

NEPAD Report Card Project Methodology

Given the expected prominence of the New Partnership for Africa's Development during the 2002 G8 summit, an analysis was undertaken of the NEPAD document as presented in October 2001. The analysis mainly addresses health-systems issues. To increase rigour, three different analysts/raters familiar with population health determinants independently identified NEPAD statements with population health significance (see the G8 matrix in Appendix 1 for categories used to code the statements). The NEPAD project used the same system as the G8 project to classify commitments – explicit commitments that could be assessed in quantitative terms, implicit commitments that are primarily assessed qualitatively, and normative positions on socio-economic relations and conditions. The NEPAD matrix classified explicit, implicit and normative commitments into three categories:

1. Explicit health commitments: NEPAD commitments that concern health directly:
   - Child mortality,
   - Maternal mortality,
   - Reproductive health services,
   - Disease control: AIDS, malaria and other communicable diseases,
   - Affordable drugs,
   - Medical: Doctors and traditional practitioners,
   - Capacity building,
   - Sustainable health-care systems,
   - Health as a means to growth and development, and
   - The poor as a priority health target.
2. Health-related commitments explicitly recognized: NEPAD commitments that explicitly acknowledge the link with health:
   - Poverty,
   - Food and food production, and
   - The environmental and energy initiative.
3. Health-related commitments not explicitly recognized: NEPAD commitments that do not specifically mention a link to health (but which address areas generally recognized as having an impact on health):
   - Safe water and sanitation,
   - People-centered development,
   - Global partnership,
   - African autonomy and Renaissance,
   - GDP target for sustainable development,
   - Debt reduction,

- Official development assistance (ODA), concessional finance and sustainable development,
- Structural adjustment policies, and
- Political domestic reforms.

Benchmark indicators for each of these commitments, primarily secondary data regarded as valid and reliable (e.g. World Bank, UN agencies, OECD) were then identified where possible. Apart from some of our own calculations using these data, the accuracy of the data from any of our sources was not checked. The choice of indicators and data is not definitive. Because the initial NEPAD document was first presented in October 2001 to a meeting of African leaders in Abuja, Nigeria, and has not yet been implemented, it is clearly not yet possible to determine whether NEPAD commitments have been fulfilled. The analysis presented here, then, should be seen as a first attempt to analyze NEPAD's health strategy. Research will continue as more documentation becomes available.

Outline of the Book

In the next chapter (Chapter 1), we provide a necessarily brief overview of the key dimensions of contemporary globalization, and a framework for describing and understanding the various causal linkages between globalization and human health. Those linkages operate through globalization's effect on various social and economic variables at the national, community and household levels. Our analysis in the remaining chapters is based on what is known, from the perspective of a variety of disciplines, about those linkages and the influence of the variables in question on human health.

In Chapter 2, we begin our analysis of the effects of G8 commitments and policies on human health with the topic of national macroeconomic policy. This choice reflects the manifold ways in which poverty and economic insecurity affect human health, both directly and through various intervening variables. In an increasingly interconnected world, the policy commitments of the largest economic players have unavoidable impacts half a world away. In the case of the structural adjustment policies that are a focus of the chapter, this is by design. Many of the policies of the G8, while moving in the right direction, are doing so on the basis of insufficient financial commitments and an unwarranted reliance on neo-liberal social and economic policy prescriptions. The absence of more comprehensive debt relief is a special concern.

Chapter 3 focuses specifically on G8 commitments as they affect health care and health systems. Although health care is far from being the only contributor to the health status of individuals or populations, it is nevertheless important – especially in the developing world, where low-cost, low-technology interventions can make major contributions to reducing the burden of disease. In turn, improved health may contribute to economic growth that improves the social determinants of health and makes more resources available to support health systems. The G8 could be doing much more, and doing it better, to improve health in the developing world.

Two of the most important social determinants of health are education and nutrition: access to each is fundamentally impaired by poverty, and each can in turn be supportive of poverty reduction, as well as directly contributing to improved health. We therefore devote Chapters 4 and 5 to G8 commitments as they affect these areas, using evidence supplied by leading international agencies – as we do in other chapters – to suggest that the resources that the G8 have committed to improving education and nutrition are, on the whole, not commensurate with the size of the tasks at hand.

Official development assistance is the primary vehicle that governments in the industrialized world use to transfer resources to the developing world. We therefore devote Chapter 6 to assessing whether, and how, G8 ODA policies support health-related development objectives and live up to commitments made at the past three summits. Disturbingly, the long-term trend is one of declining ODA from the G8 countries, and all are far from reaching the often repeated target of devoting 0.7 per cent of their gross national product (GNP) or income (GNI) to development assistance. The fact that some industrialized countries have attained this goal shows that it is not implausible – and, if the G8 had achieved it, an additional U$109 billion would have been made available in 2001 for purposes including poverty reduction, support for education and access to basic health care and improved nutrition. To put this figure in perspective, it is roughly twice the value of *all* ODA from the industrialized world.

Reduction of tariffs and other barriers to trade is a key element of contemporary globalization, and invariably a centerpiece of conventional economic policy prescriptions for development. In Chapter 7, we examine the G8 record on trade liberalization as it affects the products of the developing world, in particular the least developed countries (LDCs). We identify a remarkable consensus among observers as diverse as Oxfam, the World Bank and the IMF that improved performance on the part of the industrialized world in opening its markets, especially for agricultural products and textiles, would generate economic gains comparable in value to several times today's levels of development assistance. G8 rhetoric about commitment to open markets has, with some laudable exceptions, so far not been matched by action in the areas that matter most to developing economies – and therefore, at least potentially, to the health of those populations.

Environmental concerns are the topic of Chapter 8. Over the past few years, the G8 summits have devoted surprisingly little attention to environmental questions as they affect human health. A few areas of satisfactory performance stand out, but G8 members have been slow to ratify key international environmental agreements: Russian delay in ratifying the Kyoto Protocol on climate change and US repudiation of the protocol are especially reprehensible. The Johannesburg summit on sustainable development ('Rio +10') marked the decline of environment–development linkages as an element of the international policy agenda – ironically, 15 years after the World Commission on Environment and Development (the Brundtland Commission) emphasized the connections between environment and development.

While African data and analysis are included in several earlier chapters, Chapter 9 synthesizes and extends the previous discussion. The focus of this chapter, written by researchers based on that continent (D.S. and W.M.), is an analysis of NEPAD in light of the deterioration in health status and health systems that the continent has suffered in recent decades. NEPAD was created largely for G8 and other industrialized world audiences and, despite its 'made in Africa' branding, critics argue that it exemplifies the problems of shaping development policy around external expectations of how poorer nations should 'develop' within an increasingly globalized market. NEPAD therefore reflects the tensions between neo-liberal macroeconomic policy assumptions and health and human development identified in earlier chapters.

Finally, in Chapter 10, we summarize our findings in light of intensifying debates over the macroeconomic prescriptions presented in both G8 policy statements and the NEPAD document. We also review a few key areas of G8 (in)action that we were unable to address in any detail in our study. These, and a number of other issues arising from our earlier chapters, are brought forward as topics requiring ongoing monitoring and research.

Limitations of the Analysis

Several limitations of our analysis should be noted. The choice of indicators and data for our report card is far from definitive. We did not, for example, check on the accuracy of the data from any of our sources, beyond the identification of clear omissions and inconsistencies in the data as published. The literature review for findings that would shed light on the effects of the commitments on population health was not exhaustive, but rather drew on previous research carried out by members of the project team.

Time and timeliness are both issues. Because commitments made in a given year may take some time to implement, assessment of the extent to which G8 countries have lived up to summit commitments runs the risk of being premature. On the other hand, such commitments are normally decided upon well in advance of the summits themselves; they are not spur-of-the moment choices. In addition, the speed with which resources were mobilized and the agenda of the 2002 summit transformed after the events of 11 September 2001 suggests that the G8 countries are capable, individually and collectively, of rapid responses to issues that are regarded as high and urgent priorities.

As for timeliness, the bulk of our research was completed before the Kananaskis summit in June 2002. We have provided some commentary on post-Kananaskis actions by individual G8 countries, but we restrict any detailed data analysis to information relating to events prior to June 2002. The time lags associated with book publication mean that no published volume can keep up with the continuous flow of new developments and announcements.

Finally, a bias may have been introduced by the relative ease of tracking new announcements by Canada and, to a slightly lesser extent, the US and the UK, from our vantage point in the English-speaking world. Although we have made every effort to achieve accurate scholarship and balanced presentation, our 'report card' should be read as a work in progress and an agenda for future research.

Endnotes to the Introduction

[1] Details of the assessment are not available; only the summary data have been made public at this time, thus the estimate should be treated cautiously.

[2] These data come from a news report based on Equity International's conference presentation of their summary data (*The Globe and Mail*, 5 March 2003: A10). Again, the estimate should be treated cautiously.

[3] For a contemporary version of the prescription for adjustment with a human face, unfortunately presented without systematic reference to supporting documentation, see UNRISD (2000).

[4] Despite this, and despite the fact that Russia was not a full participant in the 1999–2001 summits, we refer to the 'G8' throughout the book, rather than the clumsier G7/G8 designation, except when the factual context clearly pertains to the G7.

[5] The G8 Research Group finds that compliance rates, typically under 40 per cent, improved dramatically with the Okinawa summit in 2000, which achieved an 80 per cent compliance rate (Kirton *et al.*, 2001). Compliance declined to 49.5 per cent post-Genoa, although with considerable issue and country variance (Kirton & Kokotsis, 2002). Their determination of compliance is based on new actions on specific commitments undertaken by G8 countries in the 12 months following issuance of the summit communiqué.

CHAPTER ONE

Globalization, Health and Development: The Right Prescription?

> Unregulated or under-regulated by governments, corporations set the terms of engagement themselves. In the Third World we see a race to the bottom: multinationals pitting developing countries against each other to provide the most advantageous conditions for investment, with no regulation, no red tape, no unions, a blind eye turned to environmental degradation. It's good for profit, but bad for workers and local communities. As corporations go bottom fishing, host governments are left with little alternative but to accept the pickings. Globalisation may deliver liberty, but not fraternity or equality (Hertz, 2001).

Introduction

G8 members' economic policies and their influence on the programs of the inter-national financial institutions shape much of contemporary globalization. To assess this influence, and how it pervasively affects health and human development, we first need to define more carefully what we mean by 'globalization.'

Over the past decade, globalization has become both a slogan and a useful historical and analytical concept. To some, it is an inescapable and primarily benign process of global economic integration, in which countries increasingly drop border restrictions on the flow of capital, goods and services. Acknowledged risks of more rapid spread of disease and pests accompany the speedier and more massive movement of goods and people, but these are not new. Risks can be managed and are more than offset by benefits in the diffusion of new ideas, technologies and steady global economic growth. To others, 'globalization' is shorthand for a technologically mediated coup by economic elites and political conservatives to create a 'new world order' based more on private corporate control than public democracy. Rich countries have overwhelmed poor ones in defining the macroeconomic policies that must be followed, which usually benefit the former at the expense of the latter. New global rules entrench private economic rights – 'liberty'[1] – but at the expense of public goods and public governance – key instruments

1

of 'equality' and 'fraternity.' Battle lines are drawn. Barricades separate the political and economic elites negotiating the terms of contemporary globalization from those who protest the very idea.

Globalization, defined at its simplest, describes a constellation of *processes* by which nations, businesses and people are becoming more connected and interdependent across the globe through increased economic integration and communication exchange, cultural diffusion (especially of Western culture) and travel. By emphasizing *processes* we draw attention to the means by which this interdependence and connectivity is occurring. Globalization is not a new phenomenon. One might actually call it a basic human drive. Jared Diamond, in *Guns, Germs and Steel* (2000), recounts how the history of humankind has been one of pushing against borders, exploring, trading, expanding, conquering and assimilating. In ancient Western times, 'global' simply meant the Middle East, once a Garden of Eden that, despoiled by overuse, became an eroding desert that drove people further east to what is now China, and west to the Mediterranean and continental Europe. In Western Renaissance times, 'global' meant exploration, colonization and exploitation of the 'New World.' As the remarkable Uruguayan journalist Eduardo Galeano showed 30 years ago in *Open Veins of Latin America* (1973), only the wealth of the exploited colonies – their resources, their peoples – allowed Western capitalism to displace feudalism. And, as some economic historians point out, this is not the first time in more recent history that capital (and capitalists) have had more interest in foreign markets than in those in their home countries: the percentage of global economic output accounted for by trade has only now returned to the levels characteristic of the late nineteenth and early twentieth centuries (Cameron & Stein, 2000), before growing income inequalities and a global economic recession helped fuel renewed protectionism and, eventually, two 'world' wars (Nye, 2002).

Contemporary Globalization

Contemporary globalization is characterized by an accelerated pace of interdependence and connectivity, aided by innovations in communications technologies. Although it arguably continues a longer historical trajectory, it also differs from previous eras in several ways:

1. *The scale and speed of cross-border movement of goods, services and (particularly) finance capital:* Over US$1.5 trillion (some estimate US$2 trillion) worth of currency transactions occur daily, an amount equivalent to more than twice the total foreign exchange reserves of all governments. Such transactions reduce the ability of governments to intervene in foreign exchange markets to stabilize their currencies, manage their economies

and maintain fiscal autonomy (UNDP, 1999); they also increase the vulnerability of national economies to short-term movements of capital in response to real or perceived changes in the relative risk of investing in various jurisdictions.

2. *The establishment of binding rules, primarily through the WTO:* Trade agreements are increasingly establishing a regime of obligations that can be enforced on national governments through the implementation of trade sanctions. Countries have also entered into dozens of other multilateral conventions and agreements on human rights and environmental protection, but few if any of these are accompanied by a similar regime based on national self-interest. This asymmetry between enforceable economic (market-based) rules and unenforceable social and environmental obligations is arguably the biggest governance challenge of the new millennium (Labonte, 1998; UNDP, 1999; Kickbusch, 2000)[2].

3. *The size of transnational corporations, several of which are economically larger than many nations or whole regions,* as measured by annual sales and annual GDP, respectively. For example, General Motors' global sales in 1997 exceeded in value the GDP of Thailand or Norway; Mitsubishi's sales in that year exceeded the GDP of Poland or South Africa; and the sales of Wal-Mart Stores exceeded the GDP of Malaysia, Israel or Colombia (UNDP, 1999: 32). This comparison is admittedly simplistic, but is does illustrate the relative scale of the institutions involved. More fundamentally, the balance of power between transnational companies and nation states is, according to many observers, shifting decisively in favour of the former, even within the industrialized world (e.g. see Hertz, 2001; Schmidt, 1995). According to one estimate, 'around 60% of international trade involves transactions between two related parts of multinationals' (Bishop, 2000: 18). The ability of transnational corporations to organize production across national borders, sometimes by using multiple tiers of sub-contractors, is an important contributor both to the emergence of genuinely global labour markets (World Bank, 1995) and to tax competition among jurisdictions, as intra-firm transfer pricing enables corporations to shift profits to low-tax countries.

4. *The apparent commitment of most countries to continue the project of global economic integration through increased market liberalization:* This commitment is built upon two decades of neo-liberal economic assumptions, reflected in the macroeconomic policies of most governments, the World Bank and IMF, and most trade agreements. It is somewhat tempered by the reluctance of many of the world's wealthiest nations to abide by these assumptions if they are not to their benefit, exemplified by the continued presence and even increase of trade-distorting domestic agricultural subsidies in the EU, Japan and the US.

5. *Social, economic, environmental and health issues are becoming 'inherently global', rather than purely national or domestic* (Labonte & Spiegel, 2002): Environmental impacts of human activities are planetary in scale and scope; disease pandemics and economic stagnation partly underpin state collapse and regional conflict (Price-Smith, 2002).

Globalization, Health and Development: Competing Arguments, Conflicting Evidence

From a health and human development perspective, several compelling pro-globalization arguments exist. The diffusion of new knowledge and technology through trade and investment, for example, can aid in disease surveillance, treatment and prevention. Information communication technologies (ICTs) are frequently cited as an overwhelmingly positive aspect of contemporary globalization: they enable more rapid scientific discovery, create virtual communities of support, increase knowledge about human rights, strengthen diasporic communities and create an international advocacy movement pushing to create new global governance structures to balance the predominance of market-driven initiatives. Broad consensus can also be observed on the positive effects of globalization on gender rights and empowerment (Chinkin, 2000; Harcourt, 2000), though with the caveat that these rights are not simply an invention of the West but previously existed (often more strongly in pre-Western colonization times) in many countries that are presumably less emancipated today (Sen, 1999).

In macroeconomic terms, the pro-globalization argument posits that increased trade and foreign investment through liberalization can increase economic growth. Growth can be used to sustain investment in necessary public goods, such as health care, education, women's empowerment programs and so on (Dollar, 2001; Dollar & Kraay, 2000). Especially in poorer countries, growth *may* also reduce poverty, leading to desirable change in the determinants of health. Improved population health, particularly amongst the world's poorest countries, is increasingly associated with improved economic growth (Savedoff & Schultz, 2000; WHO, 2001), and so the circle virtuously closes upon itself.

Critics of the pro-globalization thesis quickly respond that the virtuous circle can have a vicious undertow. This includes the more rapid spread of infectious diseases, some of which are becoming resistant to treatment, and the increased adoption of unhealthy 'Western' lifestyles by larger numbers of people (Lee, 2001). The more significant challenge is that integration into the global economy does not always or inevitably lead to economic growth and that, when it does, the result is not necessarily the reduction of poverty (Cornia, 2001; Weisbrot *et al.*, 2001; UNDP, 2000). Much depends upon pre-existing social, economic and environmental conditions within countries; and upon specific national programs and policies that enhance the capacities of citizens, such as health, education and social welfare programs (UNDP, 1999, 2000). China, Korea, Thailand, Malaysia, Indonesia and Vietnam, while dramatically increasing their role as global traders, did so primarily as exporters. They retained tariff and non-tariff barriers shielding important sectors of their domestic economies from competitive imports, maintained public ownership of large segments of banking and placed restrictions on foreign capital flows.

This is precisely how wealthier European and North American economies developed historically (Rodriguez & Rodrik, 2000; Rodrik, 1999), with the important additional resources and markets – neglected in conventional economic narratives – that were made available by colonialism (Milanovic, 2003). Trade agreements now largely prohibit poorer countries from doing the same, with only modest provisions for 'special and differential treatment' (see Box 7.2, Chapter 7) that are being actively opposed by many of the world's richest countries. Weaker economies with fewer domestic protections, largely removed through earlier World Bank and IMF 'structural adjustment' loan policies, have fared poorly under trade and investment liberalization (see Box 1.1, below). The net effect for many of these countries has been suppressed domestic economic activity, depressed wages and tax revenues, and a worsened balance of payments (International Institute for Sustainable Development, 2001). Mexico, Uruguay, Zimbabwe, Kenya, India and the Philippines, for example, all witnessed serious declines in income, and corresponding increases in poverty and poor health, among their rural populations following liberalization (Hilary, 2001).

Box 1.1: Zambia's Textiles and Kerala's Public Policies

Countries with weak domestic economies can be overwhelmed by surging, cheap imports, often from wealthier countries still subsidizing their domestic producers or their exports. Zambia provides a compelling example. In return for World Bank and IMF loans, Zambia opened its borders to cheap, often second-hand textile imports. Its domestic manufacturing, inefficient by the standards of wealthier industrialized nations, could not compete. Within eight years, 30 000 jobs disappeared and 132 of 140 textile mills closed operations, which the World Bank acknowledges as 'unintended and regrettable consequences' of the adjustment process (Jeter, 2002). Overall, 40 per cent of manufacturing jobs disappeared in the past decade, and huge numbers of previously employed workers rely on precarious street vending. In the early 1990s, user charges for schools, imposed partly because of the loss of public revenues following the collapse of the textile sector, led to increased dropout and illiteracy rates. The current government is now seeking to undo many of these policies, including elimination of user fees for education, lowering costs for public health care, reintroducing agricultural subsidies and supporting domestic industries with a potential for growth. But the task is harder than it might have been before the 'open borders' had been imposed.

The Indian state of Kerala provides another example. Like Cuba, Costa Rica, China and a handful of other countries, Kerala has high population health status despite a low per capita GDP. This somewhat anomalous relationship results from policies that, at least until recently, created relatively equitable income distribution, as well as supporting social transfers to meet basic needs, universal education, equitable access to public health and primary health care, and adequate caloric intake (Werner & Sanders, 1997; Thankappan, 2001). These pro-poor policies are now being eroded by trade liberalization. In Kerala, a media-developed Western consumerist culture, alongside tariff reductions, is rejecting locally produced goods for imported luxuries. This is weakening the local entrepreneurial base, lowering employment and reducing the level of state taxes available for social program spending and income redistribution. Liberalization in coconut and rubber products, required by WTO rules, has seen a drop in prices that 'will have serious implications for the health of Keralites, especially that of farmers' (Thankappan, 2001: 893). There is also some concern that WTO rules may cause Kerala to end its food subsidy program, which until now has succeeded in providing affordable and adequate nutrition to almost its entire population (Hilary, 2001).

A Framework for Understanding Globalization's Impacts on Health

Globalization may improve human health and development in some circumstances but damage it in others, especially when liberalization has been rapid and without government support to affected sectors and populations (UNDP, 1999; Ben-David *et al.*, 1999; Cornia, 2001). Liberalized trade in agricultural products may provide short-term economic benefit to less developed countries. This can improve human health, depending on how equitably these benefits are allocated among all citizens. But food exports in poorer countries can also increase fossil fuel-based transportation, creating short and longer-term health- and environment-damaging effects; and commodity-led export produces lower long-term economic growth than manufactured ('value-added') export (Yong Kim, Millen *et al.*, 2000). Protectionist policies, including subsidies, may preserve rural life and livelihoods – arguments frequently advanced by the EU and Japan (Labonte, 2000). This benefits the health and quality of life of rural people. But such policies can also support ecologically unsustainable forms of production and increase oligopolistic corporate control over global food production.

Trade openness might increase women's share of paid employment, which is an important element of gender empowerment (UNDP, 1999: 80). Yet much of women's employment remains low-paid, unhealthy and insecure in Export Processing Zones that often prohibit any form of labour organization and employ only single women. Public caring supports for young children have been declining in many trade-opened countries, portending future health inequalities. There is also evidence of a global 'hierarchy of care.' Women from developing nations employed as domestic workers in wealthy countries send valued hard currency back home to their families, some of which is used to employ poorer rural women in their home countries to look after the children the expatriate women have left behind. These rural women, in turn, leave their eldest daughters (often still quite young and ill-educated) to care for the family they left behind in the village, depriving them of any opportunity for personal development or social advancement (Hochschild, 2000).

Who gains and who loses? Tracing the impacts of globalization on health is a daunting and complex task. Figure 1.1, below, based upon a more extensive study (Labonte & Torgerson, 2002), provides a simplified framework for understanding how contemporary globalization can affect health. The key points conveyed by this figure, in descending order of scale, are as follows:

1. How contemporary globalization affects health depends on the historical context of particular countries, specifically their political, social and economic traditions (e.g. democratic, oligarchic, patriarchal, theocratic, dictatorial); and their stock of pre-existing endowments (e.g. level of economic development, environmental resources, human capital development).
2. Globally, the major vehicles or *processes* through which contemporary globalization operates are imposed macroeconomic policies. One category consists of the Structural Adjustment Programs (SAPS) of the World Bank and IMF, which were the precursors to and a key component of today's 'free trade' agenda, and the more recent Poverty Reduction Strategy Papers (PRSP) program of the World Bank and IMF, required for debt relief and, increasingly, for development assistance. A second category consists of enforceable trade agreements (notably those administered by the WTO) and associated trans-border flows in goods, capital and services. Third, official development assistance represents a form of wealth transfer for public infrastructure development in poorer nations. Fourth, there are

'intermediary global public goods' – the numerous yet largely unenforceable multilateral agreements we have on human rights, environmental protection, women's rights, children's rights and so on.

3. These vehicles, in turn, have both positive and negative health effects on domestic policy space, by increasing or decreasing public sector capacity or resources and regulatory authority. Key domestic policies that condition health outcomes include universal access to education and health care, legislated human and labour rights, restrictions on health-damaging products, such as tobacco, or exposure to hazardous waste and environmental protection. Liberalization, whether through trade agreements or through SAPs, lowers tariffs on imported goods. This has been particularly hard on developing countries, which derive much of their national tax revenue from tariffs and which lack the capacity to institute alternative revenue-generating sources. This affects their abilities to provide the public health, education and water/sanitation services essential both to health and to economic development. Global and regional trade agreements, in turn, are increasingly circumscribing the social and environmental regulatory options of national governments.

4. National policies and resource transfers affect the abilities of regional or local governments to regulate their immediate environments, provide equitable access to health-promoting services, enhance generic community capacities (community empowerment) or cope with increased and usually increasingly rapid urbanization.

5. At the household level, all of the above determine in large measure family income and distribution (under conditions of poverty, for example, when women control household income, children's health tends to be better), health behaviours and household expenditures (both in time and in money) for health, education and social programs.

In addition, each level affects, and is affected by, environmental pathways. Among the most important of these are resource depletion (water, land, forests), biodiversity loss, pollution, and the loss of ecosystem services such as the sequestration of carbon by forests.

Subsequent chapters in this book provide evidence on, and arguments surrounding, many of the elements in Figure 1.1. Much remains to be understood about how globalization's *vehicles* or *processes* (the 'global contexts' identified by the framework in Figure 1.1) can be harnessed to improve global health outcomes. But the experience of 20 years of increased market integration is surely enough to permit a preliminary assessment of the consequences for human health. In several chapters of the book, we present an overview of the evidence, which should always be understood with the caveat that more detailed, context-specific inquiry is needed.

Figure 1.1: A Framework for Linking Globalization and Health

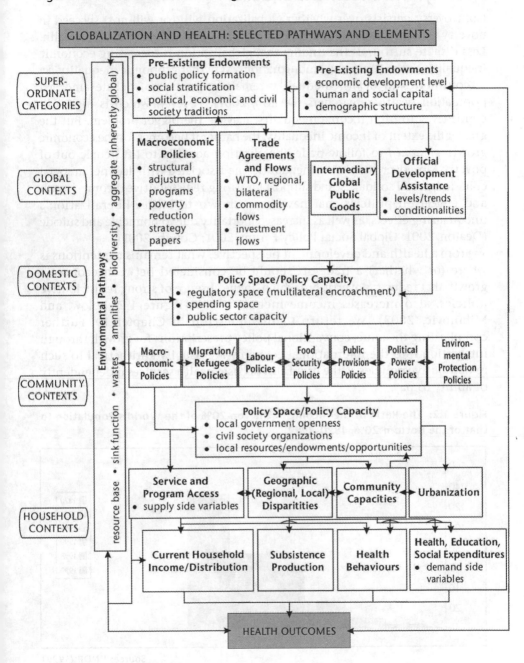

Poverty and Income Inequality

Controversy persists over whether globalization will (or will not) succeed in poverty reduction – recalling that poverty is one of the greatest threats to health. Less dispute surrounds the finding that globalization is increasing economic inequality, both within and among nations. Whether economic inequality *per se* contributes to health inequality remains a matter of debate amongst population health researchers (Deaton, 2001). Poverty, which is higher in countries with high income inequality, may be the bigger problem. But the greater the extent of income inequality, the harder it becomes for the economic growth *presumed* to follow trade liberalization actually to lift people out of poverty. Moreover, increasing inequalities *are* associated with declines in social cohesion, social solidarity and support for strong redistributive income, health and education policies that have been shown to buffer liberalization's unequalizing effects, as well as increased mortality due to homicide and suicide (Deaton, 2001; Global Social Policy Forum, 2001; Gough, 2001).

From a health and development perspective, what remains contentious is where (or whether) a trade-off should be considered between economic growth that reduces poverty, but which, in the absence of strong redistributive policies, also increases income inequality (see Figure 1.2, below, and Milanovic, 2003). We return to this question in Chapter 10. Further complicating the issue, conventional policy prescriptions for growth through integration into the international economy are usually antithetical to such redistributive policies as the provision of basic health services independently of ability to pay.

Figure 1.2: The Ratio of the Income of the Top 20% of the World's Population to that of the Bottom 20%, 1820–1999.

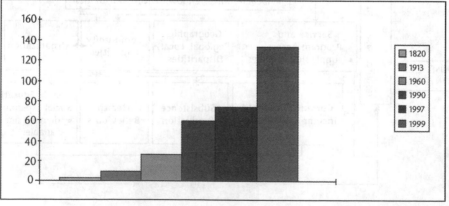

Source: UNDP (1999)

The Environment and Sustainable Development

Among the pathways linking globalization to human health via changes in the natural environment are the liberalization-induced effects of growth on resource depletion and pollution, and increased transportation-based fossil fuel emissions. As noted in Chapter 8, the past decade has provided numerous illustrations of how these pathways operate.

Potential indirect climate change effects are also associated with loosening of restrictions on foreign investment. A recent example was provided by the Brazilian currency crisis of 1998 (UNDP, 1999; De Paula & Alves, 2000). The Brazilian government lacked sufficient foreign reserves to stabilize its currency and was forced to borrow from the IMF. The rescue package was conditional on drastic public spending cuts, which included a two-thirds reduction in Brazil's environmental protection spending. This led to the collapse of a project with international funding that would have begun satellite mapping of the Amazonian rain forest as a first step in stemming its destruction. This destruction, in turn, may have a profound effect on climate change, with long-term and potentially severe health implications for much of the world's populations (Labonte, 1999). Many empirically based projections on the environmental impacts of trade liberalization show severe ecological damage (Labonte & Torgerson, 2002). The only exceptions are trade agreement requirements to reduce trade-distorting agricultural and fisheries production subsidies. These subsidies go primarily to wealthier producers within wealthy countries, wreak havoc on local production in poorer countries by flooding the market with below-cost commodities, and severely damage the environment.

The Devil is in the Details

A special issue of the *Bulletin of the World Health Organization* in 2001 was devoted to the theme of globalization and health. The journal's editor, Richard Feachem – now director of the Global Fund to Fight AIDS, Tuberculosis and Malaria (GFATM) – weighed in heavily on the pro-globalization side of the debate: 'A globalized world with rapid transit of ideas, people and money provides a setting for a new generation of successful investments in health that benefit people of all nations' (Feachem, 2001: 804).

Interestingly, the articles in the special issue were more divided and less sanguine on this prospect than was the editor-in-chief. 'Globalization is good for you' bannered one article, while 'Globalization is bad for you' headlined another. The devil, as always, lay in the details. Thus, liberalization in trade in goods may, under the 'right' domestic policy circumstances and with a good supply of human, social and environmental capital, yield health and development benefits. But liberalization in capital accounts, which is urged to promote foreign direct investment (FDI), generally wreaks havoc for the poor in poorer nations.

Research on the pathways between commercial, export-oriented agriculture and child nutrition/health demonstrates the importance of attention to detail and distributional effects (Von Braun *et al.*, 1994). For the household unit engaged in agriculture, the effects of liberalization-induced commercialization involve changes in the prices, wages and risks for the farm. Low prices for commodities may mean that more off-farm labour is needed to ensure the sustainability of the household unit. Findings from case studies of several low-income countries that had implemented various types of commercialization/liberalization schemes – including Guatemala, the Philippines, Papua New Guinea, India, Kenya, Rwanda, Zambia, Malawi, Sierra Leone and the Gambia – were mixed. In some countries, such as Rwanda and Zambia, the shift from subsistence farming to agricultural commercialization (e.g. a technological change in maize production) had favorable effects on the health and nutrition of children under five, while in other countries, such as the Philippines and Sierra Leone, the children of commercialized farmers were worse off than the children of subsistence farmers. The essential nutrition-improving component was not the level of income itself (the 'rising tide' presumed to lift all boats), but who controlled the income. Rising female-controlled, but not male-controlled, incomes were related to higher levels of caloric intakes among children, as women are more likely than men to allocate household resources towards food.

These findings underscore the importance of a gender analysis in any research examining how globalization influences health at the household or individual level. More importantly, they emphasize that sweeping claims about globalization's benefits can safely be disregarded unless the claims clearly identify the relevant *processes*, and describe the pathways through which these processes are believed to affect the outcome of interest. This perspective informs our analysis throughout the chapters that follow.

Endnotes to Chapter One

[1] And even here, liberty only in a narrow economic sense, and certainly not as Amartya Sen influentially defines freedom (liberty) as the capacity to live a life one has reason to value (Sen, 1999).

[2] O'Brien (2002: 14) extends the list of 'rules-supervisory institutions' to include the World Bank and IMF, creating a triumvirate of advocates for 'economic liberalism with little concern for social policy', relegating social policy institutions (largely the UN agencies) to 'an advisory category' relying solely upon 'argument' to see their measures adopted.

CHAPTER TWO

Macroeconomic Policy, Structural Adjustment and Debt Relief

> Economic policies are not neutral. Contrary to received opinion, they can even kill (George, 1988: 6).

Introduction

Because of the numerous causal pathways and feedback loops linking poverty and economic insecurity with ill health, we have chosen to begin our substantive discussion of how G8 commitments affect health in the developing world with an examination of the influence of the G8, directly and through international financial institutions, on domestic macroeconomic and social policy. The channels of G8 influence must, in turn, be understood with reference to 'debt crises' as they have unfolded over the last three decades, and to the role of 'structural adjustment' as a response to these crises.

According to the World Bank (2001b: 36–8), some 1.2 billion people world-wide were living on less than US$1 a day, and 2.8 billion, or close to half the world's population, were living on less than US$2 per day, in 1998. Using a somewhat different technique for estimating income levels, the UN Conference on Trade and Development (UNCTAD) has calculated that within the 39 LDCs[1] for which data are available, an estimated 81 per cent of the population lived on less than US$2 per day during the period 1995–99 (UNCTAD, 2002b: 52) and the incidence of poverty – on either measure – has actually increased in the LDCs over the last few decades. However, it should not be inferred from these figures that the LDCs are the primary locus of poverty as measured in this manner: in fact, the LDCs account for 495 million people living on less than US$2 per day, or less than one-fifth of the World Bank's estimated total. (Direct comparisons are not possible because of differences in methodology, but the magnitudes in question are nevertheless important.) It should also be noted that recent critiques have argued that the World Bank's methodology and definitions actually result in a substantial underestimate of the extent of global poverty (Reddy & Pogge, 2002), and have suggested that the methodological choices in question may have political motivations (Wilks & Lefrançois, 2002: 28–31). Since the US$2-per-day figure implies an annual per capita income roughly equivalent to the cost of two nights' deluxe hotel accommodation or a mid-priced business suit in one of the world's financial centres, the debate can safely be dismissed as one with marginal relevance to the real world of health and development.

'Debt Crises' and Structural Adjustment

The term 'structural adjustment' entered the international development lexicon in 1980, when the World Bank initiated structural adjustment loans (SALs) to help developing countries address an accumulation of economic woes. To oversimplify considerably, but not inaccurately, a combination of recession in the industrialized countries, rising oil prices and rising interest rates meant that numerous developing countries were no longer able to fulfil their governments' and firms' financial obligations to the industrialized world's banks and official development agencies. Structural adjustment became far more important after 1982, when the government of Mexico announced that it was prepared to default on billions of dollars in loans, primarily made by major US banks. The result was the first of a series of 'debt crises.'

Following the Mexican announcement, apprehensions about the stability of major banks in the industrialized world in the event of co-ordinated default – an eventuality that was admittedly unlikely, given the formidable capacity for reprisal at the disposal of banks and governments (George, 1988) – led industrialized country governments, bilaterally and through the IFIs, to provide new money for debt rescheduling. However, it must be emphasized that debt repayment was normally stretched out, rather than cancelled. One of the consequences was that, 'despite repeated rescheduling of debt by creditor countries, developing countries continue[d] to pay out more each year in debt service than the actual amounts they receive[d] in official development assistance' between 1986 and 1996 (Cheru, 1999: para. 10). The net outflow of funds became even more significant in the years that followed, as a result of the financial crisis in South Asia (UN, 2002a). Ironically, high levels of borrowing were and are often accompanied by capital flight (see Box 2.1, below), facilitated by the availability of 'offshore' financial institutions, an issue we address near the end of this chapter.

Box 2.1: Capital Flight and 'Odious Debts'

'Capital flight' refers to the process in which domestic investors shift their assets abroad, and foreign investors repatriate them, when threatened by economic uncertainty or offered the prospects of higher rates of return elsewhere. The United States, Switzerland, and a variety of less-well-known offshore financial centres are among the primary destinations of flight capital, and historically have often been eagerly receptive (Naylor, 1987).

No simple or unambiguous way of defining or measuring capital flight exists, but estimates for a number of countries and regions suggest the magnitudes involved. Using official financial statistics and several alternative formulae for calculating capital flight, Cumby & Levich (1987) estimated capital flight from Argentina, Brazil, Mexico, the Philippines and Venezuela during the period 1976–84 as between US$54.7 and US$131.8 billion. (The wide variation indicates the differences that result from using alternative bases for measurement.) During this period, those countries' debts increased by a total of US$243.1 billion. These figures mask substantial intra-country variations. For Mexico in the late 1970s and early 1980s, knowledgeable observers in the financial services industry suggested a much closer correspondence between the amounts of capital flight and external debt (George, 1988; Naylor, 1987). Loungani & Mauro (2000) estimated capital flight from Russia at US$15–20 billion per year between 1994 and 2000. Ndikumana & Boyce (2003) estimated the value of capital flight from sub-Saharan Africa between 1970 and 1996 at US$186.8 billion (in 1996 dollars), noting that during the period, 'roughly 80 cents on every dollar that flowed into the region from foreign loans flowed back out as capital flight *in the same year*, suggesting that the phenomenon of debt-fuelled capital flight was widespread' (Ndikumana & Boyce, 2003: 122; emphasis added). In economically beleaguered Argentina, it was estimated at the end of 2001 that the value of assets held abroad by Argentine residents equalled the total value of the country's foreign debt (CELS, 2003).

From one perspective, capital flight is unexceptionable: it is a mechanism investors use to apply the 'discipline of the market' to national economic policies. However, capital flight is often a vehicle for tax evasion, or a way for rulers and their close associates to sequester the proceeds of corruption. In any event, when governments are borrowing on external markets while private investors are shifting assets abroad, the effect is to reduce domestic savings and foreign exchange available for development; to increase inequalities in income and wealth, as governments must cut back services or tax the population as a whole to finance debt service charges; and to create downward pressure on exchange rates that further reduces the purchasing power of those who do not have the option of diversifying into foreign assets (Rodriguez, 1987). In 1987, economist and financial historian Thomas Naylor stated flatly that '[t]here would be no "debt crisis" without large-scale capital flight' (Naylor, 1987: 419). As the propertied and connected were able to shift their assets abroad, governments were left to work out the best deals they could with commercial lenders and the IMF, on the basis of various forms of conditionality.

In the context of debt relief for developing countries, it has been argued that lenders are not entitled, as a matter of ethics and perhaps as a matter of international law, to demand repayment of some debts that had the effect of financing capital flight. The clearest case is that of so-called odious debts incurred by despotic rulers who were looting the public treasury and moving the assets abroad (Kremer & Jayachandran, 2002a, 2002b). Even when rulers are not directly implicated, '[t]he use of foreign borrowing to finance the accumulation of private external assets raises questions as to the legal and moral legitimacy of the external debt – that is, its treatment as a public obligation as opposed to a private liability' (Ndikumana & Boyce, 2003: 108).

In a more expansive approach, the Halifax Initiative, a Canadian NGO formed at the time of the Halifax (Canada) G7 summit in 1995, called in May 2002 for the establishment by the G8 of an international mechanism with the authority to cancel 'illegitimate debts.' Its proposal did not single out capital flight, but included 'odious debts incurred to strengthen despotic regimes, debts contracted for fraudulent purposes, debts whose proceeds were stolen through corruption, debts for failed projects and debts that became unpayable as a result of a creditor unilaterally raising interest rates' (Halifax Initiative, 2002).

Thus, several arguments exist for considering the *circumstances* under which a developing country's debt was incurred, as well as the hardships associated with repayment, for purposes of debt relief. Opportunities for such inquiries at the moment are few and far between: the international bankruptcy or insolvency procedure that has been proposed by a number of NGOs (see Box 2.3, below) might address this deficiency.

A key element of the provision of financing for debt rescheduling was 'conditionality': funds were made available only if the debtor country agreed to a relatively standard package of macroeconomic policies that were designed primarily to ensure that interest payments could be maintained. Although the specifics of conditionality varied somewhat, the core elements were remarkably constant:

1. Opening domestic markets to imports, in the interests of improved efficiency, through tariff reductions and removal of import controls;
2. Integrating national economies into the global economy, with the specific aim of increasing exports, by way of exchange rate devaluation that favoured export industries and removal of controls on FDI, while;
3. Restricting domestic consumption by moving toward free market pricing. Policy measures included not only reducing 'overvalued' exchange rates, but also deregulation of food and energy prices and elimination of food price subsidies;
4. Divesting state resources in favour of the private sector through privatization and contracting out of services;

5. Reducing state expenditure (with the exception of military expenditure) through devolution of responsibilities to local communities and cost recovery for formerly public services that were not actually privatized; and
6. Reorientation of social and economic policy toward attracting private, primarily foreign, investment (adapted from Milward, 2000).

By the end of the 1980s, 'cross-conditionality' involving both the World Bank and the IMF had become routine (Walton *et al.*, 1994: 19), further ensuring the subordination of domestic policy goals to the imperative of generating revenues sufficient to meet debt obligations, even if the economy's ability to meet basic human needs (such as food or clean water) deteriorated. This often happened as a result of mandated domestic austerity measures, which also decreased access to services, including health care and education, as public expenditures were cut and user charges introduced (e.g. see Cheru, 1999; Chossudovsky, 1997; Cornia *et al.*, 1987, 1988; Creese & Kutzin, 1997; Schoepf *et al.*, 2000; Walton *et al.*, 1994; Yong Kim, Shakow *et al.*, 2000).

The impacts of SAPs have proved difficult to separate from the effects of economic crises that preceded their imposition. Many countries experienced severe economic recessions in the early 1980s that were already eroding their capacities to provide programming to support the health and livelihoods of vulnerable populations (Braveman & Tarimo, 2002). Only in a few countries strongly committed to pro-child and pro-poor policies even in difficult times (e.g. Cuba, South Korea) did 'broad trends towards improvement in child welfare continue ... almost unaffected' (Jolly & Cornia, 1984). There is less ambiguity about the generally negative effects these programs had on people's health. A review of the health consequences of structural adjustment conducted for the CMH (Breman & Shelton, 2001) found a preponderance of negative effects among 76 studies identified. A more even distribution of positive and negative findings existed among what the authors classified as 'empirical' studies, a term that was never defined. This literature review was weakened, however, by a selective and incomplete sampling of literature: the authors do not appear to have read the country case studies from the original *Adjustment with a Human Face* study (Cornia *et al.*, 1987 & 1988), nor did they consider ethnographic studies (e.g. Schoepf, 1998; Schoepf *et al.*, 2000, on AIDS in Africa) and other forms of field observation (e.g. Farmer, 1999). Although the point cannot be explored here, these omissions suggest the importance of a much more general issue: what counts as 'knowledge' in development policy discourse, and what power relations determine the answer to this question (cf. Wilks & Lefrançois, 2002). Nevertheless, Breman and Shelton (2001) found that most studies identified negative health impacts from structural adjustment in Africa.

The Need for Debt Relief and the HIPC Initiative

The urgency of debt relief as a precondition for achieving various social, economic and environmental policy objectives was identified more than a decade ago by the WCED (1987) and UNICEF (Cornia *et al.*, 1987, 1988; UNICEF, 1990). More recently, a review prepared for the Economic and Social Council of the United Nations Commission on Human Rights documented the destructive consequences of the debt crisis and the role of the industrialized world in perpetuating it, and argued for a program of debt cancellation as part of a broader package of initiatives combining sustainable economic growth with social justice (Cheru, 1999). In the same year UNCTAD (1999) argued that the 'debt overhang' of the LDCs continued to be the major obstacle to their economic growth and development. It is also a major impediment to their ability to invest in health, education, water, sanitation and other essential human development infrastructures. For example, scheduled debt service in Zambia and Tanzania exceeds 40 per cent of their governments' budgetary resources (AFRODAD, 2002). African countries as a whole are currently paying over US$15 billion annually in debt servicing charges to rich country creditors, an amount that exceeds the total aid they receive (OECD, 2002b: 258).

This background is essential to understanding the genesis and limitations of the Heavily Indebted Poor Countries (HIPC) Initiative, announced by the World Bank and IMF in 1996 as a way of providing more effective debt relief to a limited number of countries (41, 33 of which are in Africa). HIPC, and the subsequent 'enhanced' HIPC Initiative, have been the centerpiece of G8 debt relief efforts, even though the HIPC countries account for only ten per cent of the developing world's debt (UNRISD, 2000: 22).

> Debt relief – particularly the Enhanced Heavily Indebted Poor Countries (HIPC) Initiative – is a valuable contribution to the fight against poverty .... We are delighted twenty-three countries have qualified for an overall amount of debt relief of over [US]$53 billion, out of an initial stock of debt of [US]$74 billion. We must continue this progress' (Genoa Communiqué, para. 7).
>
> The Enhanced HIPC Initiative we launched in Cologne aims to increase growth, reduce poverty and provide a lasting exit from unsustainable debt, by reducing debt on the basis of strengthened policy reforms. ... This will significantly reduce their debt service, thus freeing resources for social sector expenditure, in particular education and health (Genoa Communiqué, para. 15).

A recent progress report on Enhanced HIPC notes that

[a]s of March 2002, 25 countries [have] reached their decision point[2] under the enhanced Heavily Indebted Poor Countries (HIPC) Initiative framework and are now receiving debt service relief under the Initiative which will amount to about [US]$40 billion over time, or a reduction of nearly [US]$24 billion in the net present value (NPV) of their outstanding stock of debt. This is more than 70 percent of the total relief projected to be delivered under the Initiative (World Bank, 2002b).

The same report calculated that African countries eligible for debt relief under HIPC would be able to increase their social expenditures from 4.3 per cent of GDP in 1999, to 5.5 per cent of GDP in 2002 (World Bank, 2002b: 6). Adrian Lovett of Jubilee 2000, in an address to the pre-Genoa summit meeting with NGOs (Florence, 1–3 April 2001) noted that, of the debt relief so far granted, two-thirds of the budgetary savings were going to health and education, and the rest to water, sanitation and HIV/AIDS programs. Later that year, however, a controversy arose that serves to illuminate the tensions between social expenditure priorities and the commercial interests of countries that provide development assistance – a topic examined at greater length in Chapter 6. Tanzania secured a loan to buy an expensive military air traffic control system from British Aerospace, even though the cost – according to Kevin Watkins of Oxfam – would 'wipe out about two thirds of the budget savings Tanzania would make' from the HIPC Initiative (Watkins, 2001). The purchase eventually went ahead, and indeed Tanzania was able to secure a substantial additional aid package from the UK (see Box 6.3, Chapter 6).

The G8, in other words, have lived up to their debt relief commitments. The key question involves the adequacy of those commitments. The statement issued at the start of the 2001 Genoa summit, for example, reiterated their 1999 commitment to forgive any debts associated with the loan portions of ODA to HIPC countries (Genoa Statement, para. 16). But this debt reduction will be available only once HIPC countries have reached their 'decision point', and will not be fully implemented until they achieve their 'completion point', something only five HIPC countries had accomplished by the end of 2002 (World Bank, 2003b).

Eligibility for debt relief under HIPC is currently determined based on a ratio of debt service costs to export revenues. However, a more appropriate ratio involves debt service costs to government revenues (Pettifor *et al.*, 2001: 8–10). Numerous studies have indicated that the level of debt relief provided – roughly one third of all HIPC debt – is thoroughly inadequate, given the economic challenges faced by the countries that qualify for debt relief under the terms of the initiative. For example, a US General Accounting Office analysis of seven recipient countries, published in 2000, warned that the decline in debt service for the seven countries [studied] will only 'free up' resources for additional poverty reduction if countries continue to borrow at the same level and concessional terms as in the years prior to their qualifying for debt relief. This occurs because countries previously borrowed for several reasons including debt payments, and they will need to continue borrowing after receiving debt relief in order to meet their remaining debt payments and to increase spending on poverty reduction (USGAO, 2000: 9).

Pettifor *et al.* (2001) examined a much larger number of countries and considered both uncertainties surrounding commodity prices and the economic consequences of the HIV/AIDS epidemic. They reached the same conclusion: 'Enhanced HIPC is debt rescheduling not debt reduction' (Pettifor *et al.*, 2001: 10). The current rate of debt stock reduction from debt relief is approximately 65 per cent; US$40 billion in debt relief ultimately eliminates only US$26 billion in original debt stock. The US$14 billion difference is the new debt that continues to accumulate over the period of the initiative. If this rate persists over the whole period of the HIPC program, the total debt stock eliminated will be approximately US$45 billion. But the initial debt stock for these countries in 1996 stood at over US$74 billion, with compounding interest and additional lending continually increasing it.

In other words, having received the full amount of debt relief for which they are eligible, at the end of the HIPC Initiative, the heavily indebted poor countries will remain heavily indebted poor countries. By the World Bank and IMF's own estimates, at least ten of the 26 countries involved in the HIPC program will exit it with unsustainable debt loads, and their criterion for what constitutes a 'sustainable' debt (150 per cent of a country's export earnings) has been widely critiqued (Denny, 2003a). This problem is particularly severe for several sub-Saharan African countries, notably Rwanda, Zambia, Chad, Burkina Faso, Malawi, the Gambia, Tanzania and Niger. The Enhanced HIPC Initiative, for example, will provide debt reduction equivalent to only about three years of multilateral loans to Burkina Faso, Mali, Mozambique and Uganda (World Bank, 2002b). These countries in future years will have debt repayment requirements that, with essential spending requirements, will still exceed available revenues. They will have to continue borrowing in the future to continue paying down what they borrowed in the past, *ad infinitum* (Pettifor *et al.*, 2001; EURODAD, 2001). They are also continuing to pay debt servicing each year, amounting to US$73 million in Ethiopia (currently facing one of its worst famines ever), and over US$250 million in Zambia, Mozambique and Malawi, all of which are also facing famines (Denny, 2003a). Oxfam (2001a: Figure 1) calculates that in 14 HIPC countries, annual debt servicing costs will exceed combined public spending on health and primary education even *after* debt relief is obtained.

Hanlon (2000), working backward from estimates of the amount of spending that would be required to meet a package of development goals similar to the Millennium Development Goals (MDGs) (see Box 2.2, below) throughout the developing world, estimates that approximately US$600 billion (at current value) in debt reduction would be needed in order to ensure that debt repayment did not occur at the expense of essential social spending.[3] This is roughly eight times the value of debt relief to be provided under Enhanced HIPC. Hanlon's estimates consider not only the HIPC countries, which he estimates will require debt relief worth US$180 billion if essential social spending is not to be compromised, but also many others. His calculations imply, for instance, debt relief of US$24 billion for Argentina, US$116 billion for Indonesia and US$98 billion for India – countries that cannot qualify for HIPC despite the prevalence of poverty and desperation within their borders. It should further be noted that some development NGOs have argued for even more extensive debt relief, invoking both the impossible arithmetic of debt repayment given the small amounts of development assistance available (Bond, 2001: 28, 140) and the extent to which the debt burden of poor countries consists of 'odious debt' (see Box 2.1, above) incurred by leaders in order to finance political repression or the accumulation of private fortunes. Economist Jeffrey Sachs (2000: 2), in a scathing critique of 'the world's minimalist approach to helping the poor', has called HIPC 'a program so badly mangled by the international community that millions of people around the world have protested the debt relief policies that the IMF and World Bank call their finest moment.'

Box 2.2: The International and the Millennium Development Goals

As will be seen in the next chapter, the G8 have committed to support both the International Development Goals and the later Millennium Development Goals. The IDGs and the first seven of the MDGs are virtually identical – not surprisingly, since they arose from the same multilateral consultative process (Devarajan *et al.*, 2002) (see Table 2.1, below). The full set of MDGs, as adopted by the UN General Assembly in 2000 (Resolution A/RES/55/2, United Nations Millennium Declaration), includes a considerably more expansive set of targets, under the heading of an eighth goal: a global partnership for development (see Devarajan *et al.*, 2002: 34–5). The targets specified under this goal relate, *inter alia*, to debt relief, market access, access to affordable drugs and providing productive youth employment. In this book, discussion of the MDGs is presumed to involve the first seven goals, unless otherwise specified, because of the convergence between the IDGs and the MDGs. This does not mean that Goal 8 is any less important than the first seven: indeed, the thrust of this book is that changes of the kind envisioned are especially necessary in order to achieve longer-term global improvements in population health.

Table 2.1: International Development Goals and Millennium Development Goals Compared

International Development Goals	Millennium Development Goals (Goals 1–7)
1. Reduce the proportion of people living in extreme poverty (less than US$1/day) by 2015.	Goal 1: Eradicate extreme poverty and hunger. Target 1: Halve, between 1990 and 2015, the proportion of people whose income is less than US$1/day. Target 2: Halve, between 1990 and 2015, the proportion of people who suffer from hunger.
2. Enrol all children in primary school by 2015.	Goal 2: Achieve universal primary education. Target 3: Ensure that, by 2015, children everywhere, boys and girls alike, will be able to complete a full course of primary education.
3. Eliminate gender disparities in primary and secondary education by 2005.	Goal 3: Promote gender equality and empower women. Target 4: Eliminate gender disparity in primary and secondary education preferably by 2005 and to all levels of education no later than 2015.
4. Reduce infant and child (under-five) mortality rates by two-thirds between 1990 and 2015.	Goal 4: Reduce child mortality. Target 5: Reduce by two-thirds, between 1990 and 2015, the under-five mortality rate.

5. Reduce maternal mortality ratios by three-quarters between 1990 and 2015.	Goal 5: Improve maternal health. Target 6: Reduce by three-quarters, between 1990 and 2015, the maternal mortality ratio.
6. Provide access for all who need reproductive health services by 2015.	Goal 6: Combat HIV/AIDS, malaria and other diseases. Target 7: Have halted by 2015, and begun to reverse, the spread of HIV/AIDS. Target 8: Have halted by 2015, and begun to reverse, the incidence of malaria and other major disease.
7. Implement national strategies for sustainable development by 2005 so as to reverse the loss of environmental resources by 2015.	Goal 7: Ensure environmental sustainability. Target 9: Integrate the principles of sustainable development into country policies and programs and reverse the loss of environmental resources. Target 10: Halve, by 2015, the proportion of people without sustainable access to safe drinking water. Target 11: By 2020, to have achieved a significant improvement in the lives of at least 100 million slum dwellers.

Source: IMF *et al.* (2000) for IDGs; Devarajan *et al.* (2002: 34–5) for MDGs

Development NGOs are urging a different approach to debt relief. The African Forum and Network on Debt and Development (AFRODAD), for example, argues that, instead of conditional or tied ODA, donor countries should direct all aid to write off *all* loans (total debt cancellation) for African countries – a zero debt, zero aid proposition that, with an overdue opening of Northern markets to African goods, would provide African countries with the capital and autonomy they need for both economic and human development (AFRODAD, 2002: 32).[4] We expand upon this argument in Chapter 7. The Jubilee 2000 movement, an international NGO campaign, gathered 24 million signatures on a petition urging G8 leaders to 'cancel the unpayable debts of the poorest countries by the year 2000, under a fair and transparent process' (http://www.jubilee2000uk.org/about/about.htm). The campaign's successor organization, Jubilee Research, argues for increased debt relief and, more importantly, a debt restructuring process that embodies principles similar to those that govern domestic bankruptcy procedures (see Box 2.3, below). This proposal is similar to one that emerged from NGO consultations preceding the Genoa summit, which further urged a cancellation of all debts to the World Bank and IMF owed by the LDCs (http://www.gnginitiative.net/gngreport.htm).

Canada has been the only G8 nation even to approach this position on debt cancellation/debt relief. Canada called for a total moratorium on debt payments for all HIPCs at the G7 finance ministers' meeting in Prague in 2000. However, Germany was 'particularly dismissive, of the proposal' (Kirton, 2001: 157), as reportedly was the US (*Globe and Mail*, 7 June 2002: A16). Former Canadian Finance Minister Paul Martin strongly advocated an international bankruptcy process that incorporates emergency standstills (an argument now being taken on board by the IMF, in light of Argentina's 2002 currency crisis; see Elliott and Teather, 2002) and more generous debt forgiveness (Martin, 2002). At the Prague meeting, Martin 'announced that Canada would cancel 100% of debt owed by HIPC countries to the Canadian Export Development Corporation (EDC) and the Canadian Wheat Board (CWB). Sub-Saharan Africa makes up about [C]$1.5 billion of developing country debt owed to Canada, of which [C]$1.1 billion is owed to EDC and CWB by HIPC countries' (CCIC Africa-Canada Forum, 2002: 1).

Martin's tenure as Canada's finance minister ended in early 2002. His replacement reportedly failed to lobby forcefully for such an initiative at the 2002 Halifax G7 finance ministers meeting, where 'there [seems to be] no political will among G7 countries, particularly the United States and Japan, to consider deeper and complete cancellation of ... unsustainable debts' (CCIC Africa-Canada Forum, 2002: 2), although the UK Chancellor of the Exchequer, Gordon Brown, reportedly lobbied for more generous debt relief for poor countries vulnerable to commodity price fluctuations (Elliott, 2002). The UK is also urging a '100% plus' approach, in which qualifying countries reaching their 'decision point' are retroactively reimbursed for debt service payments from the start of the initiative. The Halifax G7 finance ministers' meeting ultimately agreed to commit only US$1 billion in new HIPC funding, to cover a shortfall in its Trust Fund, and to call for 100 per cent of future World Bank loans for AIDS programs in HIPC countries to be non-repayable grant resources (Zeitz & Bryden, 2002: 3).

Box 2.3: Insolvency for Countries?

NGOs such as Jubilee Research and AFRODAD have put forward several proposals to adapt the treatment of insolvent debtors within the borders of industrialized countries to the situation of developing country debtors. Jubilee Research (Pettifor *et al.*, 2001; Pettifor, 2002) argues that such a procedure should be modeled on provisions of US federal law that deal with the bankruptcy of municipal governments. Key features of this proposal would be the opportunity to petition for an immediate standstill on debt repayments; a procedure for appointing an independent panel to mediate between creditors and debtors, whose function would include providing opportunities for inquiry into the legitimacy of the debts in question; continued access to capital on the part of the debtor country; protections against capital flight; and protections for human rights in the debtor country as part of the debt restructuring process. (It is not clear how these last two objectives would be ensured.) The IMF would assume the role of a 'gateway' to the process, but would not itself play an active role, because its own status as a creditor would (and does, according to critics) place it in a conflict of interest.

Since 1996, UNCTAD has been cautiously exploring the need for an international insolvency procedure modeled on the better-known 'Chapter 11' provisions of US bankruptcy law: the provisions that allow for-profit corporations to seek court protection from creditors while they restructure their operations, rather than simply liquidating their assets (see UNCTAD, 2001: 68, 133–49). In a different vein, AFRODAD (2002) suggests that the UN take the lead in efforts to establish an International Arbitration Court for Debt by international treaty. Instead of US bankruptcy law, AFRODAD uses as a model principles of international arbitration that are now widely incorporated into commercial contracts, and supported by several international conventions that provide for the inter-jurisdictional enforcement of arbitral awards. Such a court would, of course, only bind those countries that were parties to the proposed treaty.

Interestingly, the IMF itself has conceded the need for some form of international insolvency mechanism, starting with a widely cited speech by senior official Anne Krueger (2001). However, in their current form, the IMF's proposals for a Sovereign Debt Restructuring Mechanism (SDRM) have been criticized for expanding the already powerful role of the IMF in setting the terms and conditions under which new financing will be made (Pettifor &

Raffer, 2003). These observations suggest a more general limitation of the analogy with bankruptcy proceedings under national legislation – the idea that bankruptcy genuinely provides a 'fresh start', except for large corporations or ultra-wealthy households that can shelter many of their assets, is illusory. As a rule, bankruptcy more closely resembles a form of indentured servitude to creditors, with debtors expected (a) to liquidate saleable assets, and (b) to assign priority to meeting their debt obligations. At the household level, the health consequences can be substantial (Jacoby, 2002). In other words, the asymmetrical power relations characteristic of routine household or business bankruptcy rather closely resemble the conditionalities associated with structural adjustment as they have historically been applied to developing countries' economies. Taking the human consequences of developing country debt seriously is likely to require a different vocabulary, and more radical solutions (more radical, because they involve real large-scale resource transfers from the rich world to the poor) that involve, *inter alia*, debt cancellation rather than just new forms of rescheduling.

HIPC Conditionality: Are PRSPs Just the Reincarnation of Structural Adjustment?

Further problems arise because HIPC eligibility is contingent on the recipient government's completion of a Poverty Reduction Strategy Paper. PRSPs were launched by the World Bank and IMF in December 1999, as 'a new approach to the challenge of reducing poverty in low-income countries based on country-owned poverty reduction strategies that would serve as a framework for development assistance' (International Development Association/IMF, 2002: 5). Indeed, PRSPs are becoming a central element of the G8 approach to development policy:

> We urge multilateral development organisations and financial institutions to support developing countries' efforts to create a favourable trade and investment climate, including through the Poverty Reduction Strategy Papers (PRSPs) and the Integrated Framework (IF) (Okinawa Communiqué, para. 17).
>
> We welcome the efforts being made by HIPCs to develop comprehensive and country-owned poverty reduction strategies through a participatory process involving civil society. IFIs should, along with other donors, help HIPCs prepare PRSPs and assist their financial resource management by providing technical assistance (Okinawa Communiqué, para. 24).

Placing poverty reduction at the centre of development strategy is clearly a laudable policy direction. However, as suggested by the reference to 'creat[ing] a favourable trade and investment climate ... through the Poverty Reduction Strategy Papers', the lenders who assess PRSPs operate on the presumption that poverty reduction is best achieved through neo-liberal prescriptions for privatization, deregulation and rapid integration into the global economy – the same prescriptions that often exacerbated existing inequalities when they were incorporated into structural adjustment regimes (SAPRIN, 2002). Indeed, direct parallels exist between the PRSP process of qualifying for debt relief and earlier forms of conditionality (Cheru, 2001; IMF, 2001: 50–2; UNCTAD, 2002a: 191).

The United Nations Development Programme (UNDP), in its assessment of the PRSP process, notes that advice on the requirement for a macroeconomic framework identifying fiscal and financing policies for poverty reduction is weak, contains many unexamined assumptions and does not adequately emphasize distributional impacts of macroeconomic policies (UNDP, 2001b). UNCTAD (2002b: 197) links the PRSP process with the inadequacy of overall levels of debt relief, noting that in order to ensure that a PRSP is perceived as 'realistic', countries like Uganda and Tanzania are still investing far less than the minimum amounts required for health and social programs. The WHO goes further in analyzing serious gaps in existing PRSPs with respect to health. Among its major criticisms: PRSPs deal with ill health as a *consequence* of poverty, but not as a *cause* of poverty, particularly with respect to the effects of cost recovery or user charges for health-care services on the poor. Similarly, PRSPs address health as an outcome of development, rather than a means of development. At least implicitly, then, investments in health are regarded as secondary to investments in economic growth. Six of the ten PRSPs reviewed by the WHO referred to the need to subsidize cost-recovery health services for the poor, but failed to mention any of the well-known failures of such fee-exemption programs, even though the failures were raised in the public participatory documents associated with these PRSPs. PRSPs do not deal with such important health system issues as governance (e.g. government doctors also working privately) and expenditure levels well below the minimum needed to provide basic primary health care; and there is no indication that the PRSP process is leading to any increased commitments in health or education (WHO, 2002a).

Several development NGOs have noted that the degree of public or civil society participation in developing PRSPs has been minimal. Given the short time since their inception, and that eight full and 41 interim country PRSPs have been completed, the pace of their development perforce precludes wider civil society engagement. A recent World Bank/IMF evaluation of the PRSP process acknowledges this problem, although it also notes that public participation is slowly increasing, government 'ownership' is strengthening and there is more transparent communication between governments and their citizens as a result of the PRSP requirement (World Bank/IMF, 2002b: 6–7). Some G8 countries, such as Canada, are urging that PRSPs associated with their development assistance include gender analyses of poverty-reduction plans, an extremely important consideration for maternal/child health and for HIV/AIDS prevention (Tomlinson, 2002). There is also some evidence that countries engaged in the PRSP process are making education a higher priority in national government policies and plans (UNESCO, 2002b: 131). But the PRSP process continues to be plagued by several development assistance challenges, including lack of adequate public budget and accounting structures in most affected countries, inadequate funding for the costs of broader civil society participation, and a lack of mechanisms for ensuring that programs actually do reach and benefit the poor primarily (World Bank/IMF, 2000, 2002b).

The major concern remains that full PRSPs require integration into a comprehensive macroeconomic framework that simultaneously incorporates pro-poor and pro-growth strategies, and in fact attaches highest priority to accelerated global economic integration (Craig & Porter, 2003). Yet the World Bank and IMF acknowledge that 'the linkages between macroeconomic policies and poverty reduction are complex' (World Bank/IMF, 2000: 11). They also acknowledge that policy adjustments creating macroeconomic stability can cause short-term fiscal shortfalls, which they 'hoped ... could eventually lead to an increase in donor assistance to support larger fiscal deficits in line with the targets identified in the PRSP.' In other words, development assistance is expected to provide a safety net for the losers from policies that were adopted in order to qualify for loans from the IFIs. We note in Chapter 6 the uneven, and less than enviable, record of the G8 with respect to providing such assistance.

A critique that echoes many earlier commentaries on the effects of structural adjustment conditionality points out 'that the [PRSP] focus on short-term economic stability often comes at the expense of long-term sustainable development' (World Bank/IMF, 2000: 13). UNCTAD (2002a), in its review of the PRSP initiative, cites a public statement by a World Bank official that 'the PRSP is a compulsory process wherein the people with the money tell the people who want the money what they need to do to get the money', and suggests that this can lead to governments 'second-guessing' what the World Bank and IMF want to see, thus shaping their PRSPs as a response to earlier World Bank and IMF lending conditionalities. Cheru (2001: 12), in his assessment of PRSPs, quotes a finance minister from one of the HIPCs: 'We do not want to second-guess the Fund. We prefer to pre-empt them by giving them what they want before they start lecturing us about this and that. By so doing, we send a clear message that we know what we are doing, i.e., we believe in structural adjustment.'

A special concern has been the incorporation of user fees for primary health care and education in some PRSPs, despite even the World Bank's acknowledgment that this increases the difficulty of access for the poor (Naiman, 2001; Hilary, 2001). According to Naiman (2001), leaked World Bank documents concerning the Tanzanian interim PRSP led to NGO protest and, in the US, lobbying by certain legislators who pointed out that, under October 2000 US legislation (itself a product of intense NGO and AFL-CIO lobbying efforts), US representatives to the World Bank and IMF could not support any primary health-care or education program that included user fees. The Tanzanian interim PRSP indicated that the poor would be exempt from such fees, but NGOs and others cited extensive evidence that such exemption schemes have failed (Naiman, 2001; WHO, 2002a).

Many development NGOs insist that debt relief and ODA must be de-linked from the PRSP process. If debt relief is to provide either a meaningful general stimulus to development or the more specific fiscal flexibility necessary for investments in health and education, it cannot be contingent on the macroeconomic conditions historically imposed by lenders. Some of the G8 are moving, cautiously, in this direction. France is reported to be progressively removing conditionality on its bilateral aid (Canonne, 2002); Italy is imposing very little (Rhi-Sausi & Zupi, 2002); Japan never agreed with the emphasis of SAPs on market liberalization and privatization, believing that governments had stronger roles to play (Takayanagi, 2002); and Germany's concerns include respect for human rights, public participation in political decision-making, a social market economy and a good legal system (Dederichs-Bain, 2002). Canada, the UK and the US appear to be lining up more firmly behind the PRSP process. To the extent that G8 nations increase the multilateral portion of their ODA, the PRSP process will likely continue to increase its influence on financial relations between the G8 and poor countries.

Poverty Reduction and Foreign Direct Investment

A major goal of PRSPs (and before them SAPs) has been to create conditions favourable to attracting foreign direct investment that, in turn, would supposedly fuel new economic growth. This assumption is embedded in G8 summit statements, and is also to be found in NEPAD:

> The *New Partnership for Africa's Development* seeks to increase private capital flows to Africa, as an essential component of a sustainable long-term approach to filling the resource gap.

> The first priority is to address investors' perception of Africa as a 'high
> risk' continent, especially with regard to security of property rights,
> regulatory framework and markets (NEPAD, paras. 153–4).

Even before urging the multilateral development organizations and financial institutions to step up the pace of the PRSP process, the G8 'express[ed] concern that certain regions remain marginalized as regards foreign direct investment, and that the 48 LDCs attract less than 1% of total foreign direct investment flows to the developing countries' (Okinawa Communiqué, para. 17).

Since most African countries have adopted SAPs as the price of assistance from the IFIs and many are now following PRSPs, one would expect them to have been rewarded with a greater flow of FDI. In absolute terms, that is so. Between 1990 and 2000, FDI inflows to sub-Saharan Africa increased eight-fold, from US$834 million to US$6.67 billion. It is also so in relative terms, with sub-Saharan Africa's share of global FDI rising from 0.4 per cent to 0.5 per cent (World Bank, 2002d: 354), although the percentages are so low they are almost meaningless in the global context of financial flows, and its share of overall FDI inflows to developing countries remained stuck at four per cent.

Governments are not necessarily responsible for where firms and investors located within their borders choose to invest – although a case could be made for social responsibility requirements in the case of large institutional investors like public sector pension funds, which might include policies of investing in the developing world when consistent with the institutions' fiduciary obligations. But the evidence on FDI flows raises two questions. Firstly, are the macroeconomic policies that are being demanded of HIPC countries and other LDCs in Africa necessary to attract such investment? Secondly, is the prescription for FDI-led growth – normally understood to require major increases in exports – even appropriate for sub-Saharan Africa?

In a world of increasingly hypermobile capital, the answer to the first question may very well be 'yes,' at least in situations where countries cannot realistically expect to rely on domestic savings and development assistance as sources of capital investment. However, the potentially destructive effects of organizing economic policy around the competition for foreign investment – a few of which we discuss briefly in the next chapter, as they relate to health systems – should not be underestimated. The resulting dilemma is succinctly captured by a recent study of FDI in the developing world as a whole: '[P]rogressives often criticize FDI as a destructive force while at the same time decrying the fact that many poor countries can't seem to attract any. It may be that the only thing worse than engaging in this bidding war and getting FDI is engaging in it and not getting any' (Crotty *et al.*, 1998: 121; see also Box 2.4, below). FDI has only been successful in creating employment in developing countries when it has been forthcoming in very large amounts (e.g. Singapore, Malaysia, the Mexican *maquiladoras*), and such FDI generally takes advantage of low labour costs rather than developing new technological capacities in the host country, rendering the employment and its associated economic growth very fragile (Third World Network/UNDP, 2001: 20). This is especially true for industries characterized by commodity chains that cross multiple borders, with associated competition among contract suppliers. Stated another way, '[c]ompetition among firms, including international firms, in developing countries becomes competition among labour located in different countries' (UNCTAD, 2002c: ix), creating downward pressure on wages and disincentives to improve working conditions. More fundamentally, Tandon (2000, original emphasis) has argued that the prevailing orthodoxy that growth must be led by foreign investment does not fit the historical facts, in Africa or elsewhere: '*[T]he very assumption that FDIs are necessary for development of Africa (or for the developing countries generally) was itself at best an untested theory, and at worst a plain inversion of the truth ... it was growth that attracted FDIs, and not FDIs that brought growth.*' In any event, the social policy implications of organizing macroeconomic policy around attracting foreign investment illustrate how and why research on health and development needs to be broadly transdisciplinary, engaging specialists in development policy and political economy (to name just two fields), as well as those who normally contribute to research on international health.

Box 2.4: Capital Account Liberalization and Foreign Direct Investment

The G8, reflecting mainstream economic theory on the benefits of liberalization, frequently claim the importance of trade and investment to economic growth and poverty reduction, e.g. 'trade and investment are critical to promoting sustainable economic growth and reducing poverty' (Okinawa Communiqué, para.17). Given the low amount of savings in many developing, particularly least developed, countries, investment is assumed to be primarily foreign. A recent study of capital account liberalization, which is presumed to increase the flows of presumably beneficial FDI, found that this was so principally for *developed* but not for *developing* countries (Cobham, 2002: 169). Moreover, there are significant negative poverty impacts associated with increased FDI in developing countries when it does occur, quite apart from the problems associated with currency 'meltdowns' and conditions imposed upon the bailouts. A structural difficulty is embedded in the need for governments to prevent inflationary pressures brought on by increased FDI flows by selling bonds in their domestic currency and purchasing bonds in foreign currencies. Differences in the interest rates or fluctuations in exchange rates between these two transactions represent a cost to the developing country government; and so 'the effect of capital inflows is to seriously reduce the level of government expenditure' (Cobham, 2002: 178). Private sector growth may occur, but whether or not this translates into benefits for the poor is moot. This is not to claim that FDI is inevitably disadvantageous, but rather that its advantages are not without significant development costs.

International Finance, Tax Competition and Offshore Financial Centres

The complex issues associated with tax competition and the operations of offshore financial centres deserve the attention of the international health research and policy community for the following reasons. As we indicate in Chapter 7, many developing and least developed countries rely on tariffs for a far higher proportion of their overall tax revenues than do the industrialized countries. This pattern replicates the situation in the industrialized countries at a much earlier stage of their economic development, but trade liberalization is rapidly reducing the significance of this source of revenue without – at least over the short term – generating alternatives. When governments' fiscal capacity is simultaneously eroded by reductions in tariff revenue and by international pressures to maintain 'competitive' tax regimes in order to attract direct and portfolio investment, the effect is to make taxation to finance such policies as income support and investment in basic health and education more problematic than in previous decades (Von Furstenberg & Kirton, 2001: 248; CMH, 2001: 76). Indeed, capital flight has the potential seriously to erode the fiscal capacity even of wealthy countries (Avi-Yonah, 2000; OECD, 2001b), just as it has already compromised many developing countries (see Box 2.1, above). The financial volatility that results from the hypermobility of capital can result in economic crises, such as the collapse of the Mexican peso in 1994–95, the so-called Asian meltdown in 1997–98 and the more recent implosion of the Argentine economy, which plunged millions of people into poverty, with attendant effects on the social determinants of health (e.g. see Bello *et al.*, 1998; CELS, 2001, 2002; DePalma, 1995; Kristof, 1998a, 1998b; Myerson, 1995; Reveles & Terán, 2001; Santiso, 1999; Walton *et al.*, 1994; Weeks, 1995; Yong Kim, Shakow *et al.*, 2000).[5]

A recent report from Oxfam Great Britain (2000) estimated that developing countries might be losing as much as US$50 billion per year in tax revenues – roughly equivalent to the annual amount of ODA they receive – as a consequence of tax avoidance and inter-jurisdictional tax competition. Even these amounts pale in comparison to estimates of the total value of assets held in offshore tax havens (Oxfam, 2000: 3–5). The line between 'legitimate' diversification of household and corporate investments from tax avoidance and tax evasion is not always clearly visible. It is clear, however, that the general erosion of barriers to capital mobility – a trend to which the rise of offshore finance clearly contributes (cf. Naylor, 1987) – offers abundant opportunities for small, propertied minorities to protect assets against the redistributive consequences of national and sub-national taxation. One recent estimate is that an astounding one-quarter of the world's financial assets are being managed from or through offshore financial centres (Levin, 2003); another places the value at roughly US$8 *trillion*, which, if subjected to a 'freeloader levy' of just 3.5 per cent, would generate US$280 billion annually (Gates, 2002: 21).

The G8 leaders have attempted to address these problems, although not with specific reference either to capital flight or to the potential channels of influence on population health. In 2000, a detailed set of commitments addressed 'abuse of the global financial system' under the separate but related headings of 'money laundering'; 'tax havens and other harmful tax practices'; 'offshore financial centres'; and 'the role of IFIs' (Okinawa Statement, para. 26). More recently, in 2001, the G8 nations 'reaffirm[ed] [their] support for the multilateral effort against abuses of the global financial system and endorse[d] [their] Finance Ministers' recommendations to address this challenge' (Genoa Statement, para. 14, citing *Fighting the Abuses of the Global Financial System*, Report of G7 Finance Ministers and Central Bank Governors, Rome, 7 July 2001).

Most of these activities endorsed at Okinawa were and are actually undertaken by the OECD. The OECD's Financial Action Task Force against money laundering (FATF), whose 'initial work' was 'welcomed' at Okinawa (Okinawa Statement, para. 26), was established at the G7 summit in 1989; its mandate specifically addresses national policies with respect to the proceeds of serious crimes, including drug trafficking.[6] In 2000, the FATF published its first list of Non-Compliant Countries and Territories (NCCTs), defined with reference to a set of 25 practices said to be conducive to money laundering (FATF, 2000). By the FATF's own account, most countries it has identified as NCCTs have responded with appropriate legislative and regulatory actions (for updates, see http://www1.oecd.org/fatf/NCCT_en.html). These national policy responses to FATF have probably improved financial reporting, transparency and client identification, and thereby made certain forms of tax avoidance more difficult. However, the FATF's mandate does not include tax competition or international financial stability.

In 1996, the OECD established a project on 'harmful tax competition,' whose initial report was published in 1998 (OECD, 1998). The OECD's activities in this area were 'welcome[d]' and 'encourage[d]' by the G8 in 2000 (Okinawa Statement, para. 26), despite the US refusal to participate in May 2001 talks convened by the OECD to advance this project (Du Boff, 2002: 28). Since the publication of the 1998 report, the OECD has continued to refine the criteria for defining 'tax havens,' to the point that by April 2002, only seven countries (Andorra, Liechtenstein, Liberia, Monaco, the Marshall Islands, Nauru and Vanuatu) remained on the OECD's 'uncooperative' list (Kondo, 2002). The shortness of this list, and the absence of specific attention to the destructive social consequences of capital flight in the developing world, raises concerns that harmful tax competition is being defined less broadly than would be justified by the potentially destructive effects of the erosion of governments' fiscal capacity. A further concern is that tax competition among the OECD countries (including the G8 countries themselves) may be escaping scrutiny. Only in January 2003, for example, did the EU agree to end banking practices allowing non-residents to earn interest tax-free. Luxembourg, Austria and Belgium would not have to share banking information but would be required to impose a withholding tax on interest-earning investments; however, this would not begin until 2004 or be fully phased in until 2010 (*The Economist*, 25 January 2003: 72). A deal is still to be reached with non-EU member Switzerland, and it is not even clear that all EU members will ratify January's agreement (Denny, 2003b: 14).

The report of the UN's high level panel on financing for development (the Zedillo report), released in 2001 as background for the 2002 Monterrey conference on Financing for Development, called for considering the establishment of an International Tax Organization. The proposed organization would have a variety of roles, ranging from providing technical assistance to national governments (an activity the importance of which was acknowledged at the Okinawa summit in 2000) to sharing tax information in order to limit tax evasion on offshore investment income and actively trying to limit the use of 'excessive' tax incentives to attract multinational firms. The panel noted:

> If an ITO succeeded in curbing tax evasion and tax competition, there would be two beneficial consequences. One would be an increase in the proportion of a given volume of taxes paid by (a) dishonest taxpayers and (b) mobile factors of production (such as capital). Most people would consider this an unambiguous gain. The second consequence would be an increase in tax revenue at given tax rates (UN, 2001: 27-8).

In some of the most legally and financially sophisticated countries in the world, concern is growing about erosion of the domestic tax base as a result of offshore reincorporations motivated by tax advantages (Johnston, 2002; Rosenbaum, 2002), the rise of private banking services (e.g. USGAO, 1999) and, in the United Kingdom, the ability of the super-rich to opt for an offshore domicile with a more advantageous tax regime while remaining physically resident in Britain (Davies, 2002). For developing countries that may have limited administrative capacity, and that are exhorted to attract private investment as a central element of their growth and poverty-reduction strategies, the challenges – and the potential health consequences – are vastly greater.

Despite growing policy attention to the larger issue of financial mobility (legal and illegal), the connections among capital flight, tax competition and the social determinants of health are not yet well understood by either academic researchers or policy makers. Further research in this area, comprising both country-specific case studies and investigations of international capital flows, will be extremely important (Cobham, 2002: 182). The research task is complicated by the extreme technical complexity of the policy field, the obvious interest of users of offshore financial centres in concealing details of their operations, and the normative difficulty in distinguishing between harmful tax competition and the efforts to create investor-friendly economic environments that are a central element of many contemporary policy prescriptions.

Summary: Chapter Two

Two of the major vehicles by which G8 macroeconomic policy preferences have been imposed globally are the SAPs and PRSPs of the World Bank and the IMF, which are dominated by the G8 countries. (A third vehicle, trade liberalization, is taken up in later chapters.) The effects of SAPs on health care and health status have been studied for almost two decades, with largely negative findings. While PRSPs emphasize country 'ownership' and civil society participation, their requirements for a macroeconomic framework with recommended elements almost identical to those of SAPs have raised criticisms from civil society groups, international development organizations and several UN agencies.

SAPs were unable to alleviate the severe debt problems of many developing and most of the least developed countries. The G8's HIPC Initiative for debt relief, while freeing up some national income for use in the health, education and water/sanitation sectors, is widely criticized for being debt restructuring rather than actual relief. Many HIPC countries will exit the initiative with unsustainable debt loads. Estimated costs of effective debt cancellation for all developing countries are high, but represent only a small percentage of the net wealth of OECD donor countries. It is unlikely that countries that remain crippled by debt will ever be able to develop economically, or make any sustained progress towards the IDGs to which the G8 countries regularly commit their support. Civil society groups, and even some G8 member countries, have called for more radical approaches, including complete debt cancellation, particularly of 'odious debts,' or 'bankruptcy' proceedings structured to insulate poor and vulnerable groups while also allowing appropriate forms of economic development.

A key assumption of G8 development policy preferences is that conventional macroeconomic policies at the national level will attract the FDI that is an indispensable prerequisite for economic growth. This assumption has not been borne out empirically. When FDI materializes, it creates the risk of 'compradorization,' in which the economic development of the receiving country becomes subject to the interests of foreign investors rather than its own citizens.

Explicit or Specific Commitments: Macroeconomic Policy, Structural Adjustment and Debt Relief

- Enhanced HIPC Initiative, 23 countries qualified for overall debt relief of $53 billion, out of an initial stock of debt of $74 billion (Genoa).

  Accomplished: Yes. As of March 2002, 25 countries received debt service relief that will amount to about $40 billion over time.

  Adequacy: Enhanced HIPC is debt rescheduling, not debt reduction. Several countries will exit HIPC with unsustainable debt loads. Debt reduction is not extended to many other developing countries with large impoverished populations facing debt crises.

  Comments: Canada is the only G8 country that has suggested total debt cancellation for HIPC countries. Germany and the US have not supported this proposal. The UK and Canada have both urged some form of bankruptcy protection for heavily indebted countries, similar to protections offered private companies. The UK is promoting retroactive forgiveness of all debt service payments from the start of the HIPC initiative once countries reach their 'decision point.'

- HIPC countries to be forgiven loan portions of ODA (Cologne, reiterated at Genoa).

  Accomplished/Adequacy/Comments: Slow rate of eligibility for this forgiveness. At the end of 2002, only five HIPC countries had actually reached their 'completion point,' where this provision will apply.

- Urge multilateral development organizations and financial institutions to support the PRSPs and the Integrated Framework (Okinawa).
  Accomplished: Yes. The World Bank and IMF are promoting PRSPs. Several G8 countries are increasingly linking their ODA to PRSPs.
  Adequacy: The PRSP process, to date, has been plagued by lack of adequate public budget and lack of civil society participation; actual programs are not benefiting the poorest segments of society. PRSPs arguably represent a new form of conditionality.
  Comments: France is considering de-linking of aid (including debt relief) from conditionality. Italy imposes very little conditionality. Japan has never agreed that market liberalization is fundamental to economic success. Germany has focused its conditionality on human rights, civil society participation, social market economy and a strong legal system.
- Welcoming, supporting and encouraging of OECD efforts to improve financial transparency (especially with respect to money laundering) and reduce harmful tax competition (Okinawa).
  Accomplished: Yes, although the language of the commitments makes precise assessment difficult.
  Adequacy: The problem is the narrowness of definitions of 'tax havens,' and uncertainty about the willingness of G8 governments to improve compliance on the part of home country firms, investors and financial institutions.

Implicit or Generic Commitments: Macroeconomic Policy, Structural Adjustment and Debt Relief

- Debt relief will free up resources for social sector spending (Genoa).
  Accomplished: Yes. African countries under debt relief for HIPC are projected to increase social expenditure from 4.3% of GDP in 1999 to 5.5% of GDP in 2002.
  Adequacy: Continuing unsustainable debt loads for many HIPC countries will undermine their ability to provide health, education and essential human development services. For all developing countries, far higher levels of debt relief are required to ensure that debt repayment does not occur at the expense of social spending.
- PRSPs require macroeconomic framework with pro-growth strategies embodying several assumptions (cost-recovery, privatization, increased liberalization) associated with SAPs.
  Accomplished/adequacy: The UNDP and many NGOs believe that PRSP focus on poverty reduction is extremely weak, and macroeconomic assumptions are questionable. The WHO posits that there are serious

gaps relating to health in existing PRSPs. International development agencies point to the empirically demonstrated weaknesses of structural adjustment programs in achieving poverty reduction or improved health in the past.

Comments: Canada, the US and the UK appear committed to using PRSP or other macroeconomic orientation to prioritize allocation of ODA.

Endnotes to Chapter Two

[1] The UN Economic and Social Council classifies countries with fewer than 75 million people as LDCs if they are characterized by low GDP (currently US$900 or less per capita), weak human assets, and a high level of vulnerability. Forty-nine countries are now classified as LDCs (UNCTAD, 2002b). Note that the upper population threshold means the LDC category excludes countries that may actually have larger numbers of people than the entire population of 'official' LDCs living in comparable privation and insecurity.

[2] The 'decision point' is reached when debt relief under enhanced HIPC is approved by the Executive Boards of the IMF and World Bank.

[3] To put this apparently huge sum of US$600 billion into some perspective: it amounts to a little more than one per cent of the OECD members' total financial assets of US$53 trillion, and represents less global financial disruption than the financial meltdowns of recent years (Mexico, Asia, Russia, Brazil, Argentina), and the losses in global stock market valuations. Debt relief of this magnitude would be economically possible, if it were also deemed politically important by wealthy creditor nations.

[4] We caution that, assuming full market access and the most optimistic economic growth projections, full debt cancellation for African countries would still be insufficient to generate the public revenues required to develop the health, education and other infrastructures needed to attain the MDGs. Direct financial transfers from rich to poor nations, through ODA or other channels, would still be needed.

[5] Unemployment and poverty rates generally rise, and rarely drop to pre-crisis levels; wage rates often remain frozen while inflation rises, creating negative income effects for those still working; and 'fire-sales' of profitable and well-performing public utilities, as a condition for loan 'bail-outs,' have long-term implications for the poor (O'Brien, 2002: 174). O'Brien (2002: 172) points out another major reason why currency collapses, partly induced by liberalized capital markets, negatively affect the health and development of the poor: recapitalizing domestic banks costs governments enormous sums – some US$50 billion in Korea, US$70 billion in Indonesia and US$20 billion in Thailand. '[T]he average cost across 40 cases [of banking crises] was 12.8 percent of GDP', an enormous sum when compared to the portion of GDP allocated to health and social development budgets in many developing countries.

[6] The irony of G8 indifference to the far more serious health consequences of the (usually) legal activities of the tobacco industry is briefly discussed in Chapter 3.

CHAPTER THREE

Health and Health Systems

Just think of the so-called war on terrorism, with scores of billions of dollars hurled into the fray overnight to avenge the horrendous deaths of three thousand people. So explain to me why we have to grovel to extract a few billion dollars to prevent the deaths of over two million people every year, year after year after year? Why is the war against terrorism sacrosanct, and the war against AIDS equivocal? In the answer to that question lies the challenge for NEPAD and the true test for the G8 (Stephen Lewis, 2002, UN Special Envoy for HIV/AIDS in Africa).

Introduction

One of the basic axioms of population health is that health care is just one of the determinants of health, and far from the most important one. For this reason, the previous chapter focused on the health consequences of macroeconomic policy. However, health care is far from irrelevant. This is especially true in the developing world, where major improvements in health could be achieved by way of relatively low cost, low technology interventions, for instance, to prevent the spread of infectious diseases and reduce the toll from diarrhoea and childbirth (Spinaci & Heymann, 2001). A central concept in promoting these low-cost approaches has been a focus on the 'burden of disease', identifying those diseases associated with the largest reductions in healthy years of life.[1] The burden of disease approach yields global estimates that show sharply different disease distributions in the industrialized and developing worlds (see Table 3.1, below). In developing countries in 1996, for example, infectious and parasitic diseases accounted for 43 per cent of all deaths, as against just 1.2 per cent in developed nations, including the transition economies (WHO, 1997: 21).[2]

Table 3.1: DALY Loss by Disease Group and Country Income Level Grouping

Cause	Percentage of DALY loss		
	Entire global population	Poorest 20% of global population	Richest 20% of global population
Communicable, maternal, perinatal, nutritional (Group I)	43.9%	63.6%	10.9%
Non-communicable (Group II)	41.0%	23.3%	75.8%
Injuries (Group III)	15.1%	13.1%	13.3%
Total	100.0%	100.0%	100.0%

Source: WHO (1999) as cited in GFHR (2000)

Not only does the disease burden differ between rich and poor countries: poorer nations shoulder a much higher burden (see Table 3.2, on the next page). Only in depression, heart disease and motor vehicle accidents do high-income countries face a greater burden than low-income countries.

Access to health care is limited, first and foremost, by lack of resources. The world's LDCs spend an average of just US$11 per capita annually on health, including both public and private expenditures, to cope with their much greater burden of disease. For other low-income countries, average per capita expenditure on health is US$25 (Global Forum on Health, 2002: 5). By comparison, the CMH estimated the cost of a 'set of essential interventions,' which would not need to be the same for each country, at US$34 per capita per year. The report warned that '[i]f anything, we are on the low end of the range of estimates of the cost of such essential interventions' (CMH, 2001: 11). As if to corroborate this observation, according to the former Director-General of the WHO, '[i]t is becoming clear that health systems which spend less than [US]$60 or so per capita are not able to even deliver a reasonable minimum of services, even through extensive internal reform' (Brundtland, 2000). While the greatest predictors of population (average) health status in developing countries are income and education levels and gender equity, lack of access to essential health services creates enormous human hardship, particularly for the poor.

Table 3.2: Global Burden of Disease Distribution among Major Groups of Causes, Low-Income and High-Income Countries, 1998

Cause	Percentage of total burden of disease		
	Low-income countries (%)	High-income countries (%)	World (%)
Lower respiratory infections	6.4	1.3	6.0
Perinatal conditions	6.2	1.9	5.8
Diarrhoeal diseases	5.7	0.3	5.3
HIV/AIDS	5.5	0.9	5.1
Unipolar major depression	4.0	6.5	4.2
Ischaemic heart disease	3.3	8.8	3.8
Cerebrovascular disease	2.9	4.8	3.0
Malaria	3.1	0.0	2.8
Motor vehicle accidents	2.7	4.2	2.8
Tuberculosis	2.2	0.1	2.0
Chronic obstructive pulmonary disease	2.1	2.3	2.1
War	1.7	0.1	1.5

Source: Frenk and Murray (1999); WHO (1999)

The Global Fund to Fight AIDS, Tuberculosis and Malaria

At the Okinawa summit in 2000, the G8 appeared to take up some important aspects of the challenge of reducing the burden of disease in the developing world. They committed themselves to an 'ambitious agenda' of 'deliver[ing] three critical UN targets': reducing the number of HIV/AIDS-infected young people by 25 per cent by 2010; reducing TB deaths and prevalence of the disease by 50 per cent by 2010; and reducing the burden of disease associated with malaria by 50 per cent by 2010 (Okinawa Communiqué, para. 29). To help accomplish this, in 2001 the G8 announced:

> At Okinawa last year, we pledged to make a quantum leap in the fight against infectious diseases and to break the vicious cycle between disease and poverty. To meet that commitment and to respond to the appeal of the UN General Assembly, we have launched with the UN Secretary-General a new Global Fund to fight HIV/AIDS, malaria and tuberculosis. We are determined to make the Fund operational before the end of the year. We have committed [US]$1.3 billion. ... We welcome the further commitments already made amounting to some [US]$500 million (Genoa Communiqué, para. 15).

The Global Fund to Fight AIDS, Tuberculosis and Malaria has now been established, and has awarded its first grants, totalling US$616 million over two years to 58 programmes in 40 countries (GFATM web site, accessed 16 January 2003). Pledges received from government and the private sector to date amount to almost US$2.1 billion (see Table 3.3, below). Table 3.3 shows that the G8 exceeded their Genoa commitment of US$1.3 billion, although some countries gave proportionally more than others (Italy, the UK, France, Canada and Russia) and many of the commitments are spread over several years. Since only one round of GFATM grants has been announced, it is too early to evaluate performance with respect to the G8 commitment that the GFATM 'will promote an integrated approach emphasising prevention in a continuum of treatment and care ... with a strong focus on outcomes' (Genoa Communiqué, para.16).

It is not too early, however, to identify the urgency of finding additional resources for both treatment and prevention of HIV/AIDS, tuberculosis and malaria if the 'quantum leap' referred to in the Genoa Communiqué is to happen. The GFATM was never intended to be the sole source of support for interventions to address these three diseases. Nevertheless, the level of G8 commitment to the GFATM, relative to need, is both woefully inadequate and comparatively cheap. On a per capita basis, the US contribution amounts to US$1.78, or less than the cost of a Big Mac, and Italy's contribution – the highest among the G8 countries – to US$3.48. Using another comparison: Canada's three-year pledge, equal to US$1.10 annually, is less than the cost of a cup of coffee per Canadian per year. By contrast, contributions from Sweden and the Netherlands – not members of the G8 – amount to US$6.18 and US$7.61 per capita respectively.

Richard Feachem, Executive Director of the GFATM, although guarded in his comments, states, 'the current situation requires a substantial front-loaded capital investment to scale up existing efforts' (quoted in Nolen, 2002b). The first round funding of 58 projects committed US$1.6 billion over five years; without immediate and dramatic new donor resources, there will be little left for later funding rounds. Jeffrey Sachs, chair of the WHO CMH, which urged the scaling up of the GFATM to about US$8 billion per year by 2007 and US$12 billion by 2015, speaks more harshly, stating that the GFATM and its contributors 'are nowhere on track to actually achieving [the US$8.1 billion required over the next two years] ... the fiscal [20]03 request from the Bush administration was a shocking US$200 million for the Global Fund – that's a derisory sum, telling the rest of the world that they're just going to drop dead and it's too bad' (quoted in Nolen, 2002b).

The US$8.1 billion figure cited by these critics refers to the shortfall between the current level of commitments to the GFATM, and the UN Secretary-General's call for US$7–10 billion annually to combat the HIV/AIDS pandemic alone. According to the GFATM's web site, this call 'is based on an estimate of the total resources required annually to address the HIV/AIDS epidemic in low- and middle-income countries.' Similarly, estimates suggest that about US$2 billion is needed annually from all sources to address TB and malaria.

Activist groups have called upon some form of contribution formula to prompt more appropriate levels of contribution from the G8 countries. Using G8 country share of the total UN budget, and an annual GFATM contribution of US$10 billion, Lee (2002) calculated how much each G8 nation should be contributing (see Table 3.4, below). By this measure, all G8 countries fall well short of a 'fair share' and, while Canada and the UK appear to be doing better than several of their fellow G8 members, their contributions are meted out over three and five years respectively. Another formula, proposed by the Washington-based Global AIDS Alliance, breaks down the GFATM's present shortfall by GDP (Global AIDS Alliance, 2002). Based on estimated GFATM requirements for 2003 and 2004, the alliance calculated what each G8 country should have contributed, against what it actually contributed (see Table 3.5, below). By this metric, all G8 countries fall short. Italy sets itself apart from its G8 fellows, with Japan, Germany, the US and the UK lagging well behind. Each set of calculations presents a reasonable criterion for tithing G8 country

Table 3.3: G8 Pledges to the GFATM

Country	Amount pledged as of 7 May 2002 (US$ millions)	Value of pledge, per capita (US$)*	Proportionate value of pledge**	Comment
United States	500	1.78	▼	Largest contributor but by GDP is 18% under
Japan	200	1.58	▼	35% under
Italy	200	3.48	▲	Second highest contributor after US for FY 2002
United Kingdom	200	3.37	▲	Spread over 5 years
France	133.6	2.26	▲	
Germany	135.4	1.65	—	
Canada	100	3.28	▲	Spread over 3 years
Russia	19.2	n/a	▲	
and for comparison ...				
Sweden	55	6.18		
Netherlands	120.25	7.61		

* Based on 1999 population figures from UNDP (2001b: Table 5). Dollar figures unadjusted for purchasing power parity.   ** Source: Kirton *et al.* (2002)

Legend:

▲ = Contribution exceeds proportionate amount (country's share of G8 GDP × US$1.3 billion/total G8 commitment).

▼ = Contribution below proportionate amount.

— = Contribution equal to proportionate amount.

Table 3.4: A Fair Share for G8 Contributions to the GFATM, Based on UN Contributions

Country	Share of total UN budget (%)	Fair annual contribution based on share of UN budget (US$ millions)	Total contri-bution to date as a % of fair annual contribution*
United States	22.00	2 200	22.73
Japan	19.63	1 963	10.19
Italy	5.09	509	39.29
United Kingdom	5.57	557	35.91
France	6.50	650	20.55
Germany	9.83	983	13.77
Canada	2.57	257	38.91
Russia	1.20	120	16.67

Source: Lee (2002: Table 1)

* Some figures in this column adjusted to correspond with latest data on GFATM commitments.

annual contributions to the GFATM and, as such, is a benchmark against which future G8 commitments might be adjudicated. However Stephen Lewis, the UN Secretary-General's special envoy on HIV/AIDS in Africa, says that, '[t]he Global Fund simply does not want to deal with a formula – they don't want to nail the US' (quoted in Nolen, 2002b).

Table 3.5: G7 GFATM Contributions Based on GDP, and Actual Contributions, 2003–04

Country	Percentage of total obligation to GFAT based on GDP	Hypothetical contribution basedGDP (US$ millions)			
		2003	2004	Actual pledges for 2003 (US$ millions) (as of 1 October 2002)	2003 pledges as % of what should have been received
United States	34.8	1 488	1 610	200	13.4
Japan	16.5	704	762	0	0.0
Italy	3.8	161	174	100	62.0
United Kingdom	5.0	213	230	39	18.3
France	4.5	194	210	49	25.3
Germany	6.6	282	305	34	12.1
Canada	2.4	104	112	25	24.0

Source: Global AIDS Alliance (2002: Table 2)

To put the GFATM's urgent need for an additional U$8.1 billion into global perspective, this amount is roughly equivalent to what was spent annually on cosmetics in the US, and roughly one-sixth of what was spent on cigarettes in Europe, during the mid-1990s (UNDP, 1998: 37). It is easy to dismiss such comparisons as polemical, but they serve a critically important purpose in comparing the discretionary consumption of the few with the low cost of reducing or preventing the desperation of the many. A more timely comparison against which G8 commitments to the GFATM can be weighed is the 2002 Kananaskis summit commitment to raise up to US$20 billion over the next ten years to support projects aimed at the 'destruction of chemical weapons, the dismantlement of decommissioned nuclear submarines, the disposition of fissile materials and the employment of former weapons scientists' (Statement by the G8 leaders, Kananaskis summit, 'The G8 global partnership against the spread of weapons and materials of mass destruction'). An important undertaking, this commitment, when annualized, exceeds that made to the GFATM. As we noted in our Introduction, pandemic diseases also pose grave national and global security threats, with immediate humanitarian consequences. During his opening address to the 'G6Billion' alternate summit in Calgary in June, 2002, Stephen Lewis argued that it would be 'unconscionable' if the G8, which freed up over US$100 billion to avenge the deaths of 3 000 people in the attacks on New York and Washington, failed to free up the US$10–40 billion needed to prevent the deaths of millions of people in Africa (Lewis, 2002a). 'Unconscionably,' they did fail at Kananaskis.[4]

Essential Health Interventions as Global Public Goods

Public goods are economic amenities that are undersupplied by the market and therefore require public provision and/or financing. In common use, the concept of a public good is often associated with 'the common good,' or with such value-based goals as social equity, social justice and environmental sustainability. Its definition in economic theory is narrower, more precise, and contrasted specifically with private goods. A *private good* is one whose individual consumption is both excludable (my use of the good is not dependent on other's use) and rivalrous (my use of the good could preclude use by another) (Kaul *et al.*, 1999). This characterizes most market-based commercial exchanges of commodities, and many exchanges of services. A *public good* is one that is non-excludable (which includes most common pool resources, such as air,[5] water, biodiversity, peace and even – the classic example often used to illustrate a public good – the traffic order created by traffic lights); and, in 'pure form,' also non-rivalrous. However, many common pool resources do entail potential rivalry as supply diminishes, or efforts are made legally to convert them into private goods.

In practice, the boundary between public and private goods is harder to pin down, for several reasons. Many transactions have both private and public effects. Access to nutritious meals, for example, primarily improves individual health (a private good), but this improvement, in turn, contributes to better population health (which many public good theorist economists define as a public good). Education, as another example, improves individuals' earning capacity (a private good), but at the same time universal public education has important benefits in the quality of civic life, benefits that would be undersupplied if education were left up to individual consumer choices. Public education's effects on earnings and on a society's ability to innovate also have a public good dimension that would be foregone in a strictly *laissez-faire* society. A variant of this argument is the principal economic justification for public support of scientific research, even though such research also yields extremely important private benefits. These examples suggest that many kinds of goods can be provided in a variety of ways, and, '[w]hether – and to what extent – a good is public or private is often not a given but a matter of policy choice' (Kaul, 2001: 6).

When public goods are local (such as police and fire protection) or national (such as public defence), local or national governments, respectively, are the key providers. Global public goods (GPGs) are public goods that are underprovided by local and national governments, since the benefits accrue at least partly beyond a country's borders. Efforts to distinguish national or regional public goods from global public goods are also problematic. Aid efforts to alleviate poverty in sub-Saharan Africa will produce national or, at best, regional public good effects. But such aid might also be considered a global public good to the degree that reduced poverty rates allow for more stability, peace and security in the region, and hence globally. Individual poverty itself is not considered a public bad, but its contribution, *inter alia*, to environmental degradation or to conflict through loss of social cohesion creates a number of potential public bads, making poverty eradication, to some extent at least, a public good. Similarly, malaria control efforts are not GPGs in themselves, because the disease is regional, although with climate change the affected regions are likely to expand (McMichael, 2001: 300–2). Such control efforts might still be considered to have a public good element because malaria creates a disincentive for investment and trade, and so may reduce economic growth (Kaul, 2001; Kaul *et al.*, 1999). As the final revisions to this manuscript are made, the human and economic toll associated with the spread of Severe Acute Respiratory Syndrome (SARS) underscores the truly global dimensions of infection control as a public good. In the environmental field, the carbon sequestration benefits provided by forests exemplify public goods that may be important for health reasons, and are threatened by the private appropriation of forests for purposes of timber sales.

Despite some disagreement, then, a consensus is emerging that the fight against infectious diseases affecting poorer countries is both a GPG in itself, and requires important investments in GPGs that are beyond the means or incentives of any single government and beyond the capabilities of national-level programs (CMH, 2001: 76). GPGs for health minimally include disease eradication, disease research, control of epidemics and disease surveillance (CMH, 2001; Bradley, 2001). The category is often expanded to include air and water pollution emissions control (Sandler & Arce, 2001) and prevention of global warming (Sandler, 1999); and can be further enlarged to include poverty reduction and disaster relief (Sandler & Arce, 2001), expertise in development (Bradley, 2001) and technical assistance/training in health (CMH, 2001), to the degree that these are necessary to achieve the 'purer' GPGs of disease eradication and control of epidemics.[6]

Against this background, G8 commitments to health must be assessed with reference to a need for investment in such public goods that goes far beyond interventions to fight AIDS, tuberculosis and malaria. This was indirectly acknowledged in 2001:

> We call on MDBs [multilateral development banks] to provide support for global public goods, such as fighting infectious diseases, facilitating trade, fostering financial stability and protecting the environment. We support a meaningful replenishment of IDA[7] and, in that context, we will explore the increased use of grants for priority social investments, such as education and health (Genoa Statement, para. 13).

Interestingly, the G8 leaders did not commit their own governments directly to an increase in support for global public goods. Concern over lack of action on the '10/90' gap, however, led the Canadian Coalition for Global Health Research to lobby successfully for more explicit recognition of health research as a GPG in the Kananaskis *G8 Africa Action Plan*, which commits members to '[s]upporting health research on diseases prevalent in Africa, with a view to narrowing the health research gap, including by expanding health research networks to focus on African health issues, and by making more extensive use of researchers based in Africa' (G8, 2002: para. 6.4).

Unfortunately, lack of specificity on how *much* more this support will grow renders this statement more of an opportunity for global health advocates than a commitment by G8 governments.

Health System Infrastructure

The final report of the CMH concluded that a major increase in donor financing would be needed to support critical health interventions throughout the developing world. It identified the need for 'an additional [US]$22 billion per year by 2007 and [US]$31 billion per year by 2015' in grant financing for country-specific interventions against infectious diseases and nutritional deficiencies, which are important prerequisites for creation of GPGs. The CMH further emphasized that these amounts should be augmented by increased aid flows in other health-related areas, such as education, sanitation and water supply. Above and beyond these country-specific interventions, it called for additional grant funding of US$5 billion in 2007 and US$7 billion in 2015 for research and development on diseases of the poor and other GPGs, such as epidemiological surveillance, for a total of US$27 billion in 2007, rising to US$38 billion in 2015 – as against current ODA for health of around US$6 billion (CMH, 2001: 11).[8]

The disparity between the commitments that would be needed even for a minimal package of essential health interventions and current levels of development assistance calls into serious question the likelihood of achieving health-related development goals. For example, in 2001 the G8 committed itself to 'work with developing countries to meet the International Development Goals, by strengthening and enhancing the effectiveness of our development assistance' (Genoa Communiqué, para. 14); and recommitted itself to the updated MDGs at the 2002 Kananaskis summit (G8, 2002, para. 8).[9] The IDGs, jointly published in 2000 by the World Bank, the IMF, the OECD and the UN, call for reducing infant and under-five child mortality by two-thirds between 1990 and 2015 (IMF *et al.*, 2000: 12–13). The World Bank recently concluded, based on a scenario of 3.6 per cent annual per capita income growth in the developing countries between 2005 and 2015, that South Asia was the only region likely to achieve the target (World Bank, 2002a: 31).[10]

One of the reasons the IDG health targets are unlikely to be met is the increasing collapse of health-care infrastructure in many countries, particularly in sub-Saharan Africa. Although there are a number of contributory factors, key has been reduced public expenditure on health in at least 29 of the poorest African countries (UNDP, 2000), with all but six countries falling below the US$60 per capita figure recently advocated by the WHO Director-General (Brundtland, 2000). Some analysts argue that public health systems have been undermined by a combination of structural adjustment policies and health sector reform; their impact on sub-Saharan Africa is reviewed in Chapter 9. Whatever the reason, public health spending in developing countries, both per capita and as a percentage of GDP, remains considerably lower than in G7 countries (see Figure 3.1, below).[11] The persistence in health budgets of disproportionately high spending on tertiary and specialised services coexists with chronic underfunding of basic health services, which in many cases are unable to meet their running costs. Declining child vaccination coverage is just one indication of the deterioration of health systems, albeit one with special significance in view of our earlier discussion of GPGs. Although coverage declined in all developing continents during the 1990s, the decline in Africa is particularly troubling (Sanders *et al.*, 2002). Almost 50 per cent of African children are now not adequately vaccinated (Social Watch, 2002; Simms *et al.*, 2001; UNICEF, 2000: 89; WHO, 2002b). Perhaps the most serious reflection of the collapse of African health systems lies in the situation regarding health personnel, a point we take up later in this chapter.

It is fundamental to understand that the CMH's estimates of the minimum necessary increase in donor spending on health interventions assume that developing countries have well-functioning, well-staffed health systems accessible to those in greatest need. Although developed countries generally do better than developing countries in ensuring that the poor obtain access to health care, health care in poorer countries still tends to favour the wealthy over the poor, and hospital care over primary care. Gains from ensuring health-care access for the poor in developing countries are much more substantial than they are for the poor in wealthier nations (Wagstaff, 2001).

Figure 3.1: Average Annual Key Health Indicators and Health Expenditures in G7, Low-Income Countries and Sub-Saharan African (SSA) Countries

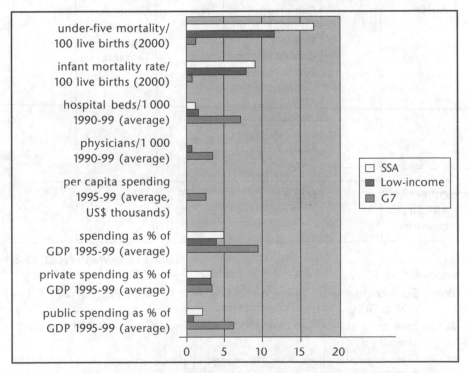

Source: World Bank (2002d: Tables 2.15 & 2.20)
Note: Where no bars appear on the graph, the numbers are so low they do not register. See data tables in Appendix 2 for actual numbers.

Table 3.6, below, shows that, despite the economic, political and social difficulties Africa has faced this past decade, many countries have attempted to increase the portion of their GDP spent on public health care. This table is a measure of effort, not of capacity, which would entail adjustments for actual GDP trends for 1990–98, taking into account population changes, improvements in health service delivery and management, and the emergence of new health problems such as the AIDS pandemic.

Table 3.6: Changes in Expenditures for Public Health Services Africa, 1990–98

Countries for which data is available	▲▲	▲	—	▼	▼▼
Sub-Saharan Africa	Senegal Zambia	Burkina Faso Botswana Cameroon Congo, Rep. of Ethiopia Gabon Ghana Guinea Mali Namibia Rwanda South Africa Swaziland	Benin Kenya Togo	Burundi Côte d'Ivoire Gambia Mozambique Nigeria Tanzania	
Other African countries		Morocco		Algeria Tunisia	

Source: Social Watch (2002: 52–4)

Legend:

▲▲   Significant progress (more than 1% change in public expenditure as % of GDP or GNP).

▲   Some progress (less than 1% change in public expenditure as % of GDP or GNP).

—   Stagnation.

▼   Some regression (less than 1% change in public expenditure as % of GDP or GNP).

▼▼   Significant regression (more than 1% change in public expenditure as % of GDP or GNP).

The absence of an effective public health-care system in poorer countries undermines the more technical disease interventions supported by the GFATM and the Global Alliance for Vaccines and Immunization (GAVI). Over 90 per cent of the first round of grants from GAVI went to research on new vaccines and injection equipment (Hardon, 2001). Although this is an important investment, an initial assessment of GAVI in four African countries reported that there are major inadequacies in health-system infrastructure, including poor staffing levels, infrequent supervision, insufficient transport and fuel, and poorly functioning refrigeration for vaccines (Brugha *et al.*, 2002). Health officials in these countries expressed concern that they would be unable to sustain the cost of vaccines should GAVI funding stop after five years. There is worry that the GAVI funding proportions (where the bulk goes to pharmaceuticals and laboratory research) will be replicated by the GFATM, compounding a problem already identified in the fund's initial assessment: 'The great burden of these three diseases [AIDS, tuberculosis and malaria] falls on Africa, and most especially on children and young adults living in sub-Saharan Africa. There, AIDS, and TB linked to AIDS, and malaria, *are straining an already frayed public health infrastructure*' (WHO, 2002d: 6; emphasis added).

Access to sufficient and affordable quantities of anti-retroviral drugs remains an issue, partly due to extended patent protection under the Agreement on Trade-Related Intellectual Property (TRIPS). As an indication of the potential gains, Brazil's policy of free, publicly funded anti-retroviral therapy – which relies as far as possible on locally manufactured drugs – is credited with substantially reducing deaths from AIDS and the incidence of opportunistic infections, while improving patient quality of life (Galvão, 2002). But without adequate resources to support the delivery of basic health care, overcoming problems of treatment supply alone may do little to control the AIDS pandemic in Africa (Attaran & Gillespie-White, 2001).

G8 Official Development Assistance to Health-Systems Development

The G8 at their 2001 Genoa meeting stated that '[s]trong national health systems will continue to play a key role in the delivery of effective prevention, treatment and care and in improving access to essential health services and commodities without discrimination' (Genoa Communiqué, para. 17).

Given the desperate condition of public health systems in many developing countries, and certainly in most sub-Saharan African nations, one might expect that ODA targeted to basic health would constitute a major plank in the G8's development assistance strategy. In the preceding chapter, we noted that the acceptance in PRSPs of cost-recovery schemes results in reduced access to

Figure 3.2: Trends in Aid to Health as % of Total ODA*

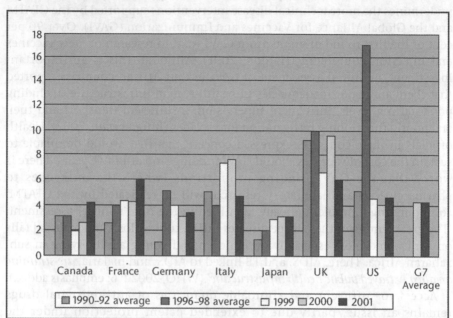

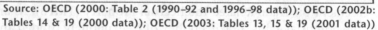

Source: OECD (2000: Table 2 (1990–92 and 1996–98 data)); OECD (2002b:
Tables 14 & 19 (2000 data)); OECD (2003: Tables 13, 15 & 19 (2001 data))

Estimates of 1999, 2000 and 2001 multilateral contributions made by authors.[13]
* Total ODA includes bilateral aid (country to country) and multilateral aid
(contributions made by donor countries to the European Commission, the World
Bank and regional development banks).
Note: Averages for 1990–92 and 1996–98 are for bilateral aid only. Data on country-
specific contributions to multilateral health aid could not be obtained or calculated
(imputed).

health care for the poor, despite efforts to exempt the poor from such schemes.
The question here is more basic: How adequately have G7 countries assisted
developing countries in creating 'strong national health systems'? Figure
3.2, above, provides data on health aid over two periods (1990–92 and 1996–
98 averages, bilateral only) and the summit years that are the focus of our
research (1999, 2000 and 2001, both bilateral and multilateral). Only two of
the G7 show any progressive increases in health aid since 2000 (France and
Canada), both of which now exceed their 1990 levels. Italy and the UK showed
increases in 2000 over 1999, but both countries also recorded a surprisingly
sharp drop the next year. Italy's low level of total development assistance
also mutes its generosity: it gives a lot of very little to health. The precipitous

drop in US aid to health in 2000, on the eve of a G8 declaration of the need to increase such assistance, is particularly disturbing.[12] G7 performance did not improve much in the following year (2001). US contributions inched up, as did Germany's. Japan's remained stagnant while Italy's and the UK's took a surprisingly sharp drop. Only Canada and France recorded any notable increases. Overall, the portion of ODA directed to health remained surprisingly low. Since 1999, 2000 and 2001 figures include multilateral aid, as well as bilateral aid, the general downwards tend from earlier years is even more disturbing.

The data in Figure 3.2 are for total health aid, which includes medical education, health policy and management, medical services such as laboratories, and medical research. The amounts directed to basic health (primary health care, infrastructure, nutrition, disease control and health education) were even smaller (see Figure 3.3, below). Here, we see that in 2001, France gave the largest proportion of its aid to health, followed closely by the UK, Italy, the US and Canada. The US, however, lead in the amount of its health aid devoted to basic health, and was the only country to exceed the G7 average. It was followed closely by Germany and Canada. France and Japan did not fare well in basic health contributions, and the UK fared little better. The UK showed a marked decline in both forms of health aid (total and basic) from the previous year, as did Italy. For all of the G7 countries, except the UK in 2000 but not in 2001, the percentage of their ODA that they allocated to health care was lower than the percentage of their GDP that they spent on the public portion of their own domestic health care (World Bank, 2002d, Table 2.15).

Total health spending, however, excludes the aid category described as 'population and reproductive health.' Not all aid analysts believe that this category should be included, since it is program- rather than sector-specific (OECD, 2000). Population and reproductive health programs, however, could improve maternal/child health outcomes and so contribute substantially to the IDGs. Figure 3.4, below, incorporates this category of aid. Here again, for both years, the US rises well above the pack. In 2001, Canada and France follow it, although Canada shows a decline in combined 'basic' and 'population health' aid from the previous year.

Because they represent percentages of ODA spending, the data in Figures 3.3 and 3.4 do not take into account the differing size of the economies of the G7 countries and so do not present health aid relative to a country's ability to pay. When total health aid is presented as a percentage of GNI (a new measure roughly similar to GDP), a different pattern appears (see Figure 3.5). (We exclude population health spending from these calculations in order to better present *sectoral* commitments.) The UK led the G7 for 2000, but fell back to a tie with France in 2001. Both France and Canada showed significant increases in 2001. The rest of the G7, though showing some increase in 2001, fell below the group average, particularly the US and Italy.

Figure 3.3: % of Total ODA* to Basic Health and Total Health, 2000–01**

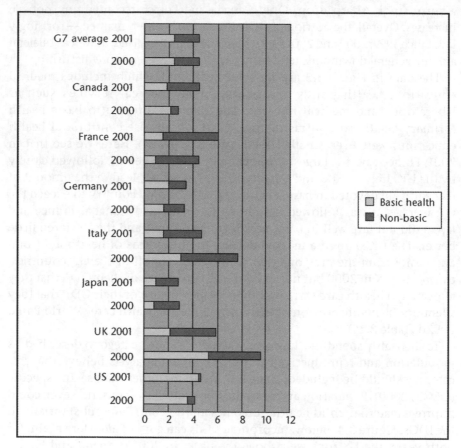

Source: OECD (2002b: Tables 14 & 19); German and Randel
(2002); OECD (2003: Tables 13, 15 & 19)

*   Estimates of multilateral contributions made by authors.
** Basic health spending is part of total health spending; the darker portion of the bar represents non-basic health spending.

Countries target their development assistance to different priorities, including population and reproductive health (notably the US), nutrition, water and sanitation, education and other important determinants of health. Given the urgency of dealing with infectious diseases, however, G8 development assistance to health systems lags as far behind need as does the group's current level of contributions to the GFATM.

Figure 3.4: % of Total ODA* to Basic Health, Population Health and Total Health, 2000–01**

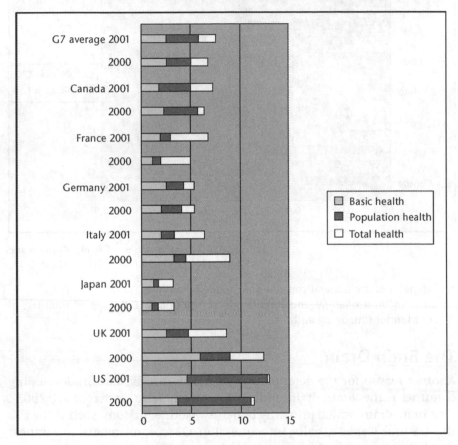

Source: OECD (2002b: Tables 14 & 19); German and Randel (2002); OECD (2003: Tables 13, 15 & 19)

*   Estimates of multilateral contributions made by authors.

** Basic health spending is part of total health spending. Population health is a separate category. The right-hand portion of the bar represents health spending that is neither 'basic health' nor 'population health.'

Figure 3.5: Total Health ODA as % of GNI, 2000–01

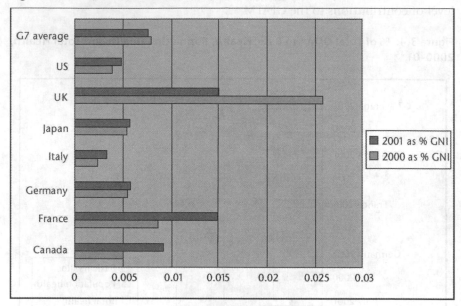

Source: OECD (2002b: Tables 14 & 19); German and
Randel (2002); OECD (2003: Tables 13, 15 & 19)

* Estimates of multilateral contributions made by authors.
* Includes both bilateral and multilateral contributions. Estimates of multilateral
contributions made by authors.

The Brain Drain

Another reason for the deterioration of health-care systems in developing
countries is the 'brain drain' of health professionals (Sanders *et al.*, 2002).
This brain drain, which primarily benefits wealthier nations, such as the UK,
the US and Canada, calls into question G8 commitments to support
developing countries in reaching health targets of the International and
Millennium Development Goals.

The WHO target for the doctor-to-population ratio is one per 1 000. The
doctor-patient ratio is currently one per 500 in wealthy countries, and only
one per 25 000 in the 25 poorest countries (Frommel, 2002),[14] a 50-fold
difference made all the more unacceptable when one considers the greater
health gain such care affords the poor in poorer countries (Wagstaff, 2001).
Current trends in the movement of health-care professionals from developing
countries to wealthy countries are quite discouraging; and the CMH

specifically cites such movement as a negative aspect of contemporary globalization (CMH, 2001: 74):

- Fifty-six per cent of all emigrating physicians move from developing to developed countries; developing countries, in turn, receive only 11 per cent of emigrating physicians, principally from other developing countries. Rates are even higher for nurses (Chanda, 2001).
- Half of Pakistan's medical graduates in any year leave the country and go to the West; very few return (Chanda, 2001: 23).
- Sixty per cent of Ghanaian doctors trained locally during the 1980s have left the country; over 21 000 Nigerian doctors are practising in the US, while there is an acute shortage of physicians in Nigeria; Zimbabwe lost almost three-quarters of all of its doctors to emigration during the 1990s (Chanda, 2001: 22).
- Over 35 per cent of trained health professionals from Africa's poorest 20 countries left for (and often were actively recruited by) countries in North America and the EU (CMH, 2001: 76).
- Zambia has lost 75 per cent of its physicians in recent years, often to South Africa as well as to developed countries (*Globe and Mail*, 5 January 2002).
- Fully one-third to a half of all graduating doctors in South Africa migrate to the US, UK and Canada, at a huge annual cost to South Africa (lost investment in education/training). Including all health personnel, the losses for South Africa reach US$37 million annually (WHO, 2001b). This exceeds the combined (multilateral and bilateral) estimated education assistance for all purposes, not just health professional training, received by South Africa in 2000 (US$35.5 million; calculations based on OECD, 2002b: Tables 13, 19 & 30).[15]

Many of the G8 countries are the beneficiaries of these losses to developing nations. Indeed, Canada, the US and the UK have actively recruited health professionals from developing countries to make up for their own undersupply in domestic production. (Italy is the only G8 country that produces a surplus of physicians and nurses.) The provincial government of Alberta, Canada, as one example, has done active recruitment of more than 40 physicians from South Africa to fill the numerous vacancies in the rural communities (Bundred & Levitt, 2000), and over half of the physicians in northern Saskatchewan, another Canadian province, are South African. The South African government in 2001 formally complained to the Canadian government about the number of its physicians being allowed to take up practice in Canada, yet in 2002 the number of South African-trained physicians in Canada increased by another 174, to total 1 738 (McClelland, 2002).

Developing countries invest about US$500 million each year in training health-care professionals, who are then recruited by or otherwise move to developed countries (Frommel, 2002).[16] This amount is equivalent to roughly 25 per cent of the total ODA that developing countries receive for health (based on OECD, 2002b: Tables 1 & 19). Meanwhile the United States, with its 130 000 foreign physicians, saved an estimated US$26 billion in training costs for nationals (Dovlo, 2001), while estimates suggest that Africa spends approximately US$4 billion annually on salaries of 100 000 foreign experts (all sectors, not only health) to 'build capacity' and/or provide technical assistance, and incurs a loss of US$184 000 per migrating African professional (Pang *et al.*, 2002; IRIN, 2002a).

The problem is not simply active recruitment by wealthier countries – a result of their own poor health-care human resource planning – or even the pull of higher earnings and greater opportunities available in such countries. There is also the push in terms of low salaries, lack of positions and little infrastructure for research or advanced training. These are problems rooted in the underdevelopment of public health systems in poorer countries. The NEPAD main document (October 2001) recognizes the brain drain problem and calls for its reversal into a 'brain gain for Africa' (para. 122). Its solutions to this problem lack detail, however, and are unconvincing (see Chapter 9). Several specific proposals have been vetted by others, and include the following:

- Wealthy countries accepting health professionals from developing countries should compensate those countries' health and health training systems for the costs of the training.
- Wealthy countries should not actively recruit health professionals from developing countries, unless these countries are producing a surplus of such professionals (such as Cuba and the Philippines).

With respect to recruitment behaviours, the UK recently adopted as guiding principles for National Health Service (NHS) recruitment that 'developing countries should not be targeted for recruitment' (Department of Health Guidance on International Recruitment, 2001). It is difficult, however, to know how well these principles are being implemented. Nurses and physicians, for example, continue to leave South Africa in large numbers for positions in the UK NHS. Indeed, some 2 114 South African nurses were registered in the UK between March 2001 and March 2002, twice the number who were registered in the previous year when the 'anti-poaching' policy went into place. The US, in turn, is attempting to recruit one million nurses by 2010 from, amongst other countries, the UK and South Africa (Carvel, 2002a).

The G8 has not dealt with this specific issue in any of its recent summits. We believe it needs to, and that it should be leading the wealthy developed nations to collaborate with developing countries to draft an enforceable international protocol to stem the South-North brain drain, perhaps using the Framework Convention on Tobacco Control as a model.[17]

Access to Essential Medicines

High pharmaceutical costs associated with the harmonization of intellectual property regimes under the TRIPS Agreement have emerged as one major barrier, among many, to improving health-care access in poor countries (Médecins sans Frontières, 2001b; 't Hoen, 1999). Another source of doubt about G8 commitments to assist developing countries in attaining the IDG targets arises from the uncertain progress made in ensuring that patents do not create economic impediments to access to essential medicines. The G8 committed to '[a]ddress ... the complex issue of access to medicines in developing countries, and assess ... obstacles being faced by developing countries in that regard' (Okinawa Communiqué, para. 30) and to 'work with the pharmaceutical industry and with affected countries to facilitate the broadest possible provision of drugs in an affordable and medically effective manner' (Genoa Communiqué, para. 17). More importantly, the Genoa Communiqué continues:

> We welcome ongoing discussion in the WTO on the use of relevant provisions in the Trade-Related Intellectual Property Rights (TRIPS) agreement. We recognize the appropriateness of affected countries using the flexibility afforded by that agreement to ensure that drugs are available to their citizens who need them, particularly those who are unable to afford basic medical care (Genoa Communiqué, para. 17).

It is unclear what verbs like 'welcome' and 'recognize' actually commit the G8 to doing, but one can infer, at least, the position that TRIPS does not (or should not) prevent access to essential medicines.

Developing countries proposed that the WTO ministerial meeting in Doha in November 2001 adopt a declaration on intellectual property affirming that nothing in the TRIPS Agreement prevents WTO members from taking measures to protect public health, clearly asserting the right to issue compulsory licensing and to use other means to decrease drug prices, such as parallel importing. Canada, the US and Japan (as well as non-G8 countries Switzerland and Australia) opposed this proposal, arguing that TRIPS already provided these flexibilities; France supported it (Stern, 2003: 25). This position, however, did not acknowledge that developing countries attempting to use these flexibilities were often faced with challenges by foreign governments and pharmaceutical companies, and that the US was pursuing bilateral 'TRIPS-plus' agreements that further limited these flexibilities. The Doha meeting eventually adopted the position of the developing countries in a Declaration on the TRIPS Agreement and Public Health stating, in part, that 'the TRIPS agreement does not and should not prevent members from taking measures to protect public health' (WTO, 2001b). The Doha TRIPS declaration further committed WTO members to recognizing a number of 'flexibilities' in interpreting TRIPS in the context of public health crises. It also mandated the WTO TRIPS Council to find a solution before the end of 2002 to the problem of ensuring access to the compulsory licensing provision in TRIPS by the majority of developing countries that lack any domestic pharmaceutical production. The EU made the first proposal (5 March 2002), focusing on two possible options. Firstly, the relevant article of the TRIPS Agreement (31f) could be amended so that the medicines can be produced elsewhere and exported to the country in need. Secondly, the TRIPS agreement could be interpreted in such a way as to allow medicines to be produced elsewhere for export to the country in need (referred to in WTO-speak as 'parallel imports').

Developing countries gave cautious support to the EU proposal, but the US opposed it and proposed, instead, a time-limited, conditional moratorium on trade disputes related to intellectual property (IP) and drugs that would apply only to the three diseases (HIV/AIDS, malaria and tuberculosis) named as examples in the declaration. Canada supported the US position (*Inside US Trade*, 2002). This position, however, contradicted the declaration's broader view of public health emergencies, which may not be restricted to the 'big three' of HIV/AIDS, malaria and tuberculosis, i.e. that '[e]ach member has the right to grant compulsory licences *and the freedom to determine the grounds upon which such licences are granted*' (WTO, 2001b: para. 5(b); emphasis added).

By late 2002, the TRIPS Council had reached near consensus on a detailed plan that would allow developing countries the right to declare what constitutes a public health emergency within their borders, and to engage in parallel importing of generic drugs from other developing countries with pharmaceutical manufacturing facilities (WTO, 2002c). The US has been the only country to reject the plan outright, reportedly on the specific direction of Vice-President Dick Cheney to the US TRIPS negotiators (*Elliott & Denny*, 2002). This stance is consistent with the US government's earlier, aggressive defence of the pharmaceutical industry's intellectual property rights against efforts by the South African government to reduce the costs of HIV/AIDS treatment (Bond, 2001: 154–76). Civil society groups, notably Médecins sans Frontières, also urge rejection of the plan, but for a different reason: the plan refers to 'national emergencies,' rather than the broader language of 'measures to protect public health.' Some African countries express the same concern (*BRIDGES Weekly Trade News Digest*, 2003). The issue is far from resolved: irrespective of how well its ultimate resolution reflects the spirit of the Doha Declaration, some G8 behaviour in the TRIPS Council has not kept faith with stated commitments.

The US is also seeking to write 'TRIPS-plus' restrictions into the intellectual property rights chapter of the Free Trade Area of the Americas Agreement, now in negotiation (Human Rights Watch, 2002). These 'TRIPS-plus' restrictions are non-WTO agreements between two or more nations in which members agree not to exercise some of their compulsory licensing rights currently permitted by the TRIPS Agreement. The US is also entering into trade talks with the Southern African Customs Union – Lesotho, Botswana, South Africa, Namibia and Swaziland – that include discussion of intellectual property rights, something NGO observers believe could be another 'TRIPS-plus' effort (*BRIDGES Weekly Trade News Digest*, 2002g).

Concern about the US trade policy agenda in the area of intellectual property and about the negative impact of the TRIPS Agreement on developing country health is becoming widespread. No less an authority than Joseph Stiglitz, the former chief economist of the World Bank and the winner of the 2001 Nobel Prize in economics, recently commented:

> When I was on the Council of Economic Advisers in the Clinton administration, we (as well as the Office of Science and Technology Policy) worried that the US trade representative, who negotiates these agreements 'on behalf' of the US, was pushing for intellectual property arrangements that could have harmful effects. The US was reflecting the interest of the drug companies more than the perspectives, for instance, of scholars or those concerned that the laws governing intellectual property should maximize growth. The US trade representative paid scant attention to our concerns – let alone those of the developing world (Stiglitz, 2002a: 28).

The World Bank's 2002 *Global Economic Prospects* report notes as part of a broader discussion of the distribution of the costs and benefits of strengthened intellectual property protection under TRIPS that

> [i]t is conceivable that patent protection will increase incentives for R&D [research and development] into treatments for diseases of particular concern to poor countries. However, because purchasing power is so limited in the poorest countries, there is little reason to

expect a significant boost in such R&D. Accordingly, many developing countries see little potential benefit from introducing patents [since] potential costs could be significant (World Bank, 2002a: 137; see also Trebilcock & Howse, 1999: 310–12).

The authors of the UNDP *Human Development Report 2000* took the problem seriously enough to warn that the TRIPS Agreement may conflict with international human rights agreements that recognize the right to share in scientific progress, because it 'dramatically reduces the possibilities for local companies to produce cheaper versions of important life-saving drugs' (UNDP, 2000: 84). NGO critiques of the TRIPS Agreement's policies as they apply both to pharmaceuticals and to living matter have been even more emphatic about the adverse distributional consequences of the current IP regime (e.g. Médecins sans Frontières, 2001b; Shand, 2001; Watkins, 2002a: 208–24).

Macroeconomic Policies and Health Care

Stiglitz's comment that the treatment of intellectual property rights in trade agreements should take into account impacts on economic growth brings us to a consideration of the broader impact of macroeconomic policies on health care. Most countries, from the US in the eighteenth and nineteenth centuries to Asian states in the twenty-first century, have grown economically by taking technologies developed by other people in other nations and copying them, often more cheaply. This opportunity is now being denied poorer countries, by virtue of the harmonization of IP regimes under TRIPS.

Detailed studies of macroeconomic adjustment policies, largely predicated on the neo-liberal tenets of globalization that continue to be endorsed by G7 (now G8) summits (Kirton & Von Furstenberg, 2001; Dallaire, 2001), find that such policies generally result in 'high inequalities in access to and utilization of health services, and the reinforcement of risks of exclusions and barriers to access of the poorest by efficiency-oriented health sector reforms' (Haddad & Mohindra, 2001: 20). Declining public expenditures on health are closely linked to privatization of health services and the imposition of user fees as part of structural adjustment packages (Arhin-Tenkorang, 2000; Melgar, 1999; Schoepf *et al.*, 2000; CMH, 2001: 121; Whitehead *et al.*, 2001; Yong Kim, Shakow *et al.*, 2000). Since ill health, often itself related to low income and economic insecurity, is one of the principal reasons that households slip further into poverty (Narayan *et al.*, 2000), the 'medical poverty trap' (Whitehead *et al.*, 2001) created by adjustment may undermine the potential for achieving economic growth through improvements in health. The contribution that interventions to improve population health can make to economic development was a central theme of the work of the CMH (2001).

Conversely, the impacts of HIV/AIDS and malaria provide especially dramatic, large-scale illustrations of the economic damage that can result from poor health (Haacker, 2002; Sachs & Malaney, 2002). With these considerations in mind, we should briefly revisit some issues of macroeconomic policy.

Neo-liberal prescriptions for reorienting economies and societies in order to attract FDI may have a variety of negative health effects. Many developing countries did not allow FDI in health services until the 1990s, when it was often required under SAPs (Chanda, 2001: 28). FDI in health services increased the presence of parallel private health-care systems in many developing countries, which eroded public health-care systems in several ways. Latin America provides a compelling example of this. Between 1990 and 1995, the share of private health expenditure rose in 15 of 22 Latin American countries (Brugha & Zwi, 2002). The scope for private health care in Latin America is considered so large that, in 1999, *The Economist* launched a new quarterly, *Healthcare Latin America*. The same year, *The Economist* ran a feature on the 'shift toward private health care,' which quoted the President of the American Association of Health Plans noting that, '450 million Latin Americans constitute a health-care market of [US]$120 billion a year – of which only 15% is spent on private insurance' (Lewis, 1999). By inference, 85 per cent of the market is ripe for privatization.[19]

Latin American governments are moving in this direction, often with World Bank or IMF prodding.[20] Peru, in 1998, committed itself to increased privatization of public services, including concessions to private companies taking over public services and increased foreign investment in health and education. Bolivia, with World Bank, IMF and US Agency for International Development (USAID) funding, is promoting a private, self-financed primary health-care model (PROSALUD). 'Regardless of the type of intervention, most [World Bank and International Development Bank] initiatives have favored the private financing and provision of health care over the former public financing and provision that predominated in most Latin American countries' (Armada *et al.*, 2001).

Evocative Latin American examples show how such privatization creates inequalities in access. Between 1974 and 1989, total private health-care expenditures in Chile rose substantially, while public health-care expenditures declined (Collins & Lear, 1995). Large segments of the poor population were left with underfunded, low-quality public health care. Although public health expenditures since the return of democratic regimes in 1990 have been increasing, growth in private health-care expenditure in Chile still outstrips that for public health care (Leon, 2002), and foreign companies now provide 60 per cent of Chile's health insurance (Wasserman & Cornejo, 2002). In Brazil, private health care provides 120 000 physicians and 370 000 hospital beds to the richest 25 per cent of the population, while the public system has just 70 000 physicians and 565 000 hospital beds for the remaining 75 per cent (Zarrilli, 2002a). Yong Kim, Shakow *et al.* (2000) describe a similar pattern of declining, and increasingly unequal, access to health care in Peru. A special need exists for an authoritative literature review and synthesis on the effects of cost recovery and privatization on access to health care in developing countries. In this context, 'privatization' must be understood both in the narrow sense of the substitution of private, for-profit health services for publicly provided serves and the broader sense of 'a new division of responsibility among the state, the family and the market for individual and social welfare' (Fudge & Cossman, 2002: 18).

Privatization, Liberalization and GATS

Liberalization of trade in services is another element of conventional development policy wisdom. The contribution of services to economic growth and wealth has increased rapidly in comparison to the production of goods. Their actual and potential contribution to trade has also grown (Sinclair, 2000). Countries differ in the degree to which they are introducing commercial operating principles into their domestic public services, or autonomously liberalizing trade in services with other nations. The WTO's General Agreement on Trade in Services (GATS) is a 'framework agreement' introduced at the conclusion of the Uruguay Round of the General Agreement on Tariffs and Trade (GATT). GATS essentially 'locks in' existing service privatization and liberalization policies. It has not itself been a driver of either privatization or liberalization, but has secured and entrenched pro-competitive policies in areas that have been autonomously liberalized.

GATS was conceived, and continues to be defended, primarily as a vehicle for the expansion of business opportunities for transnational service corporations (Hilary, 2001). The key concern is that GATS will unavoidably lead to increased privatization of such essential public services as health care, education and water/sanitation. Corporations with a major stake in service industries are exerting considerable pressure, especially in the US and EU, to use GATS to open up government services for commercial and foreign provision (Evenett & Hoekman 1999, in Sinclair, 2000). European negotiators are urging greater service liberalization because they see China as a lucrative market, as that country dismantles its previous state welfare infrastructure (Pollock and Price, 2000; see note 19, in this chapter). Private US health-care providers regard GATS as the main vehicle for overcoming obstacles to market access in countries where public funding and provision currently predominate.

The estimated annual value of the global health-care market is US$3.5 trillion (Barlow, 2001).

GATS defines four different modes of liberalization of trade in services:

1. Cross-border delivery of services (such as shipment of laboratory samples or provision of telehealth services);
2. Consumption of services abroad (so-called 'health or medical tourism'), where people from one country are treated by health services in another, and provision of professional (under- and post-graduate training at tertiary institutions abroad);
3. Commercial presence (where foreign private investors provide private hospitals, clinics, treatment centres or insurance, or have management contracts for such facilities, whether they are public or private); and
4. The presence of natural persons (the temporary movement of health professionals from one country to another).

As with globalization and trade liberalization generally, many arguments are made for liberalizing trade in health services. For example, liberalized health services can lead to new private resources to support the public system; can introduce new techniques to health professionals in developing countries; can provide such professionals with advanced training and credentials; and can introduce new and more efficient management techniques (Zarrilli, 2002b).[21] But there are powerful counter-arguments to each of these points. Notably, private investments in health services, by definition, emphasize those services for which a market exists. They are therefore likely to be concentrated in services for the affluent (Lethbridge, 2002), undermining support for universal, public provision of health services. We have already described the global crisis associated with the movement of health professionals from developing to developed countries. Trade in goods or services, generally, is presumed to benefit health by increasing the income of providers and decreasing the costs for consumers. In health, however, the goal is not increased income but equitable access to quality services, including by those who may not be able to purchase traded services. Most importantly, nothing prevents countries from allowing foreign commercial presence in their domestic services market, providing services to non-nationals or 'exporting' service providers to other countries *without* making commitments under GATS. The only effect of such GATS commitments is to make it extremely difficult for countries to change these provisions in the future.

To date, 54 WTO members have made commitments to liberalize medical and dental services, 44 for hospital services, 29 for nursing and midwifery and 17 for 'other' health services (Adlung & Carzaniga, 2001, 2002). Many of these are developing countries, whose corresponding figures are 36, 29, 12 and 15. The number of health-liberalized countries grows to 78 if one includes private health insurance. GATS has a built-in requirement for 'progressive liberalization', meaning that countries are committed to ongoing negotiations to apply the GATS rules to a wider range of services and government measures. Once these rules apply to a service sector, any changes that reduce the level of trade liberalization are subject to penalties in the form of trade compensation (CCPA, 2002). Canada and Brazil, for example, have both opened up private health insurance under GATS. Should either country ever wish to extend its public system into areas that are now covered by private insurance, and so reverse the current trend away from privatization, its GATS commitments might expose it to penalties. The same would apply to any developing country wishing to reverse its current commitments to health services privatization.

Imagine a poorer country where many essential services are now privately provided, partly in response to earlier conditionalities. Imagine further that trade liberalization does eventually promote long-term economic growth, and that the country is able to tax such growth so that it has sufficient revenue to increase its public provision of health, education or sanitary services. If it had committed itself to liberalized trade in any of these services under GATS, it might have to provide compensation in the form of trade concessions should its public programs reduce private foreign providers' share of the domestic market.

Box 3.1: GATS, Health Services, Africa and the G8: Who's Committed to What

Negotiations on GATS are ongoing, with a major round under way in 2003. Commitments under GATS can be for 'market access' (opening the market to foreign providers) and 'national treatment' (treating foreign providers the same as domestic providers). Governments can commit to none or any combination of the four modes. Their commitments can be:

*   no limitations – or full liberalization, which they designate by claiming 'none';
*   bound – which covers both existing and any future government measures; and
*   unbound – which applies only to current government measures.

Both bound and unbound commitments can have limitations placed on foreign service provision in both national treatment and market access. Countries can also stipulate 'horizontal commitments,' which are limitations that apply to a

---

larger range of service sectors. There is pressure in current GATS negotiations to make all commitments 'bound' and restrict the limitations placed on them, i.e. to move towards the 'no limitations' or full liberalization option.

GATS does offer an exception from its liberalization requirements for 'a [government] service which is supplied neither on a commercial basis, nor in competition with one or more service suppliers' (Article 1:3b). This is often cited as evidence that concern over privatization is misplaced. This clause, however, may not adequately shield public health measures from a trade challenge, since most countries allow some commercial or competitive provision of virtually all public services (Pollock & Price, 2000; Price *et al.*, 1999; Sinclair, 2000).

Only one sub-Saharan African country has made any GATS commitments involving specialized medical services, but over half a dozen have committed to full liberalization of several modes of medical and dental services, including provisions for private foreign investment. They have done so with fewer limitations than those defined by the already well-developed EC 12 members. Sub-Saharan African countries appear more reluctant to open up nursing, midwifery and other health services. It is important to recall that liberalization in health services will benefit more affluent 'consumers' with the ability to pay for them, at the expense of the poorest sectors of the population reliant upon a public system likely to lose staff and funding as the private system entrenches and expands. If domestic incomes and political will should shift in such committed countries in the future, and if the shift brings with it an improved prospect of implementing a more equitable and efficient universal, risk-pooled health-care system, future governments may find it financially impossible to pay the trade sanctions or monetized settlements required by an expanded public system's displacement of the foreign-invested private one. *It is also important to recall that there is nothing preventing present-day governments from allowing foreign commercial presence or service providers in health (or any other) services without making GATS commitments. These commitments simply make it difficult or impossible to create a stronger public system of services in the future.* There are also concerns that wealthier nations, particularly the US and the EU, will be pressuring developing countries to make more commitments to liberalize services in the present GATS negotiations (2003), in return for increased market access for their exports.

Health care is not like other commercial services. It is essential to the creation and maintenance of public goods. Public systems for health-care provision arose in most countries because private systems proved inadequate and inequitable. Whatever forms of cross-border exchanges in health (or education, or other essential public services) may be beneficial or desired, trade treaties – which are intended to promote private economic interests – are not the best place to negotiate them (CCPA, 2002). Other forms of multilateral agreements freed from commercial economic goals, such as a proposed global cultural diversity treaty supported by both Canada and France, which would remove cultural products from the WTO ambit (*Globe and Mail,* 29 November 2002: B5), are more in keeping with the G8's commitment to the health targets of the IDGs (see Box 3.2).

Box 3.2: Developing a New International Agreement on Cultural Diversity

The Okinawa Communiqué described cultural diversity as a 'source of social and economic dynamism which has the potential to enrich human life in the 21st century' and recognized 'the importance of diversity in linguistic and creative expression' (para. 39).

As far back as February 1999, the Cultural Industries Sectoral Advisory Group on International Trade (SAGIT) in Canada drafted a report urging creation of an independent international and rules-based agreement to 'manag[e] the interface between cultural objectives and trade obligations' (SAGIT, 2002: 1). The intent was not a general exemption for culture from trade agreements, but to agree upon the conditions under which governments would 'confidently pursue their legitimate domestic cultural policy objectives without fear of trade reprisals' (SAGIT, 2002: 8). Cultural goods and services are already covered under several WTO agreements, including GATT (1994), GATS and TRIPS.

In proposing that a new instrument on cultural diversity be developed outside the WTO, we recognize that the relationship between the instrument and the WTO will need to be addressed. Once the instrument has been finalized, it is envisaged that signatories to it would seek to have its principles recognized by the WTO, although the agreement would continue to be a distinct stand-alone agreement (SAGIT, 2002: 8).

The reason for a new instrument and monitoring/enforcement organization, with its own dispute settlement body and procedures, separate from the WTO, is that 'it is important that it be first and foremost a cultural instrument [and] the WTO may not be in a position to take into account what is required to ensure the preservation of cultural identities and cultural diversity' (SAGIT, 2002: 8).

Indeed, the goal of the proposed new agreement would be 'to ensure that the international trading system is compatible with the goal of preserving and enhancing cultural diversity' (SAGIT, 2002: 4). In the absence of such an agreement, governments must now ensure the reverse: that new cultural policies are compatible with trade agreements.

The SAGIT group has drafted a model text for '[a]n international agreement on cultural diversity,' which states the intent even more clearly: 'Member states have the right to take measures with respect to the creation, production, distribution and exhibition of cultural content and to the activities of cultural undertakings in order to support, promote and preserve diverse cultural expression' (Article VI, para. 1).

Foreign cultural content would be encouraged under the proposed agreement, but trade sanctions would only apply if governments expropriated without compensation existing cultural undertakings of non-nationals, or adopted policies inconsistent with international treaties respecting IP rights (e.g. TRIPS).

The draft agreement is now being circulated internationally, with the expectation that a negotiated international agreement with a sufficient number of member nations can be signed in the near future. It is thought that support from between 70 and 80 countries will be needed for discussions for adoption of its principles at the WTO to be successful (*Globe and Mail,* 29 November 2002: B5).

The countries promoting this agreement recognize that it is an ambitious undertaking, given its novelty in the current multilateral arena. Nonetheless, it provides a usefully different model for managing international beneficial exchanges in goods and services where the defining criterion is no longer cross-border liberalization, but rather a public good.

If such an agreement can be undertaken for cultural diversity, it can also be undertaken for essential public services like health care.

Tobacco Control: Deadly Silence from the G8

We shift here from emphasizing what the G8 said they would do, to an inexplicable gap in what they failed to say at all. At all three of the summits we investigated (1999, 2000 and 2001) and also the 2002 Kananaskis summit, the G8 were totally silent on the issue of tobacco control, despite tobacco's contribution to the global burden of disease. That contribution is expected to increase in the future.

In the first year of the new millennium, it is estimated that tobacco will kill approximately two million people in the developed nations and an equal number in the developing nations. By the year 2030, however, estimates are that three million per year will die from tobacco use in the developed nations and *more than seven million people per year* will die from tobacco use in the developing world.

In all nations of the world, nearly one in ten people – or more than 500 million human beings – who are now alive will die from a tobacco-related disease (Bal *et al.*, 2001: 247; see generally WHO, 1999: 65–79).

The health consequences of tobacco use are of special concern to the developing world for several reasons. Firstly, as noted, it is anticipated that most of the growth in tobacco-related disease will occur outside the industrialized world, where tobacco control initiatives have been at least partly successful. The tobacco industry, in fact, has actively sought to expand its markets in such developing regions as Latin America (PAHO, 2002b) and Asia (Niu *et al.*, 1998; O'Sullivan & Chapman, 2000), even as it attempts to undermine tobacco control efforts both nationally and internationally (Carter, 2002; Committee of Experts, 2000; Glantz *et al.*, 1996; Yach & Bettcher, 1999, 2000). The industry's marketing efforts directed at young people are of special concern, since '[n]icotine addiction takes hold almost exclusively in children and youth' and about half of teenagers in OECD countries who try smoking 'become life-long smokers, among whom one in two will die from smoking' (WHO, 1999: 70).

Secondly, tobacco-growing in developing countries – like other forms of the drug trade – may emerge as a competitor for scarce resources, such as arable land and water, as tobacco consumers quite simply outbid subsistence users. One observer relates that '[t]hroughout the two years that I lived and worked in central Mozambique I saw trees collapse because of the drought ... and I never saw maize grow successfully. I did however see fields full of healthy growing tobacco on a multinational-owned tobacco farm' (Lawlor, 2001). This is an area that clearly merits further research.

Thirdly, there are indications that trade liberalization may undermine tobacco control efforts. Chaloupka and Laixuthai (1996) concluded that liberalized trade agreements result in an overall increase in cigarette demand. A joint World Bank/WHO study demonstrated the same results more broadly, showing that the largest impact of reduced trade barriers with respect to tobacco consumption occurred in low-income countries (Taylor *et al.*, 2000). The inclusion of tobacco marketers in Canada's most recent (February 2001) trade delegation to China raised numerous complaints from health officials in government, and from health practitioners and researchers.

It could be argued that specific G8 attention to tobacco control at annual summits has not been necessary, since negotiations have been under way since 1996, under the auspices of the WHO, toward the Framework Convention on Tobacco Control (FCTC). Reportedly, developing countries took the lead in many areas of the negotiations – notably in opposing the inclusion of a trade supremacy clause that would have subordinated the public health goals of the convention to international trade agreements (Bates, 2001). Germany, the US and Japan, G8 countries with major tobacco industries, reportedly made several attempts to 'water down crucial clauses,' and the FCTC 'falls short of expectations by not banning duty-free sales and vending machines, and by failing to ban deceptive descriptors, such as "light" and "low-tar"' (Framework Convention Alliance, 2003). A draft of the FCTC was released in March 2003 for discussion at the World Health Assembly in May of that year (Intergovernmental Negotiating Body, 2003). In fact, the case for decisive G8 action is now stronger than ever. Political commitment to signature and ratification at the highest levels of the industrialized countries, in which the global tobacco industry is based, will be essential if the FCTC is to succeed. If past experience is any guide, restrictions on advertising and promotion are likely to be especially contentious. Willingness to ratify the FCTC, to devote the necessary resources to its domestic implementation, and to provide assistance to developing countries for this purpose will be one of the clearest tests of G8 leadership on global health issues in the coming years.

Summary: Chapter Three

The global pandemics of HIV/AIDS and other infectious diseases are increasing, and with them a devastating and morally unacceptable toll of human misery, economic loss, deepening poverty and regional and global insecurity. LDCs are most affected. More funds for disease prevention are urgently needed. Access to affordable drugs for treatment or management is essential. Increased aid to build functioning public health systems to administer both is critical. Retaining and supporting health professionals to run these systems and their programs is basic. On almost of all these fronts, the developing world, particularly in sub-Saharan Africa, is losing ground. The G8, while fulfilling some of its past commitments, has failed in others, and the promises it has kept come nowhere near matching the scale of the problems they were meant to help remedy.

Explicit or Specific Commitments: Health and Health Systems

- Establish global fund on AIDS, TB and malaria and initially pledge $1.3 billion (Okinawa).
- Reduce the number of HIV/AIDS-infected young people by 25%; TB deaths and prevalence by 50%; and the burden of disease associated with malaria by 50%; all by 2010 (Okinawa).
  Accomplished: Yes. GFATM was established by the time of the Genoa summit.
  Adequacy: Annual contributions are below 10% of estimated requirements. The Kananaskis summit failed to deliver any substantial new commitments. With seven years to go, achieving the 2010 targets seems remote, if not impossible.
  Comments: Italy, the UK, France, Canada and Russia gave proportionally more than other G8 countries. Every G8 country falls short of what it

actually should be giving if allocations were based on estimated need. By each metric, Italy has been the most generous G8 contributor, followed by France and Canada. The recent pledge by US President Bush for significant new annual funding for HIV/AIDS represents a unilateral, rather than multilateral, approach, largely bypassing the GFATM.

• Work to meet IDGs by strengthening and enhancing effectiveness of development assistance (Cologne, Okinawa and Genoa; reiterated as MDGs at Kananaskis).

Accomplished: No. Key health IDGs are to reduce infant and under-five mortality rates by two-thirds between 1990 and 2015, and to reduce maternal mortality rates by three-quarters between 1990 and 2015. South Asia, based on optimistic growth projections, is estimated to be the only region to achieve just one target: infant and under-five mortality reduction.

Adequacy: The G7 ODA support given to health is substantially below the estimated amounts needed to achieve targets.

Commit to address the complex issue of access to medicine in developing countries (Okinawa).

Recognize some flexibility for developing nations regarding TRIPS (Genoa).

Accomplished: Mixed.

Adequacy: The Doha Declaration on TRIPS and Public Health (2001) emphasized that TRIPS should not impede the protection of public health, and that countries had the right to determine when they could invoke compulsory licensing provisions. However, implementation was impeded by US intransigence. The problem of allowing poor countries to 'parallel import' generic drugs was referred to the TRIPS Council for resolution by 31 December 2002.

Comments: Canada, the US, and Japan initially opposed the Doha Declaration, and referred the parallel import problem to the TRIPS Council. The US remains opposed to any TRIPS amendments for parallel importing except for HIV/AIDS, tuberculosis and malaria.

Implicit or Generic Commitments: Health and Health Systems

• Strong national health systems will continue to play a key role in the delivery of effective prevention, treatment and care and in improving access to essential health services and commodities without discrimination (Genoa).

Accomplished: No. Total ODA for health was only one-sixth the low-end estimate of amounts required for essential health services related to major infectious diseases in developing countries. Many developing countries are suffering severe 'brain drain,' dramatically weakening their national health systems; the major beneficiaries are G8 countries. GATS commitments by some African countries to liberalize trade in health services could prevent the development of these national health systems. **Comments:** Many G7 countries have shown sharp declines in ODA to health since 1996/98. Only France, Italy and Japan showed any increases in health aid between 1996/98 and 2000; as a percentage of gross national income (GNI), the UK's contributions in 2000 were most generous. G7 ODA to health dropped further for 2001 in the UK and Italy, remained the same in Japan, and rose slightly in Germany. Only Canada and France showed any substantial increase. Canada is the only G7 country making no new commitments to liberalize health services under GATS, and there have been no requests for such liberalization by other countries.

- Ask the multilateral development banks to provide support for global public goods. The G8 will explore the possibility of increased grants for social investments (Genoa Statement).
  Accomplished: No. This commitment was not reiterated in the final Genoa Communiqué.
  Comments: See Box 6.2, Chapter 6.

Endnotes to Chapter Three

[1] The units used for purposes of this determination, disability-adjusted life years (DALYs), have been the topic of considerable controversy. DALYs were originally developed in an effort to provide a single metric for combining lost years of life with reduced functioning, in order to overcome the serious limitations of such crude indicators as life expectancy. Ethical critiques of the use of DALYs focus on four issues (Arnesen & Nord, 1999; Rock, 2000). Extending the life of a person with reduced functioning ('disability') counts for less than extending the life of someone with full functioning. Disability weightings used for calculating DALYs were arrived at using convenience samples of health professionals rather than community members, including people living with disabilities. The age weighting that is used for calculating DALYs assigns a lower value to a year of life lost by the very young or aged than to a year of life lost by a young adult. Finally, discounting means that a year of life lost in the future is valued less than a year of life lost today.

Defenders of DALYs note that both age and disability weightings are consistent with common clinical intuitions and practices in the context of limited resources, and that failure to discount future life years might lead to recommendations that all current treatment be deferred in favour of expenditures on research that would lower the cost or improve the effectiveness of future treatment (Murray & Acharya, 1997). They also point out that changing or removing the age weighting and discounting does not substantially change the ranking of contributors to the burden of disease. Thus, the DALY remains at best an imperfect indicator, while being widely used and useful for comparing the burden of disease across populations or societies with very different patterns of health and development. For illustrations of this point, see Gwatkin *et al.* (1999) and Prüss *et al.* (2002). At the same time, serious ethical issues arise when burden of disease figures are used as the basis for comparing the cost-effectiveness of interventions or combinations of interventions.

[2] The term 'transition economies' refers to the group of 25 Central and Eastern European countries, including Russia, which were once part of or affiliated with the USSR. China and Vietnam are also sometimes considered in this category.

[3] At the Okinawa summit, Japan committed US$3 billion over five years to an Infectious Disease Initiative. About US$700 million of this commitment has been 'implemented,' with another US$200 million contributed to the GFATM (OECD, 2002b: 108).

[4] As with many G7 commitments, evaluating compliance and adequacy is akin to chasing a moving target. An example of this is the recent pledge by US President Bush to commit US$10 billion in new funding for HIV/AIDS over the next five years (Stolberg, 2003). This pledge is subject to Congressional approval, so its future (at time of writing) is uncertain. The pledge was generally welcomed by most organizations concerned with the global pandemic, but only US$1 billion of it would be channeled through the multilateral and independent GFATM (McDonald, 2003). The rest would be administered according to US bilateral aid priorities – bilateral aid, as Chapter 6 notes, is often based more on geopolitical interests than development need. More importantly, this decision calls into question US commitment to multilateral processes, including the G8 itself.

[5] Note that although air and water are common pool resources, air and water quality are impure or ambiguous public goods. Households can purchase air quality by moving to leafy neighbourhoods upwind from pollution sources or on hillsides above the metropolitan haze; communities and societies can also purchase air quality by mandating emission reductions. Safe drinking water can be provided as a public good through pollution regulations and public investment in treatment facilities, or can be a private good purchased in a bottle.

[6] The UN report on financing for development had its own list for GPGs, which included 'peacekeeping; prevention of contagious diseases; research into tropical medicines, vaccines and agricultural crops; prevention of chlorofluorocarbon (CFC) emissions; limitation of carbon emissions; and preservation of biodiversity' (UN, 2001: 19). No individual country, the report continued, has an incentive to pay for these, hence international cooperation and collective action is required. The report estimated the annual cost to meet these GPGs at about US$20 billion (UN, 2001: 20). The need for more research on tropical diseases is sometimes described as closing the '10/90 Gap' (GFHR, 2000) – the fact that 90 per cent or more of all medical research addresses the 10 per cent of the 'burden of disease' affecting the wealthiest sectors of the global population. 'Apparently it is more profitable to develop and market Viagra than to research a new drug to treat patients with visceral leishmaniasis, a fatal disease if left untreated. Such a drug is more likely to be developed through veterinary research if it has economic potential on the pet market' (Veeken & Pécoul, 2000; see also Médecins sans Frontières, 2001a; Pécoul *et al.*, 1999; Reich, 2000).

[7] The International Development Association (IDA) is that section of the World Bank that provides funding for 79 countries with per capita incomes below US$885. Over 96 per cent of donor country disbursements to the World Bank go to the IDA. Significantly, this commitment appears in the pre-summit statement but not in the final summit communiqué. The issue of G7 ODA for health, education and other development goals, both bilateral and multilateral, is taken up in Chapter 6.

[8] A higher cost-estimate range of US$40–52 billion per year in new health funding by 2015 is provided in a summary of the report of the Working Group responsible for these estimates (Jha *et al.*, 2002). Both estimates include a US$8 billion annual allocation to the GFATM.

[9] Box 2.2 in the previous chapter presents these two sets of goals and describes their similarities and differences.

[10] The WHO Coordinates report (2002d), which provides the first assessment of progress toward meeting the goals that motivated the establishment of the Global Fund, avoided any quantitative assessment of this point.

[11] Per capita spending is so low in sub-Saharan Africa (averaging US$20/year) that it does not even track on Figure 3.1; see Appendix 2 for detailed data for this figure. Averages also overstate health care available for the poor in sub-Saharan Africa, since they include both public and private spending (World Bank, 2002d: 105).

[12] Its equally precipitous increase between 1990–92 and 1996–98 may also be an artifact of reporting. In 1995, the US began to report aid by strategic objectives rather than by individual aid activities (OECD, 2000: 6). We thus urge caution in interpreting the trend data presented. Average total ODA contributed for health by all Development Assistance Committee (DAC) members (including non-G7 members and multilateral lending) has averaged about seven per cent in recent years, up from four per cent in the mid-1970s and matching high levels reached in the mid-1980s (OECD, 2000: 6).

[13] The OECD DAC report (OECD, 2002b) provides country-specific data for bilateral aid, by key sectors. It does not, however, provide multilateral aid by country for these same key sectors. Comparing sector-specific aid trends without estimating countries' portions of 2000 aid contributed through multilateral agencies would be egregious, to say the least. Instead, we estimate total 2000 ODA (bilateral and multilateral) based on the following calculation: country-specific percentage of total aid contributed through each of the three multilateral agencies (Regional Development Banks, World Bank, European Commission) × the percentage of aid provided to the specific sector by each of the multilateral agencies. The product of these calculations is added to that country's sector-specific bilateral contribution. While reasonably accurate, there may be small margins of error: the OECD report (OECD, 2002b) itself cautions that figures for the European Commission are 'approximate.' Total 2001 ODA contributions are based on the same calculations, using provisional data from the OECD (2003). An even greater note of caution is expressed for 1999 multilateral estimates. We applied the same formula as for 2000 and 2001, but the percentage of EC aid contributions by sector is not available for 1999. We used the percentages for 2000 as a rough approximation. For this reason, we do not include 1999 in calculating G7 averages, but rely on years for which data are more reliable (2000, 2001).

[14] Similar inequalities in ratios for nurses also apply, but we did not locate precise figures. Much of the easily accessible date on the 'brain drain' applies to physicians. In using this data, we are not implying that nursing shortages are any less critical for effectively functioning health systems.

[15] We were unable to locate sector-specific ODA receipts for South Africa. Applying the percentage of ODA for education disbursed to all recipient countries and applying it to the net ODA receipts for South Africa, we arrived at our estimate of educational ODA.

[16] The scale of this South subsidy to the North is much larger when all trained professionals are considered. Fully one-third of computer professionals in California's Silicon Valley, for example, are from India, and India, despite remittances earned from its foreign-placed workers, is estimated to lose around US$700 million annually in training costs (Desai, 2001, cited in Oxfam, 2002: 45).

[17] This convention, intended to be a legally binding treaty on collective international action and cooperation on tobacco control, is being negotiated under the auspices of the WHO, and is described later in this chapter.

[18] It is difficult to assess the UK's position on this, given its intent to lobby for its own, differing plan at the 2003 G8 summit in France. This plan, closely resembling the US's position, would have drug companies sell their patent-protected treatments at 'slightly above cost,' but only for HIV/AIDS, tuberculosis and malaria, and only for sub-Saharan African and other least developed countries (Boseley, 2002).

[19] Globally, 'the growing income of developing countries is leading to increases in private care expenditures that are faster than public health care expenditures' (Lethbridge, 2002: 350). The result is an increasing number of rural poor and urban low- and even middle-income persons losing access to effective public health care, as services lose practitioners to the better-paying private system, lack basic equipment or supplies due to decreased public funding, charge user

fees or implement other cost-recovery programs, or are simply privatized (Iriart *et al.*, 2002; Xing, 2002). China's 'great leap forward in economic growth ... and great leap backward in social security' (Xing, 2002: 248) is one of the starkest examples. Since the late 1970s, as public spending on health as a share of GDP dropped by 75 per cent, over 700 000 communal rural health clinics have been turned into private, full-cost-recovery services, completely disenfranchising almost 40 per cent of the rural population. While 80 per cent of China remains rural, 80 per cent of physicians are in the urban centres that are home to its new middle- and upper-income classes (Xing, 2002: 249–50).

[20] The World Bank's International Finance Corporation (IFC), which makes loans to the private sector, for example, is aggressively marketing growth in privatized health and other services (Lethbridge, 2002; Tannenbaum, 2002). In its 'Private Sector Development Strategy,' adopted by the World Bank in 2002, the IFC envisions a larger private market in health services, with subsidy programs for the poor financed by the World Bank's IDA, which provides concessional lending or grants to developing countries (Tannenbaum, 2002). Its priorities for private health investment 'reflect a high-technology, high-income approach to health care provision' (Lethbridge, 2002: 352) and rest on 'the underlying belief that investing to meet middle-class health needs through the private sector will eventually have a significant impact on poverty,' despite there being 'no substantial evidence to support this' (Lethbridge, 2002: 352).

[21] Several developing countries, such as Cuba and India, are liberalizing health services under Modes 2 (health tourism) and 4 (export of health professionals), in order to earn valuable foreign exchange. India, which is a major exporter of health professionals and sees economic advantage in GATS Mode 4, nonetheless has a domestic deficit in the number of physicians, ranking 119 of 184 countries for which there are data (WHO, 2002c).

CHAPTER FOUR
Education

[N]o government seriously committed to achieving education for all
will be thwarted in this achievement by lack of resources (G8 Okinawa
Communiqué, para. 33).

Introduction

The connections between education and health are many, and operate both
directly and through the intervening variables of economic growth and gender
equity. Personal and household (family) income rises with education level.
In developed countries, higher education is associated with healthier living
conditions (e.g. better housing, exposure to less environmental pollution)
and healthier lifestyles. In developing countries, increased education is
associated with greater economic productivity, lower disease rates, better child
survival and increased political participation (Dutch Ministry of Foreign
Affairs, 2002). These gains are more dramatic as education levels for women
rise, and 'societies that limit girls' access to education pay a price in poorer
health, and thereby in poorer economic growth' (CMH, 2001: 75).[1] Education
levels are also associated with reduced HIV risk, particularly for girls and
women. Those countries showing the greatest lack of knowledge about HIV/
AIDS (primarily in sub-Saharan Africa and several of the former Soviet
republics) are also ones with very low and in some cases rapidly declining
rates of education spending and participation (CIDA, 2002b; World Bank,
2002c). As women's education rates and levels rise, fertility rates decline,
and life expectancies for both women and children rise (UNESCO, 2002b:
34–5). Universal primary education, UNESCO further argues, can be a
powerful social force in displacing unhealthy child labour (UNESCO, 2002b:
33).

Indeed, if ever a virtuous development circle existed, it is the link between
health and education. The healthier a child, the better able he or she is to
learn. The better educated a child becomes, the healthier he or she will grow.
The healthier and better educated people are, the more economically sufficient
and productive they will become. The more economically sufficient and
productive people become, the better able they are to reinvest their own savings
into continuing health and education that is universally accessible.

Education for All and the Dakar Framework for Action

This virtuous circle has long been recognized, first in Article 26 of the Universal Declaration of Human Rights (1948), more recently in the 1990 Declaration on Education for All (EFA) at the World Conference on Education for All, and subsequently in a series of summits throughout the 1990s (UNESCO, 2002a). The goal of education for all took on more operational shape during multilateral meetings in Dakar in 2000, which produced the Dakar Framework for Action (UNESCO, 2000). This framework identifies six education goals (see Box 4.1).

Box 4.1: The Six Dakar Goals

We hereby collectively commit ourselves to the attainment of the following goals:

- expanding and improving comprehensive early childhood care and education, especially for the most vulnerable and disadvantaged children;
- ensuring that by 2015 all children, particularly girls, children in difficult circumstances and those belonging to ethnic minorities, have access to and complete free and compulsory primary education of good quality;[2]
- ensuring that the learning needs of all young people and adults are met through equitable access to appropriate learning and life skills programmes;
- achieving a 50 per cent improvement in levels of adult literacy by 2015, especially for women, and equitable access to basic and continuing education for all adults;
- eliminating gender disparities in primary and secondary education by 2005, and achieving gender equality in education by 2015, with a focus on ensuring girls' full and equal access to and achievement in basic education of good quality;[3] [and]
- improving all aspects of the quality of education and ensuring excellence of all so that recognized and measurable learning outcomes are achieved by all, especially in literacy, numeracy and essential life skills (UNESCO, 2002b: 13).

At the Okinawa summit, which followed the Dakar meeting by only a few months, the G8 expressed its support for several of these goals:

> We reaffirm our commitment that no government seriously committed to achieving education for all will be thwarted in this achievement by lack of resources.
>
> We therefore commit ourselves to strengthen efforts bilaterally and together with international organisations and private sector donors to achieve the goals of universal primary education by 2015 and gender equality in schooling by 2005 (Okinawa Communiqué, paras. 33–4).

This second commitment is a direct quotation from paragraph 10 of the Dakar Declaration, identifying the two most important initial targets in education. These two targets (enrolling all children in primary school by 2015 and eliminating gender disparities in primary and secondary education by 2005) are also among the IDGs to which the G8 have committed their support. The G8 reaffirmed support for the Dakar Declaration at their next summit in Genoa (2001), including 'our commitment to help countries meet the Dakar Framework for Action goal of universal primary education by 2015' and that 'education, in particular universal primary education and equal access to education at all levels for girls, must be given high priority both in national poverty reduction strategies and in our development programmes' (Genoa Communiqué, para. 18). They nonetheless failed to specify the resources that would be devoted to the Dakar Framework goals.

In every region of the world, excepting the transition and Central/Eastern European countries, substantial progress has been made in both universal primary education (UPE) and gender equality since 1990 (UNESCO, 2002b: 69). UNESCO's 2001 *Monitoring Report* on progress toward the Dakar goals, however, cautioned that

> [a]t least 32 countries, of which 11 are experiencing conflict, are unlikely to meet the target of UPE [Universal Primary Education] by 2015, unless a serious effort is made for these countries.
>
> One region of particular concern is sub-Saharan Africa, where enrolment would have to increase at almost three times the effort undertaken during the period 1990–97 (UNESCO, 2001: 7).

One year later, the tally of countries unlikely to meet the UPE goal has increased to 37, with another 20 countries noted as requiring 'renewed efforts' (UNESCO, 2002b: 17). Only 21 countries remain on target. The majority of countries unlikely to meet the UPE goal are in sub-Saharan Africa, where net enrolment rates for primary education stand at only 57 per cent (UNESCO, 2002b: 45). For UPE alone, 21 countries (of which 14 are African) are further away from the Dakar goal now than in 1990 (UNESCO, 2002b: 91).

Estimating progress toward the Dakar goals using school completion rates rather than enrolment rates, the World Bank came up with an even more pessimistic assessment: '[U]se of completion rates raises the number [unlikely to meet the UPE goal] to 88 countries, out of the total 155 for which data were established. Some 35 countries are unlikely to meet the goal of eliminating gender disparities at the primary level by 2005, even when the goal is simply universal primary education and not universal primary completion' (World Bank, 2002f: 3).

There are further causes for concern. The 2003 Social Watch annual report noted that of the 153 countries (including the industrialized countries) for which information was available, 38 had regressed relative to their situation in 1990 (or, in some cases, in 2000) in the area of basic education, as determined by primary school enrolment rates and the percentage of students reaching Grade 5 (Social Watch, 2003: 73–6). The previous year's report noted that out of 116 countries for which data were then available, 33 had actually reduced the percentage of their GDP spent on education between 1990 and 1995–97 (Social Watch, 2002: 19).

Responsibility for the downward trend in some countries, and stagnation in others, cannot be laid entirely at the door of the G8, but the data do indicate the size of the challenge that lies ahead. That challenge is compounded by the effects of the HIV epidemic, which, as the World Bank (2002c) points out, threatens to undermine and reverse the modest progress that has been made toward educational goals, even while education, as we have already noted, has a particularly important role to play in combating the epidemic. Some 860 000 children in sub-Saharan Africa, for example, lost their teachers to HIV/ AIDS in 1999 (UNESCO, 2002b: 118). '[F]or a growing number of countries, HIV/AIDS is not just an additional factor that needs to be accommodated in educational planning and practice. It is now a fact of life that requires that every policy, procedure and activity should be re-worked and rethought within an AIDS-centred policy framework' (UNESCO, 2002b: 118).

This statement merely underscores the importance of the virtuous circle linking health, education and development, and the dramatic inadequacy of G8 support for the GFATM and health systems recounted in the previous chapter.

Once again, we confront the scale of the problem, and estimates of the resources required to remedy it. UNESCO cites estimates of the additional resources that would be needed to achieve the UPE goal ranging from US$8 billion to US$15 billion per year, with the higher estimate being UNESCO's own (UNESCO, 2001: 38). To put this in some perspective, these amounts, respectively, are six per cent to ten per cent of the value of US tax reductions in 2001–02 (Oxfam, 2001b). The lower estimate is roughly equal to the average annual value of tax cuts enacted in Canada between 1984 and 2000 (Yalnizyan, 2002). The World Bank, focusing on completion rather than just access rates, estimates the additional funds needed to achieve the UPE goal at US$10–30 billion, depending on the basis used for estimating costs (Devarajan *et al.*, 2002). Another World Bank calculation (World Bank, 2002f) generated a substantially lower set of cost estimates – lower, because it assumed gradual phasing-in of increased expenditures and a more substantial contribution from governments' own domestic budgets. Despite this latter assumption, 'a regional breakdown of the estimate shows the importance of intensifying support to sub-Saharan Africa: the region would require a *seven-fold* increase from its present level of aid inflows for primary education in real terms' (World Bank, 2002f: 4, original emphasis). Table 4.1, below, indicates that relying on the availability of additional funds from domestic sources is almost certainly unrealistic, at least in the case of sub-Saharan Africa. In 1998, public expenditure on education by G7 countries averaged 5.3 per cent of GDP, while for sub-Saharan African countries the comparable figure – excluding foreign aid for education – was 3.6 per cent (World Bank, 2002d: 82–5). The problem is that in poor countries, the available funds are simply inadequate to the task. As we emphasized in Chapter 2, public expenditures on all forms of social provision are often further constrained by the imperative of servicing the external debt, and the limited scope of currently available debt relief.

Table 4.1: Changes in Public Education Expenditure Africa, 1990–98

Countries for which data are available	▲▲	▲	–	▼	▼▼
Sub-Saharan Africa	Botswana Burkina Faso Congo, Rep. of Gambia Lesotho Malawi Mauritius Namibia South Africa	Burundi Chad Ethiopia Ghana Guinea Swaziland	Equatorial Guinea Madagascar	Kenya Niger Senegal Togo Uganda Zambia Zimbabwe	Gabon Mali Nigeria
Other African countries	Tunisia	Egypt		Morocco	Algeria

Source: Social Watch (2003: 79–81)

Legend:

▲▲   Significant progress (more than 1% change in public expenditure as % of GDP or GNP).

▲   Some progress (less than 1% change in public expenditure as % of GDP or GNP).

–   Stagnation.

▼   Some regression (less than 1% change in public expenditure as % of GDP or GNP).

▼▼   Significant regression (more than 1% change in public expenditure as % of GDP or GNP).

Policy Challenges, G8 Responses

UNESCO (2001: 38) identified four major challenges for the international community if the Dakar Framework's targets are to be achieved:

1. To *drastically increase support* for basic education within a context of increased support for the education sector and for overall international development assistance.

2. To ensure that *increased financial flows*, from the private sector as well as ODA, act as a catalyst for national resource mobilization and sustainable development, with due attention to the critical role of basic education.

3. To *strengthen policy coherence* and co-ordination of EFA efforts nationally and internationally.

4. To *hold national governments and the international community to their commitment* for EFA through careful monitoring of the progress towards the goals and targets of EFA (original emphases).

The UNESCO report observed that although the real value of ODA declined during the 1990s, 'education seems to have suffered relatively less within this overall declining ODA trend.' However, it also notes that 'education continues to constitute a low proportion of individual countries' development assistance' (UNESCO, 2001: 37–8).

Data from our three summit years (1999, 2000 and 2001) indicate that, as with health, education aid forms a small part of total ODA for most G7 countries (see Figure 4.1, on the next page). Overall, G7 aid for education increased slightly in 2001 from the previous year. Both France and Germany have reasonably high total education expenditures and, with Italy, show a marked upward increase since 1990. In the case of France, however, '"education" encompasses areas as broad as higher education, research, teaching of French and the promotion of the French-speaking world' (Canonne, 2002: 194). Some caution in interpreting these trends is thus warranted, the more so since the earlier two time periods (1990–92 and 1993–96) reflect only bilateral aid, and calculations for total (multilateral and bilateral) aid for France, Italy, Germany and the UK for 1999 rest on an assumption we have had to make in the absence of available data (see explanatory notes in Figure 4.1 on the next page). Education aid increased marginally in 2001 from 2000 (the two years for which data are more reliable) in the US, UK and Japan, and more substantially in Italy and France. It declined in Canada and Germany, although Canada's basic education contribution increased (see Figure 4.2, on page 86).

Figure 4.1: Trends in Aid to Education as % of Total ODA*

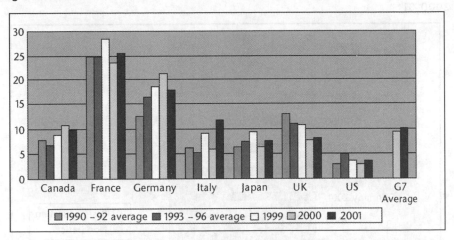

Source: UNESCO (2002b: Table 5.2); OECD (2001c: Tables 13, 15 & 19);
OECD (2002b: Tables 13, 15 & 19); OECD (2003: Tables 13, 15 & 19)

Estimates of 1999, 2000 and 2001 multilateral contributions made by authors.
* Total ODA includes bilateral aid (country to country) and multilateral aid
(contributions made by donor countries to the EC, the World Bank and Regional
Development Banks).
In 1999, the multilateral contributions for European G7 countries were approximated
using EC sector commitments in 2000, as data on EC sector commitments for 1999 are
not available.
Note: Averages for 1990–92 and 1993–96 are for bilateral aid only.

Basic education aid – that portion going to primary education, basic life skills
and early childhood education in developing countries – is surprisingly low
for all G7 countries, especially given their repeated commitments to the UPE
goal. (To avoid misleading comparisons, we restrict these data to the two
years – 2000 and 2001 – for which full and reliable data are available.) Japan
and the US showed very marginal increases in basic education aid in 2001;
only Canada and France showed a substantial rise. The other G7 countries
registered declines in basic education aid, causing the group as a whole to
rise only marginally above its 2000 level.

Figure 4.2: % of Total ODA* to Basic Education and Non-basic Education, 2000–01**

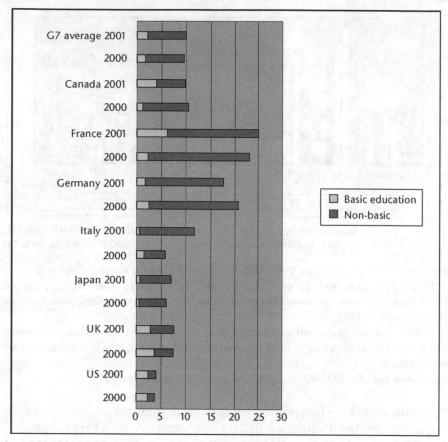

Source: OECD (2002b: Table 19); OECD (2003: Table 19).

* Estimates of multilateral contributions made by authors.
** Basic education spending is part of total education spending; the dark portion of the bar represents non-basic education spending.

The G8 further stated, 'we will develop incentives to increase school enrolment' (Genoa Communiqué, para.18). No further elaboration was provided, but the G8 committed themselves to 'establish a task force of senior G8 officials to advise us on how best to pursue the Dakar goals in co-operation with developing countries, relevant international organisations and other stakeholders,' with a report to be presented at the next summit (Genoa Communiqué, para. 19). Although the report (G8 Education Task Force, 2002) was duly released, it contained no explicit proposals for commitments to new solutions, and was disturbing in its emphasis on increased contributions from developing countries' domestic resources.

Canada was the first G8 country to announce a specific monetary commitment to the Dakar Framework, indicating a quadrupling of its basic education assistance to a total of C$555 million over five years (2000–05) (CIDA, 2002b), of which C$100 million is earmarked for Africa (CCIC, 2002: 5). By 2005, annual basic education contributions from Canada should reach C$164 million (CCIC, 2002: 5). Since Dakar (April 2000), the UK has committed £96 million to major new education initiatives in three African countries: Malawi, South Africa and Rwanda (Kirton & Kokotsis, 2002) and pledges 'significant' increases in new education aid (UNESCO, 2002b: 174). The US in July 2002 pledged to increase basic education aid by 50 per cent from 2001 to 2003, and to increase educational aid to Africa by 30 per cent over the same period (UNESCO, 2002b: 174). In September 2002, Japan pledged an additional US$2 billion in new educational aid over five years (2002–07), but outside of the G8's Dakar EFA Action Plan (UNESCO, 2002b: 174). Japan's assistance, however, will be targeted to low-income countries, including those in Africa, and appears dedicated to basic education (Ministry of Foreign Affairs, Japan, 2002).

These are positive changes. They are, however, still grossly insufficient. UNESCO (2002b: 75), complaining that the documentation from G8 bilateral aid agencies makes it difficult to sum up their new education commitments, nonetheless estimates these at about US$1 billion annually, of which US$0.3 billion will likely go to basic education. This US$0.3 billion sum is less than ten per cent of UNESCO's estimate of US$4.4 billion in new annual contributions to basic education if the UPE and gender goals are to be met by 2015 (UNESCO, 2002b: 175).

UNESCO and the G8

In Genoa, the G8 also committed its members to 'support UNESCO in its key role for universal education' (Genoa Communiqué, para. 18). It is not possible to separate out G8 funding from total support to UNESCO, but it is safe to presume that G8 countries, with the exception of the United States, are among the major contributors.[4] In that light, the concern expressed by UNESCO's Director-General about the inadequacies of the post-Genoa summit fiscal year are revealing:

> [T]he Programme and Budget for 2002–2003 was drawn up – for the third time in a row – on the basis of zero-nominal growth pegged at some US$544 million for the two years. In reality, zero-nominal growth represents a reduction in resources of 4.2% …. Clearly, the Organization cannot afford to remain on such a path of continuous belt-tightening

lest it be depleted of its vitality and ability to respond to new challenges (UNESCO, 2002b).

In fairness, the G8 did not say they would *increase* support to UNESCO in its work, but, without such an increase, their statement of support lacks any meaning.

Education and NEPAD

Like recent G8 summit communiqués, NEPAD commits participating African nations to the IDGs, which include UPE by 2015, and to remove gender disparities in primary and secondary education by 2005 (NEPAD, para. 68). As Bond (2002: 121) points out, 'cost-recovery provisions and exceedingly low state education budgets' are 'double disincentives' to achieving these goals, and are not explicitly addressed by NEPAD. Cost-recovery programs are particular barriers to women's participation. At the same time, progress in UPE had been made in many African countries in recent years and has only recently begun to regress. Gender parity in primary education in sub-Saharan Africa rose from 0.79 in 1990 to 0.89 in 1999, bettering the world average of 0.88 (affected primarily by low gender parity in South and West Asian countries) (UNESCO, 2002b: 69). The adult illiteracy rate has also decreased in all African countries for which data exist (N = 47) (Social Watch, 2002).

These positive trends, however, require perspective. As we noted earlier, 14 African countries are farther away from the UPE targets now than they were in 1990, and nine have worse gender parity (World Bank, 2002d). Many African countries still have a very high adult illiteracy rate. Twelve of the 47 reporting countries have adult illiteracy rates of less than 23.9 per cent, the world average. Almost half (N = 23) have illiteracy rates exceeding 40 per cent of the adult population (Social Watch, 2002: 42). Countries in West Africa (many of them former French colonies), countries that have been or still are in conflict, and countries with predominantly Muslim populations have particularly high illiteracy rates.

Two of the Dakar goals reference the need for basic education beyond UPE and gender parity. UNESCO has criticized NEPAD for ignoring these:

> In basic education, NEPAD refers only to the ... [g]oal of UPE by 2015, and to curriculum, quality and the use of ICTs. In view of the huge EFA needs in Africa in the area of each of the six Dakar objectives, planning for basic education needs special attention wherever the NEPAD is used as a framework for planning specific initiatives or allocating new funding (UNESCO, 2002a: 47).

This is a criticism also made of the 'Fast Track Initiative' (FTI), a program supported by the G8 Education Task Force (2002). The FTI emphasizes UPE and gender parity to the exclusion of other Dakar goals, which makes the initiative 'less satisfactory as a framework for medium- to long-term education reform' (UNESCO, 2002b: 176). It is also linked with the PRSP program, which, UNESCO cautions, renders 'the extent of national ownership of plans and policies ... uncertain' (2002b: 177; see PRSP discussion in Chapter 2). NEPAD's desire to reduce the global 'digital divide', which it shares with the G8 (see Box 4.2, below), is not unwarranted, but without more specific planning for basic education, it risks replicating within Africa the same global divide it is keen to bridge.

Box 4.2: Technology for Development

In 2000, the G8 leaders set up the Digital Opportunities Task Force (dot.force), and in 2001 they stated: 'We endorse the report of the Digital Opportunity Task Force (dot.force) and its Genoa Plan of Action that successfully fulfilled the Okinawa mandate. ... We will continue to support the process and encourage all stakeholders to demonstrate ownership, to mobilise expertise and resources and to build on this successful co-operation' (Genoa Communiqué, para. 22).

The dot.force report is to be welcomed as a recognition of the critical role that access to information and communications technology (ICT) will play in economic development (e.g. see Hewitt de Alcántara, 2001; OECD, 2001a) and in contributing to the achievement of a variety of social goals, such as those related to education and food security (International Food Policy Research Institute, 2000). Although it is too early to assess the success of the G8 in achieving the objectives outlined in the report, it is not too early to warn about the importance of two critical sets of questions.

Firstly, a fundamental weakness of technology-based prescriptions in other areas has been and continues to be the gap between market power and social need. The Genoa Communiqué's vague references to 'ownership' and to 'mobiliz[ing] expertise and resources' do not address the concrete problem of limited purchasing power as it affects both access to the results of today's scientific research and influence on the priorities of tomorrow's. It is useful to know that OECD countries, per capita, have roughly ten times as many telecommunications access paths and 100 times as many internet hosts as non-OECD countries (OECD, 2001a: 7–8), and it is not hard to imagine the social and economic effects of this divide, given the indispensability of advanced computing and telecommunication for many sectors of today's industrial and commercial economy. It is harder to imagine how the situation can soon be remedied, even in a world of dramatically falling ICT costs, without some financial support (Hewitt de Alcántara, 2001: 17–18). The UNDP Director of ICT for Development has warned that today's disparity in information infrastructure investment between the OECD and the rest of the world is unlikely to lessen in the future, given the status quo, because of revenue-related limits on 'telecoms operators' availability to support infrastructure build-out' (Gilhooly, 2001): even within the industrialized countries, internet access at the household level tends to vary with income and education (OECD, 2001a: 18).

A second set of questions is more complex, more disturbing, and can only be touched upon here, because it requires analysis of a huge literature on technology and development. Hewitt de Alcántara, in a sceptical survey of claims about development and the knowledge economy, warns that developing countries vary widely in their ability to adopt new ICTs and in the speed with which they can do so, and argues that 'nothing in the current information revolution seems to be changing the underlying dynamics of unequal development at a global level' (Hewitt de Alcántara, 2001: 14), although thoughtfully designed and implemented development assistance policies have the potential to do so. Especially in the context of NEPAD's preoccupation with ICT, it is worth asking what mechanisms will be developed to ensure equitable and meaningful participation in the potential benefits from ICTs.

Education, Child Labour and NEPAD

The Genoa summit, as part of its support for UPE and UNESCO, referenced the importance of working 'with the International Labour Organization (ILO) to support efforts to fight child labour' (Genoa Communiqué, para. 18). The issue of child labor remains one of the contentious points in trade negotiations between developed and developing countries, particularly with efforts by EU countries and, in 1999, by the US, to link labor rights to WTO agreements. Developing countries, with some justification, see this as a potential means of 'back door protectionism', although much depends on how such a linkage is operationalized and the extent of 'special and differential' phase-in periods for countries lacking the financial resources or material infrastructures allowing quick compliance (Labonte, 2002).

NEPAD does not mention children, apart from its reference to infant and under-five mortality rates. It does not mention the Convention of the Rights of the Child, nor the Worst Forms of Child Labor Convention 1999. Of the 53 African countries, 32 have ratified the 1999 convention, while no African country has denounced it. Child labor rates, while high, continue to decline (see Table 4.2).

Table 4.2: Children under 14 Working in the Labor Force (as % of Population Aged 10–14 Years)

	1970	1980	1990	1997
Africa (53 countries)	31.4	30.9	28.0	25.8
Sub-Saharan Africa (48 countries)	36.3	34.7	32.2	29.8
Sub-Saharan Africa excluding South Africa	39.1	37.2	35.5	31.7
Sub-Saharan Africa excluding South Africa and Nigeria	41.1	39.3	36.2	33.5

Source: World Bank (2000a)

Key factors internationally in child labor decline are higher rates of spending on public health (which induces parents to switch from a high-fertility, low-survival, low-education strategy to a low-fertility, high-survival, high-education one) and on education (via direct subsidies or indirectly through tax-based income redistribution policies) (Cigno *et al.*, 2002). Globalization, in the form of increased trade, may worsen child labor in countries that start out with an uneducated labor force, although the 'net effects are ... ambiguous' (Cigno *et al.*, 2002: 1587), and it reduces it in countries starting with a larger educated (post-primary level) workforce. This makes intuitive sense, since such countries would be able to import products made more cheaply by child labor in other countries.

GATS and Education

Trade liberalization, under some conditions, may have a positive effect on reducing child labour and increasing school enrolment and completion. The impact of services liberalization is less well known, but with potentially negative results. As with health-care services (Chapter 3), there is a growing developed world market in private provision, or contracted private management, of education services (Grieshaber-Otto & Sanger, 2002). Indeed, privatization and commercialization in education in many developed countries are outpacing their equivalents in health care; the global education market is estimated to be worth US$2 trillion annually (Barlow, 2001). Policies and practices include school management contracts with private companies, increased fund-raising by parents and school committees to pay for basic services and supplies in public schools, direct corporate sponsorship for public school supplies and programs, new or higher tuition costs (particularly for tertiary public education), increased numbers of private schools (religious and non-denominational), and tax deductions (indirect public subsidies) for private school fees.

Education in most countries has long been a mix of public and private provision. Private education, in turn, has usually been the prerogative of wealthier individuals and families with the income needed to afford it. As Cigno *et al.* (2002) argue for developing countries, public provision of health and education are important factors in school enrolment. User charges or other cost-recovery schemes for education, whether public or private, are associated with declines in enrolment, especially by the poor (Hilary, 2001). If private provision of education increases, an enlarged 'two-tiered' system will disproportionately benefit the wealthy and penalize the poor. It can do so in a number of ways paralleling threats to public health care: e.g. by eroding support for tax-funded public systems among the elite ('tax revolt') or by attracting teachers away from public schools to a private system with higher salaries or benefits. Countries that liberalize trade in education services without restrictions or horizontal limitations under 'national treatment' that exempt subsidies for public education could be responsible for providing similar subsidies to foreign private companies seeking to establish private schools. Even when they do make such exemptions, trade challenges could arise, with the final outcome uncertain – as it is in other areas where the disciplines of trade law could be applied to social services (Grieshaber-Otto & Sanger, 2002: 110–13).

Few African or G7 countries have so far made GATS commitments related to education. Exceptions are the fairly extensive commitments made by Lesotho, and by the EC 12 nations to permit foreign provision of private education. Nevertheless, critical questions arise about whether liberalization of trade and investment in education services liberalization under GATS is compatible with international instruments concerning the right to education. Notably, Article 26, paragraph 5 of the Universal Declaration of Human Rights (1948) declares that 'education shall be free, at least in the elementary and fundamental stage'; and Article 13, paragraph 9b of the International Covenant on Economic Social and Cultural Rights (1966) states that '[s]econdary education in its different forms, including technical and vocational secondary education, shall be made generally available and accessible to all by every means, and in particular by the progressive introduction of free education'.

Summary: Chapter Four

Education is one of the keys to improved population health and economic development. The Dakar Framework for Action (Education for All or EFA) was the first comprehensive, multilateral plan setting targets for education across the lifespan. The framework has been endorsed by individual G8 nations, and by the G8 as a group at the Okinawa (2000), Genoa (2001) and Kananaskis (2002) summits. In the group's own words, '[e]ducation is the foundation for higher living standards and democratic societies. It is an important long-term investment in peace and development. We reaffirm the importance of literacy, numeracy, and learning, and our support for the EFA initiative' (G8 Education Task Force, 2002).

The G8 have focused particularly on two of the Dakar goals, UPE and gender equality, which UNESCO describes as a minimization of expectation, a minimization that appears to have been copied by NEPAD. Despite the G8's acceptance of the importance of the EFA goals, the number of countries regressing on their UPE and gender equality goals increased since the Okinawa summit. There are numerous reasons for this. One directly bearing on the G8 is the need for increased development assistance for basic education, which, for sub-Saharan Africa, is estimated to require a seven-fold jump if the UPE goal alone is to be met. Yet, with the exceptions of France (which gives a lot to language education), Italy (which gives a lot of little) and the US (which gives little of a lot), G8 countries' aid to education, including their multilateral assistance, *declined* in 2001. Several countries since (Canada, Japan, the US, the UK) have announced increased aid for basic education, much of it targeted to Africa. This is partly a reflection of a Kananaskis summit commitment to 'significantly increase the support provided by our bilateral aid agencies to basic education for countries with a strong policy and financial commitment to the sector. Each G8 donor will make public the steps it will take to fulfill this commitment' (G8 Education Task Force, 2002). The total amounts, however, are still less than one-tenth of the annual increases which UNESCO estimates are required to reach the UPE and gender equality goals alone.

Explicit or Specific Commitments: Education

*   Affirmed commitment to education for all, including the goals of UPE by 2015 and gender equality in schooling by 2005 (Okinawa, Genoa).
    Accomplished: Will probably not be accomplished, particularly in sub-Saharan Africa.
    Adequacy: Basic education aid for all G7 nations is very low. New G8 pledges for basic education assistance will be less than 10% of new donor funding needed if UPE and gender equality goals to be met.

Comments: Both France and Germany have relatively high total education aid expenditures; this does not always translate into expenditure on primary education. Canada was the only G7 nation to announce a monetary commitment to the Dakar framework prior to the Kananaskis summit. The UK, the US and Japan have made subsequent commitments to increase education aid, targeting low-income countries (including African ones) and basic education.

- Support UNESCO in its key role for universal education (Genoa).
Accomplished: Unknown; specific G8 contributions to UNESCO budget are not available.
Adequacy: UNESCO budgets, mostly financed by the G8 nations (excluding the US), have declined in real dollar terms over the past several years.
Comments: Support is usually considered a non-explicit commitment since it is not quantified. We regard it as explicit and requiring constant if not rising financial contributions.

Implicit or Generic Commitments: Education

- Will work with the ILO to support efforts to fight child labour (Genoa).
Accomplished: Unknown.
Comments: Decreased child labour is associated with increased public health and education spending/access, and possibly with trade liberalization (market access). See Chapters 3 and 7.
- Will develop incentives to increase school enrolment (Genoa).
Accomplished: Unclear.
Comments: The G8 Education Task Force has commited itself to increased development assistance to basic education (Kananaskis). The Kananaskis Chair's Summary states, 'We agreed to increase significantly our bilateral assistance for countries *that have demonstrated a strong and credible policy and financial commitment to these goals*' (emphasis added). No other initiatives were specifically identified.

Endnotes to Chapter Four

[1] Although education spending is associated with improved health outcomes at the US$2/day poverty level, it is not so associated at the US$1/day poverty level (Wagstaff, 2001). This is probably because the burden of disease and malnutrition at deeper poverty levels precludes an ability to learn effectively, or to act upon that knowledge. On the vicious circle linking illness and impoverishment, see Narayan et al. (2000: 95–105).

[2] This goal is almost identical to Target 3, Goal 2 of the MDGs, which states: 'Ensure that, by 2015, children everywhere, boys and girls alike, will be able to complete a full course of primary schooling.'

[3] This goal is almost identical to Target 4, Goal 3 of the MDGs, which states: 'Eliminate gender disparity in primary and secondary education, preferably by 2005, and to all levels of education no later than 2015.'

[4] The United States had, as of May 2003, not rejoined UNESCO after leaving in 1984 to protest a UNESCO project designed to reduce dependence on the 'Big Four' wire services for media information (Du Boff, 2002: 29).

CHAPTER FIVE

Nutrition, Food Security and Biotechnology

Most international trade in agricultural commodities is controlled by a very few big transnational corporations, based in rich exporting countries. If a low-income country attempts to promote greater self-reliance in feeding its population and more remunerative employment for its small producers, it will often have to selectively restrict agricultural imports. [P]oor countries have few other effective policy instruments. ... Rich countries in contrast ... have a wide range of policy instruments at their disposal. ... The issue for developing countries should be seen as ... the goal of sustainable agriculture, not as one of 'free markets' versus regulated ones (Barraclough, 2000: xvii–xviii).

Introduction

According to the UN Food and Agriculture Organization (UNFAO), 'in 1997–99, there were 815 million undernourished people in the world: 777 million in the developing countries, 27 million in transition countries and 11 million in the industrialized countries' (UNFAO, 2001: 2). 'Undernourishment' in this context means daily caloric intake 'that is continuously insufficient to meet dietary energy requirements' (UNFAO, 2001: 50); it does not refer to shortages of micronutrients such as iodine, vitamin A and iron that may be critical for health, and which affect much larger numbers of people (UN ACC/SCN, 2000: 23–32; WHO, 1997: 13–14). Nutritional deficiencies represent an adverse health outcome in themselves, and clearly increase vulnerability to other stressors such as infectious disease (e.g. see Rice *et al.*, 2000). Indeed, the WHO describes malnutrition as the greatest single risk factor contributing to the global burden of disease (WHO figures published in 1995, as cited in World Bank, 2002d: 42), and more recently published figures suggest that this may even be an underestimate.[1] In developing countries, particularly LDCs, adequate nutrition may figure more importantly as a determinant of health, and therefore of economic growth and development, than even education. We noted in Chapter 3 that education spending at the US$1/day poverty level is not associated with improved health outcomes. This is probably because malnutrition and other stressors inescapable at this level of poverty affect people's abilities to learn or act upon new knowledge. At the same time, the higher a woman's education, the less likely her children are to be stunted (Smith & Haddad, 2000): the relationship between education and nutrition is dynamic. In this chapter, we provide a brief assessment of G8 responses to the health-related challenges presented by inadequate nutrition and food security. We have not attempted to place food crises in their historical context, even though knowledge of that context is often essential to understanding the continued coexistence within national and regional economies of highly productive agriculture with large numbers of people who are unable to get enough to eat (cf. Franke & Chasin, 1980; Lawrence, 1986).

Nutrition and Food Security

The 1996 World Food Summit defined food security as a situation where '[a]ll people at all times have physical and economic access to sufficient, safe and nutritional food to meet dietary needs and food preferences for an active and healthy life' (quoted by Thomson, 2001: 24). In the intervening years, progress in reducing the global prevalence of food insecurity has been at best modest, perhaps reflecting what some observers see as the marginal political status of food security issues and the associated international institutions (Amalric, 2001). The 2001 *State of Food Insecurity* report from UNFAO notes that

> FAO's latest estimates indicate that, in 1997–99, there were 815 million undernourished people in the world: 777 million in the developing countries, 27 million in transition countries and 11 million in the industrialized countries. For the developing countries, the latest figure represents a decrease of 39 million since 1990–92 (the benchmark period used at the World Food Summit), for which the revised figure is 816 million undernourished.
>
> This means that the average annual decrease [in undernourished people] now stands at about 6 million people. Clearly, there has been a slowdown in the reduction of undernourished in the world. As a consequence, to achieve the World Food Summit goal of halving the number of undernourished in developing countries by 2015, the average annual decrease required is no longer 20 million but 22 million – well above the current level of performance (UNFAO, 2001: 2).

Figure 5.1: Regional Prevalence of Undernourishment, % of Total Population

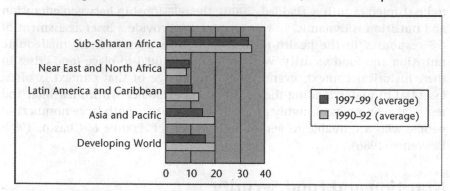

Source: UNFAO (2001: 51, Table 1)

Indeed, 'continuing at the current rate, it would take more than 60 years to reach the target' (UNFAO, 2001: iv).

These aggregate figures fail to shed light on widely varying country performances. For example, the highest *percentage* reductions in the proportion of undernourished people during the 1990s were found in Peru, Chad, Ghana and Kuwait, and the highest increases were found in Tanzania, Burundi, North Korea and the Democratic Republic of the Congo. UNFAO warns, however, that 'the majority of developing countries suffered significant increases in their *absolute number* of undernourished. This is a worrying trend, masked by the much better performances of a few' (UNFAO, 2001: 6; emphasis added).

Table 5.1, below, shows the ten 'best' and 'worst' performers, in terms of the increase or decrease in the absolute number of undernourished people. It should be read keeping in mind several things. Firstly, various factors – including population growth, changes in agricultural productivity, and changes in the level and distribution of income – can contribute to changes in undernourishment. Secondly (population) size matters. In India, 'the percentage of undernourished is estimated to have declined from 25 to 23 percent but the number of undernourished rose by 11 million, owing to rapid population growth'; conversely, 'despite China's good performance, the country is still home to the world's second largest number of undernourished people after India' (UNFAO, 2001: 5).

At the 2001 summit, the G8 made a generic commitment to 'meet the International Development Goals, by strengthening and enhancing the effectiveness of our development assistance' (Genoa Communiqué, para. 14). As we point out in the next chapter, a commitment to *increase* the amounts of aid at this summit was conspicuous by its absence. The IDGs include the goal of poverty reduction, a key indicator for which is the proportion of children under five who are underweight. However, the lack of more explicit commitments in the area of food security at the Cologne, Okinawa and Genoa G8 summits represents an omission of considerable significance in terms of human health. The *G8 Africa Action Plan* announced at the 2002 summit contains a section on food security (para. 7.3), but within a context concerned primarily with the economic development (including adoption of new biotechnologies) of Africa's agricultural sector. We comment on the relationships between agriculture, biotechnology and food security later in this chapter.

Table 5.1: Ten Countries with Largest Increases and Decreases in the Number of Undernourished People, 1990–92 to 1997–99

Decreases (best performers)		Increases (worst performers)	
Country	**Number (millions)**	**Country**	**Number (millions)**
China	76	*Democratic Republic of the Congo*	17
Peru	6	India	11
Indonesia	5	*United Republic of Tanzania*	6
Nigeria	4	Democratic People's Republic of Korea	5
Thailand	4	Bangladesh	5
Vietnam	4	Afghanistan	3
Brazil	3	Venezuela	3
Ghana	3	*Uganda*	2
Pakistan	2	*Kenya*	2
Sudan	2	Iraq	2
All others	7	All others	21

Source: UNFAO (2001: 5)
Sub-Saharan African countries are indicated in *italics*.

G7 ODA to Agriculture

The G8 further noted in 2001 that 'a central objective of our poverty reduction strategy remains access to adequate food supplies and rural development. Support to agriculture is a crucial instrument of ODA. We shall endeavour to develop capacity in poor countries, integrating programmes into national strategies and increasing training in agricultural science' (Genoa Communiqué, para. 20).

They also committed to 'target the most food-insecure regions, particularly Sub-Saharan Africa and South Asia' (Genoa Communiqué, para. 21) – apparently, given the context, for development assistance including food aid. The brief time that has elapsed since Genoa makes it impossible to assess the contributions of specific G7 countries to reducing food insecurity. The decline in such aid over the past 20 years, however, has been substantial (see Figure 5.2, below), except for those G7 countries that initially directed a low percentage of their ODA to agriculture in the first place (the UK and France).

Trends in agriculture assistance in more recent years vary considerably across G7 countries. Japan and France show sizeable increases in 2001, while Germany, Italy and the US show modest growth. The UK and Canada both register a drop, although not enough to prevent the G7 average from rising in 2001. To put the dollar figures into some context, however, US agriculture aid in 2000 was US$411 million, roughly 2.3 per cent of the US$18 billion planned annual increase in US domestic agricultural subsidies over the next ten years.

Food aid shows a different pattern, with Italy, Canada and the US (the latter two being the two largest food exporters among the G7) contributing sizable portions of their ODA in this fashion. US contributions, however, are declining; while Canadian, Italian and, to a lesser degree, French, assistance show increases in 2001. However, such aid is motivated at least partly by a desire to absorb domestic production surpluses. Here, again, perspective is valuable: combined US agricultural and food ODA in 2000 amounted to just US$1.6 billion, or 11 per cent of the amount that will be spent on new domestic agricultural subsidies (see Figure 5.4, below). The importance of industrialized country agricultural subsidies as a barrier to improving agricultural production, food security and export earnings is discussed in more detail in Chapter 7.

Figure 5.2: % of Total ODA to Agriculture, 1979–80, 1999–2001

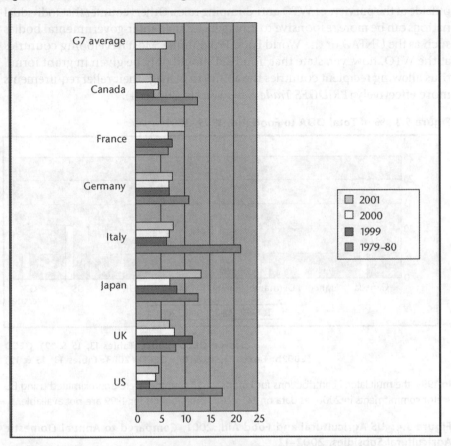

Source: OECD (2001c: Tables 13, 15 & 19); OECD
(2002b: Tables 13, 15, 18 & 19); OECD (2003: Tables 13, 15 & 19)

Estimates of 1999, 2000 and 2001 multilateral contributions made by authors.
The multilateral contributions for European G7 countries in 1999 were approximated
using EC sector commitments in 2000, as data on EC sector commitments for 1999 are
not available. 1979–80 is bilateral aid only.

These crude data do not permit an assessment of the *usefulness* of agricultural
aid: i.e. the purposes for which it is intended and whether the beneficiaries
are primarily recipient country producers and food security or donor country
producers and agro-technology companies. Non-emergency food aid, for
example, 'has damaged food production in a number of developing countries,
some of which had been carefully nurtured under assistance programs' (IMF,
2002: 2). Even emergency food aid had come under scrutiny by developing

nations. Some argue that bilateral food aid has often been used to 'dump' surpluses outside of the purview of WTO anti-dumping rules. Others counter that individual nations can be more responsive to emergencies than inter-governmental bodies such as the UNFAO or the World Food Programme. Most developing countries at the WTO, however, state that 'food aid should only be given in grant form,' thus allowing recipient countries the ability to manage their relief requirements more effectively (*BRIDGES Trade News Weekly*, 2002c: 4).

Figure 5.3: % of Total ODA to Food Aid, 1999–2001

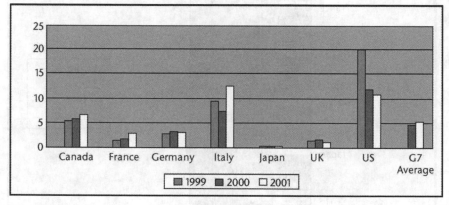

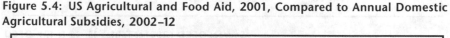

Source: OECD (2001c: Tables 13, 15 & 19); OECD (2002b: Tables 13, 15 & 19); OECD (2003: Tables 13, 15 & 19)

In 1999, the multilateral contributions for European G7 countries were approximated using EC sector commitments in 2000, as data on EC sector commitments for 1999 are not available.

Figure 5.4: US Agricultural and Food Aid, 2001, Compared to Annual Domestic Agricultural Subsidies, 2002–12

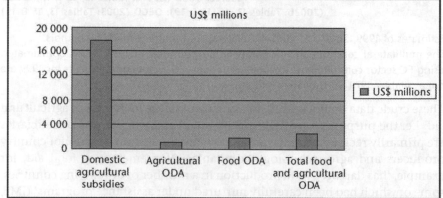

Source: OECD (2003: Tables 13, 15 & 19)

Child Malnutrition, Food Security and Africa

In absolute numbers, child malnutrition is highest in Asia (47 per cent of the world's total) and second highest in sub-Saharan Africa (35 per cent) (World Bank, 2002d: 47). The prevalence of child malnutrition has been steadily declining in Asia over the past 20 years, but has been increasing steadily in Africa, particularly over the past decade (World Bank, 2002d: 40). Of all African countries, 18 showed some improvement in recent years, three showed no change, and ten showed increased rates (Social Watch, 2002: 33). However, the inferences that can be drawn from these data are limited, because data are limited or unavailable for some countries and, for others, the 'trend' in question has been observed over a very short time (one- or two-year periods).

Available food security data (Social Watch, 2002) provide trends between 1990 and 1999, although these data concern average daily caloric intake only. Data are available for 52 African countries; trend data are available for 47 (see Table 5.2).

Table 5.2: Food Security Trends in Africa, 1990–99

Progress/ Starting point	No trend data	Significant progress	Progress	Stagnation	Regression	Significant regression	Total
A	2	3	2	1	1	1	10
B	3	2	7	0	4	1	17
C	–	7	2	2	3	1	15
D	–	0	1	0	1	0	2
E	–	2	0	0	0	0	2
F	–	3	0	1	0	2	6
Total	5	17	12	4	9	5	52

Source: Social Watch (2002: 31–2)

No data available for Equatorial Guinea.

Legend:

A: Countries that must achieve a minimum of 2 300 cal.
B: Countries that must grow one per cent per year.
C: Countries starting off with less than 2 300 cal. that can reach 2 700 cal.
D: Countries starting off with more than 2 300 cal. that can reach 2 700 cal.
E: Countries starting off with more than 2 700 cal. that can reach 3 000 cal.
F. Countries starting off with more than 2 950 cal. that can reach 3 200 cal.

The World Food Summit goal of ensuring caloric supply according to UNFAO levels should be seen in relation to undernutrition rates, which continue to be high in many African countries, despite progress in food security: in 1990, 42 countries provided less than 2 300 calories per capita daily, and 24 countries were still below the 2 300 level in 1999. This could possibly be explained by increasing maldistribution of food supplies within countries, reflecting increasing economic inequalities as an aspect of globalization.

It also has to be noted that seasonal fluctuations in food security are important for large numbers of people who rely substantially on subsistence farming. The importance of these seasonal fluctuations can be seen in countries currently affected by drought in Southern Africa, which has resulted in an estimated 13 million people facing starvation (IRIN, 2002c; Brough, 2002). Despite this, three of these countries showed progress in achieving the UNFAO food security goal between 1990 and 1999. (See Chapter 9 for a discussion of NEPAD's statements on food security.)

Again, we emphasize that responsibility for malnutrition in Africa, and in other developing and least developed countries, does not rest solely with the G8. The premise of NEPAD is that African countries shoulder their share of responsibility for resolving entrenched, health-damaging practices and conditions. Moreover, the G8 have taken steps to aid in many of these areas, albeit usually inadequate ones. But there are also many instances in which G8 practices contribute directly to the problems facing Africa's human and economic development. One such practice, involving factory fishing off Africa's coast, is described in Box 5.1.

Box 5.1: African Fish on European Dinner Plates

Food security in African countries can be undermined by G7 behaviours that have little to do with aid or trade. One recent example is provided by Mauritania, one of the poorer sub-Saharan African countries. Mauritania managed to show substantial improvements in its food security (using caloric supply as the benchmark) between 1990 and 1996 (Social Watch, 2002: 31). More recently, however, it has significantly regressed on infant mortality rates and become stagnant in under-five mortality rates (Social Watch, 2002: 27, 29). Taken together, this suggests a decline in nutritional levels since 1996.

Since 1996, according to UNEP, Mauritania became one of several countries granting fishing licenses to factory-style fishing vessels of the EU, Japan and China that were 'causing alarming reductions in fish stocks off West Africa' (Brown, 2002). (Senegal had such an agreement with the EU, but is renegotiating it for better terms.) Some 60 per cent of global fisheries are estimated to be in, or near, depletion crisis (UNEP, 1999), mostly due to industrial overfishing. Mauritania will receive US$426 million from the EU for fishing rights from 2001 to 2006, but recent overfishing has already seriously depleted fish stocks, and fish, 'the staple diet of coastal communities ... is no longer available in some places' (Brown, 2002).

This behaviour by the EU and Japan also contradicts commitments made by their environment ministers at the 1999 Schwerin meetings prior to the Cologne summit, which stated emphatically their 'grave concern at the continuing threat to the oceans and seas and their biological diversity posed' in part by 'unsustainable fishing practices' (Schwerin Communiqué, para. 23). The hypocrisy of the EU is particularly glaring, given its moves to limit fishing vessels within its own waters to protect stocks, and to commit almost US$600 million to compensate European fisherpeople affected by depleting fish stocks and increased fishing restrictions (*BRIDGES Trade News Weekly*, 2002f: 12).

Biotechnology and Food Security

While direct attention by the G8 to food security issues has been limited, documents from the last three summits show what can almost be called an obsession with the promotion of biotechnology and the removal of impediments to its rapid diffusion that might be created by food safety regulation. Thus, in 2001 the G8 stated the following:

> Every effort should be undertaken to enhance agricultural productivity. Among other things, the introduction of tried and tested new technology, including biotechnology, in a safe manner and adapted to local conditions has significant potential to substantially increase crop yields in developing countries, while using fewer pesticides and less water than conventional methods. We are committed to study, share and facilitate the responsible use of biotechnology in addressing development needs (Genoa Communiqué, para. 20).

The *potential* for agricultural biotechnology to make significant contributions to both food security and environmental conservation was noted in a recent article in *Science* by a team of scientists who emphasized the need for productivity improvements to slow the rate of land use and land-cover change as the demand for agricultural products increases (Tilman *et al.*, 2001). On the other hand, whether that potential can be realized given the current incentive structure for agricultural research, which ensures that priority is given to commercially attractive applications that may or may not have much to do with food security, is open to serious question. In this area, as in health research, 'money talks louder than need' in setting priorities for scientific research (UNDP, 1999: 68–76), and productivity improvements in the crops on which the world's poor depend seldom offer commercial returns sufficiently attractive to interest commercial investors. As the World Bank's 2003 *World Development Report* pointed out,

> [g]enes are already available that could help food production in the poorest countries if they were to be transferred into poor people's crops. These include genes that improve tolerances to salt, aluminum and manganese in soils; give plants greater resistance to insects, viruses, bacteria, and fungi; enrich beta carotene to correct vitamin A deficiency; create more nutritious oils, starches, and amino acids; and improve fatty acid profiles and digestibility for animals.
>
> Despite this promise for poor people, biotechnology in general and transgenics research in particular have barely begun to be put to work to address the problems of poor people. ... This is partly because much of the research supporting this technology is locked into patents held by a small number of multinational, vertically integrated life-science organizations, which have had little commercial interest in working on crops with limited markets, or funding research for the needs of poor producers (World Bank, 2003: 90–1).[2]

The World Bank, in turn, links this privatization of agricultural research with the limited political support that can be mobilized for public sector research in a time of low prices and – in the industrialized world – growing agricultural surpluses.

A more fundamental question is that of whether food security should be considered primarily an issue of resource scarcity (with the corollary being that it can be 'solved' by improving agricultural productivity through, for example, the diffusion of genetically modified crops) or resource distribution. Amartya Sen's (1981, 1982, 1989) path-breaking work on the political economy of famine showed that famines are not 'natural' phenomena, but rather that access to nutrition and food security is directly related either to purchasing power or to the availability of some other entitlement to food.[3] On the one hand, this may explain the absence of specific G8 commitments on the topic – it could be argued that they are addressing the issues instead by way of economic development and poverty reduction. On the other hand, both the record of 'adjustment' policy as it has affected food security (e.g. see Walton *et al.* 1994) and our own critical examination of recent G8 commitments in the areas of macroeconomic growth and poverty reduction suggest that the bleak prospect identified by the UNFAO earlier in this chapter may be the best we can expect in the absence of fundamental policy shifts. One participant in a recent effort to identify the 'top ten biotechnologies' in terms of potential health benefits in developing countries commented that 'the basic problem of poverty-related diseases cannot be addressed by providing supplements through genetically engineered food. The issue is how to have socio-economic equity and this cannot be solved through biotechnology' (quoted in Daar *et al.*, 2002: 102). Ironically, issues of 'socio-economic equity' were largely ignored in the report of this initiative.

The G8 in Genoa further claimed that they would

> strive to provide consumers with relevant information on the safety of food products, based on independent scientific advice, sound risk analysis and the latest research developments. We believe an effective framework for risk management, consistent with the science, is a key component in maintaining consumer confidence and in fostering public acceptance (Genoa Communiqué, para. 30).

In light of the cautions expressed by the UNDP and the World Bank, the recurring emphasis on consumer information about food safety and on 'science-based, rules-based' regulatory approaches to food safety (Okinawa Communiqué, para. 56) may be viewed less as an effort to improve food security than as one to protect and increase market share for agricultural producers and producers of agricultural inputs (such as genetically modified crop varieties, and the herbicides they have been designed to resist) in some industrialized countries (see Box 5.2, below). This impression is reinforced by the notable absence of G8 commitments to strengthening public sector agricultural research infrastructure or improving researchers' ability to address the needs of the developing world.

Box 5.2: The 'Beef-Hormone' Case

Consideration of a 'science-based, rules-based' system must begin from the premise that *no* regulatory regime can be purely 'science-based': regulatory regimes can be 'rules-based', but the rules must reflect the competing values that can guide public policy under conditions of scientific uncertainty (Schrecker, 2001; Walker, 1998). The contrasting interpretations of a precautionary approach to food safety that emerged from the long-running trade dispute between the EU and Canada and the United States over the issue of hormone-treated beef (Walker, 1998; Skogstad, 2001: 304–6) are a case in point. It is important, firstly, to recognize that the trade agreement in question (on sanitary and phytosanitary measures, or SPS) is not a health agreement (WTO, 1995). Its stated goal is to prevent the use of SPS as disguised barriers to trade. Indeed, 'a government that abandoned all health regulations would not be in violation of the SPS. Governments do not violate the SPS by permitting exports unsafe for the foreign consumer' (Charnovitz, 2001: 2).

The SPS require that countries base their regulatory standards on a scientific risk assessment. The WTO dispute panel rejected as inadequate the scientific

---

arguments presented to them by the European Commission, specifically ruling that the EC had failed to present an adequate risk assessment (Sullivan & Shainblum, 2001; Charnovitz, 2001). Several aspects of both the SPS agreement and the beef hormone case raised concerns within the health community.

Firstly, 'the SPS [agreement] subjects non-discriminatory domestic measures to supervision whenever they affect trade' (Charnovitz, 2001: 1). It allows exporting countries to challenge how national governments set their own domestic standards.

Secondly, these standards must be 'based on scientific principles' and cannot be maintained 'without sufficient scientific evidence' (WTO, 1995: art. 2.2). The EC bans the use of growth hormones in its domestic beef products, but Canada and the US argued that this ban was not justified on scientific grounds. The necessity test in the SPS is a 'risk assessment' (WTO, 1995, art. 5.1) and challenges under the SPS have usually succeeded because the WTO dispute panels and Appellate Body found that the challenged country had failed to undertake an adequate risk assessment proving harm. But it is not clear how the adequacy of such assessments should be adjudicated. For example, evidence that hormones were 'safe' was based on the assumption that they would always be used in accordance with 'good veterinary practice' (Charnovitz, 2001: 4); did not include studies examining the synergistic effects of growth hormones on naturally occurring hormones, or effects on infants or children more susceptible to carcinogens (Caldwell, 1997); and apparently did not take into account convincing conclusions by the International Agency for Research on Cancer that exposure to several of the hormones at issue may cause human cancer and/or have carcinogenic effects on laboratory animals (Charnovitz, 2001). Dispute panel and Appellate Body members are not scientists, yet are in a position of making judgements on the adequacy of scientific study.

Thirdly, the burden of any error in an SPS dispute panel decision is borne entirely by the affected importing country. The exporting country has nothing to lose. If hormone-treated beef is found to harm human health, the affected individuals and the EC bear the cost, not the producers or exporting country.

Fourthly, the Appellate Body in the beef-hormone dispute acknowledged that the precautionary principle may be part of customary international law – the position argued by the EC – but that the principle lacked authority in health law (unlike environmental law) and that it 'had not been written into the SPS Agreement as a ground for justifying a measure that otherwise violates the SPS' (Charnovitz, 2001: 8), i.e. the precautionary principle may have no bearing in an SPS dispute.

Article XX(b) of GATT permits exceptions to the general GATT rules 'necessary to protect human, animal or plant life or health.' The question of when general health exceptions (including the precautionary principle) are disguised forms of protectionism lies at the heart of disputes under both GATT (art. XX(b)) and the SPS.

One important means of improving the odds that trade does not trump public health in such cases is to reverse the burden of proof in all such disputes. The onus should be on the disputing country to prove that the exception was not intended to protect human or environmental health (GATT, art. XX(b)), i.e. that its intent is protectionist; or, in the case of SPS, to provide risk assessments indicating a product disallowed on health grounds in one country is safe, or at least that reasonable study has been undertaken to show it does not cause harm. This position was strongly called for by several hundred representatives of NGOs invited by the Italian Prime Minister to a major consultation prior to the 2001 Genoa summit – the first such major civil society engagement by any G7 hosting country (see *Final Report and Recommendations* from this consultation: http://www.gnginitiative.net/gngreport.htm). Interestingly, this is also a position now supported by the Government of Canada, which proposes guidelines for the precautionary principle to include that, '[g]enerally, the responsibility for providing the scientific information base (the burden of proof) should rest with the party who is taking an action associated with potential or serious harm' (Government of Canada, 2001). This was clearly not the case when Canada joined with the US against the EU in the beef hormone dispute.

Agricultural Exports and Food Security

As we have noted elsewhere, an underlying assumption in G8 development policy is that open markets lead to the economic growth that, in turn, is a means of reducing poverty and presumably enhancing food security. In Genoa, the G8 affirmed its pledge about opening its own markets to products from the LDCs, many of which are agricultural. These assumptions are even more explicit in NEPAD, which envisions Africa as becoming 'a net exporter of agricultural products' (para. 154). Trade and market access are taken up in Chapter 7. Here we wish to raise a number of economic and distributional concerns about agricultural export-led growth. We need also to underscore that, insofar as environmental aspects of increased agricultural production are concerned, the G8 have a longer history of deforestation, excess fertilizer and pesticide use and water pollution than most developing nations (UNDP, 1999).

Such growth presumes, for example, that increased food or non-food (cash crop) exports to developed countries will create sufficient income for developing countries to pay for the increased food imports they will need to offset any decline in domestic production. This is a classic liberalization argument, but supported by little empirical evidence (Murphy, 1999); rather, the costs of imported foods are often higher. Evidence also suggests that agriculture-led growth performs poorly over the long term, when compared to manufacturing-led growth, indicating that emphasis in poorer agricultural countries should be placed on 'value-added' (food processing and packaging) exports rather than raw food commodities (Gershman & Irwin, 2000). This is recognized by NEPAD, which stresses the importance of 'value added in agro-processing' (para. 153). This would require G8 countries to change their current policies on tariff escalation, by which tariffs rise with the value added to raw material imports (UNCTAD, 2002c: 37–8; IMF, 2002).

More generally, agricultural export-led development can have negative effects on poverty and income distribution in poorer nations, including reduced tax revenues for social development programs, such as health, education and sanitation (Woodward, 1996). Relatively few agricultural producers grow for the export market in developing countries, but these producers often occupy a large portion of arable land. The majority are subsistence producers or farmers who cultivate small land holdings and sell on local markets. Price effects of agricultural liberalization, without 'special and differential' treatment for domestic markets, can force many local producers into poverty, and subsistence producers onto less desirable land more readily degraded by farming.

A UNFAO study in 14 countries concluded that liberalization in the agriculture sector has led, variously, to an increase in the food import bill, a decline in local production of products facing competition from cheaper imports, and a general trend towards consolidation of farms and displacement of farm labour (Third World Network/UNDP, 2001: 8). Several developing countries, even as they argue for a radical drop in agricultural subsidies and tariffs in developed countries, are urging exemptions for themselves. This apparent double standard is warranted on health, development and ecological grounds. The economics of food production differ radically between rich and poor nations, in terms of the number of citizens employed in food production, the technological scale of such production, the size of the production surplus or deficit for domestic consumption, and so on. Several small exporter countries, for example, rely upon only one or two agricultural products. Without phase-in protection, liberalized trade in agricultural prodcts could seriously affect their domestic economies and food security.

This logic appears to have been accepted at the WTO, which, in the Doha Declaration (WTO, 2001a) committed itself to 'reductions in, with a view to phasing out, all forms of export subsidies; and substantial reductions in trade-distorting domestic support,'[4] while at the same time recognizing the need for 'special and differential treatment for developing countries ... including food security.' Developing countries are urging creation of a 'development box' under the Agreement on Agriculture (AoA) in order to do so.

Negotiations on special and differential treatment for developing countries, however, are proceeding very slowly at the WTO. The primary obstacle developing nations are facing is the reluctance by the US, Canada, Japan and the EU members – the entire G7 membership – to regard these meetings of the WTO Committee on Trade and Development as actual negotiating sessions, which is how developing countries consider them and how the process was laid out by the Doha Declaration and the WTO itself (*BRIDGES Weekly Trade News Digest*, 2002a: 7). This negotiating stance on the part of the G7 calls into question the seriousness of some of its more normative commitments on globalization and, in the words of one LDC delegate, 'would contradict the reasoning behind the whole special session exercise,' including their rhetoric about this WTO Round comprising, in part, a 'development agenda.'

How will increased agricultural trade affect greenhouse gas emissions, water shortage and contamination, or other global environmental issues; and how, over time, might this affect domestic food security? This question is most pressing for Africa, which has experienced serious soil erosion in the past decade, with declining food security, and which is the only continent where poverty rates are expected to rise over the next decade. Moreover, many of the two-thirds of the global population projected to experience moderate to high water stress by 2025 (UNEP, 1999), including many of the two billion people projected to experience extreme water scarcity (Worldwatch Institute, 2001), will reside in the 25 African countries that are, or will be, experiencing water scarcity (UNEP, 1999). Intensified agricultural production currently intensifies water use, notwithstanding the potential for bioengineered crops to be less thirsty. The potential negative water impact of intensified agricultural production in Africa is heightened by the facts that irrigation for agriculture currently accounts for 70 per cent of human water use, returning only 30–36 per cent for downstream use (UNDP *et al.*, 2000: 54), and that sub-Saharan Africa is presently the world's lowest regional user of irrigation, yet is still projected to have serious water shortages in the next two decades. The 'environmental debts' of accumulated ecological degradation, which could be enhanced by increased agriculture-led export growth, will soon outstrip the costs of many African countries' already heavy financial debts (UNEP, 1999).[5] Finally, we reiterate a caution raised in our Introduction that countries with a high percentage of their GDP derived from only a few primary commodities face a greater risk of conflict. As Chapter 9's discussion of NEPAD notes in more detail, fully 20 of 50 African countries derive more than 30 per cent of their GDP from agricultural products.

None of this is either to argue against increased market access in G8 countries for agriculture products from LDCs, or to dismiss the potential short-term gains these countries may enjoy through increased agricultural exports. Our discussion does emphasize, however, the need for careful planning of mitigating strategies for the negative externalities of increased exports on these countries; and for technical and development assistance from the G8 towards that end.

Food Security: An Epilogue

The World Food Summit originally scheduled to take place in November 2001 was rescheduled for June 2002 following the terrorist attacks on the United States. The declaration issued by the summit acknowledged that progress toward the 2015 targets had been inadequate, and 'call[ed] upon the concerned development partners to exert all necessary efforts to achieve the international development goals of the Millennium Declaration, particularly, those related to halving poverty and hunger by 2015' (UNFAO, 2002: Annex I, para. 6). NGOs active on food security issues were strongly critical of the lack of specific commitments to action (Mulvany, 2002; Rosset, 2002).

The United States came in for special criticism as the only country to submit a 'reservation' with respect to the declaration's call for the UNFAO Council to establish 'an Intergovernmental Working Group, with the participation of stakeholders, in the context of the WFS follow-up, to elaborate, in a period of two years, a set of voluntary guidelines to support Member States' efforts to achieve the progressive realisation of the right to adequate food in the context of national food security' (UNFAO, 2002: Annex I, para. 10). The basis of the US objection was that

> the issue of adequate food can only be viewed in the context of the
> right to a standard of living adequate for health and well-being, as set
> forth in the Universal Declaration of Human Rights, which includes
> the opportunity to secure food, clothing, housing, medical care and
> necessary social services. Further, the United States believes that the
> attainment of the right to an adequate standard of living is a goal or
> aspiration to be realized progressively that does not give rise to any
> international obligation or any domestic legal entitlement, and does
> not diminish the responsibilities of national governments towards their
> citizens. Additionally, the United States understands the right of access
> to food to mean the opportunity to secure food, and not guaranteed
> entitlement (UNFAO, 2002: Annex II).

We are a long way from the situation in which any of the rights set out in the Universal Declaration gives rise to a 'domestic legal entitlement.' Nevertheless, US insistence on the language of 'opportunity' made one NGO commentator wonder whether such an opportunity 'may be gained by purchasing lottery tickets at the local convenience store' (Rosset, 2002).

Summary: Chapter Five

The lack of explicit commitments, goals and strategies related to enhanced food security, especially in the regions of the world where undernourishment is most prevalent, is disturbing. And the fixation on biotechnology as a panacea for food security issues neglects crucial issues of market power, the direction of research priorities, and (potentially) environmental and consumer safety. Parallels exist here with the G8 position on the role of information and communications technology in development (see Box 4.2, Chapter 4). Strategies of using agricultural exports as the driver of economic growth similarly raise a number of complex (and unresolved) issues, requiring careful research and policy monitoring, a point we take up in our concluding chapter.

Explicit or Specific Commitments: Nutrition, Food Security and Biotechnology

* Strengthening and enhancing effectiveness of development assistance to meet IDGs (Genoa).
* Support to agriculture as a "crucial instrument of ODA" (Genoa).
  Accomplished: Uncertain – certainly not in a decisive fashion. Recent national contributions to agriculture ODA have varied; there is a long-term trend of decline.
  Adequacy: The UNFAO estimates that at the current rate of progress it will take 60 years to reach the goal of halving the number of under-nourished people (*not* eliminating undernutrition).
  Comments: The lack of more explicit commitments in the area of food security is highly disturbing. The World Food Summit 2002 was overshadowed by the attacks on the US. Food aid contributions may be driven by domestic political considerations.
* Targeting of Sub-Saharan Africa and South Asia (Genoa).
  Accomplished: This is difficult to assess; the continued high prevalence of undernutrition suggests that the response has been inadequate to the need.
  Adequacy: Child malnutrition still highest in Asia and Sub-Saharan Africa.
  Comments: It is unclear whether commitment refers to food aid or to agricultural aid. Agricultural aid as a whole increased substantially for the G7 as a group, although it declined in Canada and the UK and, for all countries, is well below 1979/80 levels. Food aid increased only marginally for the G7 as a group in 2001, but more substantially for Canada, Italy and France.

Implicit or Generic Commitments: Nutrition, Food Security and Biotechnology

- Promotion of agricultural biotechnology for increasing crop yields, food security, public acceptance (Okinawa, Genoa).

  Accomplished: Promotion is meeting with increased resistance within the G7 countries, and in many developing countries.

  Adequacy: There is a lack of clear measures to ensure that agricultural biotechnology research is actually directed toward the needs of developing countries.

  Comments: There is controversy about the realism of anticipating a biotechnology contribution to food security. The emphasis on public acceptance seems to play down potential environmental and safety hazards.

- Promoting agricultural (and other) exports as a route to poverty reduction, increasing food security is part of the G8 development model, and explicit in NEPAD (Okinawa, Cologne, NEPAD).

  Accomplished: Historically, yes in some cases, but sometimes with disastrous results (e.g. Box 5.1).

  Adequacy: Questions arise in several areas: domestic income distribution issues, diversion of resources, productive capacity to serve export markets, and environmental impacts.

  Comments: WTO negotiations are in progress on 'development box' under Agreement on Agriculture.

Endnotes to Chapter Five

[1] The WHO's *World Health Report 2002* (WHO, 2002b: chap. 4) estimates that undernutrition contributes 16.8 per cent to the total global burden of disease, as measured by DALYs (see Chapter 3). However, this estimate includes only the effects of maternal and childhood undernutrition, and of a limited number of specific nutrient deficiencies; it therefore may not reflect the contribution of adult undernutrition to ill health throughout the life course.

[2] At least one of the examples of potentially beneficial applications of biotechnology, beta-carotene-enriched rice ('golden rice') as a remedy for vitamin A deficiency, has been harshly criticized by some observers: e.g. see Crouch (2001). It seems likely that, even if it were widely and inexpensively available, this crop would function as a complement to other interventions (Dawe *et al.*, 2002).

[3] This generic point, which has been made by a variety of other authors as well (e.g. George, 1984), must be distinguished from a more historically specific, and contentious, claim on Sen's part about the role of 'democracy' in preventing famine.

[4] This section of the Doha Declaration is undermined by the recently announced US$180 billion in domestic agricultural subsidies. US Trade Representative Robert Zoellick subsequently proposed global reductions of US$100 billion in such subsidies, including reducing US subsidies by 50 per cent (*BRIDGES Weekly Trade News Digest,* 2002f: 2). This is a common ploy by wealthier countries in the WTO. Before agreeing to reduce trade-distorting tariffs or subsidies in sectors important

to their own economies, they first dramatically raise them. A group of Canadian NGOs working on food security issues argue that the persistence of such subsidies should allow developing countries to use strong countervailing measures (tariffs) 'on agricultural imports that are sold at less than the cost of domestic production' (Clark & Fried, 2003: 2).

[5] Another set of case studies projected the impacts of liberalization in the agriculture sector for the Mediterranean basin (Mediterranean Commission on Sustainable Development, 2001). The studies found that effects on traditional farming sectors (cereals and livestock) would be substantial and largely negative, with increased poverty and rural depopulation, as well as loss of biodiversity and landscape deterioration. Economic benefits would accrue to the export sector (primarily fruit and vegetables), but not without incurring negative environmental externalities such as increased pressure on water resources and increased pollution. The lower income from agricultural products will be hardest for the majority of small producers, which could increase pressure on marginal land to offset lower income with negative biodiversity and other environmental results. Socially, there would be increased risk of loss of social cohesion in the rural areas and of rural migration, which could worsen the environmental and social problems in towns along the coastline.

CHAPTER SIX

Official Development Assistance

[Development] cooperation is not a thing of the past, but it is not a thing of the present either, because there exists neither unequivocal development nor a strong desire for international cooperation (Pronk, 2000: 40).

Introduction

Official, or overseas, development assistance, often referred to as 'foreign aid,' is one of the older and more evident forms of international cooperation by which wealthier countries assist the development of poorer ones. ODA consists of transfers from industrialized country governments to governments and other institutions in the developing world. As the last three chapters argued, this assistance can be very important for the development of health, education, water, sanitation and other services and sectors essential to health. Contemporary forms of ODA date from the 1950s, when they emerged as part of the post-war economic reconstruction initiative that began with the Marshall Plan. By 1969, a UN commission (the Pearson Commission) recommended that industrialized countries acknowledge an obligation to improve economic conditions elsewhere in the world by committing 0.7 per cent of their GDP to ODA.[1] As we shall see, few countries have achieved this target, and ODA is sometimes provided with motivations that are far from altruistic.

ODA can be provided either as a grant or as a loan, but in order to be considered ODA in standard statistics, a loan must be 'concessional' – in other words, it must involve lower interest rates or more flexible repayment terms than would be available on the commercial market.[2] The industrialized countries provide aid both bilaterally and multilaterally. Bilateral aid involves a direct transfer to governments or other institutions in the developing world, through an agency like the Canadian International Development Agency (CIDA), the US Agency for International Development (USAID) or the UK Department of Foreign and International Development (DFID). Multilateral aid is provided by way of a country's contribution to such institutions as the World Bank, the regional development banks and UN agencies. It should be noted that the World Bank provides both 'soft' or concessional and 'hard' or non-concessional financing, but currently provides little aid on a direct grant basis.

Various estimates of the cost of meeting key development objectives in such areas as health and education have been cited in earlier chapters. A more comprehensive estimate prepared for the World Bank puts the cost of achieving the first seven Millennium Development Goals (see Table 2.1 in Chapter 2) at approximately US$40–70 billion per year (Devarajan *et al.*, 2002). The authors arrived at these figures using two distinct methods. Firstly, they estimated the additional amount of ODA that would be needed to raise growth rates by enough to meet the target of a 50 per cent reduction in the number of people living on US$1 a day or less by the year 2015. The presumption behind this approach was that 'the additional amount of ODA needed to achieve the poverty goal will finance, inter alia, the effort to achieve the social and environmental goals,' although this would not in fact necessarily or always be the case (Devarajan *et al.*, 2002: 16). Secondly, they estimated the direct costs that would be incurred to meet the targets in the areas of education, health and environment, but not the poverty reduction goals. The rationale was that progress in education, health and the environment has substantial benefits in terms of economic growth, and therefore of poverty reduction, although it is not possible to determine whether these benefits would in fact be sufficient to meet the poverty reduction target. The authors emphasized that 'these estimates are extremely crude, and based on a host of heroic assumptions,' and further, that financial assistance amounting to approximately a doubling of current ODA flows is a necessary, but not sufficient, condition for meeting the goals (Devarajan *et al.*, 2002: 30). The scale of the new annual investments needed nevertheless provides a basis for comparison with the anticipated annual increase in US military expenditures of US$48 billion in 2002 (Borger, 2002). This comparison is not specious, since disease and poverty are increasingly becoming global security threats.

Essential to any discussion of ODA is the realization that in most developing countries, growth achieved through domestic macroeconomic policy change, even on the most optimistic projections, will provide neither adequate opportunities for poverty reduction nor a tax base sufficient to support essential public sector investments in such areas as education, nutrition and health systems from domestic sources. As Enge (2002: 13) writes of just one country: 'Uganda ... has had a "model policy environment" for poverty reduction in the eyes of many donors, but with only modest growth levels and current rates of ODA receipts ... will face a poverty funding gap of [US]$660 million after five years and [US]$190 million after ten years.'

This point is underscored in the NEPAD, which states that 'while growth rates are important, they are not themselves sufficient to enable African countries to achieve the goal of poverty reduction,' which requires, *inter alia*, 'human capital ... health, and good stewardship of the environment'

(NEPAD, para. 64). With respect to health, NEPAD notes that it is essential that 'donors ... ensure that support for the continent is increased by at least [US]$10 billion per annum' (NEPAD, para. 124).[3] In other words, substantially increased and sustained donor aid targeted to health, education and sanitation will be required.

Trends in G8 Official Development Assistance

In *Agenda 21*, the document that emerged from the UN Conference on Environment and Development in 1992, the developed countries – including, of course, the G8 – 'reaffirm[ed] their commitments to reach the accepted United Nations target of 0.7 percent of GDP for ODA,' first proposed in 1969, and 'to augment their aid programmes in order to reach that target as soon as possible and to ensure a prompt and effective implementation of Agenda 21' (UN, 1992, Ch. 33). Recent summits have been notably silent on the 0.7 per cent target: the Genoa and Okinawa summit communiqués emphasized improving the effectiveness of aid, rather than increasing the quantity:

> We will work with developing countries to meet the International Development Goals, by *strengthening and enhancing the effectiveness* of our development assistance (Genoa Communiqué, para. 14; emphasis added).
>
> ODA is essential in the fight against poverty. We commit ourselves to *strengthening the effectiveness* of our ODA in support of countries' own efforts to tackle poverty, including through national strategies for poverty reduction (Okinawa Communiqué, para. 20; emphasis added).

This marks a retreat from the earlier Cologne summit, in which G8 countries committed themselves to improving both quality and quantity of ODA: 'We will strive gradually to *increase the volume of official development assistance* (ODA), and to put special emphasis on countries best positioned to use it effectively' (Cologne Communiqué, para. 29; emphasis added).

Box 6.1: The G8 and the Multilateral Development Banks

An increasing portion of G8 development assistance is directed through World Bank loans and grants – in some cases, in the form of debt relief under the Enhanced HIPC Initiative discussed in Chapter 2. Summit communiqués periodically refer to the World Bank and IMF, generally following on decisions made by G8 finance ministers in their meetings held prior to the summit itself. In Okinawa, for example, the G8 declared that

[t]he core role of the MDBs [multilateral development banks, i.e. the World Bank and regional development banks] should be accelerating poverty reduction in developing countries while improving the efficiency of assistance and avoiding competition with private financial flows. The MDBs should increase their resources devoted to core social investments such as basic health and education, clean water and sanitation (Okinawa Communiqué, paras. 9–10).

In 1999, regional development banks financed no expenditures on basic health; in 2000, basic health accounted for 3.0 per cent of their budgets, but the figure dropped again to zero in 2001. The figures for the World Bank are, respectively, 0.1 per cent, 1.9 per cent and 1.8 per cent – hardly a massive infusion of new investment. Basic education fared little better. Regional development banks, from a base of 0.1 per cent in 1999, increased assistance slowly to 0.8 per cent in 2000 and 1.4 per cent in 2001. World Bank figures for the same years were 1.3 per cent , 1.5 per cent and 1.3 per cent – not indicative of the new investments called for by the Okinawa Communiqué. Water and sanitation, a higher aid priority for both G7 and multilateral donors, actually *declined* as a proportion of regional development bank assistance, from 7.3 per cent (1999) to 7.0 per cent (2000) and 3.8 per cent (2001). The World Bank did slightly better, showing a positive growth from 2.4 per cent (1999) to 4.0 per cent (2000) and 4.6 per cent (2001) (all figures from OECD, 2001; 2002b; 2003: Table 19). In sum, there is no compelling evidence that the MDBs heeded the advice of the G7, which, given the dominance of the G7 in these banks' decision-making, gives cause to question the seriousness of this commitment.

A year later, when the G8 called on MDBs 'to provide support for global public goods' (see Chapter 3), they included amongst these 'fostering financial stability' (Genoa Statement, para. 13). Yet, as Box 2.4 in Chapter 2 noted, such stability is undermined by the very private financial flows the G8 is encouraging the MDBs to promote. Moreover, the International Finance Corporation (IFC) of the World Bank is actively promoting private investment in health services, ignoring evidence that this erodes access by the poor.

The G8 in Genoa also committed themselves to 'a meaningful replenishment of IDA and, in that context, we will explore the increased use of grants for priority social investments, such as education and health' (Genoa Statement, para.13). (The IDA is the World Bank section that provides funding for developing countries.) This repeats an even earlier pledge made in Cologne, where the G8 agreed 'to increase the share of grant-based financing in the ODA we provide to the least developed countries' (Cologne Communiqué, para. 27). Both commitments were partly fulfilled during the G7 finance ministers' meeting in Halifax, Canada, prior to the Kananaskis summit, which led to replenishment of the IDA with US$22 billion, and an agreement to 'increase ... the use of grants, in the range of 18 per cent to 21 per cent ... to enhance the effectiveness of IDA in helping the poorest and debt vulnerable countries combat HIV/AIDS, support the social sectors, including education, and overcome the effects of devastating conflict' (G7 Finance Ministers, 2002). The grant portion, however, was a disappointment to many development NGOs. The US had been urging a grants ratio of at least 50 per cent, to prevent putting developing nations further in debt. The European nations preferred retaining loans (which, for most African countries, bear no interest) in order to keep the fund replenished (Foot, 2002). The United States' generosity may reflect its low contribution to development assistance (both bilateral and multilateral), relative to GNI, in comparison to European G7 members (particularly the UK, France and Germany); in theory, at least, the US has more fiscal space to continue replenishing the IDA.

In fact, none of the G7 countries approaches the 0.7 per cent target – and, in contrast to the performance of some industrialized countries outside the G7, the trend has been one of declining G7 commitments to ODA over the past 15 years, during the very period of globalization that has produced, for those countries, unprecedented prosperity (see Figure 6.1, below). If we compress our comparisons to just the last two years for which, at this time, there are good data (2000 and 2001), two of the G7 actually saw their ODA *drop* (a failing grade on the 1999 Cologne commitment), with Italian and US levels of ODA showing small increases (from the lowest levels among the G7) and France, Germany and the UK remaining unchanged (OECD, 2003: Table 6a).

Figure 6.1: Total ODA as % of GNI, 1984–85 (average), 2000–01

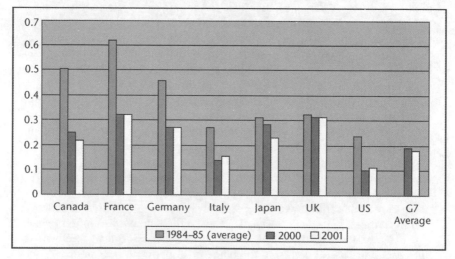

Source: OECD (2002b: Table 4); OECD (2003: Table 4)
Estimates of 2000 and 2001 multilateral contributions made by authors.

This trend is not simply a product of growth in national economies that outstripped growing, or at least constant, contributions to ODA in real dollar terms (i.e. in dollars adjusted for inflation). Figure 6.2, below, shows that for five of the G7 (Canada, France, Germany, Italy and the US), ODA relative to the size of the country's national economy declined in real dollar terms between 1993 and 2001. Japan's 2001 contribution remained essentially unchanged from its 1993 amount. Only the UK showed any signs of sharing more of the enormous amount of wealth created during the 1990s. As a group, the G7 improved over its 1997 average, but was still below its 1990 and 1994 averages.

If the G7 had met the target of spending 0.7 per cent of GNI on ODA – as Denmark, the Netherlands, Sweden, Norway and Luxembourg have done, so the target is not inherently implausible – the effect would have been to make an additional US$109 billion per year available in 2001 for improving the conditions of life outside the industrialized world. If this commitment were sustained, it might then be possible, given appropriate policy commitments and implementation capacity on the part of recipient countries, either to go beyond or to accelerate progress toward the MDGs. Based on ODA expenditures in the year 2001, the 0.7 per cent target would mean an annual increase in ODA expenditures of US$215 per resident of the United States, or US$104 per resident of Canada. The per capita value of such an annual increase corresponds to roughly a Big Mac per week in Canada, or just over 1.5 Big Macs per week in the United States, whose ODA expenditures are smallest among the G7 as a percentage of GNI (see Table 6.1).

Figure 6.2: Trends in Total ODA, 1993–2001, at 2000 Prices and Exchange Rates (US$ millions)

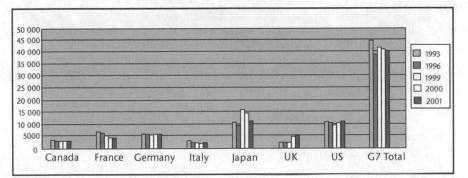

Source: OECD (2003: Table 8)

The trend to proportional declines in G7 ODA commitments becomes clearer in Figure 6.3, which takes into account inflation and changes in exchange rates.

Figure 6.3: % Change in Total ODA, 1993–2001, at 2000 Prices and Exchange Rates

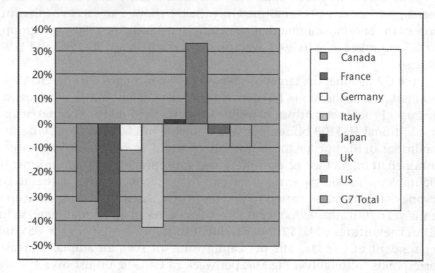

Source: OECD (2003: Table 8)

This level of added public expenditure is hardly an excessive expectation, in view of the buoyant economies of those countries over the last several years. As Sachs (2000: 1) has stated the issue in the US context, using figures from a few years ago,

> [i]n 1998, the United States foreign assistance totaled around [US]$8.8 billion, or 0.12 of one percent of the Gross National Product. And of this derisory sum, only around one-sixth went to the least developed countries. A sixth of twelve-hundredths of one-percent of GDP amounted to the grand total of around [US]$4.95 per American in 1998 for the world's least developed countries. This is [US]$4.95 per year in a country where the average income is more than [US]$30,000, and where investors have enjoyed more than [US]$7 trillion in capital gains since the start of 1996.

We make the Big Mac comparison with some hesitation, because it runs the risk of trivializing the very real levels of relative poverty, and even hunger (Schwartz-Nobel, 2002; Webber, 1992), that coexist with the myth of universal affluence in those countries. Nevertheless, just as it is very much within the capacity of those countries to address this problem domestically, so it is within their capacity to finance a commitment to improving human welfare outside their borders that is very modest in the global frame of reference.

Since the 2001 G8 summit, some countries have announced significant commitments to increasing their ODA budgets. In February 2002, the EU member countries agreed to increase their ODA spending from an average of 0.33 per cent of GNP to 0.39 per cent by 2006, which will make an extra US$7 billion per year available by 2006, if the commitments are implemented. At the International Conference on Financing for Development, held in Monterrey, Mexico, the following month, Finland, Belgium, Ireland, Luxembourg, Norway, Switzerland, the Netherlands and Sweden all announced plans to increase their ODA budgets. None of these, however, is a G7 country – and all these countries now spend as much as or more than *any* of the G7 on ODA, relative to the size of their economies (OECD, 2003: Table 4).

Only two G7 countries made commitments to increased aid at Monterrey. The US commitment, although substantial (an increase from US$10 billion to US$15 billion per year by 2006), must be weighed against the current US level of ODA (the lowest in the G7), the uncertainty of implementation, and the worrisome proviso that aid will be conditional on 'sound economic policies that foster enterprise and entrepreneurship, including more open markets and sustainable budget policies.' Canada announced that ODA budgets would increase by eight per cent a year in the coming years, with half of that growth going to Africa. Included in the African portion is a specific C$500 million fund in support of the Africa Action Plan that was later announced at the 2002 G8 summit (UN, 2002b: paras. 5–14).

In addition to declining commitments to overall ODA on the part of the G7, at least until 2002, four more specific trends are surprising and disappointing.

Firstly, the limited nature of debt relief has meant that much ODA in fact flows to debt repayment. In 1995, 'around one quarter of bilateral aid was being used to repay multilateral lenders. And for World Bank aid the position was even worse. In 1993–94, out of every [US]$3 that the World Bank offered as International Development Association (IDA) loans and grants, it reclaimed [US]$2 as debt repayment. Of the remaining dollar, the IMF pocketed part' (UNRISD, 2000: 27) (see Box 6.2, below). UNCTAD (2000: 123–6) points out that throughout the 1990s, the amount of ODA received by a developing country was directly related to the country's level of external debt. To provide one example of how this shell game works, the C$1.1 billion in debt owed by HIPC countries to its Export Development Corporation and Wheat Board that Canada has committed to cancelling (see Chapter 2) will, as countries become eligible for its cancellation over the next two to three years, be counted as part of its ODA contribution (CCIC Africa-Canada Forum, 2002).

Table 6.1: Summary of G7 ODA Commitments, 2001

Country	Value of ODA, 2001 (US$ millions)*	ODA as % of GNI, 2001*	Additional resources that would be made available by meeting the 0.7% target (US$ millions)	Population, millions	Value per capita of additional resources needed to meet the 0.7% target (US$)	Cost of a Big Mac, 2001 (US$)	Additional annual cost of meeting the 0.7% target, in Big Macs per capita	% of ODA* spent on basic education	% of ODA* spent on basic health	% of ODA* spent on water and sanitation
Canada	1 533	0.22	3 345	31.080	107.63	2.14	49	3.67	1.90	1.80
France	4 198	0.32	4 985	59.190	84.22	2.49	34	6.03	1.67	4.14
Germany	4 990	0.27	7 947	82.310	96.55	2.30	42	1.42	2.07	12.10
Italy	1 627	0.15	5 965	57.350	104.01	1.96	54	0.46	1.80	4.57
Japan	9 847	0.23	20 122	127.210	158.18	2.38	65	0.87	1.06	6.96
United Kingdom	4 579	0.32	5 438	58.790	92.50	2.85	33	2.77	2.15	2.76
United States	11 429	0.11	61 301	285.020	215.08	2.54	85	2.24	4.56	5.16
Total	109 103	0.18						2.20	2.50	5.70

Source: OECD (2003: Tables 4, 19 & 37), except Big Macs/capita calculation, based on national cost figures (for the Big Mac) from *The Economist* (2001)

* Includes both bilateral and multilateral aid commitments.

Averaged over the next three years, this will raise Canada's ODA contribution by over 20 per cent, without Canada's actually contributing any new money to development assistance (based on calculations from OECD, 2002b: Table 14): Canada will simply be contributing to the repayment of debts owed to Canadians. This problem is not, of course, restricted to ODA offered by Canada or other G7 countries, but it will persist in future in the absence of more comprehensive G8 leadership on the debt question.

Box 6.2: Canada's 'Fund for Africa'

As host of the G8 Kananaskis summit, Canada was 'first out of the gate' with a series of new initiatives for Africa's health and development. Indeed, its C$500 million 'Canada Fund for Africa' was the only substantial new commitment to the continent made in connection with the summit. An important reversal of the past decade, the fund nonetheless represents less than one-third of the C$1.6 billion in aid that might have gone to sub-Saharan African countries over the past decade, had Canada's ODA to this region remained at its 1990 level rather than experiencing its precipitous decline (CCIC, 2002). Moreover, there are several concerns raised about how the fund will be expended. An analysis of the fund undertaken by the Canadian Council for International Cooperation (CCIC), the umbrella organization of Canadian-based development NGOs, reports the following:

- C$100 million will go to private sector partnerships focusing on water, transport, pipelines and energy infrastructure.

  An additional C$50 million will go to water and sanitation projects through the 'Global Water Partnership,' comprising the World Bank, bilateral donors, private water companies and some NGOs which have a pro-privatization orientation.

  Serious questions have been raised by researchers and by civil society organizations over the ability of such partnerships to provide such health essentials as water and energy in ways that are affordable to the poor. Although results are not always negative, policies aimed at encouraging private investment in such services in Africa (Fiil-Flynn, 2001; McDonald, 2002; McDonald & Smith, 2002; Mngxitama & Eveleth, 2003; Tanoh & Cusack, 2003) and elsewhere (Herrera, 2003; Kruse & Ramos, 2003; Loftus & McDonald, 2001; Sangaralingam & Raman, 2003; Yep *et al.*, 2003) have generally resulted in higher prices and reduced access for the poor. Sometimes, as in the case of a cholera epidemic in South Africa (McDonald, 2002), the results have been immediately destructive for human health – with over 250 000 people infected and 300 fatalities (Centre for Public Integrity, 2003b: 1) – as well as adding to the general accumulation of poverty-related stressors and vulnerabilities.

- C$20 million will go to build trade capacity for export-oriented growth. This is consistent with the G8's and NEPAD's endorsements of neo-liberal economic theories of growth through increased trade liberalization. As our next chapter on trade and market access discusses, there are many empirical reservations about an export-oriented growth strategy, ranging from reliance on primary commodities (rather than manufactured products) to the lack of sufficiently strong 'special and differential' treatment (trade rule exemptions) for poorer countries to protect their domestic markets from foreign competition subsequent to liberalization. Many developed countries, however, have been reluctant to proceed with WTO negotiations on this topic (*BRIDGES Weekly Trade News Digest*, 2002e). Canada's draft 2003 negotiating strategy at the WTO explicitly states it will *not* support extending special and differential treatment for developing countries in any legally binding way, as this will allegedly create a 'two-tiered system [to which] developed countries are strongly opposed' (Government of Canada, 2002, para. 59). Yet there is growing consensus among development economists that, without a two-tiered system, poorer nations will not be able to develop internal economies in ways that will support the health of their populations, be stable over the long term or ensure the environmentally sustainable use of their natural resources (e.g. UNCTAD, 2002c).
- C$28 million will strengthen the African public sector, but in areas that 'support ... opening African economies to foreign direct investment and trade liberalization' (CCIC, 2002: 3). Only C$18 million will be devoted to strengthening governance and civil society engagement for participation in development strategies.

Secondly, as previous chapters have shown, only a small proportion of G7 ODA is directed toward health or toward the crucial health-related areas of basic education, water and sanitation. Table 6.1, above, summarizes G7 ODA for these three purposes in 2001; these figures should be viewed with the caveat that the proportion of an individual country's ODA spending on any one of these areas can vary substantially from year to year. There are some signs of increased emphasis on these crucial areas as a matter of national policy. For example, Canada is planning to increase its aid to basic health, education and nutrition, and to HIV/AIDS (Tomlinson, 2002), and the US is making global health one of its four main foci for future development assistance (Woods, 2002). There is considerable concern among development NGOs, however, that increased aid for HIV/AIDS will represent *displaced* rather than *new* assistance, coming at the expense of other programs (such as education, health infrastructure and water/sanitation) that are also very important.

Thirdly, a substantial proportion of bilateral aid continues to consist of 'tied aid' (OECD, 2002b: 245) (see Figure 6.4, below). 'Tying' of aid represents a specific form of conditionality: the recipient country must agree to use the aid for specified purposes, usually involving purchases of goods and services from the donor country.

Italy has the highest tying rate and it increased in 2001. Canada offered 68 per cent of its ODA (excluding technical cooperation and administrative costs) on a tied basis in 2001, although its record is improving marginally. Japan, Germany and the UK have very low rates of tied aid, although Japan's tied portion, like Italy's and Germany's, is going in the wrong direction.

A substantial proportion of ODA – more than 30 per cent of all Canada's bilateral aid, 58 per cent of the United States' and 61 per cent of Germany's (OECD, 2003: Table 13) – is provided in the form of technical cooperation grants. These may involve payments to people from developing countries receiving training at home or abroad, or payments to industrialized country service providers, such as consulting and engineering firms. On a regional basis, more than 50 per cent of UK aid to South Africa, Kenya, Nepal and Pakistan (Vasquez, 2002) and more than 50 per cent of German aid to African countries (Dederichs-Bain, 2002) is accounted for by technical cooperation.

Such aid is often tied, arguably with the effect of distorting recipient country priorities, as illustrated in the following example:

> The former Minister of Finance of Mozambique, Abdul Magid Osman, for example, recalled at a recent UNDP roundtable that he had declined [for budgetary reasons] a provincial governor's request for US$50,000 for 100 additional primary teachers, only to see an expatriate consultant hired for US$150,000, paid out of a technical cooperation budget (Enge, 2002: 15; citation omitted).

However, we cannot assume for purposes of calculation that technical cooperation grants are invariably tied, thus making precise calculation of the percentage of formally tied aid impossible.

The relation between ODA and levels of external indebtedness suggests a more subtle respect in which the proportion of aid that is tied may be understated by the OECD figures. A quarter of developing countries' long-term external debt is owed to export credit agencies (ECAs) in industrialized countries (World Bank, 2002e: 107), which exist solely to promote their countries' exports. It may be that a substantial proportion of ODA that is not formally tied is nevertheless offered in order to facilitate repayment of these debts, owed to agencies whose purpose and function are strictly commercial.

After protracted negotiation, in April 2001, the members of the OECD Development Assistance Committee reached an agreement on untying aid to the LDCs, as classified by UNCTAD. At the 2001 summit, the G8 'commit[ed] [them]selves to implement the landmark OECD-DAC Recommendation on Untying Aid to LDCs' (Genoa Communiqué, para. 14).

Figure 6.4: % of Bilateral Aid by Tying Status, 1999–2001

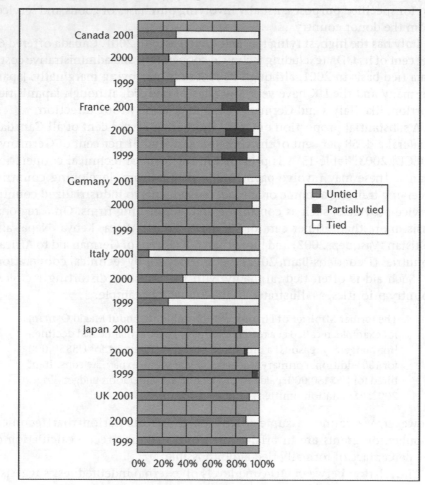

Source: OECD (2001c: Table 23); OECD (2002b: Table 23); OECD (2003: Table 23)
Data on US not provided.

However, at least two factors limit the significance of this achievement. Firstly, it applies only to the LDCs, which are not in fact the largest recipients of ODA. Secondly, not all forms of aid are untied under the terms of the agreement: food aid and investment-related technical cooperation can remain tied (OECD, 2002a: 42–3). Individual countries may take steps beyond those called for by the DAC agreement: Canada, for example, is now 'untying' its technical cooperation aid to all LDCs and sub-Saharan Africa countries, allowing individuals or organizations from those countries to bid on technical cooperation proposals (CIDA, 2002a). Nevertheless, the DAC agreement on untying aid, while a substantial accomplishment, remains only a start on the much larger task of decoupling ODA from donor country economic interests and adapting aid to the real requirements of recipient countries.

Finally, and including an imputed share of multilateral aid, G7 aid to those countries in direst need – the LDCs – declined over the past decade for all members, with the exception of the UK: Canada's drop was particularly steep (see Figure 6.5, below). This decline contradicts the G8's Cologne commitment 'to working with [developing countries], especially with the poorest countries, to eradicate poverty, launch effective policies for sustainable development and develop their capacity to integrate better into the global economy' (Cologne Communiqué, para. 27), with its implied increase in development assistance. The UK, and to a lesser extent France, however, helped raise the group average in 2000 and 2001 slightly above its 1999 rates. It is worth recalling that the 1990s were a decade of unprecedented wealth accumulation in most G7 countries. Aid to LDCs as a percentage of GNI (see Figure 6.6, below) portrays an even less generous spirit.

Figure 6.5: Aid from G7 Countries to LDCs as % of Total ODA

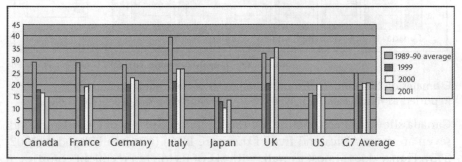

Source: OECD (2002b: Tables 4 & 31); OECD (2003: Tables 4 & 31)

Estimates of 2000 and 2001 multilateral contributions made by authors.

Figure 6.6: Aid from G7 Countries to LDCs as % of GNI

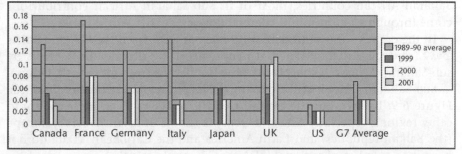

Source: OECD (2002b: Table 31); OECD (2003: Table 31)

Aid to LDCs has declined, with a corresponding increase in aid to low- and lower-middle-income nations. Where this leaves Africa, and particularly sub-Saharan Africa, is more obvious in Figure 6.7, below. While France, Italy and the UK still give a large percentage of their total aid to sub-Saharan Africa, only the US has increased targeting of sub-Saharan Africa over the past decade, though it is still below 1994–95 levels. The US, like Japan, also starts from a very low percentile. (Japan's low rate is partly explained by its geographic emphasis on Asia, where South Asian needs are also very great.) The UK marginally improved over the past five years. Italy's improvement was greater, but from a much lower total ODA rate (only 0.13 per cent of GNI). Individually, in terms of bilateral aid, the G7 countries show considerable variance (see Figure 6.8, below).

Figure 6.7: Trends in G7 Assistance to Sub-Saharan Africa as % of Total Aid

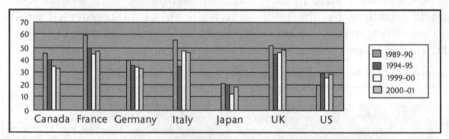

Source: OECD (2002b: Table 28); OECD (2003: Table 28)

Estimates of 2000 and 2001 multilateral contributions made by authors.
Reported as fiscal years (e.g. 1989–90) rather than calendar years (e.g. 1990).

Canada shows a sharp decline. Of the top ten recipients of UK bilateral aid, seven are from Africa and five of these are LDCs (German & Randel, 2002: 243). France does almost as well, with six of its top ten recipient counties in sub-Saharan Africa. Germany, surprisingly, shows a rapid drop, while Japan, despite its emphasis on LDCs in Asia, added one sub-Saharan African country to its list of top ten recipients in 2000. The US gives little bilateral aid to sub-Saharan African countries: most of its sub-Saharan African contributions come through support to multilateral donors, i.e. the World Bank.

In the context of overall declining rates of ODA from the G7, and shifts away from sub-Saharan Africa, it is not surprising that net aid receipts by sub-Saharan Africa fell sharply over the last decade (see Figure 6.10, below).

Sub-Saharan Africa is still receiving the largest regional portion of aid (see Figure 6.9, below), but the overall trend is for ODA to go increasingly to other regions, especially Asia and Oceania (home of Asian 'Tigers'), Europe (the Balkan republics) and Latin America and the Caribbean. (Data do not permit calculation of regional ODA for G7 countries only.)

Figure 6.8: Number of Sub-Saharan African Countries in Top 10 Recipients of Bilateral Assistance

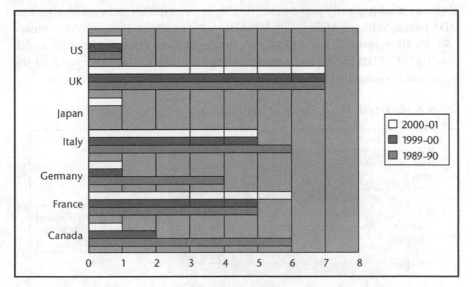

Source: OECD (2002b: Table 32); OECD (2003: Table 32)

Reported as fiscal years (e.g. 1989–90) rather than calendar years (e.g. 1990).

Figure 6.9: Trends in Regional Distribution of ODA from All Donors (%)

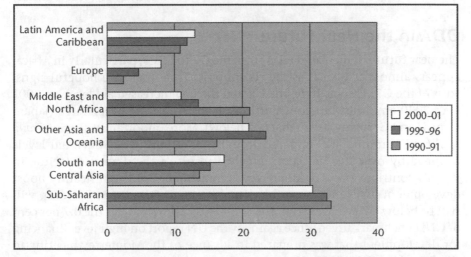

Source: OECD (2003: Table 27)

Reported as fiscal years (e.g. 1990–91) rather than calendar years (e.g. 1991).

In constant 1998 dollars, total aid to sub-Saharan Africa from G7 countries alone fell 18.8 per cent between 1988 and 1999 (CCIC Africa-Canada Forum, 2002: 3), and has only just begun to rise again. Had Canada maintained its ODA to sub-Saharan Africa at its 1990 level, for example, it would have meant C$1.6 billion more to the region over the decade – over three times its multi-year C$500 'Plan for Africa' announced with much fanfare just prior to the Kananaskis summit (CCIC Africa-Canada Forum, 2002).

Figure 6.10: Trends in G7 Total ODA Disbursements to Sub-Saharan Africa

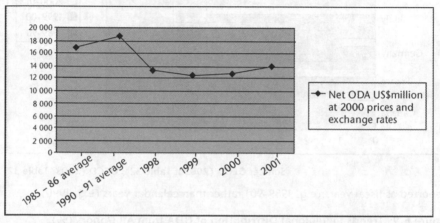

Source: OECD (2003: Table 30)

ODA in the Near Future

The near future of increased ODA from the G7 to LDCs, particularly in Africa, appears almost as dismal as the recent past. True, there are hopeful signs. Four of the G7 (France, Italy, the UK and the US) increased aid levels in 2001 over 2000 amounts, but contributions declined for the other three (Japan, Canada and Germany) (see Table 6.2, below). More importantly, for the *Group of 7* (and summits are supposed to enhance group behaviour), aid levels dropped by over five per cent, largely a result of the dramatic decline in Japan's contribution. The Monterrey commitments will significantly boost development assistance once fully implemented. ODA rates, however, will still be below G7 averages from the late 1980s and well under the 0.7 per cent of GNI benchmark urged, once again, by the UN report on high-level financing for development that was prepared in advance of the Monterrey meeting in the first place (UN, 2001: 8).

Table 6.2: Net ODA Flows, 2000–01

	2000		2001		
	ODA, US$ millions (current)*	ODA/GNI %	ODA, US$ millions (current)*	ODA/GNI %	% change in ODA, 2000–01 (real terms)**
Canada	1 744	0.25	1 533	0.22	–12.1
France	4 105	0.32	4 198	0.32	2.3
Germany	5 030	0.27	4 990	0.27	–1.0
Italy	1 376	0.13	1 627	0.15	18.2
Japan	13 508	0.28	9 847	0.23	–27.0
UK	4 501	0.32	4 579	0.32	2.0
US	9 955	0.10	11 429	0.11	15.0
G7	40 219		38 203		–5.0

Source: OECD (2003: Tables 4 & 6a)

* Includes bilateral and multilateral.
** In US$ at current prices and exchange rates.

The Politics of Aid

Despite the need for ODA, and its potential value, the development community (NGOs, academics, civil society groups) in both donor and recipient countries has sometimes questioned whether the various conditions associated with it do more long-term harm than good to poor countries. During the 1960s and 1970s, many developing countries receiving ODA also showed positive changes in key social indicators. It can be argued that these were also decades during which some recipient countries were allowed relatively more autonomy in how they chose to pursue development (Enge, 2002). With the collapse of the real or imagined Soviet threat to market capitalism, globalization has supplanted internationalism. The development discourse, first reflected in the structural adjustment policies of the IFIs and more recently by the trade agreements of the WTO, is now about adapting developing nations to the needs of the integrated global marketplace (Dallaire, 2001). This shift in emphasis is increasingly evident in the policy commitments of the G8: less is going to those in greatest need. A more general problem arises from the fact that ODA, whether offered directly or as taxpayer-financed debt relief, is unlike almost any other item of government expenditure in that it lacks a domestic political clientele, apart from the politically favoured beneficiaries of tied aid. A report prepared for the World Bank, with specific reference to Africa, observes that '[d]onors have apparently not used recipient governments' revealed commitment to tackling poverty as a basis for country aid allocations. Econometric analysis of aid shows that "donor interest variables" capturing commercial and political considerations are a major determining factor for bilateral aid allocations' (White & Killick, 2001: 118).

Box 6.3, below, briefly describes a case in which such variables arguably outweighed the reasonable belief that recipient governments should give priority to the basic needs of their citizens. Such examples, when repeated over time, have the pernicious effect of creating 'donor fatigue' even among people in the industrialized world who are inclined to favour increases in development assistance. The World Bank has suggested that

> some of the disaffection with the impact of aid on poverty reduction does not reflect the intrinsic ineffectiveness of aid, but rather the large share of aid that is allocated on the basis of 'strategic' criteria, instead of on the basis of the quality of policies and the number of poor. In this context, the end of the Cold War may have improved the opportunities for allocating aid according to poverty alleviation rather than to strategic criteria (World Bank, 2002e: 95).

If so, then the case described in Box 6.3 exemplifies a remarkable failure of leadership on the part of the G8 as a whole with respect to this opportunity.

Box 6.3: Aircraft, Air Traffic Control and Basic Needs

Early in 2002, a split within the British cabinet revealed some of the politics of development assistance and donor country interests, especially when those interests involve exporters of military hardware. Although a recipient of debt relief under HIPC, the Tanzanian government had agreed to purchase a £28 million military air traffic control system from Britain's BAE Systems, one of the world's largest defence contractors. BAE Systems actively lobbied for the granting of an export licence for the system, citing the need to preserve 250 jobs in Britain, but International Development Secretary Clare Short publicly opposed the deal. So did the World Bank, which argued that far less expensive systems would be adequate for Tanzania's civilian needs. Further complicating the matter, the purchase was financed by a low-interest loan from Barclays Bank, after the bank had 'been granted a lucrative banking licence to operate in Tanzania' (Hencke, 2002b). When the cabinet split was publicized, Short temporarily froze £10 million of British aid to Tanzania, but was ultimately overruled on the issue, and indeed announced a new aid package worth £270 million over six years as the sale went ahead. So did the Tanzanian government's purchase of a £15 million personal jet for the country's president (Denny, 2002b; Denny *et al.*, 2002; Hencke, 2002a, 2002b, 2002c, 2002d, 2002e; MacAskill, 2002; Norton-Taylor *et al.*, 2002). This case may have been unusual only because such internal disagreements are usually kept out of the public eye, but it illuminates the origins of much cynicism about ODA.

Summary: Chapter Six

Despite the political problems with ODA, massive infusions of funds are needed in developing, and especially least developed, countries. ODA, untied, with few or appropriate conditions, targeted on the basis of social need and capacity-building, is one vehicle for this infusion. Several G7 countries failed completely in their commitment to increase development assistance (over the years 1999–2001); and where increases have been forthcoming or have been announced, they remain incommensurate with the need, perhaps especially for sub-Saharan African countries.

It is important to recall that many of the LDCs, particularly in sub-Saharan Africa, will be unable to meet IDG targets for universal primary education without a seven-fold increase in their present level of aid receipts. Achieving just three of the IDG targets of poverty reduction, universal primary education and infant/maternal mortality reduction will require a *trebling* of ODA from donor countries, but commitments made at the Monterrey conference will represent just one-ninth of the amount required (Denny, 2002a: 24).

Explicit or Specific Commitments: Official Development Assistance

* Increase the volume of ODA (Cologne).
  Accomplished: No. As a group, G7 ODA as a percentage of GNI and in real dollars declined post-Cologne.
  Adequacy: Had the G7 provided ODA equivalent to 0.7% of the value of their economic production – a target that was re-affirmed at the 1992 Rio Earth Summit — an additional US $109 billion would have been available in 2001.
  Comments: The US, the UK and Italy showed marginal increases in ODA spending in 2001 over 2000 levels; Japan showed a major decline.

- Strengthen and enhance the effectiveness of ODA (Okinawa and Genoa).
  Accomplished: Difficult to assess. However, the problem of 'recycling' ODA for purposes of debt servicing remains, and debt relief from G7 countries is counted as ODA despite representing no new capital transfers.
  Adequacy: 2002 commitments to raise ODA, even when fully implemented, will represent just one-ninth of increase required to meet just three of the IDGs: poverty reduction, universal primary education, and maternal/child mortality reduction.
  Comments: Note the retreat from the 1999 (Cologne) recognition of the need to increase the value of ODA.
- Implement OECD-DAC Recommendations on Untying Aid to Least Developed Countries (Genoa).
  Accomplished: Too soon to assess. Data on the tying status of aid is not available separately for LDCs. Based on overall tying status, however, Canada and Italy have much ground to make up; Japan, Italy and Germany are increasing, rather than decreasing, their tied aid portions.
  Adequacy: OECD recommendations exclude food aid and, crucially, investment-related technical cooperation.
  Comments: Individual countries may take steps beyond those called for by the DAC agreement: Canada, for example, is now 'untying' its technical cooperation aid to all LDCs and sub-Saharan African countries.
- Replenish IDA (portion of World Bank providing funding to 79 poorest countries) (Genoa Statement).
  Accomplished: Yes: agreement to additional US $22 billion in funding. Multilateral Development Banks to increase funding for basic health, basic education and water and sanitation (Okinawa).
  Accomplished: No: The World Bank and regional development banks did not significantly increase such funding, and in some cases decreased the amounts.
  Comments: The G7 are not singularly responsible for the MDBs' decision-making, but they do hold the most influence over these banks' decisions. The World Bank's IFC, which lends to the private sector, is promoting private investment in health and other services, which could have negative impacts on access for the poor.
- Increase portion of IDA funding going to grants (Okinawa, Genoa).
  Accomplished: Yes and no. A compromise was reached in 2002 to allocate 18% to 21% of IDA financing for grants, but this does little to resolve the debt problems of developing countries.
  Comments: The US favoured a larger grant portion, EU countries favoured loans only to maintain the solvency of the IDA.

- Implicit or Generic Commitments: Official Development Assistance Target 'poorest countries' (Cologne).

Accomplished: Yes and no. The average percentage of G7 ODA going to LDCs did increase post-Cologne, but ODA to LDCs as a percentage of G7 gross national income declined post-Cologne.

Adequacy: In the context of NEPAD, it is notable that G7 ODA to sub-Saharan Africa, declined until two years ago. ODA often continues to correspond more to the strategic and economic priorities of donor countries than the development needs of poorest countries. Poverty, as measured by living on US $1/day or less, continues to increase in the least developed countries.

Comments: Recent UK increases in ODA spending, especially for LDCs and sub-Saharan African countries, set it apart from the other G7 countries.

Endnotes to Chapter Six

[1] The original plan called for 1.0 per cent of GDP, but was scaled back to the more modest 0.7 per cent. Recent comparative statistics use a slightly different figure, gross national income (GNI), against which to measure national governments' ODA expenditures.

[2] For purposes of the OECD statistics on aid flows cited in this report, a loan is only counted as ODA if the 'grant element' – i.e. the value to the recipient of lower interest rates or flexible repayment terms – is equivalent to at least 25 per cent of the nominal value of the loan.

[3] Unfortunately, NEPAD does not specify what this sum is for (essentially health interventions such as GFATM or GAVI, public health infrastructure development, some combination of both); or how the sum was arrived at. This imprecision is taken up in more detail in Chapter 9.

CHAPTER SEVEN

Trade and Market Access

Trade, along with migration, communication, and dissemination of scientific and technical knowledge, has helped to break the dominance of rampant poverty and the pervasiveness of 'nasty, brutish and short' lives that characterised the world. And yet, despite all the progress, life is still severely nasty, brutish, and short for a large part of the world population. The great rewards of globalised trade have come to some, but not to others (Amartya Sen, Honorary President of Oxfam, 2002; in Watkins, 2002a: 3).

Introduction

Because of the links between poverty and ill health, opportunities for increasing incomes in the developing world are critically important. Development policy observers, who disagree on many other points, share the view that meaningful improvements in market access for the products of the world's poorest countries would result in dramatic increases in income.[1] In keeping with their general commitment to accelerating global economic integration, the leaders of the G8 have consistently linked development objectives to shared benefits from the liberalization of trade:

> Open trade and investment drive global growth and poverty reduction. That is why we have agreed today to support the launch of an ambitious new Round of global trade negotiations with a balanced agenda (Genoa Communiqué, para. 10).
>
> We pledge to pursue policies that will contribute to global growth by enhancing strong productivity growth in a sound macroeconomic environment, through structural reform, free trade and strengthened international economic co-operation (Genoa Statement, para. 2).
>
> Sustained economic growth world-wide requires a renewed commitment to free trade. Opening markets globally and strengthening the World Trade Organisation (WTO) as the bedrock of the multilateral trading system is therefore an economic imperative. It is for this reason that we pledge today to engage personally and jointly in the launch of a new ambitious Round of global trade negotiations at the Fourth WTO Ministerial Conference in Doha, Qatar this November [i.e. November 2001] (Genoa Statement, para. 6).

138

Reduction of tariffs and non-tariff barriers to trade is one of the key institutional contributors to globalization, as well as representing a core element of the neo-liberal prescription for development policy. At the same time, trade liberalization raises, with particular force, the question: *Globalization on whose terms, and for whose benefit?* The LDCs, with ten per cent of the world's people, accounted for just 0.42 per cent of the world's exports of goods and services in 1999 – a decline of 47 per cent since 1980 (UNCTAD, 2002b: 112). Even this figure understates the degree to which the LDCs remain marginalized in the global economy, since 'in 2000, about 52 percent of total merchandise exports of the LDCs were accounted for by three countries – Angola and Yemen (both oil exporters) and Bangladesh' (UNCTAD, 2002b: 112). For developing countries as a whole, imports have tended to expand faster than exports, resulting in a deterioration of their trade balances (UNCTAD, 2002c: 51) that exacerbates their debt servicing problems. This is sometimes because import liberalization has been a key condition for receiving financial assistance from the IMF (Watkins, 2002a: 126–7).

Improving Market Access

A recent Oxfam report, which points out that the value of export earnings lost to developing countries because of trade barriers erected by the rich countries far exceeds the value of ODA, makes a compelling case for meaningful improvements in market access. It notes, for example, that '[i]f developing countries increased their share of world exports by just five per cent, this would generate [US]$350bn – seven times as much as they receive in aid. The [US]$70bn that Africa would generate through a one per cent increase in its share of world exports is approximately five times the amount provided to the region through aid and debt relief' (Watkins, 2002a: 8; see also pp. 48–9). However, G7 countries – and the industrialized world in general – have been unwilling to match their rhetorical commitments to liberalized trade with policy measures to level the playing field for developing country exporters. Oxfam has developed a Double Standards Index (DSI) that compares the EU, Canada, the United States and Japan on a number of dimensions of free trade rhetoric versus protectionist practice (Watkins, 2002a: 97–121). It is worth quoting at length from the conclusions of this exercise:

> Among the most striking findings to emerge are the following:
>
> - Thirty per cent of Canadian imports and 15 per cent of EU imports from the least-developed countries face peak tariffs (in excess of 15 per cent).
>
> - The average tariff on these 'tariff peak' items ranges from a low of 21 per cent for the USA to 40 per cent for the EU.

- Agricultural subsidies account for one-quarter of farm output in the USA, rising to 40 per cent in the EU and over 60 per cent in Japan.

- Average tariffs on processed agricultural products exported to Japan and Canada are more than three times higher than those facing unprocessed agricultural products.

- Average agricultural tariffs are close to 10 per cent in Canada and the USA, rising to more than 20 per cent in the EU and Japan.[3]

- The EU and USA have eliminated only one-quarter of the textiles and clothing import-quota restrictions that they are committed to remove under the WTO Agreement on Textiles and Clothing.

- Between them, the USA and EU launched 234 anti-dumping cases against developing countries in the five years following the end of the Uruguay Round.[4]

Taken individually, each of the trade restrictions considered in the DSI is deeply damaging to developing countries. Considered collectively, they help to explain why developing countries have been unable to increase their share of world trade, and why the links between international trade and poverty reduction are so weak.

...

The costs of Northern protectionism can be illustrated through economic models that predict the potential gains from import liberalisation. One such model shows that moving to full import liberalisation by the industrialised countries between 2000 and 2005 could generate gains of the following order:

- more than [US]$3bn each for India, China, and Brazil
- more than [US]$14bn for Latin America
- more than [US]$2bn for sub-Saharan Africa
- more than [US]$600m for Indonesia

Large as they are, even these figures understate the potential gains from reduced trade barriers. This is because they do not take into account the dynamic effects on investment and innovation that market opportunities could generate (Watkins, 2002a: 100–1; citations omitted).

The World Bank has similarly noted that while agricultural exports can reduce rural poverty and exports of textiles, clothing and other labor-intensive manufactures can reduce urban poverty, 'the world's poor face tariffs that are, on average, roughly twice as high as those imposed on the non-poor' (World Bank, 2002a: 37). To put it mildly, it is unusual for organizations that normally disagree as emphatically as the World Bank and Oxfam to agree on a key policy issue. Even more remarkable is the fact that such agreement has not been accompanied by meaningful policy change.

At the very least, a tension would appear to exist between the G8 commitment to 'offer[ing] people a fair chance to better their lives' (Okinawa Communiqué, para. 15), on the one hand, and the actual behaviour of member countries on the other. This tension has so far not been resolved by such commitments as the agreement 'to work towards duty-free and quota-free access for all products originating in the least developed countries' (Genoa Communiqué, para. 11). Canada, for example, has removed only 29 of 295 import restrictions on textiles, the US only 13 of 750 (In Common, 2001: 6), and collects five times more duty on textile imports from LDCs than it does on textile imports from the US (Wiebe, 2002).[5] The Canadian trade minister notes that the government has removed 570 tariff lines for market access by LDCs; according to Wiebe (2002), however, 'in 1999, Least Developed Countries actually exported from only 67 of these tariff lines. The total of these products was a mere [US]$543,000 – that is, less than 0.2 per cent of LDC exports to Canada in that year. The hit on the Canadian taxpayer of this largesse, as a result of foregone revenue, is a miniscule [US]$25,000' (Wiebe, 2002: A15).

Oxfam estimates that Canadian import restrictions on goods from LDCs alone cost these countries a potential US$2 billion in earnings, five times the Canadian aid to these countries (Oxfam Canada, 2002). Because of the role of non-tariff barriers, it is not clear how Canada's commitment to remove tariffs on all imports from LDCs except dairy products, poultry and eggs will improve market access. The US *Africa Growth and Opportunity Act* (AGOA) does propose access to the US market for African garments – but only if the threads used originate in the US (Oxfam Canada, 2002). The much-vaunted EU Everything But Arms initiative in 2001 provides tariff exemptions on all non-military imports from LDCs, but with the rider that tariffs on some of the most profitable developing country exports (e.g. rice, sugar and bananas) will not be fully removed for eight years (Watkins, 2002a), leading some pundits to call the initiative 'Everything But Farms.' Mozambique, for example, loses an estimated US$100 million annually because of the EU's retained tariffs on sugar (Watkins, 2002b).

Although developed countries have dropped their *average* tariffs on goods from developing countries from ten per cent in the 1980s to five per cent in 1999, they maintain very high tariff peaks on products of particular economic interest to developing countries. The EU, for example, imposes a tariff of 250 per cent on meat products; Canada and the US a tariff of 120 per cent (Watkins, 2002a: 102). Tariffs tend to increase with each value-added manufacturing or processing step over the raw product (Watkins, 2002a: 99–103). Fully processed food products face EU and Japanese tariffs twice as high as raw agricultural products; in Canada, the rate can be as much as 13 times higher (Watkins,

2002a: 103). This poses a significant barrier to agriculture-led export growth for many developing countries, and although growth in agricultural exports is far from a panacea, because of the dangers of the 'commodity trap' (UNCTAD, 2002b: 137–50), it can be one important component of an overall development strategy (see Box 7.1).

Box 7.1: Whose Free Trade? Whose Development? The WTO Banana Case

Market access for developing country agricultural products may make an important contribution to economic growth, but the devil, as always, lies in the details. In 1995, the US and several Central American countries challenged the EU over its preferential treatment of bananas from some of its members' former colonies. The WTO sided with the US, which brought the case forward on behalf of the multinational giant Chiquita corporation, a major contributor to the Democratic Party, then in control of the White House; indeed the US, after several earlier attempts by the smaller Central American countries had failed, filed its complaint at the WTO less than a day after the chairman of Chiquita donated US$500 000 to the Democratic Party (Read, 2001: 270). The WTO ruling prohibited preferential treatment by the EU for banana imports from the Caribbean, where production tends to be small and farmer-owned.

This treatment was part of the Lomé Convention, under which the EU gives financial aid and preferential market access to its former African, Caribbean and Pacific colonies. While the convention may not always make economic sense – Caribbean bananas have been ridiculed by liberalization economists for their absurdly high costs – it does make development sense, at least insofar as it represents a partial global redistribution of wealth. Without it, the economies of small island nations in the Caribbean would collapse – and there is evidence this is happening. Dominica's earnings from bananas dropped from US$25 million in 1993, to only US$9 million in 2000 (Younge, 2003: 9); St. Vincent and the Grenadines saw its banana income fall from US$120 million to US$50 million, while two-thirds of the Windward Island banana growers have gone out of business (Ryle, 2002: 26). What was once a normative decision to aid poorer countries in need became a market decision based solely on the economic criterion of efficiency. Moreover, the EU believed the convention had been successfully 'carved out' of GATT commitments.

The US and several Central American countries, however, did not dispute the convention under GATT provisions, but argued that, since packing and shipping bananas constituted *services* to which the EU had committed, the convention violated GATS.

Protected and Subsidized Agriculture

Because of the potential importance of agricultural exports to many developing country economies, direct and indirect protection for agriculture in the industrialized countries is a special problem. The effective tariff on agricultural imports levied by Japan has been calculated at 29.1 per cent, by the United States at 28.1 per cent, by the EU at 7.6 per cent, and by Canada at just 3.4 per cent (World Bank/IMF, 2002a: 12). However, tariffs are only part of the equation, and arguably a less important part than subsidies to producers in the industrialized countries. The OECD estimates that total support to agriculture in OECD countries in 2000 amounted to US$327 billion – roughly seven times the total value of the industrial countries' annual ODA budgets (World Bank, 2002a: 47). The producer support equivalent, or PSE – i.e. the value of transfers from consumers and taxpayers to support agricultural producers – has been estimated as equivalent to 35 per cent of total gross farm receipts in the EU, 59 per cent in Japan, 21 per cent in the United States, and 17 per cent in Canada (OECD estimates cited in World Bank/IMF, 2002a: 24.) Such subsidies not only limit market access, as industrialized country producers can offer artificially low prices in their domestic markets, but also lead to the production of surpluses that are then dumped on international markets, as in the case of sugar and wheat from the US and the EU. The IMF (2002) argues that world market prices depressed by US cotton subsidies (valued at US$160 000 per producer) have resulted in a loss of three per cent of GDP in Mali and Benin, and two per cent of GDP in Burkina Faso and Chad – more than twice the value of debt relief received by those countries in 2001. To state the *problematique* somewhat polemically, the industrialized world can be seen as giving with one hand (in the form of debt relief) and taking away much more aggressively (in the form of agricultural subsidies) with the other. In some cases, subsidies depress prices on international markets to the point where developing countries find their own producers competing with subsidized imports.

Ironically, one of the reasons for this outcome is that developing countries had to lower agricultural tariffs as the price of assistance from the IMF. When the WTO Agreement on Agriculture came into force in 1995, their tariffs were lower than those in developed countries. They also lacked the financial resources to subsidize their farmers. Despite their 'competitive advantage' of lower production costs, they could not compete domestically with foreign imports, while foreign markets remained largely closed to their exports due to much higher tariff rates (Third World Network/UNDP, 2001: 53–6). Mexico, Uruguay, Zimbabwe, Kenya, India and the Philippines all experienced serious declines in income, and corresponding increases in poverty and poor health, among their farming populations following liberalization (Hilary, 2001).

In Mexico, liberalization in trade and capital markets has allowed US-based Wal-Mart (now the world's largest corporation) to become the largest retailer. Although Mexico is a major corn producer, Wal-Mart sources all of its corn products from the US (Watkins, 2002a: 41–2): an impending flood of heavily subsidized imports from the US threatens Mexican corn producers.[6] Among other consequences, this is likely to result in intensified migration to the cities, which will drive down labor costs and incomes still further. The 'efficiency' of Mexican agriculture may improve, but it is not clear whether the overall economic and social (including health) impact will be positive, at least over the short to medium term.

Figures from the period 1998–2000 show the EU to have spent more than US$100 billion on agricultural subsidies, with the US and Japan together accounting for a similar amount. (Because the primary vehicle for EU agricultural subsidies is the Common Agricultural Policy [CAP], it is not meaningful to estimate agricultural subsidies for EU countries on a country-by-country basis.) However the US is the biggest spender on a per-farmer basis, spending US$20 803 per farmer as against US$16 028 in the EU (Watkins, 2002a: 112–13). The US government's recent US$180 billion farm subsidy legislation will satisfy key domestic political constituencies, but is almost certain to exacerbate the problem of markets for developing country agricultural products (Blustein, 2002). It also runs counter to the commitment made in the Doha Declaration generated by the WTO ministerial meeting in November, 2001 to 'reductions, with a view to phasing out, all forms of [agricultural] export subsidies; *and substantial reductions in trade-distorting domestic support*' (WTO, 2001a: para. 13; emphasis added). This is one instance among several of a disturbing recent US turn toward unilateralism and protectionism on trade matters.

'Since textile and clothing production often requires only simple technology and is intensive in unskilled labour, many developing countries have a strong comparative advantage in these sectors' (World Bank/IMF, 2002a: 35). In six developing countries, this sector accounts for more than half of the value of all merchandise exports (54.4 per cent in Sri Lanka, rising to a high of 88.7 per cent in Cambodia) (World Bank/IMF, 2002a: 39). However, high tariffs and quantitative restrictions on textile imports to the industrialized world create substantial impediments to such exports. When textile tariffs and subsidies are added to agricultural tariffs and subsidies, the annual cost to developing nations rises closer to US$700 billion (UNCTAD, 1999). This is more than the high-end debt cancellation cost calculated by Hanlon (2000; see Chapter 2), and several times more than high-end estimated costs of meeting the International or Millenium Development Goals.

Market Access: Necessary but Not Sufficient

The specifics of the case for improving market access for developing country agricultural and textile exports must not be taken as justifying the broader development policy claim that export-led development is the only path to economic growth and poverty reduction. Uncertainties remain about the conditions under which improved export performance can be expected to result in widely shared improvements in the social determinants of health. Still less should these specifics be taken to susbstantiate the neo-classical economic orthodoxy, part of the so-called 'Washington Consensus' in development policy (Williamson, 1990), that trade liberalization is an indispensable element of any sustainable pattern of economic growth and poverty reduction. Rodrik, writing from within mainstream academic economics, has critiqued the conventional wisdom and 'present[ed] an alternative account of economic development, one that questions the centrality of trade and trade policy and emphasizes instead the critical role of domestic institutional innovations that often depart from prevailing orthodoxy. ... Opening up the economy is hardly ever a key factor at the outset' (Rodrik, 2001: 10). In Rodrik's view (see also Watkins, 2002a: 51–2, 127–33), access to industrialized country markets is a necessary condition for development, but by no means a sufficient one. Similarly, UNCTAD (2002b: 101; emphasis added) warns, 'the current conventional wisdom that persistent poverty in LDCs is due to their low level of trade integration and insufficient trade liberalization is grossly simplistic. The persistence of generalized poverty is less related to a low level of integration into the global economy, and to insufficient trade liberalization, than to the *form* of trade integration.'

As we observed earlier, only a handful of countries (for example, some of the Asian 'Tigers') have 'grown out of poverty.' Many analysts believe this is due more to a development path that combined strategic tariff and non-tariff barriers to imports with an export orientation, rigorous controls on foreign capital flows, and various degrees of dirigisme in terms of industrial policy (Amsden, 1994; Hertzman & Siddiqi, 2000; Rodrik, 2001; Watkins, 2002a: 146–7). Furthermore, even the 'Tigers' faced dramatic increases in poverty when their economies faltered and their currencies plunged during the financial crisis of 1997–98 (Bello, 1998; Bello *et al.*, 1998; Kristof, 1998a, 1998b; Sanger & Landler, 1999; World Bank, 1999: 51-62) The consequences of the crisis, in turn, illustrate a point made by Cornia (2001) to the effect that financial liberalization may be an even more important contributor to increased economic inequality than trade liberalization, because it exposes national economies to the uncertainties created by extremely large and volatile short-term capital flows.

We return to these larger-scale issues of development policy in Chapter 10. However, none of them would need to be resolved in order to use improved market access as the starting point for making the next round of multilateral trade negotiations begun at Doha into a true 'development round,' organized around what Rodrik (2001) calls an international trade regime that puts development first (Audley & Florini, 2001; Third World Network/UNDP, 2001). Critical observers of the Doha process (Kahn, 2001; Lucas, 2001; Third World Network, 2001; Third World Network/UNDP, 2001: 97–100; Watkins, 2002b) argue that little departure occurred from past patterns in which the industrialized countries essentially strong-armed the developing world into agreeing to major concessions in exchange for few or no substantive improvements in market access.

WTO Participation

This is partly, albeit only partly, because of the dramatic disparity between rich and poor countries in access to the specialized legal and economic expertise that is a prerequisite for effective participation in the trade policy arena. Even if they are reluctant, for domestic political reasons, to level the playing field with respect to market access, the G8 have the opportunity – and some would say the obligation – to make the negotiating and dispute resolution processes as they unfold at the WTO less unbalanced. In 2001, the G8 leaders stated that 'to help developing countries benefit from open markets, we will better co-ordinate our trade related assistance to ... provide bilateral assistance on technical standards, customs systems, legislation needed for World Trade Organisation (WTO) membership, the protection of intellectual property rights, and human resource development (Genoa Communiqué, para. 12).

Table 7.1, below, shows how they have responded to one relevant initiative: the Geneva-based Advisory Centre on WTO Law that was established based on an agreement reached at the Seattle WTO Ministerial Conference. The agreement now has 32 signatories: nine developed countries, 22 developing countries, and one economy in transition. Any WTO member or country in the process of joining the WTO may join the center by acceding to the agreement; however, the 49 countries designated by UNCTAD as LDCs are entitled to the services of the center without membership. The European Commission (EC), France, Germany, Japan and the US did not sign the agreement, with the EC reportedly 'strongly opposed' to its establishment (Blackhurst *et al.*, 2001: 110).

Table 7.1: G7 Contributions to the Advisory Center on WTO Law (ACWL)

	Amount contributed, as of 25 May 2002 (US$)	Value of contribution, per capita* (US$)
United States	**	
Japan	**	
Italy	1 000 000	0.017
United Kingdom	1 850 000	0.031
France	**	
Germany	**	
Canada	1 250 000	0.041
and for comparison ...		
Sweden	1 400 000	0.157
Netherlands	2 250 000	0.142

* Based on 1999 population figures from UNDP (2001a: Table 5); dollar figures unadjusted for purchasing power parity.
** Not currently a signatory to the agreement establishing the ACWL.

The Doha Declaration recognizes the need to negotiate improved special and differential treatment for developing countries, to stem the erosion of this treatment since the Uruguay Round (UNCTAD, 2002c: 42), although discussion is bogged down by resistance from many of the developed countries, including G8 members (see Box 7.2, below). Mandates regarding 'implementation issues' in the Doha Declaration also reflect developing countries' concerns that the costs of implementing WTO agreements often impairs their own development needs (UNCTAD, 2002c: 43). Small amounts of funding assistance for developing country participation in the WTO exist (see above), intended to assist delegations from these countries, which remain very small compared to those from wealthier nations. A new Global Trust Fund to assist developing countries in post-Doha negotiations has also been established by the WTO, with about US$20 million in total funding (the only specific G8 contribution to this fund that could be ascertained was a

US$560 000 sum from Germany) (WTO, 2001c, 2002b). But these rather meagre levels of assistance do not deal with domestic costs associated with trade agreement compliance, or with 'the challenges posed by proliferating [technical] standards' (World Bank/IMF, 2002a: 17). One recent study (Finger & Schuler, 2001) found that, to comply with WTO obligations on the SPS, Argentina spent over US$80 million and Hungary over US$40 million. Mexico spent over US$30 million to upgrade intellectual property laws and enforcement.

> The figures, for just three of the six Uruguay Round Agreements that involve restructuring of domestic regulations, come to [US]$150 million ... [and could] be higher in the least developed countries .... One hundred and fifty million dollars is more than the annual development budget for eight of the twelve least developed countries for which we could find a figure for that part of the budget (Finger & Schuler, 2001: 129).

The current and future costs of WTO compliance seriously jeopardize the already weakened health, education and human rights infrastructures in many of these countries: 'for most of the developing and transition economies – some 100 countries – money spent to implement the WTO rules ... would be money unproductively invested' (Finger & Schuler, 2001: 115).

Box 7.2: Special and Differential Treatment at the WTO

The argument that there should be different standards for developed and developing nations has precedent at the WTO, in the form of multiple 'special and differential' provisions for developing and least developed countries written into many of the trade agreements. Unfortunately, most of these exemptions for poorer countries are scheduled to expire, in some instances as early as 2005, in others not until 2016. The EU, following the lead of many development NGOs, is urging that these exemptions be based on the level of economic development within a country, rather than on some arbitrary calendar date (*BRIDGES Weekly Trade News Digest*, 2002g). This was also the small victory earned by developing countries at the Doha Ministerial Round in 2001, which declared that the WTO should review 'all Special and Differential provisions ... with a view to *strengthening them*' (WTO, 2001a; emphasis added). Many developed countries, however, have been reluctant to proceed with WTO negotiations to do just that (*BRIDGES Weekly Trade News Digest*, 2002e). The 2002 World Summit on Sustainable Development made the same declaration, as has the Director-General of UNCTAD in his 2002 report. The group of LDC members of the WTO echoed the same claim in its Doha 'Development Round'

---

negotiating paper, arguing that development must be seen as the primary goal of the multilateral trading system (*BRIDGES Weekly Trade News Digest*, 2002b).

There is one overarching exception for developing countries in GATT, Article XVIII. This article allows developing countries to ignore all WTO agreements that require them to lower import tariffs and to remove quantitative restrictions on imports, both measures that reduce the level of imports allowed into the country. They can do this to protect certain key domestic industries or other economic sectors that are particularly fragile. But to do so, they must notify all other countries. These countries, in turn, can then impose reciprocal trade sanctions worth an amount equivalent to what they might lose by having their exports shut out of the developing country's market. The cost is too high for developing countries ever to use this exception (*BRIDGES Trade News Weekly*, 2002d). Removing this provision of Article XVIII, a point advocated by many developing countries, would go a long way towards the goal of the multilateral trading system being made to work for the world's poor.

Market Liberalization and Changes in Taxation

Tariffs still constitute a substantial portion of overall government revenue in many developing countries, compared to an average of only four per cent for high-income nations (World Bank, 2002d: 255). A neglected dimension of the tariff reductions adopted by many developing countries as a condition of SAPs has been the associated decline in government revenues. Between 1980 and 1997, as a percentage of total national taxes, tariff taxes fell from 48 per cent to 23 per cent in Jordan, 50 per cent to 16 per cent in Sri Lanka, and 39 per cent to 12 per cent in Botswana (World Bank, 2000b). Few countries experiencing these revenue declines have had the capacity to raise comparable revenues from other sources, and most have not experienced sufficient growth in trade to offset the drop (Hilary, 2001). In the past decade alone, for 18 of the African countries for which comparative data are available, taxes on international trade declined from 33 per cent of total tax revenue, to 30 per cent (World Bank, 2002d: 252–4). The aggregate data mask some wide variations. Cameroon *increased* its international trade share of tax revenue from 14 per cent to 28 per cent between 1990 and 1999; even steeper increases were posted by Côte d'Ivoire and Guinea. The Republic of Congo, meanwhile, saw its international trade share of tax drop from 21 per cent to six per cent, and Mauritius from 46 per cent to 26 per cent. Tariff reductions resulting from market liberalization have had, and will continue to have, a much harsher revenue impact on poorer countries.

Partly as a result of tariff reductions, overall tax revenue as a percentage of GDP is also much lower in most developing and least developed countries than it is for G7 members (see Figure 7.1, below). Declining tax capacities have been most dramatic for transition economies, but liberalization-related currency crises in Asia led to reductions of ten per cent or more in public spending for health, education and social/community services in Thailand, the Philippines, Korea and, for a time, Malaysia (UNDP, 1999). A small and declining tax base, together with tax competition and increasing difficulties in taxing mobile capital – issues we have discussed in Chapter 2 – make taxation for redistribution much harder than in previous decades (Von Furstenberg & Kirton, 2001: 248). This, in turn, increases developing countries' need for ODA or – more destructively – encourages them to resort to continued foreign borrowing.

Figure 7.1: Total Tax Revenues as % of GDP in Selected Countries, 2000

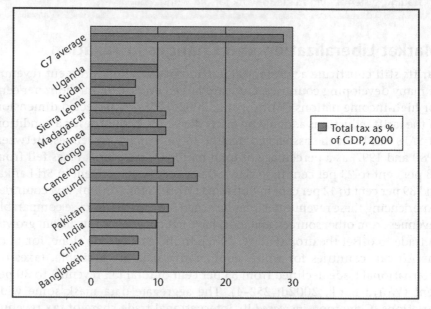

Source: World Bank (2002d: Table 5.5)

G7 average excludes France and Japan, for which data were not available.

Summary: Chapter Seven

The G8 deserve praise for launching a new round of trade negotiations in Doha. However, it is not clear whether the anticipated 'development round' will actually materialize. The failure of the G8 to open their own markets more rapidly to developing country products, despite much rhetoric about the economic benefits of trade liberalization and despite the economic boost this would provide for struggling economies, does not provide grounds for optimism. Undoubtedly, domestic economic losses in G8 countries would result, but – especially after the boom of the 1990s – the G8 are well able to absorb the costs of mitigating these. Failure to open markets is arguably a reflection of the same lack of genuine political commitment to development that has resulted in declining ODA contributions (see Chapter 6).

It must further be emphasized that in the course of their own industrialization, the G8 conspicuously failed to follow the import liberalization prescriptions they – and the IFIs – are now urging on the developing world. Recent US unilateralism on trade policy issues, exemplified by the 2002 farm subsidy legislation, is cause for special concern.

Explicit or Specific Commitments: Trade and Market Access

* Launch of a new round of global trade negotiations in November 2001, which will address developing country priorities (Genoa).
  Accomplished: Yes, launched.
  Adequacy: It remains to be seen whether the hoped-for 'development round' will materialize.
  Comments: Developing country positions on extending special and differential treatment are being opposed by many G7 countries. Progress on agricultural subsidies remains uncertain.
* Work towards duty- and quota-free market access for LDC exports (Genoa).
  Accomplished: Partially and imperfectly.
  Comments: Canadian, US and EU countries' records on this point are all compromised by protectionism.
* Provide bilateral assistance on technical, legal and human resource aspects of trade policy (Genoa).
  Accomplished: Partially and unevenly (Advisory Centre on WTO Law).
  Comments: Only Canada, Italy, and the UK among the G8 have signed the agreement establishing the Center. The per capita contributions of Sweden and Norway are more than three times Canada's, which is the highest amongst the G8.

Implicit or Generic Commitments: Trade and Market Access

* Open markets as 'bedrock of multilateral trading system' (Genoa).
* Pursue policies to contribute to global growth through, *inter alia*, free trade (Genoa).

- 'Work with developing countries to put in place policies, programmes and institutions that offer people a fair chance to better their lives' (Okinawa).
  Accomplished: Not in a way that is conducive to development. Developing country markets have been opened up; the G7 have not reciprocated in a meaningful way.
  Comments: Conspicuous failure on the part of the G8 to open their markets to developing country exports, especially agricultural products and textiles, despite rare consensus on potential development benefits. The escalation of agricultural subsidies by the US is a cause for special concern.

Endnotes to Chapter Seven

[1] This is true despite various caveats related to negative environmental and social (distributional) externalities that might be associated with such trade, especially in raw agricultural products; the potential for growth in agricultural exports to exclude smaller producers and thereby exacerbate existing economic inequalities (UNCTAD, 2002b: 128–9); and the more general perils of reliance on primary commodity exports as a development strategy (UNCTAD, 2002b: 137–50).

[2] Recall, however, that World Bank and other projections related to achievement of the IDGs and MDGs – to say nothing of the problems of the HIPCs – still require huge increases in donor aid *as well as* improved market access for goods from less and least developed countries.

[3] EU tariffs on agricultural products from LDCs are actually higher than individual European country tariffs had been (Enge, 2002: 25).

[4] Under a WTO Agreement on Subsidies and Countervailing Measures, countries are not permitted to 'dump' goods at below cost or substantially lower than market prices in other countries' domestic markets. Developed countries have used this agreement to close their borders to products from developing countries where they have a particularly cost-competitive advantage. It often takes months or years for these cases to be resolved by the WTO. In the meanwhile, the developing country has lost access to a developed country's market. In one case, an EU ban on bed linen exports from India cut Indian production by 60 per cent, resulting in the loss of thousands of jobs. Four years later, the WTO ruled that the anti-dumping measures had been unjustified, but by then the damage had been done (Oxfam Canada, 2002: 4).

[5] Indeed, Canada actually enjoys a trade surplus with sub-Saharan African countries (4.1 per cent exports to 3.2 per cent imports in 2000), primarily exporting used clothing to these countries – the very exports that helped undermine Zambia's 'inefficient' textile industries in the 1990s described in Box 1.1, Chapter 1 (CCIC Africa-Canada Forum, 2002: 7).

[6] *The Economist* has been harshly critical of what it sees as Mexico's failure to lower the costs of agricultural production, warning that 'the worst moment will come in 2008, when tariffs are eliminated on American corn' (*The Economist*, 2002: 32). At the same time, it acknowledges that the value of support for Mexican farmers is minuscule when compared with the value of producer supports in Japan, the EU or the United States.

CHAPTER EIGHT

Environment

Poverty and environmental degradation are closely interrelated. While poverty results in certain kinds of environmental stress, the major cause of the continued deterioration of the global environment is the unsustainable pattern of consumption and production, particularly in industrialized countries, which is a matter of grave concern, aggravating poverty and imbalances (UN, 1992: Ch. 4).

Introduction

The natural environment is related to human health in various ways, of which direct exposure to hazards is only one. Fifteen years ago, the report of the World Commission on Environment and Development (WCED, 1987) drew attention to the multiple feedback loops that link poverty and economic insecurity, environmental degradation, and international economic policy environment. In the 1992 *Agenda 21*, the document that emerged from the UN Conference on the Environment and Development (UN, 1992) elaborated on these themes with a high degree of sophistication, noting *inter alia* that '[a] first step towards the integration of sustainability into economic management is the establishment of better measurement of the crucial role of the environment as a source of natural capital and as a sink for the products generated during the production of man-made capital' (UN, 1992: Ch. 8). Subsequent analysis has strongly emphasized the importance for human health of making these connections at the level of public policy and policy implementation (see e.g. Butler *et al.*, 2001; McMichael, 2000; UNCTAD, 2002b: 87–97; Waltner-Toews, 2001; Waltner-Toews & Lang, 2000). The past decade has also provided numerous illustrations of how liberalization of trade and financial flows can increase the pace of environmental destruction, exacerbating inequalities in direct and indirect exposure to health hazards associated with environmental change.

For example, the combined effects of deregulation, privatization and weak governmental controls on the Indonesian logging industry have led to the loss of more than one million hectares of forest per year through logging in Indonesia. Health effects range from widespread, short-term respiratory disorders associated with extensive burning to long-term ecosystem disturbances and potential climatic change (Walt, 2000). In Uganda, trade liberalization in the form of industrial privatization and tariff reduction on fishing technology contributed to overfishing of the Nile perch in Lake Victoria, and a degradation of the lake ecosystem and water quality (UNEP, 2001). And in Argentina, trade liberalization and promotion of fisheries exports led to a five-fold growth in fish catches in the decade 1985–95. Fishing companies gained an estimated US$1.6 billion from this growth, but depletion of fish stocks and environmental degradation has produced a net cost of US$500 million (UNEP, 2001).

For purposes both of developing research strategies and of evaluating existing policies, Labonte and Spiegel (2002) have proposed an analytical framework for studying the relations between globalization (broadly defined) and population health organized around 13 categories of inherently global health issues (IGHIs). Of these categories, six (climate change, biodiversity loss, water shortage, declining fish stocks, food [in]security and deforestation) directly involve environmental policy and ecosystem change,[1] and at least two others (increasing poverty, and war and conflict) present the possibility of 'downward spirals' in which ecosystem change reflects, transmits and reinforces social conditions that are destructive of human health.

Commenting on the G8 record with respect to the environment, Bayne (2001: 33) writes that '[p]rotecting the environment becomes more effective with the advance of globalisation, in principle, as world-wide agreements become feasible. The recent record of the summits, however, has not been very positive.' This may, indeed, be something of an understatement. Only two of the IGHIs – climate change and food (in)security – are specifically and substantively addressed in the documentation from the 1999–2001 summits, and the documents reflect little awareness of the feedback loops linking globalization, poverty, environmental change and human health.

This is a short chapter, not because these feedback loops are unimportant – they are critically important, especially for the poor, who are first and worst harmed by environmental hazards and resource degradation in rich and poor countries alike – but because of the limited policy attention evident at the G8 summits we have studied. We examine four specific areas: G8 commitments to improving drinking water quality and access to sanitation; environmental assessments of export credit agencies; multilateral environmental agreements (including the Kyoto Protocol on climate change); and energy conservation and renewable energy. We conclude with a brief observation concerning the retreat from past commitments on environment and sustainable development that was evident at the Johannesburg World Summit on Sustainable Development in 2002.

Drinking Water and Sanitation

According to the WHO, inadequate access to sanitation and safe drinking water is the second most important risk factor (after malnutrition) contributing to the global burden of disease (as cited in World Bank, 2002d: 42). Earlier WHO figures indicated that 19 per cent of deaths among children under five in the developing world in 1995 were attributable to diarrhoeal disease (WHO, 1997: 21), which is closely associated with contaminated water. Reflecting the importance of water and sanitation, the IDG include increased access to potable water as one of their indicators, and the MDGs add to this increased access to sanitation.

Provision of potable water has improved, particularly for rural families (UNDP *et al.*, 2000), with access in low-income countries rising from 70 per cent to 76 per cent between 1990 and 2000 (World Bank, 2002d: 28), although some 300 million people in Africa (more than 35 per cent of the total population) were estimated to lack access to safe water in 2000 (Worldwatch Institute, 2001: 95). Sanitation lags further behind. While the portion of people with improved access in low-income countries also rose between 1990 and 2000 from 40 per cent to 45 per cent (World Bank, 2002d: 28), the absolute numbers of people without access increased from 2.6 to 3.3 billion people from 1990 to 2000 (UNEP, 1999). Sub-Saharan Africa fared slightly worse: access to safe water rose from 49 per cent to 55 per cent, while access to improved sanitation stagnated at 55 per cent (World Bank, 2002d: 28). Thus, although progress has been widespread in Africa (see Table 8.1, below) that progress is slow, and does not bode well for achieving the 2015 target of halving the proportion of people without sustainable access to safe water.

Perhaps recognizing the essential nature of safe drinking water and sanitation to all other human needs (including health), G7 aid to water supply and sanitation outstrips that for basic health and basic education combined (see Figure 8.1, below). The UK, Canada and, until 2001, the US, are particularly low donors for water and sanitation. More significantly, in light of Africa's need, the 2001 decline in the G7 average commitment to ODA in this crucial health-related area is disturbing.

In 1999, the multilateral contributions for European G7 countries were approximated using EC sector commitments in 2000, as data on EC sector commitments for 1999 are not available.

Table 8.1: Progress in Providing Access to Safe Drinking Water, Africa, 1990–2000*

Countries for which data are available	▲▲	▲	–	▼	▼▼
Sub-Saharan Africa		Cameroon Cape Verde C. African Rep. Comoros Congo, Rep. of Ethiopia Gabon Ghana Guinea Guinea-Bissau Kenya Lesotho Madagascar Mali Malawi Mozambique Namibia Niger Nigeria Senegal South Africa Sudan Zimbabwe		Benin Chad Côte d'Ivoire Mauritania Sierra Leone Togo Uganda Zambia	Rwanda
Other African countries		Algeria Morocco Saudi Arabia			

Source: Social Watch (2002: 44–5)

* Some years approximate to base-line 1990, and range from 1988 to 1995.
Legend:

▲▲ Significant progress.   ▲ Some progress.

– Stagnation.   ▼ Some regression.

▼▼ Significant regression.

Figure 8.1: % of Total Aid to Water and Sanitation, 1999–2001

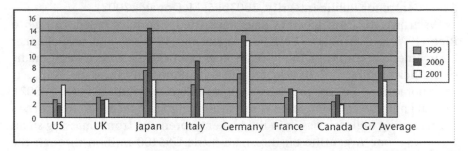

Source: OECD (2001c: Table 19); OECD (2002b: Table 19); OECD (2003: Table 19)

Privatization, Water and GATS

As disturbing as the decline in aid to water is the increasing trend to donor-assisted privatization in water and sanitation, particularly private sector management and provision. Water privatization in many poorer countries arose as a condition of SALs, which promoted privatization even when the costs would be beyond the reach of most families. Water privatization, full cost recovery and an end to public subsidy programs for water persist as conditions for IMF and World Bank loans. 'A review of IMF loan agreements across 40 countries during 2000 found that privatization or full cost recovery was a condition of 12 of them' (Hilary, 2001: 32, citation omitted). A third (N = 84) of World Bank water supply loans during the 1990s require some form of privatization, and the pace of such requirements is increasing. Fifty-eight per cent of short-term SALs between 1996 and 1999 had privatization as a condition; over 80 per cent of all World Bank-funded water projects in 2002 did the same (Centre for Public Integrity, 2003a). There is also evidence of a close relationship between private water companies and the IFIs. Former IMF Director, Michel Camdessus, on retirement in 2000, became chair of the International Panel for New Investments in Water, a project of the world's major private water companies; the World Bank owns a five per cent stake in Agua Argentinas, controlled by the huge Suez water company, and provided personnel assistance for negotiating water rate increases with the Argentine government (Centre for Public Integrity, 2003b: 4, 6).[2]

Water privatization schemes in developing countries are often associated with rapidly increased costs, which place access to water beyond the reach of most poor households. Such programs in the capital of Mauritania led to water costs consuming over one-fifth of total average household budgets for low-income families (World Bank findings quoted in Hilary, 2001: 32). In South Africa, large numbers of people have been cut off from privatized water delivery systems for various periods since the mid-1990s (Bond, 2001: 64–7; Centre for Public Integrity, 2003b: 5; McDonald, 2002).

Water privatization schemes have been tried, and have failed, in Puerto Rico (1995–99), Trinidad (1994–98), Argentina (1995–98) and several other Latin American countries. In each case, rates skyrocketed, service was sporadic or inefficient, huge deficits were created and, in most instances, the contracts were not renewed or the providers simply walked away (Shaffer *et al.*, 2002). This did not prevent companies from earning high annual profits, executives from earning high salaries or individual entrepreneurs from amassing small fortunes – one Argentine businessman made US$100 million through the sale of his shares in the private water company supplying Buenos Aires (Centre for Public Integrity, 2003c: 3). Executives of some multinational water companies, including Suez and Vivendi, or their subsidiaries, have been found guilty of bribing local officials (Centre for Public Integrity, 2003d).

There is considerable concern that GATS could be used to open up opportunities for private investment in water and sanitation services. Had this occurred at the time of the reversal of the hugely unpopular water privatization scheme in Cochabamba, Bolivia, foreign water supply companies might have been able successfully to demand massive compensation. Even without GATS protection, the companies involved – Bechtel and its consortium partner, Aguas del Tunari – are involved in lawsuits against the Bolivian government seeking compensation for lost investment (see Centre for Public Integrity, 2003b). To date, 40 countries have committed themselves to liberalizing environmental services under GATS, including 26 developing and least developed countries (WTO Services Database Online, 2002). Such commitments could 'lock in' existing policies and regulations that allow foreign private investors or companies to provide water and sanitary or other environmental services.

It is difficult without very close scrutiny of the types of services that are included in each sub-sector to determine which sets of commitments will have most bearing on water. As with education, very few sub-Saharan African countries have committed to liberalization in environmental services. Lesotho and South Africa, however, stand out: Lesotho in particular has made the most liberalization commitments in all three key sectors – health, education and environmental services – followed by South Africa. Present-day negative experiences with water privatization in South Africa do not bode well for the future. By contrast, most of the G7 have made extensive commitments in this sector, notably in mode 3, 'commercial presence' (foreign private investment). These commitments have been the source of considerable civil society critique and questioning within G7 countries.

We do not infer from this discussion that the private sector has no role to play in water provision. Our concern is that, based on experience from developing countries so far, the commodification and commercialization of water could severely limit access for the poor, with destructive consequences for population health. Public regulation of, and increased access to, water and sanitation is considered one of the main reasons for the decline in infectious diseases in nineteenth-century Europe and North America, especially among the poor (e.g. see Dubos, 1968; Szreter, 1988; Tesh, 1990). In Chapter 3 we noted the need for further review and synthesis of the literature on the effects of privatization in the context of health services and systems. A similar need exists for research on direct and indirect health impacts of privatizing water infrastructure, of a kind Canada's International Development Research Centre is now supporting through the Municipal Services Project (http://www.queensu.ca/msp) in Southern Africa.

Environmental Assessments of ECA Activities

Export credit agencies, such as Export Development Canada (EDC), the Export-Import Bank and the Overseas Private Investment Corporation (OPIC) in the United States, are agencies of industrialized country governments that provide financial assistance to purchasers of exported goods and services. To oversimplify somewhat, the assistance provided can be of several types: direct loan financing (in which the ECA lends to a developing country purchaser), guarantees of private loans (in which the ECA, on behalf of the government, assumes a contingent liability in the event of purchaser default), and insurance that protects exporters against non-payment. Even as ODA flows have been decreasing, the value of financing provided by ECAs has increased dramatically. Although precise estimates are difficult to obtain, it seems clear that the annual value of long-term export financing provided by ECAs is now considerably higher than the combined total of bilateral and multilateral development assistance, and one estimate is that ECAs now finance eight per cent of *all* global exports (Goldzimer, 2002; Rich *et al.*, 2000). In the process, ECAs have become very substantial creditors of the developing countries. As Bruce Rich of the Environmental Defense Fund points out, ECAs 'are not foreign assistance agencies. They are domestic assistance agencies. Their mission is to boost the overseas sales of their countries' multinational corporations' (Rich, 2000: 32).

For many years, NGOs have been critical of the lack of environmental standards for ECAs, calling attention to their role in financing such environmentally destructive activities as large-scale forest clearance in Indonesia, extractive industries in sub-Saharan Africa, and the construction of China's Three Gorges Dam (Fried & Soentoro, 2002; NGO Working Group, 2000, 2001; Norlen *et al.*, 2002; Rich *et al.*, 2000). To restate a point, the provision of such financing is primarily motivated not by benevolence, but rather by a desire to create or expand markets for firms in the financing country. A key element of the critique has involved lack of transparency: historically, ECAs have functioned very much on the model of private commercial corporations, without the degree of public disclosure, consultation and assessment of environmental impacts that have come to be expected from official aid agencies. The G8, reportedly with leadership from the United States, and resistance from France and Germany (Rich, 2000), have commendably recognized the importance of this issue, noting in 2001:

> We are committed to ensuring that our Export Credit Agencies (ECAs) adhere to high environmental standards. We therefore agreed in Okinawa to develop common environmental guidelines for ECAs, drawing on relevant MDB experience. Building on the progress made since last year, we commit to reach agreement in the OECD by the end of the year on a Recommendation that fulfils the Okinawa mandate (Genoa Communiqué, para. 29).

In December 2001, the OECD failed to reach complete agreement on environmental guidelines for ECAs. However, a February 2002 announcement (OECD, 2002a) indicated that 'most Member countries have unilaterally agreed to implement' a set of environmental guidelines developed by the OECD Working Party on Export Credits and Credit Guarantees. Whether all the G8 countries have adopted the guidelines is not clear. Even if they have, ongoing evaluations will be needed of whether and how the guidelines as interpreted and implemented by individual countries conform to the principles of sustainable development.

The Canadian situation illustrates this point. A recent review of new measures taken by Export Development Canada, at least in part independently of the OECD process, indicated that 'Canada retains plenty of room to avoid careful environmental assessments and public scrutiny' (Reader, 2002; see also NGO Working Group, 2003). In January 2003, a coalition of Canadian NGOs released a report highly critical of Export Development Canada's disclosure policy and lack of consistent standards for environmental review, pointing out that the agency is not required even to disclose whether it is considering financing seven large-scale industrial projects being undertaken by Canadian companies in the developing world (NGO Working Group, 2003).

Commitments on Multilateral Environmental Agreements

G8 performance on environmental issues related to health can also be assessed with respect to three major international agreements. When the Stockholm Convention on Persistent Organic Pollutants (POPs), adopted in 2001, comes into force, it will begin the process of eliminating releases of 12 chemical pollutants that are recognized as threats to human health and the environment. The Cartagena Protocol on Biosafety (to the UN Convention on Biodiversity), adopted in 2000, will create a set of procedures for managing trade in Living Modified Organisms (LMOs). Both agreements were 'welcomed' by the G8:

> We welcome the recent adoption of the Stockholm Convention on Persistent Organic Pollutants (POPs) and will strongly promote its early entry into force (Genoa Communiqué, para. 28).
> We ... welcome the conclusion of the Cartagena Protocol on Biosafety, and encourage the parties concerned to work for its early entry into force (Okinawa Communiqué, para. 64).

Although the language of these commitments is ambiguous, their supportive intent seems clear. Nevertheless, at this writing, only Canada, Germany and Japan among the G8 have ratified or acceded to the Stockholm Convention, and *none* of the G8 countries has individually ratified the Cartagena Protocol, although the EU has done so.[3] The US is not even a party to the Biodiversity Convention. In 1992, the first President Bush declined to sign the Convention on Biodiversity, citing concerns including the lack of sufficient protection for intellectual property. President Clinton subsequently signed the treaty and submitted it to the Senate for ratification, but the Senate did not act on this request (Segara & Fletcher, 2001: 2–3). Consequently, the US cannot be a party to the Cartagena Protocol, although it attends meetings of the parties to the Biodiversity Convention as an observer.

In terms of G8 performance as measured against specific summit commitments, the dominant current issue is undoubtedly the contrasting position of national governments with respect to the Kyoto Protocol for limiting greenhouse gas emissions. The protocol (to the United Nations Framework Convention on Climate Change) sets targets and timetables for cutting each developed country's emissions of the greenhouse gases that have been identified, by an overwhelming consensus among scientists (IPCC, 2001), as contributing to recent and future global climate change. It includes provisions for an emissions trading regime among industrialized countries, to accommodate situations in which it is less costly for countries to buy emissions credits than to reduce their own emissions, and also provides a 'Clean Development Mechanism' for financing emissions reductions in developing countries.

A review conducted for the WHO in 2000 found that 'climate change is likely to have wide-ranging and potentially serious health consequences' as a result of impacts including increased frequency of extreme weather events, broader distribution of vector-borne infectious diseases, localized reductions in crop yields, changes in water quality and quantity, and increased urban heat stress and air pollution (Kovats *et al.*, 2000: 16–23). This assessment was corroborated by the contributors to the health component of the third report of the Intergovernmental Panel on Climate Change (IPCC) (McMichael & Githeko, 2001), which is perhaps the largest-scale international collaboration ever assembled around a specific scientific and policy challenge. Vulnerable, low-income populations will be the first to experience adverse health effects associated with climate change (Patz & Kovats, 2002); they are also likely to have the fewest resources for effective adaptation. The rich can always turn up the air conditioner, increase the food budget, or move to higher ground; the poor have no such options. Poor countries are also less likely to have the health infrastructure necessary to cope with (for instance) the expanded range of infectious disease vectors (Githeko *et al.*, 2000).

In 2001, the position of the G8 was as follows:

> We recognise that climate change is a pressing issue that requires a global solution. We are committed to providing strong leadership. Prompt, effective and sustainable action is needed, consistent with the ultimate objective of the UN Framework Convention on Climate Change of stabilising greenhouse gas concentrations in the atmosphere (Genoa Communiqué, para. 23).
>
> We all firmly agree on the need to reduce greenhouse gas emissions. While there is currently disagreement on the Kyoto Protocol and its ratification, we are committed to working intensively together to meet our common objective (Genoa Communiqué, para. 24).

These statements should be compared with the still guarded, but more forceful, endorsements of the Kyoto Protocol at the Okinawa summit one year earlier: 'We are strongly committed to ... early entry *into force* of the Kyoto Protocol' (Okinawa Communiqué, para. 65; emphasis added); and at the Cologne summit in 1999: '[we] resolve to make an urgent start on the further work that is necessary *to ratify and make Kyoto a reality* (Cologne Communiqué, para. 11; emphasis added).

G8 performance is a study in contrasts. With the exceptions of the United States and Russia, all G8 countries have ratified or acceded to the Kyoto

Protocol,[4] although substantial opposition was expressed in Canada. Canada remains exposed to criticism for attempting to achieve Kyoto compliance without reducing actual emission levels, through such mechanisms as export credits for 'clean energy'– an approach that led one Canadian commentator to describe Canada as a 'rogue state' in the environmental policy context (Broadhead, 2001). Russia has delayed ratification, leading to concerns that the protocol – which comes into force only when ratified by countries that produce 55 per cent of global greenhouse gas emissions – may become a dead issue (MacKinnon, 2003). The United States, with the highest per capita energy-related emissions of carbon dioxide among the G8 (see Table 8.1, below), repudiated Kyoto after first signing the protocol. The positions of Canada, Russia and the United States are all contrary to commitments made by G8 environment ministers prior to the Cologne summit, to the effect that '[w]e are determined to take the lead in combating climate change and to make every effort to _change our own emission trends_ by taking effective measure domestically' (Schwerin G8 Environment Ministers Communiqué, para. 12; emphasis added).

Energy Conservation and Renewable Energy

In addition to providing comparative information on the energy intensity of the G8 economies, Table 8.1 also provides information on two reasonable, if imperfect indicators of G7 countries' willingness to improve the efficiency with which they use energy and to support a transition to renewable energy sources: the tax they impose per litre of gasoline and their investment in domestic research and development (R&D) on conservation and renewable energy. Especially striking is the relation among carbon intensity, low levels of gasoline tax and high levels of greenhouse gas emissions in Canada and the United States, suggesting abundant opportunities for reducing environmental impacts relative to comparably affluent economies and societies elsewhere in the world.

A consensus is gradually emerging that, over the longer term, industrialized economies in particular will need to reduce their current reliance on fossil fuels. Although the consensus quickly dissolves once the talk turns to the preferred replacements, in 2001 the G8 stated that '[w]e recognise the importance of renewable energy for sustainable development, diversification of energy supply, and preservation of the environment. We will ensure that renewable energy sources are adequately considered in our national plans and encourage others to do so as well' (Genoa Communiqué, para. 27).

It is too early to see how well this commitment will be honoured, but recent trend data show a schism in G7 behaviour (Table 8.2, on page 165).

Investments in renewable energy R&D over the past decade have been flat in the US and Canada, in modest decline in Germany and Italy, and in rapid and pronounced decline in the UK. Only France and Japan show increases, with France's only more recently. Data on conservation R&D are a little more encouraging for some G7 countries. Canada and the US show a rise in spending, although the US level is still below its 1995 high mark; Japan has been consistently increasing its expenditures, while Italy's performance remains flat. Germany shows a slow decline, while UK spending has plunged dramatically.

R&D spending is, at best, an imperfect indicator of the extent to which renewable energy is incorporated into 'national plans', since many more factors affect the market penetration of renewable energy. Perhaps the most important of these is the pricing structure for fossil fuels and the tax per litre of gasoline (which is several times as high in the European G8 countries as in Canada or the United States), which are perhaps the best bases for comparing the seriousness of governmental commitments to a future of reduced reliance on fossil fuels.

The G7 must also rate poorly on their ability to 'encourage others to do so as well', at least as far as the World Bank is concerned. The ratio of fossil fuel to renewable energy funding by the World Bank is 20:1, and it reportedly rejects the establishment of targets for support for renewable energy (Halifax Initiative, 2002).

The G8 in Genoa made a further commitment with respect to renewable energy more generally:

> We encourage continuing research and investment in renewable energy technology, throughout the world. Renewable energy can contribute to poverty reduction. We will help developing countries strengthen institutional capacity and market-oriented national strategies that can attract private sector investment in renewable energy and other clean technologies (Genoa Communiqué, para. 27).

One indicator of G8 seriousness on this point will be an increase in ODA commitments to renewable energy (see Table 8.3, below), which by 1999 had declined by a remarkable 80 per cent from their peak in 1995.

Also in July 2001, the G8 Renewable Energy Task Force that was formed at the Okinawa summit to examine renewable energy in developing countries (Okinawa Communiqué, para. 66) issued its report. So far, there has not been a commitment to implement the recommendations of that report (G8 Renewable Energy Task Force, 2001a), which focused on expanding the market for renewable energy on both the demand and supply sides, 'ensuring that careful account is taken of full societal costs and the broad range of benefits of alternative energy supply options,' and mobilizing effective financing for renewables.

Table 8.1: Some Key Figures on Energy R&D and Carbon Dioxide Emissions for the G7

	Tonnes of energy-related CO_2 emitted per person *	Tonnes of energy-related CO_2 per US $1 000 GDP (1995 US$) *	Tax per litre of gasoline, January 2003 (US$)	Renewable energy R&D spending as % of total, 1999 or 2000	Renewable energy R&D spending per person (US$)	Conservation R&D spending as a % of total, 1999 or 2000	Conservation R&D spending per person (US$)
Canada	16.04	0.74	0.195	7.3	0.39	24.80	1.34
France	6.00	0.21	0.805	2.0	0.20	1.90	0.18
Germany	10.01	0.32	0.856	56.3	0.68	14.20	0.17
Italy	7.30	0.36	0.763	n.a.	n.a.	n.a.	n.a.
Japan	9.14	0.22	0.486	4.1	1.32	15.70	5.02
UK	9.00	0.43	0.976	11.8	0.14	2.43	0.03
US	20.01	0.65	0.101	9.3	0.75	23.80	1.92

Source: All figures from IEA (2001: Tables 9 & B14) except column 3 (tax per litre of gasoline), which is calculated from IEA (2003).

* Excluding emissions from biomass-derived fuels, and from international marine and aviation bunkers.

n.a. = data not available.

Table 8.2: Trends in G7 Government Renewable Energy and Conservation R&D Budgets, 1989–2000 (US$ millions at 2000 prices and exchange rates)

Renewable energy

	1989	1990	1991	1992	1993	1994	1995	1996	1997	1998	1999	2000
Canada	11.8	9.8	9.4	10.8	9.7	11.2	11.0	10.9	8.4	8.7	10.6	12.0
France	7.3	7.6	6.9	6.8	4.9	4.6	4.5	4.3	2.6	3.6	11.6	n.a.
Germany	77.4	91.9	100.6	106.1	115.8	76.5	67.5	83.8	65.5	73.4	62.7	55.8
Italy	37.5	42.7	32.6	n.a.	24.1	27.3	37.3	34.8	32.1	29.9	n.a.	n.a.
Japan	132.1	131.0	127.2	121.6	126.5	116.8	117.7	120.7	119.8	132.1	140.0	167.6
UK	31.2	30.3	32.9	29.8	27.3	16.2	15.8	10.3	7.0	5.2	7.1	8.5
USA	145.1	134.5	178.9	250.7	239.9	246.4	297.8	219.6	206.6	253.7	264.2	210.7
Total *	442.4	447.8	488.5	548.2	499.0	551.6	484.4	442	506.6			

Conservation

	1989	1990	1991	1992	1993	1994	1995	1996	1997	1998	1999	2000
Canada	31.1	31.0	28.1	23.8	26.0	38.7	37.8	38.7	37.5	38.3	40.6	40.8
France	14.8	22.1	16.7	16.1	10.5	7.1	6.8	6.2	4.0	5.6	10.8	n.a.
Germany	16.1	15.5	15.6	11.0	10.4	11.9	13.7	19.8	12.9	11.6	16.4	14.1
Italy	33.9	42.1	49.0	n.a.	47.8	45.1	47.6	48.2	44.7	44.5	n.a.	n.a.
Japan	n.a.	n.a.	n.a.	n.a.	n.a.	252.5	269.6	309.9	301.6	485.1	587.5	636.9
UK	47.3	34.2	26.1	32.2	36.4	4.1	2.5	2.2	1.6	0.8	1.1	1.7
USA	203.6	224.1	258.6	332.1	349.7	476.9	552.1	442.0	406.7	436.8	490.4	538.8
Total *						836.3	930.1	867	809	1022.7		

n.a. = not available, or not available on a basis that permits meaningful comparison with previous or subsequent years.

* Calculated only for those years where figures are available for all seven countries.

Source: IEA (2001: Tables B5 & B11)

Table 8.3: G7 ODA Commitments to Renewable Energy, 1989–99 (US$ millions)

	1989	1990	1991	1992	1993	1994	1995	1996	1997	1998	1999
Canada	1.34	4.78	5.85	14.26	21.28	11.17	11.54	36.32	27.53	3.23	30.68
France	261.48	239.27	24.57	8.16	33.50	28.45	42.06	42.66	71.37	88.43	23.07
Germany		27.29	66.02	112.22	10.28	108.08	134.56	251.55	91.22	190.12	238.54
Italy	214.71	92.41	112.32	82.67	1.14	123.37	74.87	3.02	23.40	0.09	2.60
Japan	283.12	145.14	701.19	121.06	584.94	680.06	1 518.77	943.28	816.01	389.23	35.38
UK	28.68	44.67	7.94	53.26	43.36	35.93	3.12	0.39	4.33	3.64	0.09
US								10.97	3.70	7.14	6.89
Total	789.33	553.56	917.89	391.63	694.5	987.06	1 784.92	1 288.19	1 037.56	681.88	337.25

Source: G8 Renewable Energy Task Force (2001b)

Johannesburg and the Retreat from Sustainable Development

Many observers believed that the Stockholm Summit on the environment in 1972 signalled an overdue recognition on the part of the community of nations that many environmental problems are both transnational and interconnected. Twenty years later, the Earth Summit in Rio de Janeiro, following as it did the Brundtland Commission's work on environment and development (WCED, 1987), seemed to indicate a new receptiveness to integrating environmental concerns with development strategy in a way that prioritized the developing world's distinctive needs and aspirations. The sustainable development imperative pervades *Agenda 21*, the action plan developed for the summit, which, as we have noted, included such specific commitments as the widely ignored pledge to increase ODA to the 0.7 per cent figure.

Despite this lack of follow-through, expectations were high for the ten-year follow-up to the Rio Summit (Rio +10), the World Summit on Sustainable Development (WSSD) held in Johannesburg in 2002. In what seems in retrospect to have been a warning sign, the only reference made to WSSD at the 1999, 2000 and 2001 G8 summits was the commitment made in 2000 (Okinawa Communiqué, para. 65) that the G8 would 'endeavour with all [their] partners to prepare a future-oriented agenda for Rio+10 in 2002.' A few weeks before the summit, a coalition of 32 countries, including all the G8 except Russia, announced a US$2.92 billion replenishment of the Global Environment Facility (GEF), which funds developing country projects in the areas of biodiversity protection, climate change, protection of international waters and ozone depletion. However, WSSD participants made few specific commitments, primarily contenting themselves with restating the MDGs (UN, 2002c: paras. 7–8). Perhaps most notably, the commitment to establish a 'world solidarity fund to eradicate poverty' came with no dollar amounts attached, and 'stress[ed] the voluntary nature of the contributions' (UN, 2002c: para. 7(b)).

The BBC's World Service quoted an Oxfam spokesperson describing the WSSD as 'a triumph for greed and self-interest, a tragedy for poor people and the environment' (http://news.bbc.co.uk/1/hi/world/africa/2233969.stm, accessed 18 January 2003) and a published NGO commentary captured a widespread unease by concluding that '[t]he general sense is that but for some small successes the Summit is one of great disappointments. It was the largest and most expensive UN-sponsored Summit. But the Plan of Implementation is toothless, lame even. It may as well be called the Plan for Inaction' (Iyer, 2002). Although a detailed discussion of the WSSD is outside the scope of this chapter, it appears clear that sustainable development, especially the equity-driven version that featured prominently in *Agenda 21*, has slid well down the industrialized world's list of priorities.

The actual site of the summit was described in the *Guardian* as 'a purpose-built business centre ... surrounded by deep walls of police, electrified fences and miles of concrete barriers', which 'only exists because the business community has packed its bags and fled the terrible crime, impoverishment and physical degradation of the old city centre' (Vidal, 2002). Indeed, the juxtaposition of immense (and zealously guarded) wealth surrounded by desperation arguably provides a metaphor for the world order that is emerging as globalization proceeds apace. One is left to wonder whether G8 environmental policy in the future will be characterized by further retreats from the idea that environmental protection represents a shared obligation, in favour of a policy stance that regards environmental quality as just another purchasable commodity, to which rich and poor alike are entitled only to the extent that they can pay the price (on the domestic Canadian context, cf. Schrecker, 2002).

Summary: Chapter 8

Environmental issues have generally been neglected by the G8. The G8, like the other OECD countries, deserve praise for endorsing the principle of environmental review of ECA decisions. However, it is difficult to assess how much difference this stance has made 'on the ground.' Canada, Germany and Japan have ratified the Stockholm Convention on POPs, but no G8 country has individually ratified the Cartagena Protocol on Biosafety.

The United States deserves special criticism not only for failing to ratify the Biodiversity Convention, but also for repudiating the Kyoto Protocol on climate change, which has been ratified by all the other G7 countries. Russia similarly merits criticism for its delay in ratification. G8 statements of support for renewable energy sources have not been backed up either by increased ODA for this purpose or, with a few exceptions, by increased R&D commitments in their individual national budgets.

Explicit or Specific Commitments: Environment

- 'Prompt, effective and sustainable action is needed' on climate change (Genoa).
- Firm agreement on the need to reduce greenhouse gas emissions, but 'disagreement' on Kyoto protocol (Genoa, revisiting Cologne).
  Accomplished: Too soon to tell. The Kyoto Protocol was ratified by all G7 countries except the US, which repudiated after signing. Russia has signed the protocol, but not ratified it.
  Adequacy: It is too early to tell about the effectiveness of implementation. The US repudiation, the Russian hesitation and the Canadian insistence on flexibility all threaten to compromise the effectiveness of the protocol.
  Comments: Canada and the US are the highest per capita greenhouse gas emitters amongst the G7, with by far the lowest gasoline prices. Gasoline tax increases would represent an important demonstration of seriousness. However, US spending on conservation R&D more than doubled between 1989 and 2000; the US and Japan are clear leaders here. UK conservation R&D has plummeted.
- Commit to common environmental guidelines for ECAs (Genoa, revisiting Okinawa).
  Accomplished: OECD indicates that most member countries have adopted its guidelines; G8 adoption is not clear.
  Adequacy: Canadian NGOs suggest that Canada's ECA lacks transparency and consistent standards for environmental review. Research on implementation in other G7 countries is needed.
- Welcome and strongly promote early entry into force of Stockholm Convention on POPs (Genoa).
- Welcome and encourage early entry into force of Cartagena Protocol on Biosafety (Okinawa).

Accomplished: Partially and unevenly. Only Canada, Germany and Japan among the G8 have ratified or acceded to the Stockholm Convention. None of the G8 countries has individually ratified the Cartagena Protocol, although the EU has done so. The US has not even ratified the Biodiversity Convention.

Implicit or Generic Commitments: Environment

* Ensure that renewable energy sources are adequately considered in G8 national energy plans; 'encourage others to do so as well' (Genoa).
  Accomplished: Government renewable energy R&D spending 1989–2000 was stagnant in Canada, Italy and Japan; declined in Germany and the UK; rose in the US and (from a very low level) France. In per capita terms Japan is the clear leader.
  Comments: R&D spending is an incomplete measure of commitment, since market conditions, tax policy etc. are at least as important.

Encourage continuing research and investment in renewable energy technology, throughout the world (Genoa).
  Accomplished: No. G7 ODA commitments to renewable energy declined by 80% between 1995 and 1999. World Bank support for fossil fuel development was 20 times greater than its support for renewable energy.

Endnotes to Chapter Eight

[1] These 'inherently global health issues' are located in various places in the analytical framework presented in Chapter 1 (Figures 1.1 and 1.2).
[2] In July 2002, Suez terminated its 30-year contract to provide water and sewage services to Buenos Aires after the Argentine financial crisis led to an emergency decree overruling a contract clause permitting Suez to link its water prices to the US dollar. Weak regulatory practices and continuous renegotiation of the original 1993 contract allowed the Suez subsidiary Aguas Argentinas to earn a 19 per cent profit rate on its net worth, which turned into a US$500 million loss with that country's 2002 financial crisis and the loss of the Buenos Aires concession. During its nine years of water provision to the city, prices rose 20 per cent, compared to the company's promise to lower them by 27 per cent (see Public Citizen, 2003).
[3] This information is taken from the official web sites of the two agreements, http://www.pops/int and http://www.biodiv.org/biosafety respectively (accessed 17 January 2003).
[4] This information is taken from the official United Nations Framework Convention on Climate Change web site, http://www.unfccc.int/resource/convkp.html (accessed 24 February 2003).

CHAPTER NINE

Equity, Health and NEPAD:
A Case Study

Introduction

This book so far has examined some of the pathways through which the health of individuals and populations is influenced by national and global policy in domains ranging from macroeconomics to health-care financing to protection of ecosystems. The relationships are complex, sometimes converging and sometimes leading to opposing outcomes. Nevertheless, it is clear that policies developed in relation to one context – the concerns of G8 leaders and countries, for example – influence both public policy and population health in countries facing very different challenges and opportunities. In this chapter, we focus on Africa and on NEPAD. The situation of both health status and health systems in most of sub-Saharan Africa is bleak. Reviewing and re-presenting some indicators of this reality reminds us that the impacts of the complex threads we have been tracing throughout this book are both concrete and severe.

NEPAD represents one element of the complex relationship between Africa and the G8. While it is represented as a 'made in Africa' initiative, it was also very much 'made in (and for) Genoa and Kananaskis.' Examining the document and reflecting on the process of its development, as well as on the likelihood of its success, this chapter offers a case study of the intersections of contexts and approaches: what is at stake and what is decided globally and locally; how problems are framed and how proposed solutions are developed and implemented; how public policy addresses both the health sector and determinants of health. This chapter, then, speaks to the reality of (ill) health in Africa, to NEPAD as a specific response to this reality, and to the wider context of what is and is not on the political agenda of both African and G8 leaders. While NEPAD is an initiative in its own right, it can also be read as a chapter of the main narrative of this book, namely, the G8 summit story.

NEPAD addresses many issues that relate to health and development. These were identified during the development of the matrix (see Appendix 2). The explicit health commitments are dealt with in the sections of this chapter dealing with core health systems. Some of the key health-related commitments explicitly recognized, e.g. poverty, food and food security, GDP and GDP growth, are either addressed here or throughout the book. In the latter case, these have been reordered and grouped into G8 report sections that often cover several of these topics, to facilitate integration within the G8 document.

Since the presentation of NEPAD at the G8 Summit in Kananaskis, the NEPAD program of action is being refined and a summary became available in hard copy in July 2002. Within the NEPAD document, most of the content relevant to health appears in the 'program of action' section, within the 'sectoral' sub-section on human resource development. Since the publication of the NEPAD document, a draft health strategy has been developed, which was made available to us only after the manuscript for this book was nearly completed. We are pleased to note that many of our concerns raised below have been largely addressed. However, this strategy document, although finalized in August 2002, has yet to be made public and therefore its status is still unclear. The chapter concludes with our reflections on both the potential and likelihood of its successful implementation.

Global Policy, African Realities

Health and Development

Two potentially opposing views currently frame the debate concerning the relationship between health and development. These diverging views are visible throughout the policy responses discussed in this book.

Health as a Basic Human Right and Outcome of Development

'Health is a reflection of a society's commitment to equity and justice. Health and human rights should prevail over economic and political concerns' (People's Health Assembly, 2000b). Health is determined by myriad factors: 'Evidence from many countries shows that income is probably the most important of the factors outside of the health sector, while others include social inputs such as education, environmental inputs, access to clean water, and general economic measures such as food rationing and subsidies, etc.' (Bijlmakers *et al.*, 1996: 18). This approach identifies economic and political factors as the most significant determinants of health, as these factors determine who has control over resources and decision-making and who has power over whom. As Bijlmakers *et al.* put it,

> [h]istorical and contemporary experiences have shown that there is a definite but complex relationship between economic growth on the one hand and health status on the other. In general, sustained economic growth ... does lead to improved health and nutritional status, but

> there is, however, no direct correlation between health and nutrition indicators and GDP per capita because improved income distribution can accelerate improvements in health (Bijlmakers *et al.*, 1996: 17).

However, the last decades of the twentieth century have seen the increasing dominance of neo-liberal economic policies and a weakening of the state. This has been associated with increasingly unequal distribution of resources that leads to unacceptable levels of hunger, poor health and impoverishment (People's Health Assembly, 2000b: 11). Health care is being seen less as a basic right than as a product that can be sold or exchanged for profit (People's Health Assembly, 2000a).

Health as a Means to Achieve Economic Growth

The World Bank, in its 1993 *Investing in Health* report, emphasized health as an input to rather than an outcome of economic growth and development. *Investing in Health* proposed a three-pronged approach to government policies in improving health, and emphasized that health services are only one factor in explaining successes/gains made in health during the last decades. An environment enabling households to improve health – focusing on economic growth, education and gender equality – as well as diversity and competition in the delivery of health services were presented as the other two approaches (World Bank, 1993). A decade later, the Commission on Macroeconomics and Health (CMH) called for a new strategy for investing in health for economic growth, especially in the world's poorest countries (CMH, 2001).

We now turn to a recapitulation of progress and current realities in global and African health. The choice, or mix, of views about the relation between health and development significantly informs how the health situation is interpreted, and what options for action are proposed.

Progress in Global and African Health

Globally, significant gains in health status were achieved during the last decades of the twentieth century. Life expectancy increased from 46 years in the 1950s to 65.6 years in 1999 (Social Watch, 2002). The number of child deaths has been reduced from a projected 17.5 million to 12.5 million annually. Substantial control of communicable diseases such as poliomyelitis, diphtheria, measles, onchocerciasis and dracunculiasis through vaccination and other disease control measures has been achieved. Industrialised countries have seen a decline in male cardiovascular diseases.

Notwithstanding the above overall improvement in health, disaggregation of infant, under-five mortality and life expectancy data reveals that the gap in mortality rates between rich and poor countries has widened significantly.

The relative probability of dying for under-five-year-olds in developing countries compared to Western and Eastern European countries increased from a ratio of 3.4 in 1950 to 8.8 in 1990 (Legge, 1993).

Table 9.1: Relative Probability of Deaths* in the Population

Age group	1950	1980	1990
<5 years	3.4	6.4	8.8
5–14 years	3.8	6.5	7.0
15–59 years	2.2	1.8	1.7
60> years	1.3	1.4	1.4

* Relative probability of people in developing countries dying (across the ages indicated) expressed as DDC/(FSE+EME) (the ratio of demographically developing countries to the combined formerly socialist economies plus the established market economies). Calculated by Legge from data in World Bank (1993).

Health Status in Africa

While in Africa, too, health status has improved over the last 50 years, the current situation on the continent is of great concern, given the growing disparities between Africa and the rest of the world, increasing inequalities and even deteriorating indicators in many African countries.

Infant and Under-Five Mortality Rates

In 20 of the 53 African countries, an increase in infant mortality rate (IMR) occurred between 1990 and 1999. In only seven of the 53 African countries is the IMR equal to or below the world average of 45/1 000 live births; the 1999 IMR is equal to or higher than the average for developing countries (64/1 000 live births) in 37 African countries. The increases cannot be attributed to a high HIV prevalence in all cases (Mauritius, Angola, Mauritania, Benin and Niger). Eleven of the 20 countries that show an IMR increase have a per capita GDP below US$1 per day.

Nor has the under-five mortality rate (U5MR) declined in all countries; in ten countries, the U5MR showed an increase between 1990 and 2000. Only nine African countries have a 2000 U5MR below the world average (78/1 000 live births), while the 2000 U5MR is higher than the average for developing countries (93/1 000 live births) in 39 African countries (of the 51 countries for which data were available).

Life Expectancy

In 1999, 23 of 49 African countries for which trend data are available had a lower life expectancy than in 1990. The decline in life expectancy is closely linked to a high HIV prevalence rate: 21 of the 23 countries with a decline in life expectancy have an HIV prevalence rate higher than the adult HIV prevalence rate of 4.13 per cent, the average of all LDCs. The number of HIV-infected people in Africa is estimated at 28 million, approximately 70 per cent of the total of HIV-infected people globally (Collins & Rau, 2000).

Table 9.2: Adult HIV Prevalence Data in Africa

Adult HIV prevalence rate	Number of African countries
Equal or below 0.99% (world average)	10
0.99%–1.18% (average for all developing countries)	0
1.18%–4.13% (average for LDCs)	14
Higher than 4.13%	24
No data	5

Source: UNDP (2000: Table 10)

Non-Communicable Diseases

To aggravate matters, many developing countries are experiencing an 'epidemiological transition', with cardiovascular diseases, cancers, diabetes, other chronic conditions and traumas replacing communicable diseases in some social groups, but in others, coexisting with them. This constitutes an epidemiological polarization, with poorer sectors of the population experiencing high child mortality and morbidity as well as a high burden of non-communicable disease (Frenk *et al.*, 1989). In South Africa, for example, children from poor families still suffer mainly from infectious diseases, whereas increasing rates of hypertension, chronic lung diseases and diabetes affect the urban, and especially poorer, adult population (South African Demographic and Health Survey, 1998).

Health Services in Africa

Public Expenditure on Health

Public expenditure on health has increased globally from 4.7 per cent to 5.6 per cent of GDP. This increase is most notable in high-income countries. A smaller, but still significant, increase has been experienced in middle-income countries. However, low-income countries, more than half of which are African countries, have seen a reduction in public expenditure on health overall, as shown in Table 9.3.

Table 9.3: Public Health Expenditure

	Public expenditure on health as % of GDP, 1990	Public expenditure on health as % of GDP, 1996–98
46 high-income countries – GDP US$22 273 billion (no African country included)	5.3	6.4
93 middle-income countries – GDP US $4 319 billion (22 African countries included)	2.6	3.2
34 low-income countries – GDP US$1 830 billion (includes 29 African countries, excludes Somalia and Liberia)	0.9	0.8
World	4.7	5.6

Source: UNDP (2000: Table 16)

Trends in public expenditure on health, education and defence show positive signs, as can be seen in Table 9.4.

Table 9.4: Trends in Public Expenditure on Education, Health and Military, between 1990 and 1995–98

	Education (number of countries)	Health (number of countries)	Military (number of countries)
No data	10	5	11
No trend data	14	20	13
Increased expenditure	16 of 29	15 of 28	7 of 29
No change	1 of 29	7 of 28	2 of 29
Reduced expenditure	12 of 29	6 of 28	20 of 29

Source: UNDP (2000: Table 16)

Data on education expenditure are from 1990 and 1995–98, data on health expenditure are from 1990 and 1996–98, and data on military expenditure are from 1990 and 1998.

However, actual expenditure on health in Africa falls far short of the costs of a package of minimum necessary health services, as estimated by the former Director-General of the WHO (US$60), the CMH (US$34) or the World Bank (US$12) (see Table 9.5).

Only six African countries spend more than US$60 per capita per annum, and only nine countries spend more than US$34 to cover essential health services. Even using the US$12 per capita per annum package proposed by the World Bank (1993), only 19 African countries of 46 countries for which data are available spend this amount or more. These figures have profound implications for health policy implementation in Africa.

Allocation of Financial Resources to Different Levels of the Health System

Apart from a reduction in financial resources for public health expenditure, many countries have also been unable to reallocate resources significantly from tertiary and specialized services to basic health services or find increased resources to moderate the imbalance, despite warnings given as early as the mid-1960s (King, 1966). In Ghana, for instance, only 42 per cent of the health budget is allocated to district-level health service delivery, while the central Ministry of Health's budget allocation amounts to 16 per cent, tertiary facilities use almost 20 per cent and regional-level services use 23 per cent of the national health budget (Addai & Gaere, 2001).

Table 9.5: Actual Amounts of Public Health Expenditure Per Capita in Africa

	Number of countries	Names of countries
>US$60	6	Seychelles, South Africa, Mauritius, Botswana, Tunisia, Namibia
US$34–60	3	Algeria, Swaziland, Cape Verde
US$12–34	10	Gabon, Morocco, Egypt, Zimbabwe, Lesotho, São Tomé & Principe, Senegal, Republic of Congo, Côte d'Ivoire, Comoros
<$12	27	Guinea, Ghana, Mauritania, Cameroon, Gambia, Togo, Central African Republic, Uganda, Kenya, Burkina Faso, Benin, Chad, Eritrea, DRC, Nigeria, Mozambique, Madagascar, Niger, Zambia, Mali, Rwanda, Guinea-Bissau, Ethiopia, Burundi, Malawi, Tanzania, Sierra Leone
No data available	7	Libya, Angola, Equatorial Guinea, Sudan, Djibouti, Somalia, Liberia

Source: UNDP (2000)

Calculations based on 1998 GDP per capita (1995 US$) and 1998 public expenditure on health as % of GDP.

Health Sector Access

Access to health services improved considerably during the period 1980–90, but has worsened in many countries since health sector reforms, in particular user charges and other cost recovery mechanisms, were introduced. The introduction of user charges has been shown to be associated with a decline in the number of obstetric admissions and deliveries in hospitals, with an accompanying increase in perinatal mortality and maternal mortality amongst those delivering outside hospitals. Generally, utilization of health services by households with low incomes has also declined (Simms *et al.*, 2001). Health-sector performance is reflected by Expanded Programme on Immunisation (EPI) coverage data given below.

Health-Sector Performance

Vaccination coverage is considered a good indicator of health-service access and performance. As the WHO state, 'the effectiveness of immunization services is an excellent indicator of the effectiveness of the health systems' and coverage rates are a good indicator of the 'degree of efficiency of a particular reform process' (Simms *et al.*, 2001). The different components of an effective vaccination program – supervision, training, logistics – are also required for the provision of other basic services (Simms *et al.*, 2001).

Vaccination Coverage in Africa

Between 1990 and 1999, many African countries achieved an increase in vaccination coverage for all six antigens. However, a significant number of countries saw their vaccination coverage decrease and, more importantly, few countries managed to achieve coverage rates that provide 'herd immunity.' Only two countries have a measles vaccination coverage that protects the population as a whole, i.e. a higher than 95 per cent measles vaccination coverage (UNICEF, 1985: 67–8). Thirty-five countries have measles coverage below 75 per cent. A similar pattern can be seen for DPT coverage: pertussis herd immunity is only achieved when the vaccination coverage is above 95 per cent (UNICEF, 1985: 67–8). Only four African countries have achieved this coverage.

The Global Polio Eradication Initiative has organized intensive vaccination campaigns outside of the routine vaccination activities and achieved a significant reduction in the number of reported poliomyelitis cases. The campaign has also resulted in an increase in coverage in 23 countries. However, 33 countries still have polio vaccination coverage below 75 per cent.

Human Resources for Health

Health personnel account for 60–80 per cent of recurrent expenditure and are key to health systems (World Bank, 1994: 85–98). Physician and nurse to population ratios are generally low in Africa and disguise the unequal distribution of health personnel between rural and urban areas and, in some African countries between private and public sectors.

Table 9.6: BCG (Tuberculosis) Vaccination Coverage in Africa

1997–99	1997–99 coverage >75% (number of countries)	1997–99 coverage 60–75% (number of countries)	1997–99 coverage <60% (number of countries)	Total number of countries
No data	0	0	0	0
No trend data	11	1	3	15
Increase in coverage, 1990–99	14	6	2	22
Equal coverage, 1990–99	1	0	0	1
Decrease in coverage, 1990–99	6	3	6	15
Total	32	10	11	53

Source: Social Watch (2002: Table 10)

Table 9.7: DPT Vaccination Coverage in Africa

1997–99	1997–99 coverage >95% (number of countries)	1997–99 coverage 75–95% (number of countries)	1997–99 coverage <75% (number of countries)	Total number of countries
No data	0	0	0	0
No trend data	0	0	3	3
Increase in coverage, 1990–99	3	15	9	27

Equal coverage, 1990–99	1	1	1	3
Decrease in coverage, 1990–99	0	2	18	20
Total	4	18	31	53

Source: Social Watch (2002: Table 10)

Table 9.8: Polio Vaccination Coverage in Africa

1997–99	1997–99 coverage >75% (number of countries)	1997–99 coverage 60–75% (number of countries)	1997–99 coverage <60% (number of countries)	Total number of countries
No data	0	0	0	0
No trend data	6	5	5	16
Increase in coverage, 1990–99	10	4	9	23
Equal coverage, 1990–99	0	0	0	0
Decrease in coverage, 1990–99	4	1	9	14
Total	20	10	23	53

Source: Social Watch (2002: Table 10)

Table 9.9: Measles Vaccination Coverage in Africa

1997-99	1997-99 coverage >95% (number of countries)	1997-99 coverage 75-95% (number of countries)	1997-99 coverage <75% (number of countries)	Total number of countries
No data	0	0	0	0
No trend data	0	0	3	3
Increase in coverage, 1990-99	2	15	12	29
Equal coverage, 1990-99	0	0	1	1
Decrease in coverage, 1990-99	0	1	19	20
Total	2	16	35	53

Source: Social Watch (2002: Table 10)

Physician/1 000 people ratio (World Bank, 2001b):
High-income countries: 2.8/1 000
Middle-income countries: 1.8/1 000
Low-income countries: 0.5/1 000
Sub-Saharan Africa: 0.1/1 000.

Morale of health personnel in Africa is increasingly undermined, because of:

* Low remuneration;
* Inadequate staff support and supervision;
* Inadequate working and living conditions;
* The impact of HIV/AIDS, which results in both increased demand for health care as well as a high HIV prevalence amongst health workers; and
* Movement of health professionals from the public to the private sector and from developing to developed countries without appropriate replacement strategies (Dovlo, 2001; Commonwealth Secretariat, 2001).

Determinants of Health outside the Health Sector

Declines in per capita GDP occurred in 23 African countries between 1990 and 1998, while the number of countries with an average per capita GDP below US$1 per day changed from 23 of 48 countries to 23 of 50 countries, a slight improvement. However, the GDP data are aggregates that do not show the increasing gap between the rich and the poor within countries, a process that has occurred in parallel with globalization (UNDP, 2000).

Increased access to adequate housing, water and sanitation, education and improved food security, as well as to improved health care, has contributed to the gains in health status. However, much remains to be done in developing countries to achieve sustainable gains, as:

- Nearly 1.1 billion people in the developing world, approximately 25 per cent of whom lived in Africa, lacked access to a safe water supply in 2000;
- Approximately 2.4 billion people in developing countries, approximately ten per cent of whom lived in Africa, still lacked access to proper sanitation in 2000; and
- More than one billion people in developing countries lived without adequate shelter or in unacceptable housing, while at least 600 million people world-wide lived in dwellings that threaten their health and lives, and 100 million people were homeless (UNDP, 1997: 29, 42, 169, 218).

Twelve African countries have been or are still involved in conflict, while neighbouring countries are affected by the conflicts because of population movements across international borders. The breakdown in the delivery of most social services, including health care, is a frequent accompaniment of conflict.

Trends in Development of Public Health Services: Globalisation, Health and Health Services in Africa

The increased mobility of capital and labour and cheaper costs of communication have accelerated the pre-existing economic, political and social interdependence that characterizes the modern phase of globalization. Among the most important early interventions that have had the effect of further integrating developing countries into the global economy, primarily through the imposition of stringent debt repayments and the liberalization of trade, have been SAPs promoted by the IMF and the World Bank. SAPs have also resulted in significant macroeconomic policy changes, public sector restructuring and reduced social provision, with negative effects on education, health and social services for the poor: 'The majority of studies in Africa, whether theoretical or empirical, are negative towards structural adjustment and its effects on health outcomes' (Breman & Shelton, 2001).

Health Sector Reform

Health sector reform was introduced in the late 1980s. It was a reflection in the health sector of the dominant economic policies of the 'Washington Consensus' era, including key features of globalization: the dominance of market forces, the transformation of production systems and labour markets, the integration of the global economy (including insurance), and pressure on governments to reduce budgets and increase internal efficiency. In most cases, health sector reform includes the following component areas (Cassels, 1995, 1997; Breman & Shelton, 2001):

- Actions to improve the performance of the civil service;
- Decentralization of management responsibility and/or provision of health care to the local level;
- Actions to improve the efficiency of the national ministry of health;
- Universal delivery of a core set of essential services;
- Broadening health financing options – e.g. user fees, insurance schemes; introduction of managed competition between providers of clinical and support services;
- Working with the private sector through contracting, regulating and franchising different service providers; and
- Adopting sector-wide approaches to aid rational planning.

Health sector reform was seen as an intervention that would increase the efficiency and improve the functioning of health systems. At the start of the twenty-first century, an assessment of progress is, however, sobering. Questions have been raised about the sustainability of mass vaccination campaigns (Hall & Cutts, 1993), the effectiveness of health-facility-based growth monitoring (Chopra & Sanders, 1997), and the appropriateness of oral rehydration therapy (ORT) when promoted as sachets or packets and without a significant strengthening of health system infrastructure and corresponding emphasis on nutrition, water and sanitation (Werner & Sanders, 1997). For example, although Ethiopia has managed to increase polio vaccination coverage to approximately 80 per cent in 2001 from less than ten per cent in 1992, largely as a result of vaccination campaigns, five suspected cases of polio have been reported recently in a remote area (IRIN, 2001). A systematic review has pointed out the lack of evidence for the effectiveness of directly observed therapy for TB (DOTS) in the absence of well-functioning health services and community engagement (Volmink & Garner, 1997). Only when these core service activities are embedded in a more comprehensive approach (which includes paying attention to social equity, health systems and human capacity development), are real and sustainable improvements in the health status of populations seen (Halstead *et al.*, 1985; Fitzroy *et al.*, 1990).

Human Resources for Health: A Key Challenge

In many African countries, tertiary health facilities (teaching and specialist hospitals) have continued to retain high proportions of the health budget (Addai & Gaere, 2001). These general trends in resource allocation reflect and have contributed to a misdistribution of staff, many of whom prefer to work in well-resourced tertiary care facilities and in urban areas. Eventually, as these facilities have also deteriorated, they have joined the brain drain into the private sector or to other countries (Dovlo, 1999).

The haemorrhage of health professionals from African countries is easily the single most serious human resource problem facing health ministries today. This drain occurs from developing countries to the developed world but also to the relatively better-off developing countries. For example, South Africa, despite its own emigration problems, is the recipient of large numbers of doctors from other African countries. Some 20 per cent of doctors (approximately 6 000) on the South African Medical Register in 1999 were expatriates (Commonwealth Secretariat, 2001). The population to physician ratios in Africa are amongst the highest in the world: Uganda has one doctor per 24 000 people (Bundred & Levitt, 2000), while vacancy rates for physicians in Ghana, Lesotho, Namibia and Malawi were 42.6 per cent, 7.6 per cent, 26 per cent and 36.3 per cent respectively in 1998 (Dovlo, 2001; Dovlo & Nyonator, 1999; Browne, 2000; WHO Lesotho Country Team, 1994).

The recipient countries of the 'brain drain' are few. Agreements to manage the process and the numbers as well as the involvement of the 'exporting' countries in the recruitment and selection process could ameliorate the situation and ensure some remittance of earnings. For example, in 1996 and 1998, Ghana's Ministry of Health entered into agreements with the Ministry of Health in Jamaica and with some recruitment agencies in the United Kingdom, aimed mainly at restricting numbers recruited so as to avoid collapse of services and to ensure health professionals' return after an agreed period (Commonwealth Secretariat, 2001).

The NEPAD Report Card Project

Structure of NEPAD

The NEPAD document contains the following sections:
* Introduction;
* Africa in today's world;
* The new political will of African leaders;
* Appeal to the peoples of Africa;
* Programme of action;
* A new global partnership;
* Implementation of the New Partnership for Africa's Development;
* Conclusion.

NEPAD's Programme of Action is divided into three sections, which deal with:
a) Conditions for sustainable development (including peace, security, democracy, and political and economic governance);
b) Sectoral priorities (including infrastructure, human resource development (which includes poverty reduction, education, the brain drain and health), agriculture, environment, culture, science and technology); and
c) Mobilizing resources (including capital flows and market access).

Health is not NEPAD's primary focus; development is. The main goal is to eradicate poverty by meeting the IDGs formulated in 1999 for the new millennium. Nonetheless, NEPAD does contain health commitments that are explicitly recognised, as well as non-health factors that are explicitly acknowledged as having an impact on health.

These acknowledgements are important, because NEPAD is not being assessed in terms of criteria that have been externally imposed on it. The authors of NEPAD themselves recognize the interconnectedness of health and development.

Basic Principles of NEPAD: Neo-liberal Macroeconomic Policies

NEPAD in its overall thrust appears to accept uncritically a neo-liberal economic paradigm. While we cannot engage in detail with all of the aspects and implications of this, it is of concern that, for example in NEPAD, para. 24, SAPs are presented as having provided a 'partial solution' and that some 'countries achieved sustainable higher growth under [SAPs]' – whereas there is much evidence that SAPs have had a negative impact on both the economies of African countries and their health sectors, as described in earlier sections of this report (Breman & Shelton, 2001; Bijlmakers *et al.*, 1996).

The NEPAD position on globalization is not always clear. Some paragraphs clearly contradict each other:

> para. 28: While globalization has increased the cost of Africa's ability to compete, we hold that the advantages of an effectively managed integration present the best prospects for future economic prosperity and poverty reduction.
>
> para. 40: Experience shows that, despite the unparalleled opportunities that globalization has offered to some previously poor countries, there is nothing inherent in the process that automatically reduces poverty and inequality.

Conception, Design and Formulation, and Consultation Process

The NEPAD document is a merger of two separately conceived plans, the Millennium Africa Recovery Plan (MAP) developed by South Africa, and the OMEGA plan, developed by the Senegalese Head of State. The OMEGA plan largely focused on infrastructural improvements, while MAP focused on economic policies aimed at sustainable development through stimulating economic growth on the continent. The formulation and subsequent merger of the two plans into NEPAD were achieved without participation of ordinary African citizens. Consultation with African civil society and think tanks only started after NEPAD and its predecessors had been presented at the Genoa G8 summit of 2001 and the World Economic Forum in New York in 2002 (Bond, 2002). Despite the fact that many Africans have yet to make their first telephone call, the NEPAD document was, until recently, only accessible through NEPAD's web site. Furthermore, NEPAD sectoral implementation plans have not been made available to the public. Only in July 2002 were hard copies of NEPAD's Initial Action Plan and the Summary of the NEPAD Action Plan available. Detailed sectoral plans are currently being formulated, but again, civil society is largely precluded from participating in this process.

Position of NEPAD on Health

The position taken throughout the NEPAD document is that health is a means to achieve economic growth. It does not clearly recognize health as a basic human right or as an outcome of equitable development. The following paragraphs are indicative of this position:

> para. 64: The challenge for Africa ... is to develop the capacity to sustain growth at levels required to achieve poverty reduction and sustainable development. This, in turn, depends on other factors such as infrastructure ... human capital ... health, and good stewardship of the environment.

> para. 128: Health ... contributes to increase in productivity and, consequently, to economic growth. The most obvious effects of health improvement ... are the reduction in lost working days ... the increase in productivity ... and the chance to secure better-paid jobs.

Living and working conditions, social service delivery and food security have not improved for a large number of African people, and the majority live below absolute poverty levels. 'Old' diseases, such as TB and malaria, and 'new' diseases, in particular HIV/AIDS, affect large numbers of people, while African countries' health systems have been undermined to the extent that they are unable to provide even for the most basic health needs of their populations (Simms *et al.*, 2001; Sanders *et al.*, 2002).

NEPAD does not pay sufficient attention to these issues. While NEPAD in its health-sector objectives and actions 'encourages African countries to give higher priority to health in their own budgets and to phase in such increases in expenditure to be mutually determined,' it is difficult to see how this will happen in the current economic climate on the continent. As Stephen Lewis, UN special envoy for HIV/AIDS, recently said about NEPAD,

> '[f]or all its talk of trade, and investment, and governance, and corruption, and matters relating to financial architecture, there is only pro forma sense of the social sectors, only modest reference to the human side of the ledger. And in a fashion quite startling, in fact disturbingly startling, NEPAD hardly mentions HIV/AIDS at all. ... unless we deal with HIV/AIDS, all the proud declarations of NEPAD are doomed (Lewis, 2002).

NEPAD Statements and Commitments Explicitly Relevant to Health

This section considers the overarching goals of NEPAD's Programme of Action (para. 68) that concern the IDGs directly related to health as well as para. 123 (objectives for the health sector) and para. 121 (reversing the brain drain). The last has been included here because personnel are a vital component of health systems.

International Development Goals (NEPAD, para. 68)

The NEPAD Programme of Action is the 'new and radical' approach for Africa (NEPAD, para. 70). It aims to achieve a seven per cent annual GDP growth rate, and the International Development Goals (IDGs) (NEPAD, para. 68). The IDGs are considered a standard by which to measure progress (World Bank, 2001b: 3). However, the World Bank, in the same document, acknowledges that sub-Saharan Africa is unlikely to achieve the poverty reduction goal:

> Even if we achieve the goal of cutting global poverty rates in half, the number of people living in extreme poverty will fall by only one third. China and India will see the largest improvements, but in Sub-Saharan Africa the number will rise. ... If they [China and India] do [maintain average GDP per capita growth of 3.7 per cent per annum], the goal of reducing poverty rates to half the 1990 level will be achieved in all regions except sub-Saharan Africa.

As shown earlier in this chapter, the three IDGs that deal with health directly – reduction in infant and under-five mortality rates, reduction in maternal mortality ratios and universal access to reproductive health services – are unlikely to be achieved. The necessary conditions for achieving a significant reduction in infant and under-five mortality continue to involve not only improved health services, but also provision of adequate water, sanitation and housing; addressing food insecurity and consequent malnutrition; education, in particular improving participation of girls in schooling; and, last but not least, dealing with the HIV/AIDS pandemic and conflicts.

Public sector health spending has increased, but in most countries remains far below minimum recommended levels. Governments have been unable to provide adequate health services because of inadequate funding in the face of an increased demand owing to HIV/AIDS, high attrition rates of health personnel due to high HIV prevalence levels, and increasing migration of health professionals to developed countries. Other communicable disease control programs have not seen an increase in funding, be it from national governments or from foreign donors, apart from the recently launched GFATM and the Global Alliance for Vaccines and Immunization.

Infant and Under-Five Mortality Rates

The World Bank states that the IDGs' target of a two-thirds reduction in infant and under-five mortality rates will depend on:

* Halting the spread of HIV/AIDS;
* Increasing the capacity of developing countries' health systems to deliver more health services; and
* Ensuring that technological progress in the medical field spills over to benefit the developing world (World Bank, 2001a).

Comparisons of declines in IMR and U5MR globally and in sub-Saharan Africa is shown in Tables 9.10 and 9.11.

Table 9.10: % Declines in IMR, 1960–99

	IMR 1960–81	% decline 1960–81	IMR 1981–99	% decline 1981–99	% decline 1960–99
World	127 to 78	38.5	78 to 57	26.9	55.1
Sub-Saharan Africa	156 to 126	19.2	126 to 107	15.1	31.4

Source: UNICEF (1983, 1993, 2000)

Table 9.11: % Declines in U5MR, 1960–99

	U5MR 1960–81	% decline 1960–81	U5MR 1981–99	% decline 1981–99	% decline 1960–99
World	198 to 91	54	91 to 82	9.9	58.6
Sub-Saharan Africa	258 to 203	21.3	203 to 173	14.8	32.9

Source: UNICEF (1983, 1993, 2000)

Dramatic improvements occurred during the period between 1960 and 1999, e.g. in medical technologies such as in diagnostic equipment, equipment and drugs for treatment, vaccines, access to water and sanitation, and education. However, the global gains in IMR and U5MR during these 40 years are still below what the IDGs aim for during the 25-year period between 1990 and 2015. The gains on the African continent during this 40-year period amounted to 33 per cent – significant progress, but still 50 per cent below the IDG target set for the period between 1990 and 2015.

Maternal Mortality

The challenges of meeting the IDG target of a 75 per cent reduction in the maternal mortality ratio (MMR = maternal deaths per 100 000 live births) are similarly far removed from reality. Many women still lack access to health services to monitor pregnancies and receive adequate obstetrical care. Accuracy of reported information on maternal deaths continues to be a major cause for concern. Testimony to this is that almost all African countries report

MMR in units of hundreds. Maternal deaths and MMRs are not reported by all countries and are generally based on reports from national authorities. Only periodically do the WHO and UNICEF evaluate the situation on antenatal and obstetrical care to make adjustments for acknowledged problems of under-reporting (in particular in countries with inadequate access to health services) and misclassification, i.e. deaths of women of reproductive age that are not specifically related to pregnancy or delivery.

Data provided by the UNDP are incomplete, but show the following:
* In countries with high Human Development Index rank (46 countries, no African country), MMR ranges between 0 and 150, with the majority of countries reporting an MMR <10.
* In countries with medium Human Development Index rank (93 countries, 22 African countries), MMR ranges between 0 and 600.
* In countries with low Human Development Index rank (35 countries, 29 sub-Saharan African countries), MMR ranges between 350 and 1 100 (UNDP, 2000).

The *World Development Indicators 2002* provides 1995 data which are 'modeled estimates' (World Bank, 2002d), i.e. are estimated with a statistical method using data on fertility, birth attendance and HIV prevalence. Using this method, the MMRs range between two and 2 300. Unfortunately, trend data that would allow measuring progress in reaching the IDGs target are not available. The World Bank 1995 data show that in 39 of the 50 African countries with available data, the MMR is higher than 500 maternal deaths per 100 000 live births.

Table 9.12: Maternal Deaths/100 000 Live Births

1995 MMR	Number of countries
<100	3
100–500	8
500–1 000	18
>1 000	21

Source: World Bank (2002d)

Access to Reproductive Health Services for All Who Need Them by 2015

Reproductive health care includes a large number of services. The only indicator introduced to measure progress towards achieving this target is contraceptive prevalence. This indicator should be considered inadequate, because it measures both 'modern' and 'traditional' contraceptive methods, it often excludes unmarried women and it excludes men as users of contraceptive methods. Apart from MMR and contraceptive prevalence, data on the number of births attended by skilled health personnel are collected, but are scant. No data are available for 13 of the 53 countries, while trend data are only available for 19 of the 40 countries with data from either 1990 or 1999. The available data show that an increase in births attended by skilled health personnel occurred in 11 countries, while eight countries showed a reduction. However, the percentage of births attended by skilled health workers is below 50 per cent in 13 of the 22 countries with 1999 data. In nine countries, this percentage is above 50 per cent, with four countries having a percentage higher than 80.

The above evidence raises questions about the wisdom/value of adopting the IDGs in NEPAD's Programme of Action. The usefulness of setting goals is not in dispute and it would be difficult for Africa not to endorse the IDGs, as it would exclude Africa from the rest of the world. However, the goals of a program of action need to be realistically achievable, and it is not clear that NEPAD has recognized the seriousness of the constraints on achieving the IDGs.

The Health Sector in NEPAD

NEPAD's Programme of Action deals with health and the health sector in its paragraphs 123, 124, 125, 126 and 128. The objectives and plan of action for the health sector can be found in paragraphs 123 and 124. However, the most important articles that underpin NEPAD objectives for the health sector are the following:

> Health, defined by the WHO as a state of complete physical and mental well-being, contributes to increase in productivity and, consequently, to economic growth. The most obvious effects of health improvement on the working population are the reduction in lost working days due to sick leave, the increase in productivity and the chance to secure better-paid jobs. Eventually, improvement in health and nutrition directly contributes to improved well-being as the spread of diseases is controlled, infant mortality rates are reduced and life-expectancy is higher. The link with poverty reduction is clearly established (NEPAD, para. 128).

In the health sector, Africa compares very poorly with the rest of the world. In 1997, child and juvenile [*sic*] death rates were 105 and 169 per 1,000, as against 6 and 7 per 1,000 respectively in developed countries. Life expectancy is 48.9 years, as against 77.7 years in developed countries. Only 16 doctors are available per 100,000 inhabitants, as against 253 in industrialised countries. Poverty, reflected in very low per capita incomes, is one of the major factors limiting the population's capacity to address their health problems (NEPAD, para. 126).

Africa is home to major endemic diseases. Bacteria and parasites carried by insects, the movement of people and other carriers thrive, favoured as they are by weak environmental policies and poor living conditions. One of the major impediments facing African development efforts is the widespread incidence of communicable diseases, in particular HIV/AIDS, tuberculosis and malaria. Unless these epidemics are brought under control, real gains in human development will remain an impossible hope (NEPAD, para. 125).

One of the most telling statements in these paragraphs is related to the direct link NEPAD makes between the strength of the health sector and infant and under-five mortality and life expectancy. It is clear that the health sector has a role in and can contribute to the reduction of IMR and U5MR and in increasing life expectancy. However, most determinants of health and ill-health lie outside of the health sector, as we have pointed out above. There is also a strong reliance on the GFATM to provide the necessary funds. The GFATM is one of two recently established joint public and private initiatives (JPPIs) that bring together public and corporate funding in the fight against these diseases. Are these JPPIs an opportunity or a threat for Africa?

The Global Fund for the Fight against AIDS, Tuberculosis and Malaria

While the establishment of the GFATM is welcome, there is concern that Africa's mixed experience of health policy implementation in the past 20 years should inform the utilization of these new resources. As a recent *British Medical Journal* editorial stated, '[t]he dominant fear ... was that this new public-private partnership fund would (yet again) be donor led. As a result undue emphasis would be put on supplying drugs rather than building up capacity to implement and sustain effective treatment and preventive programmes' (Richards, 2001). What is as yet unclear is how the GFATM will achieve its goals in the absence of strong health systems, resulting from undermining by cuts in public expenditure under the SAPs, the health sector reforms, and international policies and agreements that have led to increased migration of skilled health workers from the public to the private sector and from developing to developed countries.

Many agree that prevention efforts have to be given emphasis in the absence of cures and limited access to therapy. However, many also acknowledge that HIV/AIDS, TB and malaria are 'straining an already frayed health infrastructure' with 75 per cent of AIDS deaths, 22 per cent of TB deaths and 90 per cent of malaria deaths occurring in sub-Saharan Africa, where ten per cent of the world's population lives (WHO, 2002d). The sustainability of the GFATM's efforts is also questioned: 'Long-term sustainability can only be achieved if the fund can be used to support system development and improve the delivery of health services' (Ireland & Webb, 2001). This view was supported by Stephen Lewis in a speech at the People's Summit in Calgary: 'The importance of health services is re-emerging as pivotal for their role in dispensing commodities and care and ensuring therapy adherence by people living with these infections. Health facilities must be re-vitalised' (Lewis, 2002).

The Global Alliance for Vaccines and Immunization (GAVI)

This initiative, supported by the Bill and Melinda Gates Foundation, was launched in January 2000. The first disbursements were made in 2000–01. The reservations expressed in the context of GAVI were similar to those for the GFATM: success will, to a large extent, depend on the strength of health systems to deliver routine vaccination services (Starling *et al.*, 2002). Experience shows that those reservations were justified: 90 per cent of funds were allocated to the introduction of new vaccines (DPT + Hep B or DPT + Hep B + HIB) and single-use injection materials, while only ten per cent of funds were allocated to strengthening vaccination services (Hardon, 2001). GAVI funds are disbursed through a separate fund, not via the sector-wide approaches for health and development (SWAps) basket funding mechanisms, because of possible delays in the implementation of the program. But more importantly, countries only receive funding through GAVI if new vaccines (either the quadravalent or pentavalent vaccine) and single-use syringe needles + disposal boxes are accepted. The support for health systems mainly concerns training of staff involved in vaccination service delivery. As one bilateral donor put it, '[a]lthough GAVI is integrated into routine immunization, it comes with a vertical training programme .... Donors encourage global initiatives that run counter to a systems approach and do not build capacity in governments .... GAVI runs the risk of being too much about commodities and supply, with insufficient emphasis on systems' (Starling *et al.*, 2002).

Also in the context of GAVI, serious concerns have been raised about long-term sustainability: the additional costs of the introduction of the new pentavalent vaccine for the national vaccination programme in Ghana are estimated at US$7.1 million. In Tanzania, estimated Expanded Programme on Immunization costs (for vaccine supply) would rise from US$2.2 million to US$9.9 million with the inclusion of quadravalent vaccine (Starling *et al.*, 2002).

One can conclude that the two funds have managed to garner much-needed support for interventions to tackle an important group of communicable diseases that mainly, although not exclusively, affect poor populations, many of whom live on the African continent. However, the issue of long-term sustainability has been studied inadequately, in particular given the current weakness of health systems on the continent. The focus on 'Global Fund diseases' could once again lead to vertical programs and a focus on technologies in isolation from health systems.

Health Sector Objectives

The health-sector objectives read as follows (NEPAD, para. 123):

- To strengthen programmes for containing communicable diseases, so that they do not fall short of the scale required in order to reduce the burden of disease;
- To have a secure health system that meets needs and supports disease control effectively;
- To ensure the necessary support capacity for the sustainable development of an effective health care delivery system;
- To empower the people of Africa to act to improve their own health and to achieve health literacy;
- To successfully reduce the burden of disease on the poorest people of Africa;
- To encourage co-operation between medical doctors and traditional healers.

The above six health sector objectives are not logically ordered, and unclear formulations are introduced, such as 'secure' health systems and 'health literacy.'

It is proposed that NEPAD change the sequence of objectives to:

- To improve work and living conditions of Africa's population (this would include objectives related to water and sanitation, housing, environment, etc.);
- To strengthen health systems so that these meet needs and support disease control effectively;

- To strengthen programs for containing communicable diseases, so that they do not fall short of the scale required in order to reduce the burden of disease;
- To ensure the necessary support capacity for the sustainable development of an effective health-care delivery system;
- To empower the people of Africa to act to improve their own health and to achieve health literacy; and
- To encourage cooperation between medical doctors and traditional practitioners.

Proposed Health Sector Actions

The proposed health-sector actions (NEPAD, para. 124) read as follows:

- Strengthen Africa's participation in processes aimed at procuring affordable drugs, including those involving the international pharmaceutical companies and the international civil society, and explore the use of alternative delivery systems for essential drugs and supplies;
- Mobilize the resources required to build effective disease interventions and secure health systems;
- Lead the campaign for increased international financial support for the struggle against HIV/AIDS and other communicable diseases;
- Join forces with other international agencies such as the World Health Organisation (WHO) and donors to ensure that support for the continent is increased by at least US $10 billion per annum;
- Encourage African countries to give higher priority to health in their own budgets and phase in such increases in expenditure to a level to be mutually determined;
- Jointly mobilize resources for capacity-building in order to enable all African countries to improve their health infrastructures and management.

It is proposed that the above actions be rearranged and modified to read as follows:

- Mobilize the resources required to strengthen (build effective disease interventions and secure) health systems;
- Encourage African countries to give higher priority to health in their own budgets and to phase in such increases in expenditure to a level to be mutually determined;
- Strengthen Africa's participation in processes aimed at procuring affordable drugs and explore the use of alternative delivery systems for essential drugs and supplies; and

- Jointly mobilize resources for capacity-building in order to enable all African countries to improve their health infrastructures and management.

It is further proposed that the following two action points be combined:
- Lead the campaign for increased international financial support for the struggle against HIV/AIDS and other communicable diseases;
- Join forces with other international agencies such as the WHO and donors to ensure that support for the continent is increased by at least US$10 billion per annum.

For NEPAD to make a meaningful contribution towards the health of African people, it is further proposed:
- That the IDGs be translated into realistic African Development Goals that take into account the starting point and are measured against compliance to pledges and commitments made by NEPAD and G8/OECD member states;
- That the introduction of the JPPIs (GFATM and GAVI) be carried out with a strong focus on the strengthening of health systems, as these are essential and a prerequisite if these initiatives are to succeed;
- That research and development focuses on relevant health technologies and health systems' performance; and
- That investment be mobilized for partnerships with NGOs and civil society, and with training institutions.

The most important action of NEPAD should focus on strengthening health systems so that health-care needs of the population can be met and underlying socio-economic determinants of ill health are addressed. This implies health systems that are inclusive of effective disease interventions, and are comprehensive in nature.

Reversing the Brain Drain

A critical component of health systems is human resources. As noted in Chapter 3, the growing loss of skilled health workers through international migration has become a major policy issue for developing countries. NEPAD has made the reversal of the brain drain one of its priorities (paras. 121–2) in its Human Resource Development Initiative, which is welcomed. A variety of economic and social factors affect the retention and equitable distribution of human resources. In many African countries, health professionals are concentrated in urban areas, while the majority of people live in rural areas. Migration of health professionals, in particular physicians and nurses, from developing to developed countries is a problem that is increasingly being recognized globally. According to Pang *et al.* (2002), an estimated 23 000 qualified academic professionals (not only health professionals) emigrate from Africa annually, a figure substantiated by research carried out on the African continent (IRIN, 2002b).

Factors that contribute to migration are many and are classified in two groups: the 'push' and 'pull' factors. Push factors refer to the situation in the exporting country and include remuneration, capacity to produce adequate numbers of health professionals, support and supervision, work and living conditions, social and political security, post-colonial and cultural links, and a tradition of mobility (Dovlo, 2001; Commonwealth Secretariat, 2001). Pull factors relate to conditions in importing countries and include the high demand for health professionals, job and career opportunities, remuneration differentials, training opportunities, and perceived freedom from undue political and administrative influences on matters professional (Dovlo, 2001; Commonwealth Secretariat, 2001; IRIN, 2002b).

GATS, recently introduced by the WTO, sets out to liberalize trade in services, including trade in health services (WTO, 1995; Hong, 2000). GATS includes four different modes of supply of trade in services. Mode 4 concerns migration directly, as it refers to the supply of a service 'by a service supplier of one Member, through presence of *natural persons* of a Member in the territory of any other Member' (WTO, 1995, emphasis in original; Bettcher *et al.*, 2000; WHO, 2001; Adlung & Carzaniga, 2001). GATS's mode 2 refers to 'consumption of services abroad' and includes under- and postgraduate training at foreign educational institutions. Mode 2 is a contributor to migration: some data indicate that as many as 50–70 per cent of persons who received such training opportunities failed to return home after completion (Dovlo, 2001; Hilary, 2001; Adlung & Carzaniga, 2001).

The costs for undergraduate training of health professionals are mainly borne by governments. Data on actual costs of training of doctors available for African countries show that these are considerable: in Ghana, tuition for medical school attendance costs the government an estimated US$20 000 per student (Bundred & Levitt, 2000), Nigeria spends an estimated US$30 000 to train a physician, while South Africa's undergraduate medical training costs approximately US$61 500 (Dovlo, 2001).

The NEPAD objectives to reverse the brain drain are (NEPAD, para. 121):

- To reverse the brain drain and turn it into a 'brain gain' for Africa;
- To build and retain within the continent critical human capacities for Africa's development;
- To develop strategies for utilising the scientific and technological know-how and skills of Africans in the diaspora for the development of Africa.

The first objective is not really an objective, but rather the desired outcome of the initiative. The issues addressed in the third objective need clarification. Different systems have different priorities, which influence the orientation of the skills of professionals. How many Africans in the diaspora still possess the appropriate skills to assist in the implementation of NEPAD's Programme of Action? How will this be assessed? Will this really lead to reversing the brain drain as currently experienced?

Actions related to above objectives are as follows (NEPAD, para. 122):

- Create the necessary political, social and economic conditions in Africa that would serve as incentives to curb the brain drain and attract much needed investment;
- Establish a reliable database on the brain drain, both to determine the magnitude of the problem, and to promote networking and collaboration between experts in the country of origin and those in the diaspora;
- Develop scientific and technical networks to channel the repatriation of scientific knowledge to the home country, and establish cooperation between those abroad and at home;
- Ensure that the expertise of Africans living in the developed countries is utilized in the execution of some of the projects envisaged under NEPAD.

The proposed actions of NEPAD to address the brain drain are welcomed. However, the focus is on Africans in the diaspora, technological and scientific skills, and the push factors leading to migration. No mention is made of international macroeconomic policies and trade agreements that perpetuate the current trend of migration to developed countries, with little gain for the continent. No attention is given to high attrition rates influenced by the high HIV/AIDS infection rates amongst professionals in many sectors, leading to brain loss. Yet, the high attrition rates in these sectors will affect NEPAD's ability to achieve its 'health sector' objectives, in particular the strengthening of health systems.

We therefore propose that NEPAD strengthen its appeal to G8 and OECD member states to assist in reversing the brain drain. In particular, we suggest:

- That G8/OECD member states are called upon to improve their health human resource planning;
- That G8/OECD member states acknowledge the economic benefits they reap from migration; and
- That G8/OECD member states establish mechanisms that ensure full return of developing countries' investments in the production of [health] professionals, in addition to ensuring that trade agreements truly benefit developing countries.

Health-Related, Explicitly Recognized Commitments

Poverty

While growth rates are important, they are not by themselves sufficient to enable African countries to achieve the goal of poverty reduction (NEPAD, para. 64). NEPAD's long-term objective is 'to eradicate poverty in Africa and to place African countries, both individually and collectively, on a path of sustainable growth and development and thus halt the marginalization of Africa in the globalization process' (NEPAD, para. 67).

Africa is unlikely to achieve the IDG target that aims to reduce by 50 per cent the proportion of people living in extreme poverty. The most likely scenario under present macroeconomic arrangements is that the number of people living in extreme poverty on the African continent will increase (World Bank, 2002a: 30–1). Although poverty rates declined during the 1990s, driven by high growth rates in particular in China and, to a lesser extent, India, an estimated 1.2 billion of the world's population live on less than US$1 per day. In 1999, an estimated 575 million Africans lived on less than US$2 daily, with the vast majority – approximately 500 million, or 87.5 per cent – living on less than US$1 per day (calculated using population figures and GDP data from UNDP, 2000).

GDP Growth Rate of Seven Per Cent and Income Inequality

Africa's GDP grew faster during 2001 than that of any other developing region, at a rate of 4.3 per cent, as against 3.5 per cent in 2000. However, the aggregate figure masks wide disparities among countries, and is still well below the seven per cent that is proposed in NEPAD (IRIN, 2002c). Between 1990 and 1998, growth rates were as shown in Table 9.13.

Table 9.13: GDP Growth Rates, 1990–98

GDP growth rate	Number of countries
No data	5 of 53
<0%	7 of 48
0–2%	10 of 48
2–4%	16 of 48
4–7%	13 of 48
>7%	2 of 48

Source: UNDP (2000)

Given this trend during the 1990s, it is questionable how Africa can achieve the NEPAD goal of seven per cent annual growth to be sustained over 15 years and the target of a 50 per cent reduction in extreme poverty, unless massive investment occurs.

Food and Food Production

NEPAD acknowledges the poor state of Africa's agriculture systems (NEPAD, para. 129), an important reason for the food insecurity experienced on the continent. At the time of writing, an estimated 13 million people in Southern Africa are facing serious food shortages because of prolonged drought, political instability, corruption and market-based agricultural reforms (IRIN, 2002d). Agriculture is an important contributor to Africa's GDP, as is shown in Table 9.14, below. The breakdown in the table reflects the fact that agriculture contributes 4.8 per cent to world GDP, an average of 13.5 per cent in developing countries, and an average of 32.7 per cent in all LDCs. In many African countries, agriculture accounts for a greater proportion of GDP than the LDC average.

Table 9.14: Agriculture as % of GDP

Agriculture as % of GDP (1998)	Number of countries	Names of countries
<4.8	4 of 50	Seychelles, South Africa, Botswana and Djibouti
4.8–13.5	11 of 50	Gabon, Mauritius, Namibia, Tunisia, Algeria, Cape Verde, Republic of Congo, Angola, Lesotho, Ghana, Eritrea
13.5–32.7	15 of 50	Swaziland, Morocco, Egypt, Côte d'Ivoire, Zimbabwe, Senegal, Guinea, Zambia, Mauritania, Gambia, São Tomé & Principe, Kenya, Equatorial Guinea, Madagascar, Nigeria
>32.7	20 of 50	Cameroon, Comoros, Togo, Central African Republic, Benin, Rwanda, Sierra Leone, Uganda, Mali, DRC, Niger, Chad, Burkina Faso, Guinea-Bissau, Burundi, Sudan, Tanzania, Malawi, Mozambique, Ethiopia
No data	3 of 53	Libya, Somalia, Liberia

Source: UNDP (2000)

However, the current food crises on the continent are indicative of how fragile the agricultural sector and production remain, exposed as they are to climate change and seasonal influences.

Nutritional Status in Africa

'Nutrition is an important ingredient of good health. The average daily intake of calories varies from 2384 in low-income countries to 2846 in middle-income countries, to 3390 in countries of the Organisation for Economic Co-operation and Development (OECD)' (NEPAD, para. 125). The target of achieving a 50 per cent reduction in global undernutrition by 2015, set at the World Food Summit in 1996, will fail according to the latest report of the UNFAO, and will not even be reached in 2030 (Brough, 2002). Available food security data (Social Watch, 2002) provide trends between 1990 and 1999. These data show that 42 countries start off with less than 2 300 calories per capita daily, with 24 countries still below the 2 300 calories per capita level in 1999.

As noted in Chapter 5, despite some progress in food security, sub-Saharan Africa is the only region of the world in which child malnutrition is on the increase. In terms of the population as a whole, 34 per cent of the people of sub-Saharan Africa remain undernourished, and the absolute number grew from 167.7 million to 194 million during the 1990s (UNFAO, 2001: 52). In a few countries, increases in undernourishment were dramatic: e.g. during the 1990s, undernourishment increased from 36 per cent to 64 per cent in the DRC, from 48 per cent to 66 per cent to 75 per cent in Somalia (UNFAO, 2001: 52-3).

The current food crises, exacerbated by conflict, HIV/AIDS, and political and economic mismanagement (Brough, 2002) and aggravated by protectionist measures in the industrialized countries (agricultural subsidies in particular), do not bode well for NEPAD's aim to achieve food security, to improve agricultural performance and achieve a 50 per cent reduction in undernutrition.

Conclusion

Given the sobering reality on the African continent with regard to health and development, NEPAD has set itself targets that are impossible to achieve without a fundamental change in the current global and African economic context. The unequivocal support the G8 extended to the NEPAD initiative during the Kananaskis summit has not been translated into monetary support. The G8 Plan of Action has promised aid and debt relief as well as support for democracy, human rights and the promotion of the equality of women. This plan further proposes the supply of life-saving drugs and the eradication of polio by 2005 to assist in achieving the health objectives. This falls far short of the commitments required.

NEPAD has been presented as a plan 'by Africans for Africa.' It needs to refocus on how it deals with the issues outlined earlier in this chapter. Where it concerns health, we propose that the overall NEPAD goal be changed to the following: 'To successfully reduce the burden of disease on the poorest people of Africa.' We further recommend:

- That the IDGs be translated into realistic African Development Goals that take into account the baseline indicators, and that progress towards achievement is carefully monitored;
- That restoring and strengthening health systems to meet the health-care needs of the population and addressing underlying socioeconomic determinants of ill health become the focus of its health strategy;
- That a strong health system should utilize effective technologies, but be comprehensive in nature, including preventive and promotive actions;
- That there be more investment in health and health-related sectors' infrastructure and recurrent expenditure;
- That particular attention be paid to health and health-related personnel, including retention strategies, training, support and supervision; and
- That commitments to NEPAD by G8 member states and NEPAD signatories be monitored against commitments made by G8 and African Union member states.

We conclude that, without challenging the causes of poverty and inequity and without addressing the functioning of health systems, NEPAD's health project as currently conceived is unlikely to achieve its goals.

CHAPTER TEN

Promises Kept and Broken, Right or Wrong

Drawing the poorest countries into the global economy is the surest way to address their fundamental aspirations. ... The most effective poverty reduction strategy is to maintain a strong, dynamic, open and growing global economy (Genoa Communiqué, para. 3).

Experience shows that, despite the unparalleled opportunities that globalisation has offered to some previously poor countries, there is nothing inherent in the process that automatically reduces poverty and inequality (NEPAD, para. 40).

It is becoming increasingly clear that globalization, as the US is promoting it, is intensely unpopular. Why...? The answer is that globalization, American-style, has left many of the poorest in the developing world even poorer (Stiglitz, 2002b: 18–19).

We must question the prevailing logic of a system that essentially enables the movement of capital, but not of people, across boundaries; a financial system that essentially rewards unemployment and consolidates a notion of jobless economic growth; a system that rewards rampant over-consumption rather than grappling with the more complex challenge of sustainable development. Instead, we continue to witness the extension of market principles into more and more realms and a stubborn reluctance to rethink the TINA (There Is No Alternative) principle. In my part of the world, there is a Zulu name, THEMBA, which means hope. We use this to remind ourselves that 'There Must Be An Alternative' (Naidoo, 2003).

Introduction

In this, our concluding chapter, we summarize our responses to the two questions that run through this book: Have the G8 countries kept their promises? Are the prescriptions the G8 promotes for global integration the right ones for health and development? (Or, returning to the synopsis on this question presented in Chapter 1, for *whose* health and development are they the right prescription?) We also identify some important issues to which we have given only cursory attention – these present fertile ground for further study. We conclude with some thoughts about the prospects for a global order that places markets in the service of human development, rather than the other way around.[1]

Promises Kept, Promises Broken

Few international development observers believe the 2002 Kananaskis summit delivered on any of the key health and human development goals its host country, Canada, had intended and African countries, in particular, had hoped for. The summit was preoccupied with a narrow, military definition of security, committing its members to 'raise up to [US]$20 billion ... over the next 10 years' for 'the destruction of chemical weapons, the dismantlement of decommissioned nuclear submarines, the disposition of fissile materials and the employment of former weapons scientists' (G8 Global Partnership Against the Spread of Weapons and Materials of Mass Destruction Fund). While ridding the world of such weapons may be an important task, by contrast, and including funds committed before the summit, Africa and NEPAD walked away with a much smaller US$6 billion pledge.

But the Kananaskis summit is not the focus of this book; rather, it is the three summits leading up to the 2002 G8 meeting. As our earlier chapters recount, promises 'broken' outnumber those 'kept'; indeed, the final tally is a failing ratio of 2:1. Table 10.1, below, is our 'report card' in its most distilled form, including both explicit (specific) and implicit (generic) commitments, with the chapters in which we made the assessment.

Table 10.1: 'Report Card' on G8 Promises Kept and Broken

Promises kept (9)	Chapter	Promises broken (18)	Chapter
New funding was provided for enhanced debt relief.	2	HIV/AIDS, tuberculosis and malaria mortality rates are unlikely to be reduced by 25%, 50% and 50% respectively (partly because GFATM contributions are far below the amount required).	3
The PRSP process is now used by multilateral institutions (World Bank and IMF). (Although the PRSP process is widely critiqued for its macroeconomic assumptions that replicate many of the – now largely discredited – SAL conditions.)	2	Work towards IDGs through enhanced and effective development assistance is not occurring (ODA levels are far below the amounts required).	3

Debt relief is freeing up social spending space in LDCs.	2	Flexibility in TRIPS agreement, and eased access to essential medicines in poorest countries is not being fully supported (US refuses to accept compromise in TRIPS Council of WTO).	3
The GFATM was established and 'primed' with US$1.3 billion initial contributions.	3	'Strong' national health systems are not being supported (G7 ODA to health lower now than in 1996–98).	3
Agricultural biotechnology for increasing crop yields is being promoted (although use of genetically modified food crops in agriculture or food aid is opposed by many developing nations).	5	Multilateral banks have not increased their support to global public goods.	3
The IDA (part of the World Bank lending to poorest countries) was replenished with US$22 billion.	6	Universal primary education and gender equality education goals will not be met (G7 ODA to education, especially basic education, very low; even with new ODA pledges, the total is less than 10% the estimate of the required aid).	4
The portion of IDA going to grants increased – but not to the level some G8 countries wanted.	6	Support to UNESCO's basic education efforts has not occurred; the agency's funding, much of it supplied by the G6 (the US still does not fund UNESCO), has declined in recent years.	4

Poorest countries received increased portion of ODA budgets, 2000–01.	6	Nutrition-related targets of the IDGs and MDGs are unlikely to be met (partly because of low level of ODA for agriculture and food aid; partly appropriation of food sources in poor countries for consumers in G8 countries, notably the EU and Japan).	5
A new round of global trade talks was launched in 2001.	7	Volume of ODA did not increase from 2000 to 2001.	6
		Multilateral banks did not increase their funding for health, education and sanitation from 1999–2001.	6
		Poorest countries received less ODA as a percentage of G7 gross national income, 2000–01.	6
		Many G8 countries are opposing developing country positions on new round of global trade talks as a 'development round.'	7
		Duty- and quota-free market access for goods from LDCs is still not fully implemented in G8 countries.	7
		Trade-distorting agricultural subsidies dramatically hurtful to developing countries are still retained by the US, Japan and EU; and in the case of the US, dramatically increased after committing in the WTO Doha meetings to reducing such subsidies.	7

		Bilateral assistance to developing countries for more equitable participation in WTO negotiations is supported by some, but actively opposed by other, G8 nations.	7
		Kyoto Protocol on climate change repudiated by the US; Russia has signed the protocol but not (as of writing, March 2003) ratified it.	8
		Only Canada, Germany and Japan have ratified the Stockholm Convention on Persistent Organic Pollutants.	8
		Only EU G8 countries have ratified the Cartagena Protocol on Biosafety. The US has not even ratified the Convention on Biodiversity.	8

Yet this simple list belies two more basic concerns. Firstly, even the promises 'kept' pale beside the nature of the problems to which they relate. Secondly, and taking the argument one level deeper, are the G8 promises appropriate, or are they rooted in a paradigmatic economic orthodoxy that is positively destructive of human health and well-being?

Promises Right, Promises Wrong

The official statements from G8 summits presuppose that globalization, with its neo-liberal underpinnings, is working for the world's poor. NEPAD, even while adopting most of the premises of neo-liberal development strategy (Bond, 2002), appears less sanguine about the beneficence of the market's 'invisible hand.' Joseph Stiglitz joins the ranks of an increasing number of mainstream economists questioning whether the neo-liberal economic prescription is the right one.

A recent 'scorecard' on the past 20 years of globalization compares numerous health, economic and development indicators for the 'pre-globalization' period (1960–80) and the rapidly globalizing period (1980–2000) (Weisbrot *et al.*, 2001; for a similar analysis, see Milanovic, 2003). During the latter period, GDP growth per capita declined in all countries, but declined most rapidly for the poorest 20 per cent of nations. The rate of improvement in life expectancy declined for all but the wealthiest 20 per cent of nations, indicating increasing global disparity. Infant and child mortality improvements slowed, particularly for the poorest 40 per cent of nations. The rate of growth of public spending on education (as a share of GDP) also slowed for all countries, and the rate of growth for school enrolment, literacy rates and other educational attainment measures slowed for most of the poorest 40 per cent of nations, with the sharpest drop in the poorest 20 per cent.

This study's authors caution that this does not prove a causal link between globalization, or liberalization, and a slowdown in development progress. As most researchers now accept, and as we suggested in Chapter 1, only detailed, multilevel national studies will begin to tease apart causal patterns or relationships. But it certainly calls into question the orthodoxy that underpins the 'global governance' economic platform of the G7. As Weisbrot (2002) recently commented, '[t]he claim that "globalisation has caused extensive poverty" is ... quite reasonable, unless one can show that the structural and policy changes associated with the globalisation of the last two decades have had nothing to do with the economic slowdown of this era.' Milanovic (2003: 673), in his assessment, notes, 'in the first period [1960–78], two out of four poorer regions grew faster than WENAO [Western Europe, North America, Oceania countries], while in the second [1978–98], all of them grew slower than WENAO.'

At the core of many of our critiques of G8 development policies is their adherence to a set of propositions about development derived directly from neo-classical economics, but supported, at best, by weak and highly contested empirical evidence. Milanovic's (2003: 679) critique of these propositions is especially blunt: 'Maintaining that globalization as we know it is the way to go and that, if the Washington consensus policies have not borne fruit so far, they will surely do so in the future, is to replace empiricism with ideology.' Two such propositions deserve special attention because of their implications for health and health policy.

The first, which is found in dogmatic form in the World Bank's 'Social protection sector strategy' paper (Holzmann *et al.*, 2000), holds that the primary justification for social policy is correcting for market failure. In that document, which is especially disturbing because of the World Bank's financial leverage and ideological hegemony, the basic task of social policy is (re)defined, without reference to redistribution, as 'social risk management'

(p. 9). 'In an ideal world with perfectly symmetrical information and complete, well-functioning markets, all risk management arrangements can and should be market-based (except for the incapacitated)' (p. 16). Such market-based arrangements can be either formal, as exemplified by the purchase of insurance (p. 24) or informal, as exemplified by marriage (p. 13). If intervention to help the non-incapacitated poor is justified, it is only because of the market failures resulting from the fact that the poor 'are more vulnerable than other population groups because they are typically more exposed to risk and have little access to appropriate risk management instruments' (p. 10). Some public health measures are justified, according to the World Bank, as is spending on formal education ('the best risk reducer') and on early childhood development services, which 'provide an exceptional opportunity to reduce risks and improve human capital in general' (p. 26). However, within neo-classical economics, such policies are justified not on the basis that they increase human well-being or reduce human suffering, but rather because they correct for market imperfections exemplified by the fact that parents cannot borrow against a child's future earnings to finance his or her education (Cigno *et al.*, 2002: 1581), and will therefore underinvest in education.

The second is that the preferred, and possibly only, route to improved health on a global basis lies through policies that will increase economic growth in the developing world. It is important not to underestimate the importance of growth; indeed, we have emphasized in this book the growth-enhancing potential of a number of policies, notably increased investment in basic health care and the reduction of trade barriers that protect industrialized country markets in agricultural products and textiles. In fact, however, the current development policy model appears to be one that promotes growth only in ways that are (a) consistent with the financial interests of the industrialized world, and (b) require minimal or no redistribution of income and wealth from the rich world to the poor. Certainly, that is the message conveyed by the long-term decline in ODA flows from the G7 countries, even as their wealth has greatly increased.

A variant of this proposition that is seldom articulated, but is implicit in the conditionalities imposed by IFIs, is that long-term gains (in health and other areas) from the adoption of growth-enhancing policies justify the short-term pain associated with structural adjustment and a variety of other policies that undermine key social determinants of health. On a population basis, the evidence is overwhelming that the surest way of improving the health of a population, other things being equal, is to raise its level of income (Sieswerda *et al.*, 2001; World Bank, 1992: 10–12, 50–5; 1993: 7, 34, 39–42). Policies that tolerate or even increase short-term inequalities, so the implicit argument proceeds, are justified so long as they contribute to long-term economic growth at the national level. In a rare instance where this position has been made explicit, World Bank researchers addressing the dramatic declines in health status in Central Europe and the former Soviet Union argue that: '[i]n the long run, the transition towards a market economy and adoption of democratic forms of government should ultimately lead to improvements in health status .... In the short run, however, one could expect that health status would deteriorate' as incomes drop, inequalities widen, stress increases, basic health services break down and already inadequate regulation of environmental and workplace hazards deteriorates (Adeyi *et al.*, 1997: 133).

Advocates of this position might cite Barrington Moore's bleak conclusion that 'the poor bear the heaviest costs of modernization under both socialist and capitalist auspices. The only justification for imposing the costs is that they would become steadily worse without it' (Moore, 1966: 410). However, there is, as we have pointed out, considerable uncertainty about the effectiveness of free markets and open borders as a route to growth. Some of the most conspicuous development success stories of the recent past opted instead for a quite different approach, and no G8 country without a colonial empire followed this path during the early stages of its own industrialization. Even if we concede, for purposes of argument, the validity of the neo-liberal prescription for growth, we must ask: How long is the long term? How long may the pain last, and how severe may it be, before it ceases to be justified by subsequent gains? And in view of such declarations of purpose on the part of the international community as 'the attainment by all peoples of the world by the year 2000 of a level of health that will permit them to lead a socially and economically productive life' (WHO, 1978: para. 5), do the poor majority of the world's people not have a claim to healthy lives that need not be vindicated with reference to their future economic productivity? This is the ethical dimension, the consideration of distributive justice that must be incorporated into current and future critiques of development policy and its relation to human health.

This critique is relevant even to 'progressive' approaches like that of the CMH, which argued for major increases in health-related development assistance, on the basis that investment in health is an investment in future development: it can initiate virtuous cycles of human capital formation and growth. The approach is empirically well grounded, yet without further elaboration it invites a form of triage in which the countries and regions that receive investments in health will primarily be those in which 'development' offers the greatest promise of economic returns for the industrialized world, e.g. because of the availability of expanding consumer markets or the availability of healthy and relatively skilled, yet low-cost labor as an attraction to foreign investors. Even within particular countries, the approach invites distinctions between those populations whose improved health is most likely to yield attractive returns on investment and those people and territories that simply cannot, for a variety of reasons, generate the returns that would justify investing in their health on strictly economic grounds.

John Williamson, who coined the term 'Washington Consensus' to describe official wisdom on development policy *circa* 1989, has noted that in codifying the consensus he 'deliberately excluded from the list anything which was primarily redistributive, as opposed to having equitable consequences as a by-product of seeking efficiency objectives, because [he] felt the Washington of the 1980s to be a city that was essentially contemptuous of equity concerns' (Williamson, 1993: 1329). Our analysis suggests that with some exceptions, the contemptuous attitude to which Williamson referred appears to have diffused throughout the official levels of the G7, and is stronger than ever in post-NAFTA, post-WTO Washington. But *it is not universal,* as shown by the divergence among industrialized country ODA levels, by the fact that some countries have met and surpassed the 0.7 per cent target while US ODA languishes at about one-seventh that amount, and by the research of the NGOs that have played such a prominent role in placing global health concerns on the policy agenda. Future research must not only document the health consequences of the neo-liberal agenda's disdain for redistributive measures that do not offer financial rewards, but challenge that agenda on a conceptual level in terms of what it implies about human worth and worthlessness.

Areas for Further Research

This brings us to consider areas where further research or synthesis could be useful. In addition to those areas identified in previous chapters (privatization and cost recovery as they affect health systems and water infrastructure), we were unable to devote the time and resources necessary to a thorough investigation of labour market flexibility. We discuss each of these below.

1. Labour Market Flexibility, Economic Insecurity and Human Health

Economic insecurity can affect human health in a variety of ways. Most obviously, it can reduce access to prerequisites for health such as education, nutrition and health care (see generally Narayan *et al.*, 2000). Economic insecurity can be associated with increased exposure to hazards on the job: Quinlan *et al.* (2001) reviewed studies of occupational injury and illness in industrialized countries, and found that in 76 of the 93 published studies 'precarious employment' (temporary or contract work, self-employment, telecommuting, part-time work etc.) was associated with an increase in work-related illness or injury. More subtly, the stresses associated with economic insecurity may have negative impacts on health that accumulate during the life course (Carroll *et al.*, 1994; Davey Smith *et al.*, 1994).[2]

The 'flexibilization' of labour is arguably one of the major contributors to economic insecurity, and to income and wealth inequality, especially in the Anglo-American world. Communications from the last few summits are ambivalent on the tension between flexibilization and social provision. On the one hand, there is the view that 'economic performance and social inclusion are mutually dependent' (Genoa Communiqué, para. 32), that 'social safety nets' (Cologne Communiqué, para. 14) are important, and that '[i]t is therefore particularly important to maintain investment in basic social services during times of crisis' (Cologne Communiqué, para. 21). On the other hand, there is an insistence on the need for 'more adaptable labour markets' (Okinawa Communiqué, para. 9) through 'elimination of structural rigidities in labour, capital and product markets, the promotion of entrepreneurship and innovation, investment in human capital, reform of the tax/benefit systems to strengthen economic incentives and encourage employment, and development of an innovative and knowledge-based society' (Cologne Communiqué, paras. 12–13).

The tension between these two objectives is particularly clear in the Cologne Communiqué's reference to the need 'to strike a sustainable balance between social support programs and greater personal responsibility and initiative' (para. 20).[3]

In their domestic social and economic policies, many industrialized countries have resolved the tension firmly in favour of policies that increase insecurity and inequality, whether or not that was the intention. A key text here is US Federal Reserve Board Chairman Alan Greenspan's March 1997 testimony to the Joint Economic Committee of the US Congress, in which he commented as follows:

> Atypical restraint on compensation increases has been evident for a few years now. Almost certainly, it reflects a number of factors, including the sharp deceleration in health care costs and the heightened pressure on firms and workers in industries that compete internationally. Domestic deregulation has also intensified the competitive forces in some industries. But ... I believe that job insecurity has played the dominant role. For example, in 1991, at the bottom of the recession, a survey of workers at large firms by International Survey Research Corporation indicated that 25 percent feared being laid off. In 1996, despite the sharply lower unemployment rate and the tighter labor market, the same survey organization found that 46 percent were fearful of a job layoff (Greenspan, 1997).

In Canada, research conducted for the federal government shows that the economic security of Canada's population as a whole, measured with reference to the risks of unemployment, ill health, single parent poverty and poverty in old age, has deteriorated almost continuously since 1973 (Osberg & Sharpe, 1999: 40–52), even before taking into account the steady rise in household debt levels. A report prepared for the Vanier Institute of the Family, based on Statistics Canada data, found that slight rises in average Canadian family income recorded in the late 1990s, after a decade of steady decline, were entirely the result of the fact that family members were working more hours, and more family members were working (Sauvé, 2001).

The same situation exists in the US, where average working hours per year increased from 1 942 in 1990 to 1 978 per year in 2001 – equivalent to a full extra week of work. This is the highest figure of all industrialized countries. Of other G7 countries, Canadian and Japanese workers put in 100 fewer hours per year, Britons 250 fewer hours, and Germans 500 fewer hours. Nor are productivity and economic growth necessarily dependent on long working hours. During the 1990s, Ireland, the 'Celtic Tiger,' saw its average number of hours worked per year drop from 1 728 to 1 520 (ILO figures cited in Ellison, 2001). Sklar *et al.* (2002) found that, as in Canada, longer working hours in the US are partly a response to declining real wages, particularly for those working near the bottom end of the job market. Inflation-adjusted minimum wage rates in the US in 2001 were only 66 per cent of what they had been in 1968.

Throughout the developing world, the literature similarly documents increases in economic insecurity for large portions of the population as a consequence both of SAPs and of financial crises precipitated by the hypermobility of capital. We provided two examples of this (Zambia and the Indian state of Kerala) in Chapter 1. China offers another, where reportedly over 200 million workers migrating from impoverished rural areas are employed in privately-run factories, often backed by foreign investment, and lacking access to many of the labour protections afforded the 80 million workers still employed in China's shrinking state industries (Pan, 2002). Among workers who may put in 16 hour days for months on end, a new illness is being described: *guolaosi* or, literally, 'overwork death.' This is the other face of precarious employment.

While we advise caution in simple cross-national comparisons, it is nonetheless interesting that the ILO finds a gradient in the annual rate of 'inter-sectoral employment flows' (an indicator of job insecurity) and the rapidity of trade liberalization. Countries liberalizing quickly experienced twice the annual rate of such employment flows (Torres, 2001: 33). A recent study of the effects of IMF programs on income distribution, which the author claims corrects for methodological weaknesses in earlier research, concludes that such programs increase income inequality, primarily by redistributing it from labor to capital (Vreeland, 2002). This effect arises partly from liberalization's impact on previously protected but less efficient (or less heavily subsidized) sectors, the contraction of employment in the public sector, and the imposition of wage freezes and other policies to increase labor market flexibility. These policies may not directly violate ILO core labor conventions, but they do place labor at a disadvantage.

Vreeland further notes that a primary objective of the IMF is 'high quality growth,' defined by former IMF Managing Director Michael Camdessus as occurring when 'the benefits of *positive* economic growth are distributed across *all* income groups' (Vreeland 2002: 133, original emphasis).

> Previous research shows that IMF programs lower economic growth, and this study demonstrates that the adverse effects are concentrated on labor. Indeed, despite negative economic growth, the income of 'the privileged few' increases. Thus, according to the characterization of Camdessus, the form of growth promoted by the IMF must be considered of the 'lowest quality' (Vreeland, 2002: 133).

If Vreeland's findings stand up to further scrutiny, they should inform the position the G8, with their majority of IMF votes, take in future lending decisions.

Box 10.1: Globalization, Labor Standards and the G8

The G8 leaders have made a limited number of commitments that directly address labor standards. In 2000, they 'welcome[d] the increasing cooperation between the International Labour Organisation (ILO) and the International Financial Institutions (IFIs) in promoting adequate social protection and core labour standards. We urge the IFIs to incorporate these standards into their policy dialogue with member countries' (Okinawa Communiqué, para. 16).

The previous year, the G8 leaders stated:

> We commit ourselves to promote effective implementation of the International Labor Organization's (ILO) Declaration on Fundamental Principles and Rights at Work and its follow-up. We also welcome the adoption of the ILO Convention on the Elimination of the Worst Forms of Child Labor. We further intend to step up work with developing countries to improve their capacity to meet their obligations. We support the strengthening of the ILO's capacity to assist countries in implementing core labor standards (Cologne Communiqué, para. 25).

The 2000 G8 labor ministers' meeting in Turin, Italy, part of the 'ramp up' to the Genoa summit in 2001, went even further, committing members to 'enhance respect for core labor standards' (Chair's Conclusions, para. 16).

Labour standards are especially important as elements of a strategy for poverty reduction and health improvement in an international economy increasingly driven by mobile FDI (Watkins, 2002a: 189–96). This is why further research is needed, on an ongoing basis. However, it is noteworthy that only France and the United Kingdom among the G8 have ratified all seven core ILO conventions on labour rights (see Table 10.2, below), especially in light of the earlier G7 commitment made at the Lyons Summit (1996) to 'respect international labor standards' (Dallaire, 2001: 100).

Table 10.2: G8 Labor Relations and Status of Fundamental ILO Conventions

	C 87	C 98	C 100	C 105	C 111	C 138	C 182
Canada	x		x	x	x		x
France	x	x	x	x	x	x	x
Germany	x	x	x	x	x	x	
Italy		x	x	x	x	x	x
Japan	x	x	x			x	x
Russian Federation	x	x	x	x	x	x	
United Kingdom	x	x	x	x	x	x	x
United States				x			x

Source: Ratification status (as of 18 December 2001):
Social Watch (2002: 59–60)

C 87: Freedom of Association and Protection of the Right to Organize
Convention, 1948
C 98: Right to Organize and Collective Bargaining Convention, 1949
C 100: Equal Remuneration Convention, 1951
C 105: Abolition of Forced Labour Convention, 1957

C 111: Discrimination (Employment and Occupation) Convention, 1958
C 138: Minimum Age Convention, 1973
C 182: Worst Forms of Child Labor Convention, 1999

While there is little relationship between union density and ILO ratification – except that the US is low in both – some research finds that it is associated with improved income distribution, employment rates and social policy outcomes under increased liberalization of global markets (Global Social Policy Forum, 2001; Gough, 2001). Although systematic comparative research on the policies of G8 governments towards organized labour is not easy to find, recent work by the International Confederation of Free Trade Unions (ICFTU) strongly suggests that several G8 countries have pursued anti-union policies in the interests of containing public expenditure and/or enhancing private sector competitiveness (ICFTU, 2001, 2002). A few findings from the most recent ICFTU report follow; no data on France or Italy were provided.

Canada: Provinces can limit who has the right to join unions. Strikes are often ended by legislation. Use of replacement workers during strikes is permitted, except in the province of Quebec.

Germany: Civil servants do not have the right to strike. Teachers do not have the right to collective bargaining.

Japan: Public sector workers have very limited trade union rights; Japan has continually ignored ILO recommendations to reform its public sector trade union laws. Restrictions on labour rights also apply to state-run companies.

Russia: Public sector workers have only a limited right to strike. The new labour code favours short-term contracts over long-term employment. Replacement labour during strikes is permitted. Anti-union activity is high, particularly in foreign-owned companies.

UK: The ILO continues to express concern over a continuing ban on all solidarity actions by trade unions; restrictions on the right of unions to enforce democratically decided rules; and use of prison labour.

US: Forty per cent of public sector workers are denied collective bargaining rights, and most public sector workers are denied the right to strike. At least ten per cent of workers organizing unions are illegally fired.

Finally, while welcoming dialogue between the ILO and the IFIs, the G8 have been silent on what role the ILO might play at the WTO. Trade liberalization can have an enormous impact on labour markets, for good or for bad. Informing decisions about the pacing of liberalization, and what domestic regulatory policies might aid in the transition to globally competitive markets, seems

218

inherently logical. Yet the ILO, despite several efforts, has so far been unable to obtain even official observer status at WTO meetings. The economic weight the G8 countries bring to the nominally democratic WTO has not been used to change this situation.

2. Arms Control, the G8 and Africa

The G8 have acknowledged that the international arms trade exacerbates conflict in the developing world and poses an obvious threat to the health and development of people living in, or fleeing, countries in conflict. At Okinawa, the G8 expressed a commitment to reducing the flow of arms exports, particularly to conflict-ridden regions:

> The UN Conference on the Illicit Trade in Small Arms and Light Weapons in All Its Aspects next year requires strong support to ensure a successful outcome, including earliest possible agreement on the Firearms Protocol. We invite the international community to exercise restraint in conventional arms exports, and are committed to work jointly to this end. We invite our Foreign Ministers to examine further effective measures to prevent conflicts (Okinawa Communiqué, para. 73).

The same summit claimed in broadly normative terms that 'poverty can best be overcome in resilient, *peaceful*, and democratic societies' (para. 14). No similar commitment or comments were reiterated the next year in Genoa, perhaps because, according to Amnesty International, the UN Programme of Action 'was stripped of any meaningful human rights protection by countries, including the USA, China and Russia' (Amnesty International, 2002). Not coincidentally, these three countries are the world's leading exporters of arms to developing countries.

The majority of global arms transfers are from developed to developing countries, accounting for 68.3 per cent of all arms sales agreements during the period 1994–2001 (Grimmett, 2002). The US has been the main actor in these arms agreements, receiving US\$35.7 billion for arms transfers to the developing world during the period 1998–2001. Russia, the second largest arms supplier to developing nations, received US\$19.8 billion over the same period. The four major West European arms suppliers (France, the United Kingdom, Germany, Italy) saw their collective share of arms transfer agreements with developing countries drop precipitously from 11.5 per cent of the world's total in 2000, to only 3.1 per cent in 2001, arguably in keeping with the spirit of their Okinawa commitment (Grimmett, 2002).

Africa has been host to some of the most brutal and bloody wars in the past few decades. African states receive the majority of their arms from Russia

(31.5 per cent during 1998–2001) and China (14.3 per cent during the same period). The four European G8 countries were responsible for 2.9 per cent of these arm transfers to Africa, and the US for 2.6 per cent. Total transfers were valued at US$3.5 billion for 1998–2001, an increase from US$2.7 billion during the period 1994–97 (Grimmett, 2002). Once these arms reach Africa, they are often traded among African nations, including those with poor human rights records or perpetrating war crimes. Arms shipments – official or otherwise – facilitate the persistence of civil wars or allow certain governments, such as the Sudanese government, to abuse and attack their own citizenry (Amnesty International, 2002). Amnesty International has repeatedly voiced concern about European nations, particularly Germany and Italy, supplying small arms to African nations guilty of human rights violations. The Horn and Central Africa, areas of high domestic conflict, continue to be armed with weapons supplied by EU member states, although the value has been significantly reduced, from US$700 million in 1985 to less than US$50 million in 1995 (Benson, n.d.).

Canada also has substantially reduced its supply of arms to developing countries, according to official Canadian government figures (Nolen, 2002a). These figures, however, do not include Canada's sales to the United States, the world's largest military exporter, or to the sub-systems that Canada supplies. There are no restrictions on Canadian military sales to the US and neither country is obligated to report any of its cross-border arms trade. Official arms trade figures also only include finished systems, leaving Canada's supply of sub-systems and unfinished parts to developing countries unrecorded (Nolen, 2002a). Another point of concern is Canada's continued arms exports to countries such as Zimbabwe and Indonesia, both of which have very poor human rights records and tenuous political situations (Hurst, 2003). Finally, arms trade figures do not include the military training provided to developing countries by members of the G8. For example, from 1995–98, the US provided military personnel training for at least 34 of Africa's 53 nations, largely under the Pentagon's Joint Combined Exchange Training (JCET) program. This training has been fairly indiscriminate. Many of the African participants in the JCET program have been or are currently engaged in brutal wars. Interestingly, the US has provided military training to opposing factions in the on-going war in the DRC (Hartung & Moix, 2000).

We admit to skimming only the surface of this issue. It is an issue complicated by the frequent use of 'third country' transfers, by which arms sold to a questionable country or regime that, if reported publicly, would be politically embarrassing, are sold to a more 'respectable' country acting as a conduit. One could adopt the stance of the US National Rifle Association – that guns do not kill people, people kill people – which has some merit considering the brutality associated with attacks using simple knives, clubs or machetes in many countries in conflict. Small arms and 'conventional weapons,' however, though only weapons of 'immediate' rather than 'mass' destruction, have the capacity to increase greatly the number of victims per incident. (Think about the shooting incidents at Austin's University of Texas, Montreal's École Polytechnique and Colorado's Columbine High School for a simple demonstration of this point.) The role of the G8 in supplying such weapons to countries in conflict – officially, illicitly or simply indirectly – is, as we have indicated, an important matter for future study.

3. Other Key Research Questions

Besides these two underdeveloped themes, other connections between contemporary globalization, health and development, and G8 commitments and behaviours require more detailed and sustained scrutiny. We have cited, for example, a number of studies that suggest or document the adverse effects of privatization, cost recovery and user fees in developing country health systems (Arhin-Tenkorang, 2000; Collins & Lear, 1995; Leon, 2002; Melgar, 1999; Schoepf *et al.*, 2000; WHO, 2001: 121; Wasserman & Cornejo, 2002; Whitehead *et al.*, 2001; Yong Kim, Shakow *et al.*, 2000; Zarrilli, 2002a). However, time and resource limitations prevented us from carrying out a systematic, authoritative and genuinely multidisciplinary literature review on this topic, nor were we able to locate one in the published literature. Such a review would represent an important contribution to public discussion of development policy and health. It would also need to look beyond health systems *per se* to consider the political economy of social provision as a whole, and the extent to which other economic factors may either mitigate or magnify the effects being observed; i.e. assess its findings against integrating frameworks such as Figure 1.2 in Chapter 1. This is an important part of the broader project of interrogating neo-liberalism.

Labonte and Spiegel (2002), in their discussion of 'inherently global health issues' associated with contemporary globalization, identified several questions in need of more nuanced examination and routine monitoring. Many of these were intimated in several of this book's chapters; we consolidate them in Table 10.3. We also emphasize that this is a very partial and incomplete list. It serves more as notice of the types of questions that have been given too little attention in many of the debates surrounding globalization, and certainly within the communiqués emanating from the G8.

Table 10.3: Priority Burden of Disease Research Questions Associated with Inherently Global Health Issues

Inherently global health issue	Priority burden of disease research questions
Climate change	1. What impact will increasing trade in goods have on fossil fuel consumption and climate change, and related infectious disease rates (e.g. malaria)? 2. What effect is increased fossil fuel consumption having on ground-level ozone production, respiratory illness and motor vehicle accident rates, particularly for poorer and more vulnerable populations?
Biodiversity loss	1. How are indigenous peoples who are more reliant on biodiversity for food, economy and health affected by increased economic harvesting of single foods and forestry crops or species? 2. What are the health effects of genetically modified organisms (GMOs) based on GMO impacts on biodiversity protection and food security?
Water shortage	1. How will the trajectories of the future economic growth of poorer nations affect the safety and sustainable supply of water, and subsequent water-related illnesses? 2. How will water supply and pricing policies reflecting market-based costs affect water access and the burden of disease associated with 'hydrological poverty' for poorer groups, particularly within poorer nations?
Fisheries depletion	1. What are the environmentally mediated human health effects of increased fish farming? 2. How is liberalization in fish products affecting food security for indigenous peoples, or poorer populations partly or wholly reliant on non-commercial fishing, and with what burden of disease outcomes?
Deforestation	1. How is deforestation affecting human health in the short term via changes in disease vectors (e.g. pooling water and malaria), burning (respiratory illness), accidents (particularly in under-regulated nations) and use of herbicides and other chemicals in reforestation?

	2. What are the distributional (poverty, inequality) effects of economic gains associated with deforestation, and how is this affecting health?
Increasing poverty/ inequality	1. What *a priori* conditions allow trade liberalization to promote economic growth in poverty-reducing, disparity-reducing ways?
	2. What compensatory public policies (ranging from retraining, to improved social safety nets, to longer phased-in tariff removals) for 'liberalization shocks' would best maintain health-enhancing social and environmental conditions, including poverty reduction?
	3. What are the long-term implications of increasing inequalities on ethnic conflict or regional warfare, and how is this abetted or constrained by trade liberalization or other macroeconomic interventions?
Financial instability	1. What are the impacts of financial instability on the abilities of governments to provide essential health, education and other health-enhancing services, particularly to the poorest population?
Digital divide	1. What are the occupational and environmental hazards associated with increased production of digital technologies, where are they occurring and who is at greatest risk of exposure?
Taxation	1. What impact is liberalization having on national tax capacities, especially for poorer nations, with what effects on the abilities of governments to provide essential health, education and other health-enhancing services, particularly to the poorest population?
	2. What are the distributional (poverty, inequality) effects of changes in national tax capacities?
Food (in)- security	1. What effects will agricultural export-led development have on poverty and income distribution profiles in poorer nations, public tax regimes and associated social development programs, such as health care and education?
	2. What are the probable environmental effects of increased crop production, particularly for African countries where soil degradation, depletion of nitrogen cycles and water shortages are already severe, and how will this affect medium and longer-term food security and health?

Trade in health-damaging products	1. What is the impact of the Framework Convention on Tobacco Control on reducing trade in and use of tobacco products, tobacco use rates and tobacco-related diseases? 2. What are the health impacts of the increased movement of toxic/hazardous waste between countries, particularly in poorer countries lacking the technology and regulatory capacity to ensure safer disposal?
Governance	1. How are liberalization and macroeconomic adjustment programs affecting governments' abilities to provide health, educational and welfare services or programs to the poorer members of their citizenry? 2. What impact is this having on measures on health status (both absolute and distributional), and the rates of change in these measures? 3. How are trade agreements affecting governments' regulatory abilities to create healthier social and environmental conditions, especially those influencing the burden of disease?
War and conflict	1. How can health-related interventions contribute to primary prevention (averting conflict) and secondary prevention (alleviating the impact of health effects) of war and conflict? 2. What is the relationship between disease rates/pandemics and risk of conflict, and what interventions best mitigate that risk?

Conclusion: The G8 and the Question of Global Governance

We began this book by citing the claim that the G8 is emerging as the centre of effective global governance (Kirton, 1999). This observation was made before the Republicans gained the US Presidency and Congress in 2000, and began to move away from the cautious multilateralism that characterized the previous administration. It nonetheless returns us to a theme we foreshadowed in Chapter 1: the major governance crisis we currently face is one in which there is an

> increasing dissociation between economic power organized on a world basis by global networks of industrial, financial and service enterprises, and political power that remains organized at the national and regional levels only. This dichotomy is rapidly leading to a situation where the world is governed, not only in the economic sphere but in other spheres as well, by groups of private networks of stateless and unaccountable firms (Emmerij, 2000: 61).

Governance, as distinct from *government*, presupposes some form of partnership between elected government representatives or their appointees and individuals representing different stakeholder constituencies. These partnerships can range from being merely consultative and token, to more formal structures, such as the accreditation process used for NGOs by UN agencies such as ECOSOC (the Covenant Committee on Economic, Social and Cultural Rights), to near or full joint decision-making, as in joint ventures or 'private–public partnerships', national or international roundtables or standards-setting bodies such as *Codex Alimentarius*. What constitutes 'good governance' is a matter of much debate; what should be the final architecture of the emerging shapes of global governance even more so. We do not purport to engage in this debate in any detail or with any systematic rigour, assigning that task to the 'further study' category of follow-up. We do offer some initial comments, however, on a few of the key challenges posed by global governance, and the G8's performance to date.

The G8 have commented on at least two different facets of governance. In Genoa, for example, they advocated the idea of 'public–private partnerships' (Genoa Communiqué, para. 13). The '3-Ps', as earlier chapters noted, remains a controversial proposition amongst health scholars, particularly when applied to health and social service delivery (Ollila, 2003; Pollock *et al.*, 2002; for contrasting opinions see Buse & Waxman, 2001; Buse & Walt, 2000). The G8 also concluded their Okinawa summit in 2000 by noting that 'we must engage in a new partnership with ... non-governmental organisations' (Okinawa Communiqué, para. 4). They delivered on this observation the following year, when the Italian government, host of the 2001 summit, funded a two-day meeting with almost 200 representatives from NGOs, the academic community and multilateral organizations. What impact this had on the decision-making during the Genoa summit is not known. This formal consultation process was not, however, adopted by the Canadian government the following year, which, dissuaded by street demonstrators in Genoa and elsewhere, convened the summit in a remote national park with limited access, declared the previously public site off-limits to the public during the summit, and employed a large constabulary to enforce its decision.

The G8 have also weighed in on the 'good governance' debate itself, first in Cologne, where the HIPC debt relief initiative is couched in terms of support for 'good governance (Cologne Communiqué, para. 29), but most clearly, and emulating similar pronouncements from the IFIs, at the Genoa 2002 summit:

> [W]e shall help developing countries promote:
>
> • accountability and transparency in the public sector
>
> • legal frameworks and corporate governance regimes to fight corruption
>
> • safeguards against the misappropriation of public funds and their diversion into non-productive uses
>
> • access to legal systems for all citizens, independence of the judiciary, and legal provisions enabling private sector activity
>
> • active involvement of civil society and Non Governmental Organisations (NGOs)
>
> • freedom of economic activities (Genoa Communiqué, para. 6).

These comments, in contrast to the caution expressed by Emmerij (2000), largely exclude reference to the corporate sector, focusing almost exclusively on the public sector. While few would take exception to these components of good governance, it is revealing that 'freedom of economic activities' warrants special mention, but guarantees of core human or labor rights, or of other existing international conventions with important health and development impacts, *inter alia*, do not.[5] The emphasis on the economic over the social, cultural and environmental reflects the neo-liberal assumptions on which the G8 continue to base much of their deliberations and global prescriptions.

Setting aside our earlier critical comments on these assumptions, the G8's statements on governance are directed either to national levels or, when more global in scope, primarily to the IFIs (but only to encourage them to promote certain qualities of national governance as loan or grant requirements), to the WTO (but only to encourage it to continue the project of global economic liberalization) or to certain other multilateral organizations, such as the ILO or UNESCO (but only to encourage them to 'keep up the good work'). The larger question of what *new* forms of *global governance* should be created, or how global governance might be improved, particularly with respect to management of Table 10.3's 'inherently global health issues' – i.e. global governance for *health and development* rather than for economic liberalization – is notable by its absence.

The need for a new framework for global governance is increasingly recognized, perhaps more so since two wars involving Iraq have revealed the difficulty of negotiating multilateral solutions when one actor is sufficiently powerful to quite literally 'call the shots.' One of the axioms of effective inter-sectoral collaboration gleaned from years of inter-organizational research is that it is virtually impossible when one of the 'stakeholders' has the capacity to act unilaterally in 'the problem domain' (Gray, 1989). How this problematic will eventually resolve at a global level is unknown. Emmerij (2000: 58), however, maintains that:

> We urgently need the equivalent of the (welfare) state at the global level. At the end of the nineteenth century, capitalism had become an economic opportunity and a social problem at the national level. Extreme riches sided with appalling poverty. It took strong and imaginative people like Otto von Bismarck (hardly a radical) to start the building of a national welfare state to balance the raw power of the marketplace, to construct an income floor below which nobody could fall, and hence to ensure a more equitable distribution of income. Nation-states were strong and national decisions mattered in a world economy that was largely organized along national lines. The private sector became less free and more civilized.
>
> Now, a century later, globalizing markets are gradually giving global private enterprises the freedom that their national predecessors had at the end of the nineteenth century. ... [A] paradoxical situation again exists, but this time at a global level. We have a booming economy propelled by energetic and dynamic global enterprises coexisting with nation-states that are growing poorer and have to downsize the welfare fabric patiently constructed over the decades .... What is now needed is a new Bismarck to redefine the economic responsibility of the state and the social responsibility of the business community.

This is, we acknowledge, a truncated account of a complex political era, one that is also very Eurocentric and lacking in acknowledgement of the role of social movement groups (unions, women's organizations and other progressive reformers of various persuasions) in bending the hand of the likes of Bismarck in certain welfare directions. Western democracies' twentieth-century welfare states were as much a product of social mobilization and political struggle, from the shop floor to the legislature, with the streets in between, as they were of reasoned or enlightened policy-making. But Emmerij's plea, while not particularly novel, is gaining in volume.

The heart of this plea is distributive justice, a consideration that has not been central to the recent commitments of the G8. We can see this from their parsimonious support of health and education; from the inadequacy of their debt relief initiative; from their failures to support developing country concerns and proposals in world trade talks; from their reluctance to give poor countries market access in areas that might work to the advantage of the poor, if at a slight cost to sectors within the industrialized countries; and in their generally inadequate response to fundamental health- and life-threatening challenges to the environmental commons. We also see this in areas where the G8 are silent – on tobacco, as we have noted already, but perhaps most strikingly on the number of proposals that have been advanced for some form of global taxation and wealth redistribution. The so-called 'Tobin' or financial transactions tax, for example, would, at one per cent, raise over US$720 billion annually 'with minimal impact on capital markets, low distortion effects and ease of administration' (Wachtel, 2000: 88), as well as having the potentially positive effect of slowing harmful speculative capital flows. UNCTAD recommends that such a tax be divided, with half going to countries whose currencies are being traded and half into a fund for redistribution from rich to poor countries (cited in Wachtel, 2000: 88).[6]

The G8 have been extremely vocal on the need for a global system of continuous wealth creation. They have been remarkably mute on the necessity for a global system of wealth redistribution. The G8, in sum, appear to be exercising their nascent role in global governance to the advantage of the members of their exclusive club, and for certain groups of citizens within their member countries. Tom Barry (2001: 2), of the Foreign Policy In Focus group, and another observer of the G8's claim to global governance, expressed it rather pithily: 'How can such an elite club fairly shape an agenda that will affect all peoples and nations?' With respect to such an agenda that begins seriously to redress the human health and development catastrophes arising in the wake of contemporary globalization, the G8's response can best, if disturbingly, be described as 'fatal indifference.'

Endnotes to Chapter Ten

[1] Cf. Falk (1996: 13) on the need for a 'regulatory framework for global market forces that is people-centred rather than capital-driven.'

[2] A rapidly expanding body of evidence indicates the biological plausibility of such cumulative impacts (e.g. Evans & English, 2002; Lupie *et al.*, 2000; McEwen, 2000a, 2001; McEwen & Magarinos, 2001; Steptoe *et al.*, 2002).

[3] Words matter, and the invocation of 'personal responsibility and initiative' recalls the US *Personal Responsibility and Work Opportunity Reconciliation Act* of 1996, which ended the guarantee of at least minimal support to US families with dependent children without any commensurate action to ensure that the 'work opportunities' available would actually provide a living wage. They didn't (Blank, 1997: 52–79).

[4] We recognize that ratification of these conventions does not necessarily mean full compliance with them; it is an imprecise indicator at best.

[5] Elliott (2001) identifies at least three such conventions: The Convention on the Elimination of All Forms of Racial Discrimination (CERD), in which parties undertake to guarantee everyone's 'right to public health, medical care, social security and social services'; the Convention on the Elimination of All Forms of Discrimination Against Women (CEDAW), in which parties agree to 'take all appropriate measures' to ensure, on a basis of equality, men and women 'access to health care services, including those related to family planning'; and the Convention on the Rights of the Child (CRC), which includes a series of items related to children with disabilities,

special needs, the matter of an adequate standard of living, access to facilities to treatment and rehabilitation, and so on.

[6] Examples of other proposals include: a small tax on FDI, levied in proportion to the receiving country's lack of compliance with core labour standards (the right to form a union and proscriptions against child, bonded or prison labor), with the proceeds used to enact such standards within the receiving country; a global unitary tax (to avoid the problems of tax havens and transfer pricing schemes); and a carbon tax (based on per capita consumption of fossil fuels and biomass).

EPILOGUE

The attacks on New York and Washington in September 2001 meant that the security of the G8 countries against terrorist threats dominated the 2002 and 2003 summits. In this brief epilogue, we first deal with more specifically health-related areas and then comment briefly on the limits of the definition of security that the G8 have adopted.

At the 2002 Kananaskis summit, G8 leaders 'welcomed and endorsed' the conclusions of the G8 Education Task Force, which reaffirmed the importance of the Dakar goals, while noting that their achievement currently seems unlikely and that special attention should be paid to gender equity and to the situation of disadvantaged children, i.e. working children, those affected by AIDS and violent conflict, and those in rural areas. Although developing countries were exhorted to demonstrate their own commitment to education and to pay more attention to issues of quality, no specific commitments of additional financial resources were made. Instead, the Monterrey commitments were simply reiterated. Given the history of declining levels of ODA that we have documented, and the far more impressive performance in this respect by industrialized countries outside the G8, this admonition is curious, to say the least. The ability of developing countries to finance expenditures on education and on other basic social services, including health care, is also constrained by the continued burden of debt repayment. Here, the G8 made no commitments beyond those associated with the Enhanced HIPC Initiative, although they did emphasize the importance of full financing for the initiative and of securing the agreement of all relevant official and commercial creditors to providing debt relief. However, the passive tone of the G8 recommendations, which assign a leadership role to the World Bank and IMF, is not in keeping with the dominant role played by the G8, perhaps most especially the United States, in those institutions.

Potentially, the most significant health-related element of Kananaskis was the unveiling of the G8 Africa Action Plan, which sets out the anticipated G8 role with respect to the implementation of NEPAD. A detailed critique of this document, which contains a number of positive measures – notably a commitment to fund the G8 share of the shortfall in financing for the Enhanced HIPC Initiative and a tentative commitment to allocate half or more of the new development assistance promised at Monterrey to Africa – cannot be undertaken here. The conditionality attached to this latter commitment should be noted: it refers to 'African nations that govern justly, invest in their own people and promote economic freedom.' This leaves open the possibility that 'economic freedom', as defined by the G8, may actually entail disinvestment in people. More fundamentally, the Action Plan, by its very nature, cannot overcome what some critics see as the basic flaws and internal contradictions of NEPAD (see Chapter 9 and Bond, 2002). And it remains difficult to understand why many African countries facing disease pandemics and collapsed health systems on such a scale that the future of any form of governance is moot should be denied assistance unless they measure up to conditions increasingly beyond their reach.

The 2003 summit at Evian, overshadowed by divisions concerning the US invasion of Iraq, continued the previous year's preoccupation with security. At the same time, it produced 'a cornucopia of specific commitments ... in 14 separate communiqués' (Kirton & Kokotsis, 2003), including action plans on the marine environment, water supplies, famine and health. Notably, the G8 committed finance ministers to report in September on a proposal by Britain's Chancellor of the Exchequer to create a new International Finance Facility that would double the overall value of ODA provided by the industrialized world (Brown, 2003; Elliott, 2003; H.M. Treasury, 2003). Although an Oxfam spokesperson identified this as 'one of the few positive outcomes of Evian' (Elliott, 2003), no specific financial commitment was mentioned – an instance of the general pattern in which

> the Evian G8 leaders added little [money] to ensure that their many promises would actually be kept. Whereas Kananaskis in 2002 had been one of the greatest G8 global fundraisers ever, mobilizing US$27 billion [albeit with US$20 billion of this amount earmarked for 'security,'] Evian ended with only one tenth of that amount near at hand. Even the US$3 billion Evian tried to lock in for the global health fund had to await a subsequent European summit and donations from the Japanese, Russians and others, before the pledged and hoped-for money would become real. In many other areas, the communiqués frankly noted the need for major new moneys, but failed to identify how, when or from where they would be obtained (Kirton & Kokotsis, 2003).

This failure on the part of the G8 underscores the need for continued in-depth, critical monitoring of the health implications of G8 (in)actions – an activity for which we will be seeking partners and collaborators in the months and years ahead. Such monitoring is particularly important because the 'security' with which the G8 are now concerned is primarily that of their own populations – a small and disproportionately rich minority of the world's people – and their own commercial interests, whether those involve France's transnational water utilities or the United States' pharmaceutical firms. Neither before nor after Evian was there evidence of significant commitment to expand the importance attached to issues of greatest concern to the developing world in the next round of trade negotiations, now scheduled to begin in September 2003 (Monbiot, 2003; Watkins, 2003). We have noted in Chapter 3 the continued intransigence of the United States with respect to the Doha commitments on TRIPs and pharmaceuticals.

Ironically, the results of a poll of 'opinion leaders' in rich and poor countries, commissioned by the World Bank and released in June 2003, suggest that elites believe broad and narrow conceptions of security to be connected. Even while being generally positive about the effects of globalization, the individuals polled expressed concern about the growing gap between rich and poor, both within and among countries (Princeton Survey Research Associates, 2003: 12). More strikingly:

> Confronted with the reality that nearly half the world's population subsists on less than [US]$2 a day, opinion leaders from around the world are in very strong agreement that poverty reduction is key to achieving global peace and stability. Overwhelming majorities in developing and industrial countries alike believe that a major effort to decrease poverty around the world is essential for reducing global tensions (Princeton Survey Research Associates, 2003: 17).

Redefining 'security' in this way would not neglect the prospect of future terrorist acts, which remains real. At the same time, equal emphasis would be placed on policies to enhance the life chances of (for example) millions of children in sub-Saharan Africa left orphaned by AIDS, of the Argentine woman whom the recent economic collapse had left with nothing to feed her children but soup made with the dried bones of a dead cow (Faiola, 2002), and of the Mexican woman who now owes US$638 300 on a house worth US$45 000, because of the dramatic rise in interest rates following the collapse of the peso in 1994 (Moreno, 2002). In different ways, globalization has threatened the health and future of these people and countless others, and it is safe to say that terrorism – at least the kind of terrorism the leaders of the G8 have in mind – is well down the list of threats to their security.

Clearly, there is potential to use security as the starting point for defining an international order that is, in Richard Falk's words, 'people-centred rather than capital driven.' For the moment, however, 'fatal indifference' remains accurate as a description of the G8 leaders' attitudes toward achieving health for all.

REFERENCES

ActionAid, CAFOD, Christian Aid, Consumers International, FIELD, Oxfam, RSPB and WDM. 2001. 'Recommendations for ways forward on institutional reform of the World Trade Organisation'; http://www.trade-info.cec.eu.int/civil_soc/documents/meeting/me-20-wto_c01.pdf (accessed 27 May 2003).

Addai, E. and Gaere, L. 2001. *Capacity-Building and Systems Development for Sector-Wide Approaches (SWAps): The Experience of the Ghana Health Sector*. Accra: DFID; http://www.sti.ch/pdfs/swap154.pdf (accessed 27 May 2003).

Adeyi, O., Chellaraj, G., Goldstein, E., Preker, A. and Ringold, D. 1997. 'Health status during the transition in central and eastern Europe: Development in reverse?' *Health Policy and Planning*, 12: 132–45.

Adlung, R. and Carzaniga, A. 2001. 'Health services under the GATS.' *Bulletin of the World Health Organization*, 79: 352–64.

Adlung, R. and Carzaniga, A. 2002. 'Health services under the General Agreement on Trade Services.' In C. Vieira and N. Drager (eds), *Trade in Health Services: Global, Regional and Country Perspectives*. Washington, DC: PAHO, pp. 13–33; http://www.paho.org/English/HDP/HDD/06Adlu.pdf (accessed 27 May 2003).

African Forum and Network on Debt and Development (AFRODAD). 2002. 'The efficacy of establishing an international arbitration court for debt.' Technical Paper No. 2002/1, AFRODAD; http://www.afrodad.org/html/Technical%20Paper.pdf (accessed 27 May 2003).

Amalric, F. 2001. 'Strategically speaking: The World Food Summit, five years later [with responses by commentators]. *Development*, 44(4): 6–16.

Amnesty International. 2002. 'G8: Failing to stop the terror trade.' Amnesty International On-line, 24 June; http://www.amnesty.org (accessed 3 September 2002).

Amsden, A. 1994. 'Why isn't the whole world experimenting with the East Asian model to develop? Review of The East Asian miracle.' *World Development*, 22: 627–33.

Arhin-Tenkorang, D. 2000. 'Mobilizing resources for health: The case for user fees revisited.' Paper No. WG3:6, Commission on Macroeconomics and Health; http://www.cmhealth.org/docs/wg3_paper6.pdf_(accessed 27 May 2003).

Armada, F., Muntaner, C. and Navarro, V. 2001. 'Health and social security reform in Latin America: The convergence of the World Health Organization, the World Bank and transnational corporations.' *International Journal of Health Services*, 31(4): 729–68.

Arnesen, T. and Nord, E. 1999. 'The value of DALY life: Problems with ethics and validity of disability-adjusted life years.' *British Medical Journal*, 319: 1423–5.

Attaran, A. and Gillespie-White, L. 2001. 'Do patents for antiretroviral drugs constrain access to AIDS treatment in Africa?' *Journal of the American Medical Association*, 286: 1886–92.

Attaran, A. and Sachs, J. 2001. 'Defining and refining international donor support for combating the AIDS pandemic.' *The Lancet*, 357: 57–61.

Audley, J. and Florini, A. 2001. 'Overhauling the WTO: Opportunity at Doha and beyond.' Policy Brief 6. Washington, DC: Carnegie Endowment for International Peace; http://www.ceip.org/files/pdf/pb6-AudleyFlorini.pdf (accessed 27 May 2003).

Avi-Yonah, R. 2000. 'Globalization, tax competition, and the fiscal crisis of the welfare state.' *Harvard Law Review*, 113: 1573–676.

Bal, D.G., Glynn, T.J. and Woolam, G.L. 2001. 'Tobacco wars: The successes, the challenges, and some failures.' *Cancer*, 91: 247–51.

Barlow, M. 2001. *The Free Trade Area of the Americas and the Threat to Social Programs, Environmental Sustainability and Social Justice in Canada and the Americas*. Ottawa: Council of Canadians; http://www.canadians.org/campaigns/campaigns~tradepub~ftaa2.html (accessed 12 November 2001).

Barraclough, S. 2000. *Meanings of Sustainable Agriculture: Some Issues for the South*. Geneva: South Centre.

Bates, C. 2001. 'Developing countries take the lead on WHO convention.' *Tobacco Control*, 10: 209.

Bayne, N. 2001. 'Managing globalisation and the new economy: The contribution of the G8 summit.' In J.J. Kirton and G.M. von Furstenberg (eds), *New Directions in Global Economic Governance*. Ashgate: Aldershot, pp. 23–38.

Bello, W. 1998. 'The end of a "miracle": Speculation, foreign capital dependence, and the collapse of the Southeast Asian economies.' *Multinational Monitor*, 19, January/February; http://www.rrojasdatabank.org/bello.htm (accessed 27 May 2003).

Bello, W., Cunningham, S. and Kheng Poh, L. 1998. *A Siamese Tragedy: Development and Disintegration in Modern Thailand*. London: Zed Books.

Ben-David, D., Nordstrom, H. and Winters, L.A. 1999. *Trade, Income, Disparity and Poverty*. Special Studies 5. Geneva: WTO; http://www.wto.org/english/res_e/booksp_e/disparity_e.pdf (accessed 27 May 2003).

Benson, W. n.d. 'Undermining development: The European arms trade with the Horn of Africa and Central Africa.' International Action Network on Small Arms; http://www.iansa.org/documents/research/res_archive/ngo37.htm (accessed 15 January 2003).

Bettcher, D.W., Yach, D. and Guindon, E. 2000. 'Global trade and health: Key linkages and future challenges.' *Bulletin of the World Health Organization*, 78: 521–34.

Bijlmakers, L.A., Basset, M.T. and Sanders, D.M. 1996. 'Health and structural adjustment in rural and urban Zimbabwe.' *The Scandinavian Institute of African Studies, Research Report No. 101*. Uppsala: Nordiska Afrikainstitutet.

Bishop, M. 2000. 'The mystery of the vanishing taxpayer: A survey of globalisation and tax.' *The Economist*, 29 January.

Blackhurst, R., Lyakurwa, B. and Oyejide, A. 2001. 'Options for improving Africa's participation in the WTO.' In B. Hoekman and W. Martin (eds), *Developing Countries and the WTO: A Pro-Active Agenda*. Oxford: Blackwell, pp. 95–114.

Blank, R. 1997. *It Takes a Nation: A New Agenda for Fighting Poverty*. Princeton: Princeton University Press.

Bloom, D. and Williamson, J.G. 1998. 'Demographic transitions and economic miracles in emerging Asia.' *World Bank Economic Review*, 12(3): 419–55.

Blustein, P. 2002. 'Who really pays to help U.S. farmers?' *The Washington Post*, 6 May.

Bond, P. 2001. *Against Global Apartheid: South Africa Meets the World Bank, IMF and International Finance*. Cape Town: University of Cape Town Press.

Bond, P. (ed.). 2002. *Fanon's Warning: A Civil Society Reader on the New Partnership for Africa's Development*. Trenton: Africa World Press.

Bonnel, R. 2000. 'Economic analysis of HIV/AIDS.' Background Paper for the Africa Development Forum 2000. World Bank/UNAIDS, September; http://www.iaen.org/files.cgi/435_HIVEconAnalysisADF.pdf (accessed 27 May 2003).

Borger, J. 2002. 'Defence spending given $2.1 trillion budget.' *The Guardian*, 5 February.

Boseley, S. 2002. 'Short leads cost-price drugs plan for poorer countries.' *The Guardian Weekly*, 5–11 December.

Boseley, S. and Denny, C. 'Prescription for world's poorest stays unwritten.' *The Guardian*, 20 February.

Bradley, D. 2001. 'The biological and epidemiological basis of global public goods for health.' Paper No. WG2:15, CMH; http://www.cmhealth.org/docs/wg2_paper15.pdf (accessed 27 May 2003).

Braveman, P. and Tarimo, E. 2002. 'Social inequalities in health within countries: Not only an issue for affluent nations.' *Social Science and Medicine*, 54: 1621–35.

Breman, A. and Shelton, C. 2001. 'Structural adjustment and health: A literature review of the debate, its role-players and presented empirical evidence.' Paper No. WG6:6, Commission on Macroeconomics and Health; http://www.cmhealth.org/docs/wg6_paper6.pdf (accessed 27 May 2003).

BRIDGES Weekly Trade News Digest, 6(19), 22 May 2002a.

BRIDGES Weekly Trade News Digest, 6(23), 18 June 2002b.

BRIDGES Weekly Trade News Digest, 6(24), 25 June 2002c.

BRIDGES Weekly Trade News Digest, 6(31), 18 September 2002d.

BRIDGES Weekly Trade News Digest, 6(34), 18 October 2002e.

BRIDGES Weekly Trade News Digest, 6(38), 7 November 2002f.

BRIDGES Weekly Trade News Digest, 6(39), 14 November 2002g.

BRIDGES Weekly Trade News Digest, 7(5), 12 February 2003.

Broadhead, L.A. 2001. 'Canada as a rogue state: Its shameful performance on climate change.' *International Journal*, 56(Summer): 461–80.

Brough, D. 2002. 'World far short of goal to halve hunger.' *Cape Times, Business Report International*, 21 August.

Brown, G. 2003. 'An assault on poverty is vital too.' *The Guardian*, 13 February.

Brown, P. 2002. 'Europe's catch-all clause.' *The Guardian Weekly*, 29 March–3 April: 26.

Browne, A. 2000. *Current Issues in Sector-Wide Approaches for Health Development: Uganda Case Study*. Geneva: WHO, Inter-Agency Group on Sector-Wide Approaches and Development Cooperation.

Brugha, R., Starling, M. and Walt, G. 2002. 'GAVI, the first steps: Lessons for the Global Fund.' *The Lancet*, 359: 435–8.

Brugha, R. and Zwi, A. 2002. 'Global approaches to private sector provision: Where is the evidence?' In K. Lee, K. Buse and S. Fustukian (eds), *Health Policy in a Globalising World*. Cambridge: Cambridge University Press, pp. 63–77.

Brundtland, G. 2000. 'Speech to Winterthur Massive Effort Advocacy Meeting.' Geneva: WHO, 3 October; http://www.who.int/directorgeneral/speeches/2000/english/20001003_massive_effort. html (accessed 1 February 2003).

Buchan, J. and O'May, F. 1999. 'Globalisation and healthcare labour markets: A case study from the United Kingdom.' *Human Resources for Health Development Journal*, 3(3), pp. 199–209.

Bundred, P. and Levitt, C. 2000. 'Medical migration: Who are the real losers?' *The Lancet*, 356: 245–6.

Burns, J. 1998. 'Profit rules Indian shore where ships go to die.' *The New York Times*, 9 August.

Buse, K. and Walt, G. 2000. 'Global public–private health partnerships: Part II – What are the issues for global governance?' *Bulletin of the World Health Organisation*, 78: 699–709.

Buse, K. and Waxman, A. 2001. 'Public–private health partnerships: A strategy for WHO.' *Bulletin of the World Health Organisation*, 79: 748–54.

Butler, C., Douglas, R. and McMichael, A.J. 2001. 'Globalisation and environmental change: Implications for health and health inequalities.' In R. Eckersley, J. Dixon and R. Douglas (eds), *The Social Origins of Health and Well-Being*. Melbourne: Cambridge University Press, pp. 34–50.

Caldwell, D.J. 1997. *Responsible Trade: Don't Trade Away Our Food Safety*. Washington, DC: Sierra Club; http://www.sierraclub.org/trade/environment/hormone.asp (accessed 24 March 2002).

Cameron, D. and Stein, J. 2000. 'Globalization, culture and society: The state as place amidst shifting spaces.' *Canadian Public Policy*, XXVI, Supplement: S15–S34.

Canadian Centre for Policy Alternatives (CCPA). 2002. 'Putting health first: Canadian health care reform, trade treaties and foreign policy'; http://www. healthcare commission.ca (accessed 14 December 2002).

Canadian Council for International Cooperation (CCIC). 2002. 'New initiatives for Africa: A Canadian response to NEPAD: A CCIC Briefing Note.' Ottawa: CCIC; http://www.ccic.ca/devpol/africa_canada_forum/acf7_ccic_briefing_note_on_g8_cdn_(Initiatives).pdf (accessed 27 May 2003).

Canadian Council for International Cooperation (CCIC) Africa-Canada Forum. 2002. *Canadian Economic Relations with Sub-Saharan Africa: Recent Trends.* Ottawa: CCIC Africa-Canada Forum; http://www.ccic.ca/devpol/africa_canada_forum/acf8_revised_sept_can_econ_rel_africa.pdf (accessed 27 May 2003).

Canadian International Development Agency (CIDA). 2002a. *Canada Making a Difference in the World: A Policy Statement on Strengthening Aid Assistance.* Ottawa: CIDA; http://www.acdi-cida.gc.ca/aideffectiveness (accessed 27 May 2003).

Canadian International Development Agency (CIDA). 2002b. *CIDA's Action Plan on Basic Education.* Ottawa: CIDA; http://www.acdi-cida.gc.ca/cida_ind.nsf/b2a5f300880e7192852567450078b4cb/e4fc8a9ac2b9b129852569ba005550bc/$FILE/ATT14SU0/BEActionPlan.pdf (accessed 27 May 2003).

Canonne, A. 2002. 'France.' In J. Randel, T. German and D. Ewing (eds), *The Reality of Aid 2002*. Manila: IBON Foundation, pp. 192–5.

Carroll, D., Davey Smith, G. and Bennett, P. 1994. 'Some observations on health and socio-economic status.' *Journal of Health Psychology*, 1: 23–39.

Carter, S. 2002. 'Mongoven, Biscoe & Duchin: Destroying tobacco control activism from the inside.' *Tobacco Control*, 11: 112–18.

Carvel, J. 2002a. 'Alarm as US woos nurses from NHS.' *The Guardian Weekly*, 25–31 July: 8.

Carvel, J. 2002b. 'NHS poaching nurses at expense of poor nations.' *The Guardian Weekly*, 23–29 May: 9.

Cassels, A. 1995. 'Health sector reform: Key issues in less developed countries.' *Journal of International Development*, 7: 338.

Cassels, A. 1997. *A Guide to Sector-Wide Approaches for Health Development: Concepts, Issues and Working Arrangements* (WHO/ARA/97.12). Geneva: WHO.

Center for Public Integrity. 2003a. 'Promoting privatization'; http://www.icij.org/dtaweb/water (accessed 28 February 2003).

Center for Public Integrity. 2003b. 'Cholera and the age of the water barons'; http://www.icij.org/dtaweb/water (accessed 28 February 2003).

Center for Public Integrity. 2003c. 'The "aguas tango": Cashing in on Buenos Aires' privatization'; http://www.icij.org/dtaweb/water (accessed 28 February 2003).

Center for Public Integrity. 2003d. 'Water and power: The French connection'; http://www.icij.org/dtaweb/water (accessed 28 February 2003).

Centro de Estudios Legales y Sociales (CELS). 2001. 'Argentina: New excuses for old abuses.' In Social Watch, *Social Watch Report No. 5, 2001*. Montevideo: Instituto del Tercer Mundo, pp. 82–3; http://www.socialwatch.org.

Centro de Estudios Legales y Sociales (CELS). 2002. 'Argentina: The eruption of a model.' In Social Watch, *Social Watch Report No. 6, 2002: The Social Impact of Globalisation on the World*. Montevideo: Instituto del Tercer Mundo, pp. 82–3; http://www.socialwatch.org.

Centro de Estudios Legales y Sociales (CELS). 2003. 'Argentina: In the hands of the oligopoly of foreign capital.' In Social Watch, *The Poor and the Market: Social Watch Report 2003*. Montevideo: Instituto del Tercer Mundo, pp. 82–3; http://www.socialwatch.org.

Chaloupka, F.J. and Laixuthai, A. 1996. 'US trade policy and cigarette smoking in Asia.' NBER Working Paper 5543. Washington, DC: National Bureau of Economic Research.

Chanda, R. 2001. 'Trade in health services.' Paper WG4:5, Commission on Macroeconomics and Health; http://www.cmhealth.org/docs/wg4_paper5.pdf (accessed 27 May 2003).

Charnovitz, S. 2001. *The Supervision of Health and Biosafety Regulation by World Trade Rules*. Washington, DC: Global Environment and Trade Study; http://www.gets.org/gets/library/admin/uploadedfiles/Supervision_of_Health_and_Biosafety_Regulat_3.htm (accessed 26 March 2001).

Cheru, F. 1999. *Effects of Structural Adjustment Policies on the Full Enjoyment of Human Rights: Report by the Independent Expert Submitted in Accordance with Commission Decisions 1998/102 and 1997/103, E/CN.4/1999/50*. New York: Economic and Social Council, UN Commission on Human Rights; http://www.unhchr.ch/Huridocda/Huridoca.nsf/TestFrame/f991c6c62457a2858025675100348aef?Opendocument (accessed 10 August 2002).

Cheru, F. 2001. *The Highly Indebted Poor Countries (HIPC) Initiative: A Human Rights Assessment of the Poverty Reduction Strategy Papers (PRSP)*. Report submitted to the United Nations Economic and Social Council, E/CN.4/2001/56. New York: UN; http://www.hri.ca/fortherecord2001/documentation/commission/e-cn4-2001-56.htm (accessed 27 May 2003).

Chinkin, C. 2000. 'Gender and globalization.' *UN Chronicle*, 37(2); http://www.un.org/Pubs/chronicle/2000/issue2/0200p69.htm (accessed 21 January 2003).

Chopra, M. and Sanders, D. 1997. 'Is growth monitoring worthwhile in South Africa?' *South African Medical Journal*, 87: 875–8.

Chossudovsky, M. 1997. *The Globalization of Poverty: Impacts of IMF and World Bank Reforms*. London: Zed Books.

Cigno, A., Rosati, F. and Guarcello, L. 2002. 'Does globalization increase child labor?' *World Development*, 30: 1579–89.

Clark, S. and Fried, M. 2003. *Fair Trade for Hungry Farmers*. Ottawa: Canadian Food Security Policy Group; http://www.oxfam.ca/news/MakeTradeFair/ FairTrade forFarmers.pdf (accessed 27 May 2003).

Cobham, A. 2002. 'Capital account liberalization and poverty.' *Global Social Policy*, 2(2): 163–88.

Cohen, S. 2000. *Failed Crusade: America and the Tragedy of Post-Communist Russia.* New York: Norton.

Collier, P. 2000. *Economic Causes of Civil Conflict and Their Implications for Policy.* Washington, DC: World Bank; http://www.worldbank.org/research/conflict/papers/civilconflict.htm (accessed 15 January 2003).

Collier, P. and Hoeffler, A. 2001. *Greed and Grievance in Civil War.* Washington, DC: World Bank; http://econ.worldbank.org/files/12205_greedgrievance_23oct.pdf (accessed 15 January 2003).

Collins, J. and Lear, J. 1995. *Chile's Free Market Miracle: A Second Look.* Oakland: Food First Books.

Collins, J. and Rau, B. 2000. 'AIDS in the context of development.' Programme on Social Policy and Development Paper No. 4. Geneva: UNRISD; http://www.unrisd.org/80256B3C005BCCF9/httpNetITFramePDF?ReadForm&parentunid= 329E8ACB59 F4060580256B61004363FE&parentdoctype=paper&netitpath=80256B3C005BCCF9/ (httpAuxPages)/329E8ACB59F4060580256B61004363FE/$file/collins.pdf (accessed 27 May 2003).

Commission on Macroeconomics and Health (CMH). 2001. *Macroeconomics and Health: Investing in Health for Economic Development.* Geneva: WHO; http://www3.who.int/whosis/cmh/cmh_report/report.cfm?path=cmh,cmh_report&language=english (accessed 27 May 2003).

Committee of Experts on Tobacco Industry Documents. 2000. 'Tobacco company strategies to undermine tobacco control activities at the World Health Organization.' Geneva: WHO; http://repositories.cdlib.org/tc/reports/WHO7/ (accessed 27 May 2003) .

Commonwealth Secretariat. 2001. *Migration of Health Workers from Commonwealth Countries: Experiences and Recommendations for Action.* London: Commonwealth Secretariat.

Cornia, G.A. 1987. 'Economic decline and human welfare in the first half of the 1980s.' In G.A. Cornia, R. Jolly and F. Stewart (eds), *Adjustment with a Human Face: Protecting the Vulnerable and Promoting Growth,* Vol. 1. Oxford: Clarendon Press.

Cornia, G.A. 2001. 'Globalization and health: Results and options.' *Bulletin of the World Health Organization,* 79: 834–41.

Cornia, G.A. and Court, J. 2001. *Inequality, Growth and Poverty in the Era of Liberalization and Globalization.* Helsinki: United Nations University World Institute for Development Economics Research (WIDER); http://www.wider.unu.edu/publications/policy-brief.htm (accessed 27 May 2003).

Cornia, G., Jolly, R. and Stewart, F. (eds). 1987 (Vol. 1) and 1988 (Vol. 2). *Adjustment with a Human Face: Protecting the Vulnerable and Promoting Growth.* Oxford: Clarendon Press.

Costello, A., Watson, F. and Woodward, D. 1994. *Human Face or Human Facade? Adjustment and the Health of Mothers and Children.* London: Institute of Child Health.

Craig, D. and Porter, D. 2003. 'Poverty Reduction Strategy Papers: A new convergence.' *World Development,* 31: 53–69.

Creese, A. and Kutzin, J. 1997. 'Lessons from cost recovery in health.' In C. Colclough (ed.), *Marketizing Education and Health in Developing Countries*. Oxford: Oxford University Press, pp. 37–62.

Crotty, J., Epstein, G. and Kelly, P. 1998. 'Multinational corporations in the neo-liberal regime.' In D. Baker, G. Epstein and R. Pollin (eds), *Globalization and Progressive Economic Policy*. Cambridge: Cambridge University Press, pp. 117–43.

Crouch, M.L. 2001. 'From golden rice to terminator technology: Agricultural biotechnology will not feed the world or save the environment.' In B. Tokar (ed.), *Redesigning Life? The Worldwide Challenge to Genetic Engineering*. Montreal: McGill-Queen's University Press, pp. 22–39.

Cultural Industries Sectoral Advisory Group on International Trade (SAGIT). 2002. 'An international agreement on cultural diversity: A model for discussion'; http://www.dfait-maeci.gc.ca/tna-nac/sagit-paper-en.asp (accessed 25 February 2003).

Cumby, R. and Levich, R. 1987. 'On the definition and magnitude of recent capital flight.' In D. Lessard and J. Williamson (eds), *Capital Flight and Third World Debt*. Washington, DC: Institute for International Economics, pp. 27–67.

Daar, A., Martin, D., Nast, S., Smyth, A., Singer, P. and Thorsteinsdóttir, H. 2002. *Top 10 Biotechnologies for Improving Health in Developing Countries*. Toronto: Joint Centre for Bioethics, University of Toronto; http://www.utoronto.ca/jcb/_genomics/top10ng.pdf (accessed 1 April 2003).

Dallaire, S. 2001. 'Continuity and change in the global monetary order.' In J.J. Kirton and G.M. von Furstenberg (eds), *New Directions in Global Economic Governance*. Ashgate: Aldershot, pp. 113–26.

Davey Smith, G., Blane, D. and Bartley, M. 1994. 'Explanations for socio-economic differentials in mortality.' *European Journal of Public Health*, 4: 131–44.

Davies, N. 2002. 'How the richest man in Britain avoids tax.' *The Guardian*, 11 April.

Dawe, D., Robertson, R. and Unnevehr, L. 2002. 'Golden rice: What role could it play in alleviation of vitamin A deficiency?' *Food Policy*, 27: 541–60.

Deaton, A. 2001. 'Health, inequality and economic development.' Paper WG1:3, Commission on Macroeconomics and Health; http://www.cmhealth.org/docs/wg1_paper3.pdf (accessed 27 May 2003)

Dederichs-Bain, B. 2002. 'Germany.' In J. Randel, T. German and D. Ewing (eds), *The Reality of Aid 2002*. Manila: IBON Foundation, pp. 196–201.

Denny, C. 2002a. 'Aid tap finally begins to turn in right direction.' *The Guardian Weekly*, 25 April–1 May: 24.

Denny, C. 2002b. 'Tanzanian aid back on track after air control system row.' *The Guardian*, 4 July.

Denny, C. 2003a. 'Hypocrisy that underlines HIPC.' *The Guardian Weekly*, 23–29 January: 23.

Denny, C. 2003b. 'Italy scuppers EU's deal to end cross-border tax cheating.' *The Guardian Weekly*, 13–19 March: 14.

Denny, C., Elliott, L. and Hencke, D. 2002. 'Short defies cabinet on African defence deal.' *The Guardian*, 20 March.

DePalma, A. 1995. 'In Mexico, hunger and woe in crisis.' *The New York Times*, 15 January, section 1.

Department of Health Guidance on International Recruitment. 2001; http://www.doh.gov.uk./international-recruitment/index.htm (accessed 31 January 2002).

De Paula, R.L.F. and Alves, A.J. 2000. 'External financial stability and the 1998–99 Brazilian currency crisis'; http://www.adenauer.com.br/HTML/Textos~e/atuais-e-1-html (accessed 8 December 2000).

Devarajan, S., Miller, M. and Swanson, E. 2002. *Goals for Development: History, Prospects and Costs*. Washington, DC: World Bank; http://econ.worldbank.org/files/13269_wps2819.pdf (accessed 30 May 2002).

Diamond, J. 2000. *Guns, Germs and Steel*. London: Random House.

Dollar, D. 2001. 'Is globalization good for your health?' *Bulletin of the World Health Organization*, 79: 827–33.

Dollar, D. and Kraay, A. 2000. *Growth is Good for the Poor*. Washington, DC: World Bank; http://www.worldbank.org/research (accessed 8 December 2000).

Dovlo, D. 1999. *Report on Issues Affecting the Mobility and Retention of Health Workers/Professionals in Commonwealth African States*. Unpublished Consultancy Report prepared for the Commonwealth Secretariat, London.

Dovlo, D. 2001. 'Retention and deployment of health workers and professionals in Africa.' Paper presented at the Consultative Meeting on Improving Collaboration between Health Professions and Governments in Policy Formulation and Implementation of Health Sector Reform, Addis Ababa. Harare: WHO-Afro.

Dovlo, D. and Nyonator F. 1999. 'Migration of graduates of the Ghana Medical School: A preliminary rapid appraisal.' *Human Resources for Health Development Journal*, 3(1): 40–51.

Du Boff, R. 2002. 'If you still don't see the US as a rogue nation ....' *CCPA Monitor*, 8(9): 28–9.

Dubos, R. 1968. *Man, Medicine and Environment*. London: Pall Mall Press.

Dutch Ministry of Foreign Affairs. 2002. 'Education for all the world's children.' Press Release, 8 April.

Economist, The. 2001. 'Big Mac currencies index.' 19 April.

Economist, The. 2002. 'Mexico's farmers: Floundering in a tariff-free landscape.' 30 November.

Edwards, B. 2001. 'IMF and World Bank to labor unions: Drop dead.' *NACLA Report on the Americas*, 34, January–February: 4–5, 49.

Elliott, L. 2002. 'Protesters win a battle, but not the war.' *The Guardian Weekly*, 3–9 October: 11.

Elliott, L. 2003. 'G8 gives fillip to Brown's $100bn remedy for global poverty.' *The Guardian*, 5 June.

Elliot, L. and Denny, C. 2002. US wrecks cheap drugs deal. *The Guardian*, December 21.

Elliott, L. and Teather, D. 2002. 'IMF aims to protect countries facing financial meltdown.' *The Guardian Weekly*, 3–9 October: 11.

Elliott, R. 2001. *TRIPS and Rights: International Human Rights Law, Access to Medicines, and the Interpretation of the WTO Agreement on Trade-Related Aspects of Intellectual Property.* Montreal: Canadian HIV/AIDS Legal Network and AIDS Law Project, South Africa; http://www.aidslaw.ca/Maincontent/issues/cts/TRIPS-brief.htm (accessed 27 May 2003).

Ellison, M. 2001. 'US workers suffer labour pains as they put in record hours at work.' *The Guardian Weekly*, 3 September.

Emmerij, L. 2000. 'World economic changes at the threshold of the twenty-first century.' In J.N. Pieterse (ed.), *Global Futures: Shaping Globalization*. London: Zed Books, pp. 53–62.

Enge, E. 2002. 'Political overview.' In J. Randel, T. German and D. Ewing (eds), *The Reality of Aid 2002*. Manila: IBON Foundation, pp. 4–22.

Equity International. 2003. 'Summit features important announcements.' Press Release. Washington, DC: Equity International; http://www.globalsecurity.bz/news/detail.asp?id=170 (accessed 27 May 2003).

European Network on Debt and Development (EURODAD). 2001. *Putting Poverty Reduction First: Why a Poverty Approach to Sustainability Must Be Adopted*. Brussels: EURODAD; http://www.eurodad.org/uploadstore/cms/docs/PuttingPoverty ReductionFirst.pdf (accessed 11 June 2003).

Evans, G.W. and English, K. 2002. 'The environment of poverty: Multiple stressor exposure, psychophysiological stress, and socioemotional adjustment.' *Child Development*, 73: 1238–48.

Faiola, A. 2002. 'Despair in once-proud Argentina: After economic collapse, deep poverty makes dignity a casualty.' *The Washington Post*, 6 August: A01.

Falk, R. 1996. 'An inquiry into the political economy of world order.' *New Political Economy*, 1: 13–26.

Farmer, P. 1999. *Infections and Inequalities*. Berkeley: University of California Press.

Feachem, R. 2001. 'Globalization: From rhetoric to evidence.' *Bulletin of the World Health Organization*, 79: 804.

Field, M., Kotz, D. and Bukhman, G. 2000. 'Neoliberal economic policy, "state desertion," and the Russian health crisis.' In J. Yong Kim, J. Millen, A. Irwin and J. Gershman (eds), *Dying for Growth: Global Inequality and the Health of the Poor*. Monroe: Common Courage Press, pp. 155–73.

Fiil-Flynn, M. 2001. 'The electricity crisis in Soweto.' MSP Occasional Paper No. 4. Kingston, Ontario: Municipal Services Project, Queen's University; /http://qsilver.queensu.ca/~mspadmin/pages/Project_Publications/ Series/PapersNo4.pdf (accessed 27 May 2003).

Financial Action Task Force (FATF). 2000. *Report on Non-Compliance Countries and Territories*. Paris: FATF Secretariat; http://www1.oecd.org/fatf/pdf/NCCT_en.pdf (accessed 11 June 2003).

Finger, J.M. and Schuler, P. 2001. 'Implementation of Uruguay Round commitments: The development challenge.' In B. Hoekman and W. Martin (eds), *Developing Countries and the WTO: A Pro-Active Agenda*. Oxford: Blackwell, pp. 115–30.

Fitzroy, H., Briend, A. and Fauveau, V. 1990. 'Child survival: Should the strategy be redesigned? Experience from Bangladesh.' *Health Policy Planning*, 5: 226–34.

Foot, R. 2002. 'G7 ministers approve $22 billion in funding for poorest nations.' *The National Post*, 17 June: A4.

Framework Convention Alliance. 2003. 'Statement of the Framework Convention Alliance: Tobacco treaty advances strong measures; full implementation key.' Geneva: Framework Convention Alliance; http://www.fctc.org/press33.shtml (accessed 27 May 2003).

Franke, R.W. and Chasin, B.H. 1980. *Seeds of Famine: Ecological Destruction and the Development Dilemma in the West African Sahel*. Totowa: Rowman & Allanheld.

Frenk, J., Bobadilla, J.L., Sepulveda, J. and Lopez Cervantes, M. 1989. 'Health transition in middle-income countries: New challenges for health care.' *Health Policy and Planning*, 4: 29–39.

Frenk, J. and Murray, C.J.L. 1999. 'Overview of the health situation in the world and perspective for 2020.' Paper presented at Forum 3 of the Global Forum for Health Research, Geneva, June.

Fried, S. and Soentoro, T. 2002. *Summary of Export Credit Agency Finance in Indonesia*. Washington, DC: Environmental Defense Fund; http://www.environmentaldefense. org/pdf.cfm?ContentID=2351&FileName= ECAmining.pdf (accessed 27 May 2003).

Frommel, D. 2002. 'Global market in medical workers.' *Le Monde diplomatique*, May.

Fudge, J. and Cossman, B. 2002. 'Introduction: Privatization, law, and the challenge to feminism.' In B. Cossman and J. Fudge (eds), *Privatization, Law, and the Challenge to Feminism*. Toronto: University of Toronto Press, pp. 3–40.

G7 Finance Ministers. 2002. 'Statement of the G7 finance ministers, Halifax, Nova Scotia, June 15, 2002'; http://www.library.utoronto.ca/g7/finance/fm061502.htm (accessed 26 February 2003).

G8. 2002. *G8 Africa Action Plan*; http://www.g7.utoronto.ca/summit/2002kananaskis/ afraction-e.pdf (accessed 27 February 2003).

G8 Education Task Force. 2002. *Report of the G8 Education Task Force*; http:// www.g7.utoronto.ca/summit/2002kananaskis/education.html (accessed 28 January 2003).

G8 Renewable Energy Task Force. 2001a. *Final Report*; http://www.renewabletaskforce. org (accessed 28 January 2003).

G8 Renewable Energy Task Force. 2001b. 'Annexes'; http://www.renewabletaskforce. org (accessed 28 January 2003).

Galeano, E. 1973. *Open Veins of Latin America: Five Centuries of the Pillage of a Continent.* New York: Monthly Review Press.

Gallup, J. and Sachs, J. 2000. 'The economic burden of malaria.' Working Paper No. 52. Cambridge, MA: Center for International Development, Harvard University, July; http://www.cid.harvard.edu/cidwp/052.htm (accessed 27 May 2003).

Galvão, J. 2002. 'Access to antiretroviral drugs in Brazil.' *The Lancet*, 360: 1862–5.

Gates, J. 2002. '21 ways neoliberalism is redistributing wealth worldwide.' *The CCPA Monitor*, 8: 19–22.

George, S. 1984. *Ill Fares the Land: Essays on Food, Hunger and Power*. Washington, DC: Institute for Policy Studies.

George, S. 1988. *A Fate Worse than Debt*. London: Penguin.

German, T. and Randel, J. 2002. 'Never richer, never poorer.' In J. Randel, T. German and D. Ewing (eds), *The Reality of Aid 2002*. Manila: IBON Foundation, pp. 145–57.

German, T., Randel, J., Ewing, D. (eds). 2002. *The Reality of Aid 2002: An Independent Review of Poverty Reduction and International Development Assistance*. Manila: IBON Foundation.

Gershman, J. and Irwin, A. 2000. 'Getting a grip on the global economy.' In J. Yong Kim, J. Millen, A. Irwin and J. Gershman (eds), *Dying for Growth: Global Inequality and the Health of the Poor*. Monroe: Common Courage Press, pp. 11–44.

Gilhooly, D. [Director, ICT for Development, UNDP] 2001. 'Digital opportunities and the digital divide.' Presentation to OECD Forum 2001 on Sustainable Development and the New Economy, Paris, 14–16 May. New York: UNDP; http://www1.oecd.org/forum2001/briefings/index.htm (accessed 27 May 2003).

Githeko, A.K., Lindsay, S.W., Confalonieri, U.E. and Patz, J.A. 2000. 'Climate change and vector-borne diseases: A regional analysis.' *Bulletin of the World Health Organization*, 78: 1136–47.

Glantz, S.A., Slade, J., Bero, L.A., Hanauer, P. and Barnes, D. 1996. *The Cigarette Papers*. Berkeley: University of California Press.

Global AIDS Alliance. 2002. 'Filling the funding gap to save lives: A proposal for an "Equitable Contributions Framework" for the Global Fund'; http://www.globalaidsalliance.org/Fund_report.html (accessed 15 January 2003).

Global Forum for Health Research (GFHR). 2000. *The 10/90 Report on Health Research 2000*. Geneva: GFHR; http://www.globalforumhealth.ch/report.htm (accessed 24 August 2001).

Global Forum on Health Research (GFHR). 2002. *The 10/90 Report on Health Research 2001–2002*. Geneva: GFHR; http://www.globalforumhealth.org/pages/index.asp (accessed 3 February 2003).

Global Social Policy Forum. 2001. 'A North-South dialogue on the prospects for a socially progressive globalization.' *Global Social Policy*, 1(2):147–62.

Goldzimer, A. 2002. 'Globalization's most perverse secret: The role of export credit and investment insurance agencies.' Paper presented at the Alternatives to

Neoliberalism Conference, 23–24 May. Washington, DC: Environmental Defense Fund; http://www.new-rules.org/Globalizations_Most_Perverse Secret.pdf (accessed 2 January 2003).

Gough, I. 2001. 'Globalization and regional welfare regimes: The East Asian case.' *Global Social Policy*, 1(2): 163–90.

Government of Canada. 2001. 'A Canadian perspective on the precautionary approach/principle: Proposed guiding principles'; http://www.dfait-maeci.gc.ca/tna-nac/booklet-e.asp (accessed 10 May 2002).

Government of Canada. 2002. 'Final draft mandate for WTO negotiations.' Cabinet Memorandum, 7 August.

Gray, B. 1989. *Collaborating: Finding Common Ground for Multiparty Problems*. San Francisco: Jossey-Bass.

Green, A. 1992. *An Introduction to Health Planning in Developing Countries*. Oxford: Oxford University Press.

Greenspan, A. 1997. 'Testimony before Joint Economic Committee, United States Congress.' Washington, DC: Federal Reserve Board, 20 March; http://www.federalreserve .gov/boarddocs/testimony/1997/199703202.htm (accessed 27 May 2003).

Grieshaber-Otto, J. and Sanger, M. 2002. *Perilous Lessons: The Impact of the WTO Services Agreement (GATS) on Canada's Public Education System*. Ottawa: Canadian Centre for Policy Alternatives.

Grimmett, R. 2002. *Conventional Arms Transfers to Developing Nations, 1994–2001*. Washington, DC : Congressional Research Service; fpc.state.gov/documents/organization/12632.pdf (accessed 27 May 2003).

Guardian Weekly, The. 2002. 'Budget 2002. Chancellor's £40bn "kiss of life" to NHS angers employers as national insurance rises by 1%. Brown gambles all on health service.' 25 April–1 May.

Gwatkin, D.R., Guillot M. and Heuveline, P. 1999. 'The burden of disease among the global poor.' *The Lancet*, 354: 586–9.

Haacker, M. 2002. *The Economic Consequences of HIV/AIDS in Southern Africa*. WP02/38. Washington, DC: IMF; http://ideas.repec.org/p/imf/imfwpa/0238.html (accessed 22 December 2002).

Haddad, S. and Mohindra, K. 2001. *Macroeconomic Adjustment Policies, Health Sector Reform, and Access, Utilisation and Quality of Health Care: Studying the Macro-Micro Links*. Montreal: University of Montreal/International Development Research Centre.

Halifax Initiative. 2002. 'Open letter to the G7 finance ministers.' Halifax, Nova Scotia: Halifax Initiative; http://www.halifaxinitiative.org/hi.php/General/299 (accessed 3 January 2003).

Hall, A.J. and Cutts, F.T. 1993. 'Lessons from measles vaccination in developing countries.' *British Medical Journal*, 307: 1294–5.

Halstead, S.B., Walsh, J.A. and Warren, K. (eds). 1985. *Good Health at Low Cost*. New York: Rockefeller Foundation.

Hanlon, M. 2000. 'How much debt must be cancelled?' *Journal of International Development*, 12: 877–901.

Harcourt, W. 2000. 'Communicable diseases, gender and equity in health'; http://www.hsph.harvard.edu/Organizations/healthnet/Hupapers/gender/hartigan.html. (accessed 16 January 2003).

Hardon, A. 2001. 'Immunization for all? A critical look at the first GAVI partners meeting.' *HAI Europe*, 6(1): 1–8.

Hartung, W.D. and Moix, B. 2000. *Deadly Legacy: U.S. Arms to Africa and the Congo War*. New York: Arms Trade Resources Center; http://www.worldpolicy.org/projects/arms/reports/congo.htm (accessed 27 May 2003).

Hencke, D. 2002a. 'Short renews attack on air traffic deal.' *The Guardian*, 14 February.

Hencke, D. 2002b. 'Ministers at odds over £28m deal.' *The Guardian*, 20 March.

Hencke, D. 2002c. 'Short to visit Tanzania as fraud claims fly.' *The Guardian*, 26 June.

Hencke, D. 2002d. '£15m jet sparks new Tanzania row.' *The Guardian*, 22 July.

Hencke, D. 2002e. 'Short defends personal jet for Tanzania's president.' *The Guardian*, 27 July.

Herrera, M. 2003. 'Nicaragua: A nation in the dark.' In Social Watch, *The Poor and the Market: Social Watch Report 2003*. Montevideo: Instituto del Tercer Mundo, pp. 148–9; http://www.socialwatch.org.

Hertz, N. 2001. 'Why we must stay silent no longer.' *The Observer*, 8 April.

Hertzman, C. and Siddiqi, A. 2000. 'Health and rapid economic change in the late twentieth century.' *Social Science and Medicine*, 51: 809–19.

Hewitt de Alcántara, C. 2001. 'The development divide in a digital age: An issues paper.' Technology, Business and Society Programme Paper No. 4. Geneva: UNRISD; http://www.unrisd.org/unrisd/website/document.nsf/(httpPapers ForProgrammeArea)/19B0B342A4F1CF5B80256B5E0036D99F?OpenDocument (accessed 27 May 2003).

Hilary, J. 2001. *The Wrong Model: GATS, Trade Liberalisation and Children's Right to Health*. London: Save the Children; http://www.wtowatch.org/library/admin/uploadedfiles/Wrong_Model_GATS_Trade_Liberalisation_and_Chil.htm (accessed 27 May 2003).

H.M. Treasury (United Kingdom). 2003. 'International Finance Facility.' London: HMSO, January; http://www.hm-treasury.gov.uk/media//CA634/ACF6FB.pdf (accessed 27 May 2003).

Hochschild, A.R. 2000. 'Global care chains and emotional surplus value.' In W. Hutton and A. Giddens (eds), *Global Capitalism*. New York: New Press, pp. 130–46.

Holzmann, R., Jørgensen, S., Doryan, E., Van Adams, A., Ruby, A., Rutkowski, M., Arriagada, A., Tzannatos, Z. and Zagha, R. 2000. 'Social protection sector strategy:

From safety net to springboard.' Washington, DC: World Bank; http://wbln0018.worldbank.org/HDNet/hddocs.nsf/2d5135ecbf351de6852566a90069b8b6/1628e080eb4593a78525681c0070a518/$FILE/complete.pdf (accessed 27 May 2003).

Hong, E. 2000. 'Globalisation and the impact on health: A third world view.' Penang: Third World Network; http://www.twnside.org.sg/heal.htm (accessed 15 January 2003).

Human Rights Watch. 2002. *The FTAA, Access to HIV/AIDS Treatment and Human Rights*. New York: Human Rights Watch; http://www.hrw.org/press/2002/10/ftaa1029-bck.htm (accessed 27 May 2003).

Hurst, L. 2003. 'Arms trade: Our dirty secret.' *The Toronto Star*, 8 February: A25.

Iannariello, M., Stedman-Edwards, P., Reed, D. and Blain, R. 2000. *Environmental Impact Assessment of Macroeconomic Reform*. Geneva: World Wildlife Fund Macroeconomics Program Office.

In Common. 2001. *Trade and Poverty: What Role for Canada?* Ottawa: Canada Council for International Cooperation.

Intergovernmental Panel on Climate Change (IPCC). 2001. *Climate Change 2001: The Scientific Basis. Contribution of Working Group I to the Third Assessment Report of the Intergovernmental Panel on Climate Change*, J.T. Houghton *et al.* (eds). Cambridge: Cambridge University Press.

Inside US Trade. 2002. 'EU and US split over scope of TRIPS exception for public health.' 8 March; http://lists.essential.org/pipermail/ip-health/2002-March/002756.html (accessed 27 May 2003).

Intergovernmental Negotiating Body on the WHO Framework Convention on Tobacco Control. 2003. 'Draft WHO Framework Convention on Tobacco Control.' A/FCTC/INB6/5. Geneva: WHO; http://www.who.int/gb/fctc/PDF/inb6/einb65.pdf (accessed 22 March 2003).

International Confederation of Free Trade Unions (ICFTU). 2001. *Annual Survey of Violations of Trade Union Rights, 2001*. Brussels: ICFTU; http://www.icftu.org/ (accessed 14 February 2003).

International Confederation of Free Trade Unions (ICFTU). 2002. *Annual Survey of Violations of Trade Union Rights, 2002*. Brussels: ICFTU; http://www.icftu.org/ (accessed 14 February 2003).

International Development Association/IMF. 2002. *Review of the Poverty Reduction Strategy Paper (PRSP) Approach: Main Findings*. Washington, DC: IMF; http://www.imf.org/External/NP/prspgen/review/2002/031502a.pdf (accessed 15 March 2003).

International Energy Agency (IEA). 2001. *Energy Policies of IEA Countries: 2001 Review*. Paris: IEA/OECD.

International Energy Agency (IEA). 2003. *End-User Petroleum Product Prices and Average Crude Oil Import Costs, January 2003*. Paris: IEA.

International Food Policy Research Institute (IFPRI). 2000. 'Bridging the digital divide.' *IFPRI News & Views*, September; http://www.ifpri.org/2020/newslet/nv_0900/nv_0900.pdf (accessed 27 May 2003).

International Institute for Sustainable Development. 2001. 'Summary of the WTO Symposium on Issues Confronting the World Trading System. *Sustainable Development*, 55(1); http://www.iisd.ca/linkages/download/pdf/sdsdvol55num1.pdf (accessed 27 May 2003).

International Labour Organisation (ILO). 2002. *Key Indicators of the Labour Market, 2001–2002*. Geneva: ILO; http://www.ilo.org/public/english/support/publ/pindex.htm.

International Monetary Fund (IMF). 2001. *Structural Conditionality in Fund-Supported Programs*. Washington, DC: Policy Development and Review Department, IMF; http://www.imf.org/external/np/pdr/cond/2001/eng/struct/ (accessed 27 May 2003).

International Monetary Fund (IMF). 2002. 'Improving market access: Toward greater coherence between aid and trade.' Issues Brief. Washington, DC: IMF; http://www.imf.org/external/np/exr/ib/2002/032102.htm (accessed 27 May 2003).

International Monetary Fund (IMF), OECD, UN and World Bank Group. 2000. *2000 – A better world for all: Progress towards the International Development Goals*; http://www.paris21.org/betterworld (accessed 11 February 2003).

Ireland, E. and Webb, D. 2001. *No Quick Fix: A Sustained Response to HIV/AIDS and Children*. London: Save the Children, UK; available at http://www.scfuk.org.uk/hiv/publications.html (accessed 27 May 2003).

Iriart, C., Waitzkin, H. and Trotta, C. 2002. 'Global policies, health care systems and social movements in Latin America: A lesson from Argentina.' *Global Social Policy*, 2(3): 245–8.

Integrated Regional Research Network (IRIN). 2001. 'Ethiopia: Campaign to eradicate polio suffers setback.' Nairobi: UN Office for the Coordination of Humanitarian Affairs; http://www.irinnews.org/report.asp?ReportID=17681&SelectRegion=Horn_of_Africa&SelectCountry=ETHIOPIA (accessed 27 May 2003).

Integrated Regional Research Network (IRIN). 2002a. 'Africa: Brain drain reportedly costing US$4 billion a year.' Nairobi: UN Office for the Coordination of Humanitarian Affairs; http://www.irinnews.org/report.asp?ReportID=27536&SelectRegion=Africa&SelectCountry=AFRICA (accessed 27 May 2003).

Integrated Regional Research Network (IRIN). 2002b. 'Africa: Africa's 2001 growth faster than other developing countries.' Nairobi: UN Office for the Coordination of Humanitarian Affairs; http://www.irinnews.org/report.asp?ReportID=28749&SelectRegion=Africa&SelectCountry=AFRICA_(accessed 27 May 2003).

Integrated Regional Research Network (IRIN). 2002c. 'Malawi: Agricultural reforms hurt food security – report.' Nairobi: UN Office for the Coordination of Humanitarian Affairs; http://www.irinnews.org/report.asp?ReportID=29139&SelectRegion=Southern_Africa&SelectCountry=MALAWI (accessed 27 May 2003).

Iyer, S.R. 2002. 'Moves to strengthen sustainable-development institutions blocked.' *Third World Resurgence*, 145–6, September-October; http://www.twnside.org.sg/title/twr145e.htm (accessed 18 January 2003).

Jacoby, M.B. 2002. 'Does indebtedness influence health? A preliminary inquiry.' *Journal of Law, Medicine and Ethics*, 30: 560–71.

Jeter, J. 2002. 'The dumping ground: As Zambia courts western markets, used goods arrive at a heavy price' *The Washington Post*, 22 April: A1.

Jha, P., Mills, A., Hanson, K., Kumaranayake, L., Conteh, L., Kurowski, C., Nguyen, S., Cruz, V., Ranson, K., Vaz, L., Yu, S., Morton, O. and Sachs, J. 2002. 'Improving the health of the global poor.' *Science*, 295: 2036–9.

Johnston, D.C. 2002. 'Tax treaties with small nations turn into a new shield for profits.' *The New York Times*, 16 April.

Jolly, R. and Cornia, G.A. (eds). 1984. *The Impact of World Recession on Children*. New York: Pergamon.

Kahn, J. 2001. 'The rich-poor division is in stark relief in talks for trade agenda.' *The New York Times*, 1 November.

Kaul, I. 2001. 'Public goods: Taking the concept to the 21st century.' Paper prepared for the Auditing Public Domains project, Robarts Centre for Canadian Studies, York University, Toronto; http://www.robarts.yorku.ca/pdf/apd_kaulfin.pdf (accessed 14 February 2003).

Kaul, I., Grunberg, I. and Stern, M. 1999. 'Introduction.' In I. Kaul, I. Grunberg and M. Stern (eds), *Global Public Goods: International Cooperation in the 21st Century*. New York: UNDP/Oxford University Press.

Kickbusch, I. 2000. 'The development of international health policies – Accountability intact?' *Social Science and Medicine*, 51: 979–89.

King, M. (ed.) 1966. *Medical Care in Developing Countries. A Symposium from Makerere*. Oxford: Oxford University Press.

Kirton, J. 1999. 'Explaining G8 effectiveness.' In M.R. Hodges, J.J. Kirton and J.P. Daniels (eds), *The G8's Role in the New Millenium*. Ashgate: Aldershot, pp. 45–68.

Kirton, J. 2001. 'Guiding global economic governance.' In J.J. Kirton and G.M. von Furstenberg (eds), *New Directions in Global Economic Governance*. Ashgate: Aldershot, pp. 143–67.

Kirton, J. and Kokotsis, E. 2002. *Keeping Genoa's Commitments: The 2002 G8 Research Group Compliance Report, June 2002*; http://www.g7.utoronto.ca/g7/evaluations/ (accessed 7 June 2002).

Kirton, J. and Kokotsis, E. 2003. 'Impressions of the G8 Evian Summit.' Toronto: G8 Research Group, University of Toronto, 3 June; http://www.g8.utoronto.ca/evaluations/2003evian/assess_kirton_kokotsis.html (accessed 27 June 2003).

Kirton, J., Kokotsis, E. and Juricevic, D. 2001. *The 2001 G8 Compliance Report: Revised Version, July 7, 2001*; http://www.g7.utoronto.ca/g7/evaluations/ (accessed 2 February 2002).

Kirton, J. and Von Furstenberg, G. 2001. 'New directions in global economic governance: Challenges and responses.' In J.J. Kirton and G.M. von Furstenberg (eds), *New Directions in Global Economic Governance*. Ashgate: Aldershot, pp. 1–19.

Kondo, S. [Deputy Secretary-General, OECD]. 2002. 'Ending tax haven abuse.' Paris: OECD; www.oecd.org/pdf/M00028000/M00028566.pdf (accessed 3 February 2003).

Kovats, R.S., Menne, B., McMichael, A.J., Corvalan, C. and Bertollini, R. 2000. *Climate Change and Human Health: Impact and Adaptation*. Geneva: WHO.

Kremer, M. and Jayachandran, S. 2002a. 'Odious debt.' Brookings Institution Working Paper. Washington, DC: Brookings Institution; http://www.brookings.edu/views/papers/kremer/200204.htm (accessed 29 December 2002).

Kremer, M. and Jayachandran, S. 2002b. 'Odious debt.' Policy Brief No. 103. Washington, DC: Brookings Institution.

Kristof, N. 1998a. 'Asia feels strain most at society's margins.' *The New York Times*, 8 June.

Kristof, N. 1998b. 'As Asian economies shrink, women are squeezed out.' *The New York Times*, 11 June.

Krueger, A. 2001. 'International financial architecture for 2002: A new approach to sovereign debt restructuring.' Address to National Economists' Club Annual Members' Dinner, Washington, DC, 26 November. Washington, DC: IMF; http://www.imf.org/external/np/speeches/2001/112601.htm (accessed 23 November 2002).

Kruse, T. and Ramos, C. 2003. 'Bolivia: Water and privatisation: Doubtful benefits, concrete threats.' In Social Watch, *The Poor and the Market: Social Watch Report 2003*. Montevideo: Instituto del Tercer Mundo, pp. 88–9; http://www.socialwatch.org.

Labonte, R. 1998. 'Healthy public policy and the World Trade Organization: A proposal for an international health presence in future world trade/investment talks.' *Health Promotion International*, 13(3): 245–56.

Labonte, R. 1999. 'Globalism and health: Threats and opportunities.' *Health Promotion Journal of Australia*, 9(2): 126–32.

Labonte, R. 2000. 'Brief to the World Trade Organization: World trade and population health.' *International Journal of Health Promotion and Education*, 6(4): 24–32.

Labonte, R. 2002. 'International governance and World Trade Organization reform.' *Critical Public Health*, 12(1): 65–86.

Labonte, R. and Spiegel, J. 2002. 'Setting global health priorities for funding Canadian researchers: A discussion paper prepared for the Institute on Population and Public Health'; http://www.spheru.ca (accessed 14 December 2002).

Labonte, R. and Torgerson, R. 2002. *Frameworks for Analyzing the Links between Globalization and Health*. Mimeo, Draft Report to WHO, Geneva. SPHERU, University of Saskatchewan; http://www.spheru.ca (accessed 14 December 2002).

Lawlor, D. 2001. 'Water, tobacco, and global inequalities.' *Journal of Epidemiology and Community Health*, 55: 852.

Lawrence, P. (ed.). 1986. *World Recession and the Food Crisis in Africa*. London: James Currey.

Leblanc, D. 2002. 'Man of action aims to make a difference in Africa.' *The Globe and Mail* (Toronto), 13 April: A4.

Lee, K. 2001. 'Globalization: A new agenda for health?' In M. McKee, P. Garner and R. Scott (eds), *International Co-operation in Health*. Oxford: Oxford University Press, pp. 13–30.

Lee, M. 2002. 'Africa shortchanged: The Global Fund and the G8 agenda.' *Behind the Numbers*, 4(4), 20 June; http://www.policyalternatives.ca/publications/btn4-4.pdf (accessed 27 May 2003)

Legge, D.M. 1993. 'Investing in the shaping of world health policy.' Paper presented at AIDAB, NCEPH and PHA Workshop to discuss Investing in Health, 31 August, Canberra.

Leon, F. 2002. 'The case of the Chilean health system, 1983–2000.' In C. Vieira and N. Drager (eds), *Trade in Health Services: Global, Regional and Country Perspectives*. Washington, DC: PAHO, pp. 155–84; http://www.paho.org/English/HDP/HDD/20Fran.pdf (accessed 27 May 2003).

Lethbridge, J. 2002. 'International Finance Corporate health care policy briefing.' *Global Social Policy*, 2(3): 349–53.

Levin, M. 2003. 'Outlook for OFCs.' *Offshore Finance Canada*, 8(1): 52–4.

Lewis, J. 1999. 'The Americas shift towards private health care.' *The Economist*, 8 May: 27–9.

Lewis, S. 2002. 'Keynote address to the G6B People's Summit, 21 June 2002'; http://www.g6bpeoplessummit.org (accessed 15 September 2002).

Loftus, A.J. and McDonald, D. 2001. 'Of liquid dreams: A political ecology of water privatization in Buenos Aires.' *Environment & Urbanization*, 13: 179–99.

Loungani, P. and Mauro, P. 2000. 'Capital flight from Russia.' Paper presented to the Conference on Post-Election Strategy, Moscow, 5–7 April. Washington, DC: Research Department, IMF; http://www.imf.org/external/pubs/ft/seminar/ 2000/invest/pdf/loung.pdf (accessed 19 September 2002).

Lucas, C. [Member of the European Parliament]. 2001. 'Doha spells disaster for development.' *The Observer*, 18 November.

Lupie, S.J., King, S., Meaney, M.J. and McEwen, B.S. 2001. 'Can poverty get under your skin? Basal cortisol levels and cognitive function in children from low and high socioeconomic status.' *Development and Psychopathology*, 13: 653–76.

MacAskill, E. (2002). 'Tanzania confirms air traffic contract.' *The Guardian*, 4 March.

MacKinnon, M. 2003. 'Russian stall could kill Kyoto pact, activists say.' *The Globe and Mail* (Toronto), 1 March: A15.

Martin, P. 2002. 'Foreign debt: There's a better way.' *The Globe and Mail* (Toronto), 8 May 8: A15.

McClelland, C. 2002. 'South Africa brain drain costing $5 billion – and counting.' *Canadian Medical Association Journal*, 167(7): 793.

McDonald, D. 2002. 'No money, no service.' *Alternatives Journal*, 28(2): 16–20.

McDonald, D. and Smith, L. 2002. 'Privatizing Cape Town: Service delivery and policy reforms since 1996.' MSP Occasional Paper No. 7. Kingston, Ontario: Municipal Services Project, Queen's University; http://qsilver.queensu.ca/~mspadmin/pages/Project_Publications/Series/7.htm (accessed 27 May 2003).

McDonald, S. 2003. 'Bush criticized for not giving AIDS money to Global Fund.' *British Medical Journal*, 326: 299.

McEwen, B.S. 2000a. 'The neurobiology of stress: From serendipity to clinical relevance.' *Brain Research*, 886(1–2): 172–89.

McEwen, B.S. 2000b. 'Allostasis and allostatic load: Implications for neuropsychopharmacology.' *Neuropsychopharmacology*, 22:108–24.

McEwen, B.S. 2001. 'From molecules to mind: Stress, individual differences, and the social environment.' *Annals of the New York Academy of Science*, 935: 42–9.

McEwen, B.S. and Magarinos, A.M. 2001. 'Stress and hippocampal plasticity: Implications for the pathophysiology of affective disorders.' *Human Psychopharmacology*, 16(1): S7–S19.

McMichael, A.J. 2000. 'Global environmental change in the coming century: How sustainable are recent health gains?' In D. Pimentel, L. Westra and R. Noss (eds), *Ecological Integrity: Integrating Environment, Conservation and Health*. Washington, DC: Island Press, pp. 245–60.

McMichael, A.J. 2001. *Human Frontiers, Environment and Disease: Past Patterns, Uncertain Futures*. Cambridge: Cambridge University Press.

McMichael, A.J. and Githeko, A. 2001. 'Human health.' In J.J. McCarthy, O.F. Canziani, N.A. Leary, D.J. Dokken and K.S. White (eds), *Climate Change 2001: Impacts, Adaptation, and Vulnerability. Contribution of Working Group II to the Third Assessment Report of the Intergovernmental Panel on Climate Change*. Cambridge: Cambridge University Press, pp. 451–85.

Médecins sans Frontières (MSF). 2001a. *Fatal Imbalance: The Crisis in Research and Development for Drugs for Neglected Diseases*. Geneva: Campaign for Access to Essential Medicines/MSF; http://www.accessmed-msf.org/prod/publications.asp?scntid=30112001115034 &contenttype=PARA& (accessed 27 May 2003).

Médecins sans Frontières (MSF). 2001b. *A Matter of Life and Death: The Role of Patents in Access to Essential Medicines*. Geneva: Campaign for Access to Essential Medicines/MSF; http://www.msf.org/countries/page.cfm?articleid=47871B51-83A7-4960-BDD40D60958FC49F (accessed 27 May 2003).

Mediterranean Commission on Sustainable Development. 2001. *Free Trade and the Environment in the Euro-Mediterranean Context, First Synthesis Report*. Valbonne: Blue Plan Regional Activity Centre; http://www.planbleu.org/indexa.htm (accessed 27 May 2003).

Melgar, J. 1999. 'Ailing Philippine health: Proof of market failings.' *Development*, 42(4): 138–41.

Milanovic, B. 2003. 'The two faces of globalization: Against globalization as we know it.' *World Development*, 31: 667–83.

Milward, B. 2000. 'What is structural adjustment?' In G. Mohan, E. Brown, B. Milward and A.B. Zack-Williams (eds), *Structural Adjustment: Theory, Practice and Impacts.* London and New York: Routledge, pp. 24–38.

Ministry of Foreign Affairs, Japan. 2000. 'Japan's concrete actions to follow up the Okinawa Infectious Diseases Initiative'; http://www.mofa.go.jp/policy/economy/summit/2000/genoa/infection3.html (accessed 16 January 2003).

Ministry of Foreign Affairs, Japan. 2002. 'Japan's latest education assistance initiatives: Education for All'; http://www.mofa.go.jp/policy/oda/category/education/action/05.html (accessed 11 June 2003).

Mngxitama, A. and Eveleth, A. 2003. 'South Africa: The widening gap between rich and poor.' In Social Watch, *The Poor and the Market: Social Watch Report 2003.* Montevideo: Instituto del Tercer Mundo, pp. 168–9; http://www.socialwatch.org.

Monbiot, G. 2003. 'Africa's scar gets angrier.' *The Guardian*, 3 June.

Moore, B. 1966. *The Social Origins of Dictatorship and Democracy*. Boston: Beacon Press.

Moreno, J. 2002. 'Homeowner's dream becomes personal nightmare.' *Houston Chronicle*, 5 September; http://www.houstonchronicle.com (accessed 27 June 2003).

Mulvany, P. 2002. *Hunger – A Gnawing Shame*. Report from World Food Summit: Five years later. Intermediate Technology Development Group; http://www.ukabc.org/wfs5+report.pdf (accessed 3 March 2003).

Murphy, S. 1999. *The Coming WTO Round on Agricultural Trade: Perspectives and Trends*. Minneapolis: Institute for Agriculture and Trade Policy.

Murphy, S. 2000. *Agriculture, Trade and Developing Countries: Where to After Seattle?* Minneapolis: Institute for Agriculture and Trade Policy.

Murray, C.J.L. and Acharya, A.K. 1997. 'Understanding DALYs.' *Journal of Health Economics*, 16: 703–30.

Myerson, A. 1995. 'Out of a crisis, an opportunity.' *The New York Times*, 26 September.

Nafziger, E.W. and Auvinen, J. 2002. 'Economic development, inequality, war and state violence.' *World Development*, 30: 153–63.

Naidoo, K. 2003. 'Civil society, governance and globalisation: World Bank Presidential Fellows Lecture.' Washington, DC: World Bank; http://lnweb18.worldbank.org/essd/essd.nsf/0/943999D14D69CEB585256CC900838324?OpenDocument (accessed 27 May 2003).

Naiman, R. 2001. 'Why we must open the meetings of the IMF and World Bank boards: The case of user fees on primary healthcare in Tanzania'; http://www.foreignpolicy-infocus.org/commentary/0106userfee_body.html (accessed 4 January 2002).

Narayan, D. 2001. 'Consultations with the poor from a health perspective.' *Development*, 44(1): 15–21.

Narayan D., Chambers, R., Shah, M. and Petesch, P. 2000. *Voices of the Poor: Crying Out for Change*. New York: Oxford University Press for the World Bank.

Naylor, R.T. 1987. *Hot Money: Peekaboo Finance and the Politics of Debt.* Toronto: McClelland & Stewart.

Ndikumana, L. and Boyce, J.K. 2003. 'Public debts and private assets: Explaining capital flight from sub-Saharan African countries.' *World Development,* 31: 107–30.

New Partnership for Africa's Development (NEPAD). 2001. Abuja, 21 October.

NGO Working Group on the Export Development Corporation. 2000. *Reckless Lending, Volume I: How Canada's Export Development Corporation Puts People and the Environment at Risk.* Halifax, Nova Scotia: Halifax Initiative; http://www. halifaxiniative.org/Reckless5.pdf (accessed 15 February 2003).

NGO Working Group on the Export Development Corporation. 2001. *Reckless Lending, Volume II: How Canada's Export Development Corporation Puts People and the Environment at Risk.* Halifax, Nova Scotia: Halifax Initiative; http://www. halifaxiniative.org/final1.pdf (accessed 15 February 2003).

NGO Working Group on Export Development Canada. 2003. *Seven Deadly Secrets: What Export Development Canada Doesn't Want You to Know.* Halifax, Nova Scotia: Halifax Initiative; http://www.halifaxiniative.org/updir/5_pam_secrets.pdf (accessed 15 February 2003).

Niu, S.R., Yang, G., Chen, Z., Wang, J., Wang, G., He, X., Schoepff, H., Boreham, J., Pan, H. and Peto, R. 1998. 'Emerging tobacco hazards in China: 2. Early mortality results from a prospective study.' *British Medical Journal,* 317: 1423–4.

Nolen, S. 2002a. 'Economic downturn curbs arms sales to developing countries.' *The Globe and Mail* (Toronto), 10 August: A11.

Nolen, S. 2002b. 'Global AIDS fund is short $8-billion.' *The Globe and Mail* (Toronto), 12 October: A14.

Norlen, D., Cox, R., Kim, M. and Glazebrook, C. 2002. *Unusual Suspects: Unearthing the Shadowy World of Export Credit Agencies.* Oakland: Pacific Environment; http:// www.pacificenvironment.org/PDF/UsualSuspects.pdf (accessed 12 February 2003).

Norton-Taylor, R., White, M. and Hencke, D. 2002. 'Tanzania cash for BAE system on hold pending inquiry.' *The Guardian,* 21 March.

Nye, J.S. 2002. *The Paradox of American Power: Why the World's Only Superpower Can't Do It Alone.* Oxford: Oxford University Press.

O'Brien, R. 2002. 'Organizational politics, multilateral economic organizations and social policy.' *Global Social Policy,* 2: 141–62.

Ollila, E. 2003. *Global Health-Related Public-Private Partnerships and the United Nations.* Helsinki: Globalism and Social Policy Programme, STAKES; http://www.stakes.fi/ gaspp/publications/brief2_summary.htm (accessed 27 May 2003).

Organization for Economic Co-operation and Development (OECD). 1998. *Harmful Tax Competition: An Emerging Global Issue.* Paris: OECD; www.oecd.org/pdf/ M00004000/M00004517.pdf (accessed 22 November 2002).

Organization for Economic Co-operation and Development (OECD). 2000. *Recent Trends in Official Development Assistance to Health.* Paris: OECD; www.cmhealth.org/

docs/oda_to_health.pdf (accessed 27 May 2003).

Organization for Economic Co-operation and Development (OECD). 2001a. *Understanding the Digital Divide.* Paris: OECD; www.oecd.org/pdf/M00002000/ M00002444.pdf (accessed 27 May 2003).

Organization for Economic Co-operation and Development (OECD). 2001b. *OECD's Project on Harmful Tax Practices: The 2001 Progress Report.* Paris: Centre for Tax Policy and Administration, OECD; www.oecd.org/pdf/M00021000/M00021182.pdf (accessed 27 May 2003).

Organization for Economic Co-operation and Development (OECD). 2001c. 'Development Co-operation: 2000 Report.' *DAC Journal,* 2(1): entire issue.

Organization for Economic Co-operation and Development (OECD). 2002a. 'Information note on export credit agencies and common approaches to the environment.' Room Document No. 1, prepared for OECD Global Forum on International Investment, Conference on Foreign Direct Investment and the Environment: Lessons to be Learned from the Mining Sector, 7–8 February. Paris: OECD; http://www.oecd.org/pdf/M00025000/M00025577.pdf (accessed 27 May 2003).

Organization for Economic Co-operation and Development (OECD). 2002b. 'Development co-operation: 2001 report.' *DAC Journal,* 3(1): entire issue.

Organization for Economic Co-operation and Development (OECD). 2003. 'Development Co-operation: 2002 Report.' *DAC Journal,* 4(1): entire issue.

Osberg, L. and Sharpe, A. 1999. 'An index of economic well-being for Canada.' Paper R-99-3E. Ottawa: Applied Research Branch, Strategic Policy, Human Resources Development Canada.

O'Sullivan, B. and Chapman, S. 2000. 'Eyes on the prize: Transnational tobacco companies in China 1976–1997.' *Tobacco Control,* 9: 292–302.

Oxfam. 2000. *Tax Havens: Releasing the Hidden Billions for Poverty Eradication.* Oxford: Oxfam GB; http://www.oxfam.org.uk/policy/papers/taxhvn/tax.htm (accessed 27 May 2003).

Oxfam. 2001a. *G8: Failing the World's Children.* Washington, DC: Oxfam International; http://www.oxfam.org/eng/pdfs/ pp0107_G8_Failing_the_Worlds_Children.pdf (accessed 27 May 2003).

Oxfam. 2001b. *Where's the Money? G8 promises, G8 failures.* Washington, DC: Oxfam International; http://www.oxfam.org/eng/pdfs/ pp0107_G8_Where_is_the_money.pdf (accessed 27 May 2003).

Oxfam Canada. 2002. *Oxfam Canada Submission on Market Access.* Ottawa: Oxfam Canada.

Pan, P. 2002. 'Worked till they drop: Few protections for China's new laborers.' *The Washington Post,* 13 May: A1.

Pan American Health Organization (PAHO). 2002a. *Health and Hemispheric Security.*

Washington: PAHO; http://www.paho.org/English/HDP/hdr-up-Nov.pdf (accessed 27 May 2003).

Pan American Health Organization (PAHO). 2002b. *Profits Over People: Tobacco Industry Activities to Market Cigarettes and Undermine Public Health in Latin America and the Caribbean*. Washington: PAHO; http://www.paho.org/English/HPP/HPM/ TOH/ profits_over_people.pdf (accessed 27 May 2003).

Pang, T., Lansang, M.A. and Haines, A. 2002. 'Brain drain and health professionals: A global problem needs global solutions.' Editorial. *British Medical Journal*, 324: 499–500.

Patrick, K. 2003. 'Bush to ask Canada for more AIDS money.' *The Globe and Mail* (Toronto), 17 May: A17.

Patz, J.A. and Kovats, R.S. 2002. 'Hotspots in climate change and human health.' *British Medical Journal*, 325: 1094–8.

Pécoul, B., Chirac, P., Trouiller, P. and Pinel, J. 1999. 'Access to essential drugs in poor countries: A lost battle?' *Journal of the American Medical Association*, 281: 361–7.

People's Health Assembly. 2000a. Untitled Draft Discussion Paper. Dhaka: Gonomudran Limited.

People's Health Assembly. 2000b. 'Health in the era of globalisation: From victims to protagonists.' Dhaka: PHA Secretariat; http://www.ldb.org/iphw/pha2000.pdf (accessed 27 May 2003).

Pettifor, A. 2002. *Chapter 9/11? Resolving International Debt Crises – The Jubilee Framework for International Insolvency*. London: Jubilee Research; http:// www.jubileeplus.org/analysis/reports/jubilee_framework.pdf (accessed 27 May 2003).

Pettifor, A. and Raffer, K. 2003. *Report of the IMF's Conference on the Sovereign Debt Restructuring Mechanism*. London: Jubilee Research; http://www.jubilee2000uk.org/ (accessed 24 March 2003).

Pettifor, A., Thomas, B. and Telatin, M. 2001. *HIPC – Flogging a Dead Process*. London: Jubilee Plus Coalition; http://www.jubileeplus.org/analysis/reports/ flogging_process_text.htm (accessed 27 May 2003).

Pinstrup-Andersen, P. 1987. 'Macroeconomic adjustment policies and human nutrition: Available evidence and research needs.' *Food and Nutrition Bulletin* 9(1): 69–86.

Pollock, A. and Price, D. 2000. 'Rewriting the regulations: How the World Trade Organisation could accelerate privatisation in health-care systems.' *The Lancet*, 356: 1995–2000.

Pollock, A., Shaoul, J. and Vickers, N. 2002. 'Private finance and "value for money" in NHS hospitals: A policy in search of a rationale?' *British Medical Journal*, 324: 1205–9.

Price, D., Pollock, A. and Shaoul, J. 1999. 'How the World Trade Organisation is shaping domestic policies in health care.' *The Lancet*, 354: 1889–91.

Price-Smith, A. 2002. *The Health of Nations: Infectious Disease, Environmental Change, and Their Effects on National Security and Development.* Cambridge, MA: MIT Press.

Princeton Survey Research Associates. 2003. *The Global Poll: Multinational Survey of Opinion Leaders 2002, Full Report.* Washington, DC: World Bank, May; http://www.siteresources.worldbank.org/NEWS/Resources/globalpoll.pdf (accessed 12 June 2003).

Pronk, J. 2000. 'Globalization: A developmental report.' In J.N. Pieterse (ed.), *Global Futures: Shaping Globalization.* London: Zed Books, pp. 40–52.

Prüss, A., Kay, D., Fewtrell, L. and Bartram, D. 2002. 'Estimating the burden of disease from water, sanitation, and hygiene at a global level.' *Environmental Health Perspectives*, 110: 537–42.

Public Citizen. 2003. 'Fiasco: Buenos Aires.' http://www.citizen.org/cmep/Water/cmep_Water/reports/argentina/articles.cfm?ID=9207 (accessed 22 April 2003).

Puckett, J., Byster, L., Westervelt, S., Gutierrez, R., Davis, S., Hussain, A. and Dutta, M. 2002. *Exporting Harm: The High-Tech Trashing of Asia.* Seattle: Basel Action Network; http://www.ban.org (accessed 10 August 2002).

Quinlan, M., Mayhew, C. and Bohle, P. 2001. 'The global expansion of precarious employment, work disorganization, and consequences for occupational health: A review of recent research.' *International Journal of Health Services*, 31: 335–414.

Read, R. 2001. 'The anatomy of the EU-US WTO banana trade dispute.' *The Estey Centre Journal of International Law and Trade Policy*, 2(2): 257–82.

Reader, R. 2002. 'See no evil.' *Alternatives Journal*, 28, Spring: 28–30.

Reddy, S.G. and Pogge, T.W. 2002. 'How not to count the poor.' New York: Columbia University, 15 August; http://www.hsph.harvard.edu/hcpds/Reddy%20count.pdf (accessed 7 January 2003).

Reich, M. 2000. 'The global drug gap.' *Science*, 287, 1979–81.

Reinicke, W. 1998. *Global Public Policy: Governing without Government?* Washington, DC: Brookings Institute.

Reveles, R.A. and Terán, A.S. 2001. 'Mexico: Among the most unequal.' In Social Watch, *Social Watch Report No. 5, 2001.* Montevideo: Instituto del Tercer Mundo, pp. 130–1; http://www.socialwatch.org.

Rhi-Suasi, J. and Zupi, M. 2002. 'Italy.' In J. Randel, T. German and D. Ewing (eds), *The Reality of Aid 2002.* Manila: IBON Foundation, pp. 206–10.

Rice, A., Sacco, L., Hyder, A. and Black, R. 2000. 'Malnutrition as an underlying cause of childhood deaths associated with infectious diseases in developing countries.' *Bulletin of the World Health Organization*, 78: 1207–21.

Rich, B. 2000. 'Exporting destruction.' *The Environmental Forum*, November-December: 32–41; http://www.environmentaldefense.org/documents/636_D1943_Forum.pdf (accessed 3 January 2003).

Rich, B., Horta, K. and Goldzimer, A. 2000. 'Export credit agencies in sub-Saharan Africa: Indebtedness for extractive industries, corruption and conflict.' Washington,

DC: Environmental Defense Fund; http://www.environmentaldefense.org/documents/638_ACF666.pdf (accessed 6 January 2003).

Richards, T. 2001. 'New global health fund.' *British Medical Journal*, 322: 1321-2.

Rock, M. 2000. 'Discounted lives? Weighing disability when measuring health and ruling on "compassionate" murder.' *Social Science and Medicine*, 51: 407-17.

Rodriguez, F. 1987. 'Consequences of capital flight for Latin American debtor countries.' In D. Lessard and J. Williamson (eds), *Capital Flight and Third World Debt*. Washington, DC: Institute for International Economics, pp. 129-44.

Rodriguez, F. and Rodrik, D. 2000. 'Trade policy and economic growth: A skeptic's guide to the cross-national evidence.' Discussion Paper 2143. London: Centre for Economic Policy Research.

Rodrik, D. 1999. *The New Global Economy and Developing Countries: Making Openness Work*. Baltimore: Johns Hopkins University Press .

Rodrik, D. 2001. *The Global Governance of Trade as if Development Really Mattered*. New York: Bureau for Development Policy, UNDP, October; http://www.undp.org/mainundp/propoor/docs/ pov_globalgovernancetrade_pub.pdf (accessed 27 May 2003).

Rosenbaum, D.E. 2002. 'Taking on offshore tax havens.' *The New York Times*, 6 May.

Rosset, P. 2002. 'U.S. opposes right to food at World Summit.' *World Editorial & International Law*, 30 June; http://www.foodfirst.org/media/opeds/2002/usopposes.html (accessed 22 November 2003).

Ryle, S. 2002. 'Consumers must be prepared to pay more to end banana war.' *The Guardian Weekly*, 5-11 December: 26.

Sachs, J. 2000. 'A new global consensus on helping the poorest of the poor.' Keynote Address to the Annual World Bank Conference on Development Economics. Washington, DC: World Bank, 19 April; http://orion.forumone.com/ABCDE/files.fcgi/210_Sachs.pdf (accessed 2 January 2003).

Sachs, J. and Malaney, P. 2002. 'The economic and social burden of malaria.' *Nature*, 415: 680-5.

Sanders, D., Dovlo, D., Meeus, W. and Lehmann, U. 2002. 'Public health in Africa.' In R. Beaglehole (ed.), *Global Public Health: A New Era*. Oxford: Oxford University Press.

Sandler, T. 1999. 'Intergenerational public goods: Strategies, efficiency and institutions.' In I. Kaul, I. Grunberg and M. Stern (eds), *Global Public Goods: International Cooperation in the 21st Century*. New York: UNDP/Oxford University Press, pp. 20-50.

Sandler, T. and Arce, D. 2000. 'A conceptual framework for understanding global and transnational goods for health.' Paper WG2:1, Commission on Macroeconomics and Health; http://www.cmhealth.org/docs/wg2_paper1.pdf (accessed 27 May 2003).

Sangaralingam, M. and Raman, M. 2003. 'Malaysia: The high cost of private monopolies.' In Social Watch, *The Poor and the Market: Social Watch Report 2003*. Montevideo: Instituto del Tercer Mundo, pp. 128-9; http://www.socialwatch.org.

Sanger, D. and Landler, M. 1999. 'Asian rebound derails reform as many suffer.' *The New York Times*, 12 July.

Santiso, J. 1999. 'Wall Street and the Mexican crisis: A temporal analysis of emerging markets.' *International Political Science Review*, 20: 49–71.

Sauvé, R. 2001. *The Current State of Family Finances – 2000 Report*. Ottawa: Vanier Institute of the Family.

Savedoff, W. and Schultz, T.P. (eds). 2000. *Wealth from Health: Linking Social Investments to Earnings in Latin America*. Washington, DC: Inter-American Development Bank.

Schmidt, V.A. 1995. 'The New World Order, Incorporated: The rise of business and the decline of the nation-state.' *Daedalus*, 124(2): 75–106.

Schoepf, B. 1998. 'Inscribing the body politic: AIDS in Africa.' In M. Lock and P. Kaufert (eds), *Pragmatic Women and Body Politics*. Cambridge: Cambridge University Press, pp. 98–126.

Schoepf, B., Schoepf, C. and Millen, J. 2000. 'Theoretical therapies, remote remedies: SAPs and the political ecology of poverty and health in Africa.' In J. Yong Kim, J. Millen, A. Irwin and J. Gershman (eds), *Dying for Growth: Global Inequality and the Health of the Poor*. Monroe: Common Courage Press, pp. 91–126.

Schrecker, T. 2001. 'Using science in environmental policy: Can Canada do better?' In E. Parson (ed.), *Governing the Environment: Persistent Challenges, Uncertain Innovations*. Toronto: University of Toronto Press, pp. 31–72.

Schrecker, T. 2002. 'Place, class, and the privatized environment.' In S. Boyd, D. Chunn and R. Menzies (eds), *Toxic Criminology: Environment, Law and the State in Canada*. Halifax, Nova Scotia: Fernwood, pp. 45–57.

Schwartz-Nobel, L. 2002. *Growing Up Empty: The Hunger Epidemic in America*. New York: Harper Collins.

Segara, A.E. and Fletcher, S.R. 2001. *Biosafety Protocol for Genetically Modified Organisms: Overview*. Washington, DC: Congressional Research Service, Library of Congress, 18 January; http://www.usembassy.at/en/download/pdf/biosafety.pdf (accessed 27 May 2003).

Sen, A. 1981. *Poverty and Famines: An Essay on Entitlement and Deprivation*. New York: Oxford University Press.

Sen, A. 1982. 'The food problem: Theory and policy.' *Third World Quarterly*, 4: 447–59.

Sen, A. 1989. 'Food and freedom.' *World Development*, 17: 769–81.

Sen, A. 1999. *Development as Freedom*. New York: Knopf.

Sen, K. and Bonita, R. 2000. 'Global health status: Two steps forward, one step back.' *The Lancet*, 356: 577–81.

Shaffer, E., Brenner, J. and Yamin, A. 2002. *Comments Regarding the Free Trade Area of the Americas Negotiations: Effects on Universal Access to Health Care and Water Services*.

San Francisco: Center for Policy Analysis on Trade and Health; http://lists.essential.org/pipermail/ip-health/2002-September/003458.html (accessed 27 May 2003).

Shand, H. 2001. 'Gene giants: Understanding the "Life Industry".' In B. Tokar (ed.), *Redesigning Life? The Worldwide Challenge to Genetic Engineering.* London: Zed Books, pp. 222–37.

Sieswerda, L., Soskolne, C., Newman, S., Schopflocher, D. and Smoyer, K. 2001. 'Toward measuring the impact of ecological disintegrity on human health.' *Epidemiology*, 12: 28–32.

Simms C., Rowson, M. and Peattie, S. 2001. *The Bitterest Pill of All: The Collapse of Africa's Health Systems.* London: Medact/Save the Children; http://193.129.255.93/pressrels/PDFS/Bitterpill.pdf (accessed 23 November 2002).

Sinclair, S. 2000. *GATS: How the World Trade Organization's New 'Services' Negotiations Threaten Democracy.* Ottawa: Canadian Centre for Policy Alternatives.

Sklar, H., Mykyta, L. and Wefald, S. 2002. *Raise the Floor: Wages and Policies that Work for All of Us.* Boston: South End Press.

Skogstad, G. 2001. 'Internationalization, democracy, and food safety measures: The (il)legitimacy of consumer preferences?' *Global Governance*, 7: 293–316.

Smith, L. and Haddad, L. 2000. *Overcoming Child Malnutrition in Developing Countries: Past Achievement and Future Choices.* Washington, DC: International Food Policy Research Institute.

Social Watch. 2002. *Social Watch Report No. 6, 2002: The Social Impact of Globalisation in the World.* Montevideo: Instituto del Tercer Mundo; http://www.socialwatch.org.

Social Watch. 2003. *The Poor and the Market: Social Watch Report 2003.* Montevideo: Instituto del Tercer Mundo; http://www.socialwatch.org.

South African Demographic and Health Survey. 1998. *Preliminary Report.* Pretoria: Medical Research Council, Department of Health, MACRO International Inc.

Spinaci, S. and Heymann, D. 2001. 'Communicable disease and disability of the poor.' *Development*, 44(1): 66–72.

Starling, M., Brugha, R. and Walt, G. 2002. *New Products into Old Systems: The Global Alliance for Vaccines and Immunization (GAVI) From a Country Perspective.* London: Save the Children UK and London School of Hygiene and Tropical Medicine; http://www.savethechildren.org.uk/development/latest/Gavi_report_text.pdf (accessed 27 May 2003).

Steptoe, A., Feldman, P.J., Kunz, S., Owen, N., Willemsen, G. and Marmot, M. 2002. 'Stress responsivity and socioeconomic status: A mechanism for increased cardiovascular disease risk?' *European Heart Journal*, 23: 1757–63.

Stern, B. 2003. 'WTO fails to deliver agreement on drugs.' *The Guardian Weekly*, 2–8 January: 25.

Stewart, F. 1991. 'The many faces of adjustment.' *World Development*, 19: 1847–64.

Stiglitz, J. 2002a. 'A fair deal for the world.' *The New York Review of Books*, 49, 23 May: 24–8.

Stiglitz, J. 2002b. 'The roaring nineties.' *The Atlantic Online*, October; http://www.theatlantic.com/issues/2002/10/stiglitz.htm (accessed 17 March 2003).

Stolberg, S. 2002 'World Health Organization calls for higher taxes on tobacco.' *The New York Times*, 28 February.

Stolberg, S. 2003. 'Bush proposal on AIDS funds shows concern about security.' *The New York Times*, 29 January.

Structural Adjustment Participatory Review International Network (SAPRIN). 2002. *The Policy Roots of Economic Crisis and Poverty: A Multi-Country Participatory Assessment of Structural Adjustment.* Washington, DC: SAPRIN; http://www.saprin.org/SAPRI_Findings.pdf (accessed 27 May 2003).

Sullivan, T. and Shainblum, E. 2001. 'Trading in health: The World Trade Organization (WTO) and the international regulation of health and safety.' *Health Law in Canada*, November.

Szreter, S. 1988. 'The importance of social intervention in Britain's mortality decline c. 1850–1914: A re-interpretation of the role of public health.' *Social History of Medicine*, 1(1): 1–41.

Takayanagi, A. 2002. 'Japan.' In J. Randel, T. German and D. Ewing (eds), *The Reality of Aid 2002.* Manila: IBON Foundation, pp. 211–14.

Tannenbaum, D. 2002. 'Obsessed: The latest chapter in the World Bank's privatization plans.' *Multinational Monitor*, September; http://www.multinationalmonitor.org/mm2002/02september/sept02corp1.html (accessed 2 January 2003).

Tandon, Y. 2000. 'The role of foreign direct investments in Africa's human development.' Paper prepared for UN Conference on Trade and Development. Oslo: Solidaritetshuset; http://www.solidaritetshuset.org/rorg/dok/arkiv/ytfdi1.htm (accessed 4 April 2003).

Tanoh, G. and Kusack, K. 2003. 'Ghana: The struggle over water.' In Social Watch, *The Poor and the Market: Social Watch Report 2003.* Montevideo: Instituto del Tercer Mundo, pp. 110–11; http://www.socialwatch.org.

Taylor, A., Chaloupka, F., Guindon, E. and Corbett, M. 2000. 'The impact of trade liberalization on tobacco consumption.' In P. Jha and F. Chaloupka (eds), *Tobacco Control Policies in Developing Countries.* Oxford: Oxford University Press, pp. 343–64.

Tesh, S. 1990. *Hidden Arguments: Political Ideology and Disease Prevention Policy.* New Brunswick: Rutgers University Press.

Thankappan, K.R. 2001. 'Some health implications of globalization in Kerala, India.' *Bulletin of the World Health Organization*, 79: 892–3.

Third World Network. 2001. 'Everything but development: The Doha WTO outcome and process.' *Third World Resurgence*, No. 135–6, November-December; http://www.twnside.org.sg/title/focus27.htm (accessed 3 November 2002).

Third World Network/UNDP. 2001. *The Multilateral Trading System: A Development Perspective.* New York: Bureau for Development Policy, UNDP; http://www.undp.org/mainundp/propoor/docs/multitradesystem.pdf_(accessed 27 May 2003).

't Hoen, E. 1999. 'Access to essential drugs and globalization.' *Development*, 42(4): 87–91.

Thomson, A. 2001. 'Food security and sustainable livelihoods: The policy challenge.' *Development*, 44(4): 24–8.

Thorbecke, E. and Charumilind, C. 2002. 'Economic inequality and its socioeconomic impact.' *World Development*, 30: 1477–95.

Tilman, D., Fargione, J., Wolff, B., D'Antonio, C., Dobson, A., Howarth, R., Schindler, D., Schlesinger, W.H., Simberloff, D. and Swackhamer, D. 2001. 'Forecasting agriculturally driven global environmental change.' *Science*, 292: 281–4.

Tomlinson, B. 2002. 'Canada.' In J. Randel, T. German and D. Ewing (eds), *The Reality of Aid 2002*. Manila: IBON Foundation, pp. 173–7.

Torres, R. 2001. *Towards a Social Sustainable World Economy: An Analysis of the Social Pillars of Globalization*. Geneva: ILO.

Trebilcock, M.J. and Howse, R. 1999. *The Regulation of International Trade* (2nd edition). London: Routledge.

United Nations (UN). 1992. *Agenda 21*. New York: UN Division for Sustainable Development; http://www.un.org/esa/sustdev/documents/agenda21/english/agenda21toc.htm (accessed 28 November 2002).

United Nations (UN). 2000. *Fourth Report on the World Nutrition Situation*, ACC/SCN. Geneva: UN Administrative Committee on Coordination, Sub-Committee on Nutrition (ACC/SCN), in collaboration with IFPRI; http://www.unsystem.org/scn/Publications/rwns/4RWNS.html (accessed 22 October 2002).

United Nations (UN). 2001. *High-Level International Intergovernmental Consideration of Financing for Development*, A/55/1000. New York: UN; http://www.un.org/esa/ffd/a55-1000.pdf (accessed 27 May 2003).

United Nations (UN). 2002a. *International Financial System and Development: Report of the Secretary-General*, A/57/151. New York: UN; http://ods-dds-ny.un.org/doc/UNDOC/GEN/N02/469/61/PDF/N0246961.pdf?OpenElement (accessed 27 May 2003).

United Nations (UN). 2002b. *Follow-up Efforts to the International Conference on Financing for Development: Report of the Secretary-General*, A/57/319. New York: UN; http://www.un.org/esa/ffd/a57-319-ffd-followup.pdf (accessed 27 May 2003).

United Nations (UN). 2002c. *Report of the World Summit on Sustainable Development*, A/CONF.199/20. New York: UN; http://www.johannesburgsummit.org/html/documents/summit_docs/131302_wssd_report_reissued.pdf (accessed 22 March 2003).

United Nations Children's Fund (UNICEF). 1983. *The State of the World's Children 1984*. Oxford: Oxford University Press.

United Nations Children's Fund (UNICEF). 1985. *Universal Child Immunization by 1990*. Geneva: Assignment Children, UNICEF.

United Nations Children's Fund (UNICEF). 1990. *The State of the World's Children 1990*. New York: Oxford University Press.

United Nations Children's Fund (UNICEF). 1993. *The State of the World's Children 1994*. Oxford: Oxford University Press.

United Nations Children's Fund (UNICEF). 2000. *The State of the World's Children 2001*. Oxford: Oxford University Press.

United Nations Conference on Trade and Development (UNCTAD). 1999. *The Least Developed Countries 1999 Report*. New York: UNCTAD.

United Nations Conference on Trade and Development (UNCTAD). 2000. *Trade and Development Report 2000: Global Economic Growth and Imbalances*. New York: UNCTAD.

United Nations Conference on Trade and Development (UNCTAD). 2001. *Trade and Development Report 2001*. New York: UNCTAD.

United Nations Conference on Trade and Development (UNCTAD). 2002a. 'The PRSP approach and poverty reduction in the least developed countries.' In IMF and World Bank, *External Comments and Contributions on the Joint Bank/Fund Staff Review of the PRSP Approach, Volume I: Bilateral Agencies and Multilateral Institutions*. Washington, DC: IMF, pp. 187–96; http://www.imf.org/external/np/prspgen/review/2002/comm/v1.pdf (accessed 1 February 2003).

United Nations Conference on Trade and Development (UNCTAD). 2002b. *Escaping the Poverty Trap: The Least Developed Countries Report 2002*. New York: UNCTAD; http://www.unctad.org/Templates/webflyer.asp?docid=2026&intItem ID=1397&lang=1&mode=downloads (accessed 17 December 2002).

United Nations Conference on Trade and Development (UNCTAD). 2002c. *Trade and Development Report 2002*. New York: UNCTAD.

United Nations Development Programme (UNDP). 1997. *Human Development Report 1997*. New York: Oxford University Press.

United Nations Development Programme (UNDP). 1998. *Human Development Report 1998*. New York: Oxford University Press.

United Nations Development Programme (UNDP). 1999. *Human Development Report 1999: Globalization with a Human Face*. New York: Oxford University Press.

United Nations Development Programme (UNDP). 2000. *Human Development Report 2000: Human Rights and Human Development*. New York: Oxford University Press.

United Nations Development Programme (UNDP). 2001a. *Human Development Report 2001: Making New Technologies Work for Human Development*. New York: Oxford University Press.

United Nations Development Programme (UNDP). 2001b. *UNDP Review of the Poverty Reduction Strategy Paper (PRSP)*; http://www.worldbank.org./poverty/strategies/review/index.htm (accessed 25 January 2002).

United Nations Development Programme (UNDP), United Nations Environment Programme (UNEP), World Bank and World Resources Institute. 2000. *World Resources 2000–2001*. Washington, DC: World Resources Institute.

United Nations Educational, Scientific and Cultural Organization (UNESCO). 2000. *The Dakar Framework for Action*. Paris: World Education Forum; http://unesdoc.unesco.org/images/0012/001211/121147e.pdf (accessed 27 May 2003).

United Nations Educational, Scientific and Cultural Organization (UNESCO). 2001. *Monitoring Report on Education for All 2001*. Paris: UNESCO; http://www.unesco.org/education/efa/monitoring/monitoring_rep_contents.shtml (accessed 27 May 2003).

United Nations Educational, Scientific and Cultural Organization (UNESCO). 2002a. *Education for All: An International Strategy to Operationalize the Dakar Framework for Action on Education for All (EFA)*; http://www.unesco.org/education/efa/global_co/global_initiative/strategy_2002.pdf (accessed 27 May 2003).

United Nations Educational, Scientific and Cultural Organization (UNESCO). 2002b. *EFA Global Monitoring Report, 2002: Is the World on Track?* Paris: UNESCO; http://www.unesco.org/education/efa/global_co/policy_group/hlg_2002_monitoring_complete.pdf (accessed 27 May 2003).

United Nations Environment Programme (UNEP). 1999. *Global Environment Outlook 2000*. London: Earthscan.

United Nations Environment Programme (UNEP). 2001. 'Trade agreements must consider environmental issues.' Information Note 01/18. Nairobi: UNEP; http://www.unep.org/Documents/Default.asp?DocumentID=196&ArticleID=2803 (accessed 27 May 2003).

United Nations Food and Agriculture Organization (UNFAO). 2001. *The State of Food Insecurity in the World 2001*. Rome: UNFAO; http://www.fao.org/docrep/003/y1500e/y1500e00.htm (accessed 10 January 2003).

United Nations Food and Agriculture Organization (UNFAO). 2002. *Report of the World Food Summit: Five Years Later*. Rome: UNFAO; http://www.fao.org/worldfoodsummit/english/index.html (accessed 10 January 2003).

United Nations Research Institute for Social Development (UNRISD). 2000. *Visible Hands: Taking Responsibility for Social Development*. Geneva: UNRISD; http://www.unrisd.org/80256B3C005BCCF9/(httpPublications)/FE9C9439D82B525480256B670065EFA1?OpenDocument&panel=additional (accessed 27 May 2003).

United States General Accounting Office (USGAO). 1999. *Money Laundering: Observations on Private Banking and Related Oversight of Selected Offshore Jurisdictions*. Testimony before Permanent Subcommittee on Investigations, Committee on Government Affairs, US Senate, GAO/T-GGD-00-32. Washington, DC: USGAO, November.

United States General Accounting Office (USGAO). 2000. *Developing Countries: Debt Relief Initiative for Poor Countries Faces Challenges*, GAO/NSIAD-00-161. Washington, DC: USGAO.

Vasquez, B. 2002. 'UK.' In J. Randel, T. German and D. Ewing (eds), *The Reality of Aid 2002*. Manila: IBON Foundation, pp. 242–6.

Veeken, H. and Pécoul, B. 2000. 'Drugs for "neglected diseases": A bitter pill.' *Tropical Medicine and International Health*, 5: 309–11.

Vidal, J. 2002. 'In a glittering citadel where poverty seems to belong to another world.' *The Guardian*, 26 August.

Volmink, J. and Garner, P. 1997. 'Systematic review of randomised controlled trials of strategies to promote adherence to tuberculosis treatment.' *British Medical Journal*, 315: 1403–6.

Von Braun, J., Bouis, H. and Kennedy, E. 1994. 'Conceptual framework.' In J. von Braun and E. Kennedy (eds), *Agricultural Commercialization, Economic Development, and Nutrition*. Baltimore: Johns Hopkins University Press, pp. 11–36.

Von Furstenberg G.M. and Kirton, J. 2001. 'The challenges ahead.' In J.J. Kirton and G.M. von Furstenberg (eds), *New Directions in Global Economic Governance*. Ashgate: Aldershot, pp. 243–53.

Vreeland, J.R. 2002. 'The effect of IMF programs on labor.' *World Development*, 30: 121–39.

Wachtel, H. 2000. 'The mosaic of global taxes.' In J.N. Pieterse (ed.), *Global Futures: Shaping Globalization*. London: Zed Books, pp. 83–97.

Wagstaff, A. 2001. 'Poverty and health.' Paper WG1:5, Commission on Macroeconomics and Health; http://www2.cid.harvard. edu/cidcmh/wg1_paper5.pdf (accessed 28 February 2002).

Walker, V.R. 1998. 'Keeping the WTO from becoming the "World Trans-science Organization": Scientific uncertainty, science policy, and factfinding in the growth hormones dispute.' *Cornell International Law Journal*, 31: 251–320.

Walt, G. 2000. 'Globalisation of international health.' *The Lancet*, 351: 434–44.

Waltner-Toews, D. 2001. 'An ecosystem approach to health and its applications to tropical and emerging diseases.' *Cadernos de Saúde Pública*, 17 (Supplement): 7–36.

Waltner-Toews, D. and Lang, T. 2000. 'A new conceptual base for food and agricultural policy: The emerging model of links between agriculture, food, health, environment and society.' *Global Change and Human Health*, 1: 116–30.

Walton, J., Seddon, D., Daines, V., Herring, R., Parfitt, T., Riley, S., Shefner, J. and Udayagiri, M. 1994. *Free Markets and Food Riots: The Politics of Global Adjustment*. Cambridge, MA: Blackwell.

Wasserman, E. and Cornejo, S. 2002. 'Trade in health services in the region of the Americas.' In C. Vieira and N. Drager (eds), *Trade in Health Services: Global, Regional and Country Perspectives*. Washington, DC: PAHO, pp. 121–43; http://www.paho.org/English/HDP/HDD/18HDP.pdf (accessed 27 May 2003).

Watkins, K. 2001. 'This deal is immoral, Mr. Blair.' *The Guardian*, 21 December.

Watkins, K. 2002a. *Rigged Rules and Double Standards: Trade, Globalisation, and the Fight Against Poverty*. Washington, DC: Oxfam International; http://www.maketradefair.com/assets/english/Report_English.pdf (accessed 27 May 2003).

Watkins, K. 2002b. 'Main development from WTO talks is a fine line in hypocrisy.' *The Guardian*, 26 August.

Watkins, K. 2003. 'EU must act now to give global trade a chance.' *The Guardian*, 9 June.

Webber, M. 1992. *Food for Thought: How Our Dollar Democracy Drove 2 Million*

Canadians into Foodbanks to Collect Private Charity in Place of Public Justice. Toronto: Coach House Press.

Weeks, J. 1995. 'The contemporary Latin American economies: Neoliberal reconstruction.' In S. Halebsky and R.L. Harris (eds), *Capital, Power, and Inequality in Latin America*. Boulder: Westview, pp. 109–35.

Weisbrot, M., Baker, D., Kraev, E. and Chen, J. 2001. *The Scorecard on Globalization 1980–2000: Twenty Years of Diminished Progress*. Centre for Economic and Policy Research; http://www.cepr.net/globalization/scorecard_on_globalization.htm (accessed 29 September 2002).

Weisbrot, M. 2002. 'Why globalisation fails to deliver.' *The Observer*, 28 July.

Werner, D. and Sanders, D. 1997. *Questioning the Solution: The Politics of Primary Health Care and Child Survival*. Palo Alto: HealthWrights.

White, H., and Killick, T. 2001. *African Poverty at the Millennium: Causes, Complexities, and Challenges*. Washington, DC: World Bank.

Whitehead, M., Dahlgren, G. and Evans, T. 2001. 'Equity and health sector reforms: Can low-income countries escape the medical poverty trap? *The Lancet*, 358: 833–6.

Wiebe, J. 2002. 'Put your tariffs where your mouth is.' *The Globe and Mail* (Toronto), 3 April: A15.

Wilks, A. and Lefrançois, F. 2002. *Blinding with Science or Encouraging with Debate? How World Bank Analysis Determines PRSP Policies*. London: Bretton Woods Project; http://www.brettonwoodsproject.org/topic/adjustment/blinding/blindful.pdf (accessed 27 May 2003).

Williamson, J. 1990. 'What Washington means by policy reform.' In J. Williamson (ed.), *Latin American Adjustment: How Much Has Happened?* Washington, DC: Institute for International Economics, pp. 7–38.

Williamson, J. 1993. 'Democracy and the "Washington Consensus".' *World Development*, 21: 1329–36.

Woods, E. 2002. 'USA.' In J. Randel, T. Germany and D. Ewing (ed.), *The Reality of Aid, 2002*. Manila: IBON Books, pp. 246–9.

Woodward, D. 1996. 'Effects of globalization and liberalization on poverty: Concepts and issues.' In *Liberalization: Effects of International Economic Relations on Poverty*. UNCTAD PA/4/Rev 1. New York and Geneva: UNCTAD.

World Bank. 1992. *World Development Report 1992: Development and the Environment*. New York: Oxford University Press.

World Bank. 1993. *World Development Report 1993: Investing in Health*. New York: Oxford University Press.

World Bank. 1994. *Better Health in Africa: Experience and Lessons Learned*. Washington, DC: World Bank; http://www.worldbank.org/afr/pubs/bhaen.pdf (accessed 27 May 2003).

World Bank. 1995. *World Development Report 1995: Workers in an Integrating World.* New York: Oxford University Press.

World Bank. 1999. *Global Economic Prospects and the Developing Countries, 2000.* Washington, DC: World Bank.

World Bank. 2000a. *African Development Indicators 2000.* Washington, DC: World Bank.

World Bank. 2000b. *World Development Indicators 2000.* Washington, DC: World Bank.

World Bank. 2001a. *World Development Report 2000/2001: Attacking Poverty.* New York: Oxford University Press.

World Bank. 2001b. *Global Economic Prospects and the Developing Countries, 2001.* Washington, DC: World Bank.

World Bank. 2001c. *World Development Indicators 2001.* Washington DC: International Bank for Reconstruction and Development/World Bank.

World Bank. 2002a. *Global Economic Prospects and the Developing Countries 2002: Making Trade Work for the World's Poor.* Washington, DC: World Bank.

World Bank. 2002b. *Financial Impact of the HIPC Initiative: First 25 Country Cases.* Washington, DC: HIPC Unit, World Bank.

World Bank. 2002c. *Education and HIV/AIDS: A Window of Hope.* Washington, DC: World Bank.

World Bank. 2002d. *World Development Indicators 2002.* Washington, DC: World Bank.

World Bank. 2002e. *Global Development Finance: Financing the Poorest Countries, Vol. 1: Analysis and Summary Tables.* Washington, DC: World Bank.

World Bank. 2002f. *Education for Dynamic Economies: Action Plan to Accelerate Progress Towards Education for All.* DC2002-0005/Rev1, prepared for the Joint Ministerial Committee of the Boards of Governors of the World Bank and the IMF on the Transfer of Real Resources to Developing Countries. Washington, DC: World Bank; http://lnweb18.worldbank.org/DCS/devcom.nsf/9dfe2a10d8acb5df852567ec00544e90/b90050b78fbc831685256b8f00729cde/$FILE/DC2002-0005-1.pdf (accessed 27 May 2003).

World Bank. 2003a. *Sustainable Development in a Dynamic World: Transforming Institutions, Growth and Quality of Life, World Development Report 2003.* New York: Oxford University Press.

World Bank. 2003b. *HIPC Initiative: Status of Country Cases Considered under the Initiative.* Washington, DC: World Bank; http://www.worldbank.org/hipc/progress-to-date/status_table_Apr03.pdf (accessed 11 June 2003).

World Bank/IMF. 2000. *International Monetary Fund and International Development Association: Poverty Reduction Strategy Papers – Progress in Implementation.* Washington, DC: World Bank/IMF; http://www.worldbank.org./poverty/strategies/review/index.htm (accessed 5 May 2001).

World Bank/IMF. 2002a. *Market Access for Developing Country Exports – Selected Issues*. Washington, DC: World Bank/IMF; http://www.imf.org/external/np/pdr/ma/2002/eng/092602.pdf (accessed 16 December 2002).

World Bank/IMF. 2002b. 'Review of the PRSP experience'; http://www.worldbank.org./poverty/strategies/review/index.htm (accessed 25 January 2003).

World Commission on Environment and Development (WCED). 1987. *Our Common Future*. New York: Oxford University Press.

World Health Organization (WHO). 1978. 'Declaration of Alma-Ata.' International Conference on Primary Health Care, Alma-Ata, USSR, 6–12 September. Geneva: WHO; http://www.who.int/hpr/archive/docs/almaata.html (accessed 22 January 2003).

World Health Organization (WHO) Lesotho Country Team. 1994. *Health Services in Lesotho: A Study of Possible Cooperation with South Africa*. Maseru: WHO.

World Health Organization (WHO). 1997. *World Health Report 1997: Conquering Suffering, Enriching Humanity*. Geneva: WHO.

World Health Organization (WHO). 1999. *World Health Report 1999: Making A Difference*. Geneva: WHO.

World Health Organization (WHO). 2001. 'Assessment of trade in health services and GATS.' Background Note, 20 December.

World Health Organization (WHO). 2002a. *Health in PRSPs: WHO Submission to World Bank/IMF Review of PRSPs*; http://www.worldbank.org./poverty/strategies/review/index.htm; reproduced in IMF and World Bank, *External Comments and Contributions on the Joint Bank/Fund Staff Review of the PRSP Approach, Vol I: Bilateral Agencies and Multilateral Institutions*. Washington, DC: IMF, pp. 217–46; http://www.imf.org/external/np/prspgen/review/2002/comm/v1.pdf (accessed 25 January 2003).

World Health Organization (WHO). 2002b. *World Health Report 2002*. Geneva: WHO.

World Health Organization (WHO). 2002c. *WHO Estimates of Health Personnel: Physicians, Nurses, Midwives, Dentists, and Pharmacists (around 1998)*. Geneva: WHO; http://www3.who.int/whosis/health_personnel/health_personnel.cfm (accessed 15 March 2003).

World Health Organization (WHO). 2002d. *Coordinates 2002: Charting Progress Against AIDS, Tuberculosis and Malaria*. Geneva: WHO; http://www.unaids.org/publications/documents/care/acc_access/Coordinates2002.pdf (accessed 27 May 2003).

World Trade Organization (WTO). 1994. 'Agreement on the Application of Sanitary and Phytosanitary Measures'; http://www.wto.org/english/docs_e/legal_e/legal_htm.

World Trade Organization (WTO). 1995. *Opening World Markets for Services: Legal Texts and Commitments: The Texts of GATS*. Geneva: WTO.

World Trade Organization (WTO). 2001a. 'Ministerial declaration.' WT/MIN(01)/DEC/1. Geneva: WHO, 20 November; http://www.wto.int/english/thewto_e/minist_e/min01_e/mindecl_e.htm (accessed 27 May 2003).

World Trade Organization (WTO). 2001b. 'Declaration on the TRIPs agreement and public health.' WT/MIN(01)/DEC/2. Geneva: WTO, 20 November; http://www.wto.org/english/thewto_e/minist_e/min01_e/mindecl_trips_e.htm (accessed 18 September 2002).

World Trade Organization (WTO). 2001c. 'Germany contributes DM1 million to the WTO technical assistance fund.' Press Release 264, 19 December; http://www.wto.org/english/news_e/pres01_e/pr264_e.htm_(accessed 27 May 2003).

World Trade Organization (WTO). 2002a. 'Council for Trade in Goods: Committee on Trade-Related Investment Measures: Communication from Brazil and India.' G/C/W/428; G/TRIMS/W/25, 9 October.

World Trade Organization (WTO). 2002b. 'Governments pledge CHF 30 million to Doha Development Agenda Global Trust Fund.' Press Release 279, 11 March; http://www.wto.org/english/news_e/pres02_e/pr279_e.htm (accessed 27 May 2003).

World Trade Organization (WTO). 2002c. 'Implementation of paragraph 6 of the Doha Declaration on the TRIPS Agreement and public health.' Note from the Chairman, Council for TRIPS, WTO; JOB (02)217, 16 December.

WTO Services Database Online. 2002. http://tsdb.wto.org/wto/ (accessed 24 November 2002).

Worldwatch Institute. 2001. *Vital Signs 2001*. New York: Norton.

Xing, L. 2000. 'Shifting the "burden": Commodification of China's health care.' *Global Social Policy*, 2: 248–52.

Yach, D. 2001. 'Chronic disease and disability of the poor: Tackling the challenge.' *Development*, 44: 59–65.

Yach, D. and Bettcher, D. 1999. 'Globalization of tobacco marketing, research and industry influence: Perspectives, trends and impacts on human welfare.' *Development*, 42(4): 25–30.

Yach, D. and Bettcher, D. 2000. 'Globalisation of tobacco industry influence and new global responses.' *Tobacco Control*, 9: 206–16.

Yalnizyan, A. 2002. *Paying for Keeps: Securing the Future of Public Health Care*. Ottawa: Canadian Centre for Policy Alternatives.

Yep, S.C., Arias, J.A. and Freiere, P.P. 2003. 'Ecuador: Adjustments, debt and privatisations: What will become of our rights?' In Social Watch, *The Poor and the Market: Social Watch Report 2003*. Montevideo: Instituto del Tercer Mundo, pp. 104–5; http://www.socialwatch.org.

Yong Kim, J., Millen, J., Irwin, A. and Gershman, J. (eds). 2000. *Dying for Growth: Global Inequality and the Health of the Poor*. Monroe: Common Courage Press.

Yong Kim, J., Shakow, A., Bayona, J., Rhatigan, J. and Rubín de Celis, E. 2000. 'Sickness amidst recovery: Public debt and private suffering in Peru.' In J. Yong Kim, J. Millen, A. Irwin and J. Gershman (eds), *Dying for Growth: Global Inequality and the Health of the Poor*. Monroe: Common Courage Press, pp. 127–54.

Younge, G. 2003. 'No refuge from reality.' *The Guardian Weekly*, 26 December 2002–1 January 2003: 9.

Zarrilli, S. 2002a. 'The case of Brazil.' In C. Vieira and N. Drager (eds), *Trade in Health Services: Global, Regional and Country Perspectives*. Washington, DC: PAHO, pp. 143–55; http://www.paho.org/English/HDP/HDD/19Zarr.pdf (accessed 27 May 2003).

Zarrilli, S. 2002b. 'Identifying a trade-negotiating agenda.' In C. Vieira and N. Drager (eds), *Trade in Health Services: Global, Regional and Country Perspectives*. Washington, DC: PAHO, pp. 71–81; http://www.paho.org/English/HDP/HDD/11Zarr.pdf (accessed 27 May 2003).

Zeitz, P.S. and Bryden, D. 2002. 'Turning their backs on Africa: President George W. Bush and G7 countries fail to confront global AIDS genocide'; http://www.globalaidsalliance.org/G7report.html (accessed 15 January 2003).

APPENDIX 1

G7 and G8 Health-Related Commitments Matrix, 1999–2001

Introductory Comments

The matrix includes only the initial statements and final communiqués from the 1999, 2000 and 2001 summits. However, endnotes are included, providing the URLs for numerous documents and policy efforts that are referred to in the documents that have been analysed. The content of these documents, some of which were generated as part of the summit process and others of which were produced in other contexts, has been incorporated into our analysis.

Two exclusions from our coverage of the summit documents need to be explained.

We have not included commitments related to arms control and disarmament. Although these have obvious and crucial effects on human health that are perhaps especially obvious with respect to the G8 countries' role in the highly lucrative global trade in small arms, we concluded that they required sufficient specialized expertise to be the topic of a separate research project.

We have also not included commitments related to the so-called war on (illicit) drugs. Once again, there are important effects on human health. However, we view as far more important the total silence at the last three summits on the issue of tobacco control, and would like to draw readers' attention to the unquestioned lethality of the global tobacco trade and its anticipated contribution to the burden of disease outside the industrialized world, where tobacco control has achieved limited legitimacy as a policy objective.[1]

One inclusion similarly demands explanation.

The connection between human health and international financial policy, including tax competition and offshore financial centres, is not initially obvious. However, economic dislocations at the national level that result from international financial crises (e.g. in the course of the so-called Asian meltdown in the late 1990s) can plunge millions of people into poverty, with attendant effects on the social determinants of health. Further, capital flight has the potential seriously to erode the fiscal capacity even of wealthy countries, and to debilitate poor ones to the extent that they are unable to provide even the most basic forms of security for their citizens. Stated another way, in conjunction with high levels of foreign debt, international institutions and financial networks that facilitate capital flight enable elites to socialize the costs of private capital accumulation, while the most basic determinants of health are allowed to deteriorate for the majority of the population.

G7 and G8 Health-Related Commitments Matrix, 1999–2001 ($ = US$ throughout)

	A. Commitments that can be assessed in quantitative or dichotomous terms (e.g. expenditure figures, agreement reached or not reached) *	B. Commitments about which adequate data exist for assessment, but which can be assessed only in qualitative narrative or terms	C. Commitments that reflect a basic, but contested, normative vision of the relations among markets, development and health
	* Note that commitments may be evaluated quantitatively even if they do not specify numerical targets: e.g. a commitment to the importance of renewable energy for sustainable development can be evaluated quantitatively if figures for domestic R&D spending and ODA on renewables are available.		
Document	Note: Some commitments span columns because they fall into two, or even all three, of the above categories		
	General commitments		
G8 Communiqué, Genoa, 22 July 2001	As democratic leaders, accountable to our citizens, we believe in the fundamental importance of open public debate on the key challenges facing our societies. We will promote innovative solutions based on a broad partnership with civil society and the private sector. We will also seek enhanced co-operation and solidarity with developing countries, based on a mutual responsibility for combating poverty and promoting sustainable development. We are determined to make globalisation work for all our citizens and especially the world's poor. Drawing the poorest countries into the global economy is the surest way to address their fundamental aspirations (paras. 2–3).		

G8 Communiqué, Okinawa, 23 July 2000	We must engage in a new partnership with non-G8 countries, particularly developing countries, international organisations and civil society, including the private sector and non-governmental organisations (NGOs) (para. 4).
G8 Communiqué, Cologne, 20 June 1999	The challenge is to seize the opportunities globalization affords while addressing its risks to respond to concerns about a lack of control over its effects. We must work to sustain and increase the benefits of globalization and ensure that its positive effects are widely shared by people all over the world. We therefore call on governments and international institutions, business and labor, civil society and the individual to work together to meet this challenge and realize the full potential of globalization for raising prosperity and promoting social progress while preserving the environment (para. 2).
	Debt relief
G8 Communiqué, Genoa, 22 July 2001	Debt relief – particularly the Enhanced Heavily Indebted Poor Countries (HIPC) Initiative – is a valuable contribution to the fight against poverty, but it is only one of the steps needed to stimulate faster growth in very poor countries. We are delighted twenty-three countries have

	qualified for an overall amount of debt relief of over US$53 billion, out of an initial stock of debt of US$74 billion. We must continue this progress (para. 7).
G7 Statement, Genoa, 20 July 2001	In addition to the policies we are pursuing in our own economies, we agreed today that co-operation on three further elements is important to a strengthened global economy: ... • actions to ensure that the poorest countries are not left behind, including the implementation of the Heavily Indebted Poor Countries (HIPC) Initiative (para. 4).
G7 Statement, Genoa, 20 July 2001	The Enhanced HIPC Initiative we launched in Cologne aims to increase growth, reduce poverty and provide a lasting exit from unsustainable debt, by reducing debt on the basis of strengthened policy reforms. ... This will significantly reduce their debt service, thus freeing resources for social sector expenditure, in particular education and health. We have all agreed as a minimum to provide 100% debt reduction of official development assistance (ODA) and eligible commercial claims for qualifying HIPC countries. We urge those countries that have not already done so to take similar steps, and we underline the need for the active and full participation of all bilateral creditors in providing timely debt relief to HIPCs (paras. 15-16).

G8 Communiqué, Okinawa, 23 July 2000	We welcome the efforts being made by HIPCs to develop comprehensive and country-owned poverty reduction strategies through a participatory process involving civil society. IFIs should, along with other donors, help HIPCs prepare PRSPs and assist their financial resource management by providing technical assistance. We are concerned by the fact that a number of HIPCs are currently affected by military conflicts which prevent poverty reduction and delay debt relief. We call upon these countries to end their involvement in conflicts and to embark quickly upon the HIPC process. We agree to strengthen our efforts to help them prepare and come forward for debt relief, by asking our Ministers to make early contact with the countries in conflict to encourage them to create the right conditions to participate in the HIPC Initiative. We will work together to ensure that as many countries as possible reach their Decision Points, in line with the targets set in Cologne, giving due consideration to the progress of economic reforms and the need to ensure that the benefits of debt relief are targeted to assist the poor and most vulnerable. We will work expeditiously together with HIPCs and the IFIs to realise the expectation that 20 countries will reach the Decision Point within the framework of the Enhanced HIPC Initiative by the end of this year. In this regard, we welcome the establishment of the Joint Implementation Committee by the World Bank and the IMF. We for our part will promote more responsible lending and borrowing practices to ensure that HIPCs will not again be burdened by unsupportable debt. We note the progress made in securing the required financing of the IFIs for effective implementation of the Enhanced HIPC Initiative, and welcome pledges including those to the HIPC Trust Fund. We reaffirm our commitment to make available as quickly as possible the resources we have pledged in the spirit of fair burden sharing (paras. 24–5).
G7 Statement, Okinawa, 21 July 2000	We welcome the efforts being made by HIPCs to develop comprehensive and country-owned poverty reduction strategies through a participatory process involving civil society. We encourage those HIPCs that have not yet done so to embark quickly on the process and thus fully benefit from the debt reduction. We are concerned by the fact that a number of HIPCs are currently affected by military conflicts which prevent poverty reduction and delay debt relief. We call upon these countries to end their involvement in conflicts and to

embark quickly upon the HIPC process. We agree to strengthen our efforts to help them prepare and come forward for debt relief, by asking our Ministers to make early contact with the countries in conflict to encourage them to create the right conditions to participate in the HIPC Initiative. We will work together to ensure that as many countries as possible reach their Decision Points, in line with the targets set in Cologne, giving due consideration to the progress of economic reforms and the need to ensure that the benefits of debt relief are targeted to assist the poor and most vulnerable. In this regard, we welcome the establishment of the Joint Implementation Committee (JIC) by the World Bank and the IMF, and strongly urge both HIPCs and IFIs to accelerate their work toward the implementation of the Initiative. IFIs should, along with other donors, help HIPCs prepare PRSPs and assist their financial resource management by providing technical assistance.

We reaffirmed our commitment to provide 100% debt reduction of ODA claims, and newly commit to 100% debt reduction of eligible commercial claims. We welcome the announcement made by some non-G7 countries that they too will provide 100% debt relief, and we urge other donors to follow suit.

We note the progress made in securing the required financing of the IFIs for effective implementation of the Enhanced HIPC Initiative, and welcome pledges and the initial contributions, including those to the HIPC Trust Fund. We reaffirm our commitment to make available as quickly as possible the resources we have pledged. In this context, we recognise the importance of fair burden sharing among creditors (paras. 20–3).

G8 Communiqué, Cologne, 20 June 1999	We have decided to give a fresh boost to debt relief to developing countries. In recent years the international creditor community has introduced a number of debt relief measures for the poorest countries. The Heavily Indebted Poor Countries (HIPC) framework has made an important contribution in this respect. Recent experience suggests that further efforts are needed to achieve a more enduring solution to the problem of unsustainable debt burdens. To this end we welcome the 1999 Köln Debt Initiative,[3] which is designed to provide deeper, broader and faster debt relief through major changes to the HIPC framework. The central objective of this initiative is to provide a greater focus on poverty reduction by releasing resources for investment in health, education and social needs. In this context we also support good governance and sustainable development (para. 29).

| G7 Statement, Cologne, 18 June 1999 | We welcome and endorse the Report of our Finance Ministers on the Köln Debt Initiative. The proposals contained in this report will lead to a deeper debt reduction through more ambitious targets, faster debt relief through greater flexibility in the timing of delivery of agreed debt relief packages, and a stronger focus on early cash flow relief by the International Financial Institutions. We also ask the Paris Club and other bilateral creditors to forgive commercial debt up to 90 % and more in individual cases if needed to achieve debt sustainability, in particular for the very poorest among these countries. In addition to these amounts, we call for full cancellation on a bilateral basis, through various options, of Official Development Assistance (ODA) debt. For poor countries not qualifying under the HIPC Initiative, the Paris Club could consider a unified 67 per cent reduction under Naples terms and, for other debtor countries, an increase of the existing limit on debt swap operations.

… We recognize that these changes will entail significant costs, in particular arising from debt owed to the IFIs. We are prepared to support a number of mechanisms to meet these costs, recognizing the importance of maintaining an adequate concessional lending capacity by the IFIs:

• To meet the IMF's costs, the Fund should mobilize its resources, while maintaining an appropriate level of reserves, through the use of premium interest income, the possible use of reflows from the special contingency account or equivalent financing, and the use of interest on the proceeds of a limited and cautiously phased sale of up to 10 million ounces of the IMF's gold reserves.

• The Multilateral Development Banks (MDBs) should build on the work they have begun to identify and exploit innovative approaches which maximize the use of their own resources.

• The costs to the IFIs will also require bilateral contributions. We have pledged substantial contributions to the existing HIPC Trust Fund. We will consider in good faith contributions to an expanded HIPC Trust Fund.

• In meeting the costs, we call for appropriate burden sharing among donors, taking into account all relevant aspects, including the magnitude and quality of ODA already extended and past ODA forgiveness, and recognizing the contributions of countries with high ODA loans outstanding relative to GDP (paras. 11–13). | |
| G7 Statement, Cologne, | On the basis of this framework, we call on the IFIs and the Paris | |

18 June 1999	Club to provide faster, deeper and broader debt relief, to work with the HIPC countries to ensure that three quarters of eligible countries have reached their decision point by the year 2000, and to assist the very poorest countries to embark on the HIPC process as soon as possible. Concrete proposals should be agreed by the time of the next Annual Meetings of the IMF and the World Bank (para. 15).

Development assistance

G8 Communiqué, Genoa, 22 July 2001	We will ... continue to provide effective development assistance to help developing countries' own efforts to build long-term prosperity. Consistent with the conclusions of the LDC III Conference and the Millennium Declaration, we support a strategic approach centred on the principles of ownership and partnership (para. 5).
G8 Communiqué, 22 Genoa 2001	We will work with developing countries to meet the Inter-

		national Development Goals, by strengthening and enhancing the effectiveness of our development assistance (para. 14).
G8 Communiqué, Genoa, 22 July 2001	We commit ourselves to implement the landmark OECD-DAC Recommendation on Untying Aid to LDCs ... (para. 14).	
G7 Statement, Genoa, 20 July 2001		We call on MDBs to provide support for global public goods, such as fighting infectious diseases, facilitating trade, fostering financial stability and protecting the environment. We support a meaningful replenishment of IDA and, in that context, we will explore the increased use of grants for priority social investments, such as education and health (para. 13).
G8 Communiqué, Okinawa, 23 July 2000	ODA is essential in the fight against poverty. We commit ourselves to strengthening the effectiveness of our ODA in support of countries' own efforts to tackle poverty, including through national strategies for poverty reduction. We will take a long-term approach favouring those countries where governments have demonstrated a commitment to improve the well-being of their people through accountable and transparent management of resources devoted to development.	

To achieve increased effectiveness of ODA, we resolve to untie our aid to the Least Developed Countries on the basis of progress made in the Organisation for Economic Co-operation and Development (OECD) to date and a fair burden-sharing mechanism that we will agree with our OECD partners. We believe that this agreement should come into effect on 1 January 2002. In the meantime, we urge those countries which maintain low levels of untying of ODA to improve their performance. We will also seek to demonstrate to the public that well-targeted ODA gets results, and on that basis will strive to give increased priority to such assistance (para. 20).		
G7 Statement, Okinawa, 21 July 2000	The core role of the MDBs should be accelerating poverty reduction in developing countries while improving the efficiency of assistance and avoiding competition with private financial flows. The MDBs should increase their resources devoted to core social investments such as basic health and education, clean water and sanitation. The Comprehensive Development Framework (CDF) and the Poverty Reduction Strategy Papers (PRSPs) should become the basis for programmes that have strong ownership by the recipient countries. All the MDBs should allocate their support increasingly on the basis of borrower performance (paras. 9–10).	
G8 Communiqué, Cologne, 20 June 1999	We will strive gradually to increase the volume of official development assistance (ODA), and to put special emphasis on countries best positioned to use it effectively (para. 27).	
G8 Communiqué, Cologne,	To ease future debt burdens and facilitate sustainable development,	

20 June 1999		we agree to increase the share of grant-based financing in the ODA we provide to the least developed countries (para. 27).
G8 Communiqué, Cologne, 20 June 1999		We reaffirm our support for the OECD mandate to finalize a recommendation on untying aid to the least developed countries. We call on OECD members to bring this effort to a successful conclusion as soon as possible (para. 27).
Domestic political reforms		
G8 Communiqué, Genoa, 22 July 2001		[W]e shall help developing countries promote: • accountability and transparency in the public sector • legal frameworks and corporate governance regimes to fight corruption • safeguards against the misappropriation of public funds and their diversion into non-productive uses • access to legal systems for all citizens, independence of the judiciary, and legal provisions enabling private sector activity • active involvement of civil society and Non-Governmental Organisations (NGOs) • freedom of economic activities (para. 6).
G8 Communiqué, Cologne, 20 June 1999		We will continue to provide substantial support and assistance to developing and transition economies in support of their own efforts to open and diversify their economies, to democratize and improve governance, and to protect human rights (para. 27).

Education	
G8 Communiqué, Genoa, 22 July 2001	Education is a central building block for growth and employment. We reaffirm our commitment to help countries meet the Dakar Framework for Action[8] goal of universal primary education by 2015. We agree on the need to improve the effectiveness of our development assistance in support of locally-owned strategies. Education – in particular, universal primary education and equal access to education at all levels for girls – must be given high priority both in national poverty reduction strategies and in our development programmes. Resources made available through the HIPC Initiative can contribute to these objectives. We will help foster assessment systems to measure progress, identify best practices and ensure accountability for results. We will also focus on teacher training. Building on the work of the G8 Digital Opportunities Task Force (dot.force),[9] we will work to expand the use of information and communications technology (ICT) to train teachers in best practices and strengthen education strategies. ... We encourage MDBs to sharpen their focus on education and con-centrate their future work on countries with sound strategies but lacking sufficient resources and to report next year to the G8. We support UNESCO in its key role for universal education. We will also work with the International Labour Organisation (ILO) to support efforts to fight child labour and we will develop incentives to increase school enrolment (para. 18).
G8 Communiqué, Genoa, 22 July 2001	We will establish a task force of senior G8 officials to advise us on how best to pursue the Dakar goals in co-operation with

	developing countries, relevant international organisations and other stakeholders. The task force will provide us with recommendations in time for our next meeting (para. 19).
G8 Communiqué, Okinawa, 23 July 2000	Building on the Cologne Education Charter,[16] we therefore support the Dakar Framework for Action[11] as well as the recommendations of the recently concluded follow-up to the Fourth World Conference on Women,[12] and welcome the efforts of developing countries to implement strong national action plans. We reaffirm our commitment that no government seriously committed to achieving education for all will be thwarted in this achievement by lack of resources. We therefore commit ourselves to strengthen efforts bilaterally and together with international organisations and private sector donors to achieve the goals of universal primary education by 2015 and gender equality in schooling by 2005. We call on IFIs, in partnership with developing countries, to focus on education in their poverty reduction strategies and provide greater assistance for countries with sound education strategies. These strategies should maximise the potential benefits of IT in this area through distance learning wherever possible and other effective means (paras. 33–4).
G8 Communiqué, Cologne, 20 June 1999	Basic education, vocational training, academic qualifications, lifelong upgrading of skills and knowledge for the labor market, and support for the development of innovative thinking are

		essential to shape economic and technical progress as we move towards a knowledge-based society. They also enrich individuals and foster civic responsibility and social inclusion (para. 15).		
G8 Communiqué, Cologne, 20 June 1999		In support of these goals, we agree to pursue the aims and ambitions set out in the Köln Charter (para. 16).[13]		
G8 Communiqué, Cologne, 20 June 1999		We commit ourselves to explore jointly ways to work together and through international institutions to help our own countries as well as developing nations use technology to address learning and development needs, for example, through distance learning (para. 18).		
		Environment, energy and sustainable development		
G8 Communiqué, Genoa, 22 July 2001		We confirm our determination to find global solutions to threats endangering the planet. We recognise that climate change is a pressing issue that requires a		

	global solution. We are committed to providing strong leadership. Prompt, effective and sustainable action is needed, consistent with the ultimate objective of the UN Framework Convention on Climate Change of stabilising greenhouse gas concentrations in the atmosphere. We are determined to meet our national commitments and our obligations under the Convention through a variety of flexible means, drawing on the power of markets and technology. In this context, we agree on the importance of intensifying co-operation on climate-related science and research. We shall promote co-operation between our countries and developing countries on technology transfer and capacity building (para. 23).	
G8 Communiqué, Genoa, 22 July 2001	We all firmly agree on the need to reduce greenhouse gas emissions. While there is currently disagreement on the Kyoto Protocol and its ratification, we are committed to working intensively together to meet our common objective (para. 24).	

G8 Communiqué, Genoa, 22 July 2001	We recognise the importance of renewable energy for sustainable development, diversification of energy supply, and preservation of the environment. We will ensure that renewable energy sources are adequately considered in our national plans and encourage others to do so as well. We encourage continuing research and investment in renewable energy technology, throughout the world. Renewable energy can contribute to poverty reduction. We will help developing countries strengthen institutional capacity and market-oriented national strategies that can attract private sector investment in renewable energy and other clean technologies (para. 27).	
G8 Communiqué, Genoa, 22 July 2001	We welcome the recent adoption of the Stockholm Convention on Persistent Organic Pollutants (POPs) and will strongly promote its early entry into force (para. 28).	
G8 Communiqué, Genoa, 22 July 2001	We are committed to ensuring that our Export Credit Agencies (ECAs) adhere to high environmental standards. We therefore agreed in Okinawa to develop common environmental guidelines for ECAs, drawing on relevant MDB experience. Building on the progress made since last year, we commit to reach agreement in the OECD by	

	the end of the year on a Recommendation that fulfils the Okinawa mandate (para. 29).	
G8 Communiqué, Okinawa, 23 July 2000	We ... welcome the conclusion of the Cartagena Protocol on Biosafety, and encourage the parties concerned to work for its early entry into force (para. 64).	
G8 Communiqué, Okinawa, 23 July 2000	We will endeavour with all our partners to prepare a future-oriented agenda for Rio+10 in 2002. We are strongly committed to close co-operation among ourselves and with developing countries to resolve as soon as possible all major outstanding issues, with a view to early entry into force of the Kyoto Protocol. To that end, we are determined to achieve a successful outcome at the Sixth Conference of the Parties to the Framework Convention on Climate Change (COP6), in order to achieve the goals of the Kyoto Protocol through undertaking strong domestic actions and supplemental flexibility mechanisms (para. 65).	
G8 Communiqué, Okinawa, 23 July 2000	We invite stakeholders to join in a Task Force to prepare concrete recommendations for considera-tion at our next Summit[14] regarding sound ways to better encourage the use of renewables in deve-loping countries (para. 66).	
G8 Communiqué, Okinawa, 23 July 2000	Export credit policies may have very significant environmental impacts. We welcome the adop-tion of the OECD work plan to	

	be completed by 2001. We reaffirm our commitment to develop common environmental guidelines, drawing on relevant MDB experience, for export credit agencies by the 2001 G8 Summit. We will co-operate to reinvigorate and intensify our work to fulfil the Cologne mandate (para. 68).	
G7 Statement, Okinawa, 21 July 2000	We look to the MDBs to play a leadership role in increasing the provision of global public goods, particularly for urgently needed measures against infectious and parasitic diseases including HIV/AIDS, as well as environmental degradation (para. 11).	
G8 Communiqué, Cologne, 20 June 1999	To underscore our commitment to sustainable development we will step up our efforts to build a coherent global and environmentally responsive framework of multilateral agreements and institutions. We support the outcome of the G8 Environment Ministers' meeting in Schwerin[15] and will expedite international cooperation on the establishment,	

		general recognition and continual improvement of environmental standards and norms (para. 31).
G8 Communiqué, Cologne, 20 June 1999		We agree that environmental considerations should be taken fully into account in the upcoming round of WTO negotiations. This should include a clarification of the relationship between both multilateral environmental agreements and key environmental principles, and WTO rules (para. 31).
G8 Communiqué, Cologne, 20 June 1999		We agree to continue to support the Multilateral Development Banks in making environmental considerations an integral part of their activities and we will do likewise when providing our own support. We will work within the OECD towards common environmental guidelines for export finance agencies. We aim to complete this work by the 2001 G8 Summit (para. 32).
G8 Communiqué, Cologne, 20 June 1999		We reaffirm that we consider climate change an extremely serious threat to sustainable development. We will therefore work towards timely progress in implementing the Buenos Aires Plan of Action with a view to early entry into force of the Kyoto Protocol. In particular, we encourage decisions on the operation of the Kyoto mechanisms and on a strong and effective compliance regime. We underline the importance of taking action to reduce greenhouse gas emissions through rational and efficient use of energy and through other cost-effective means. To this end, we commit ourselves to develop and implement domestic measures including under the UN Framework Convention on Climate Change. We also agreed to exchange experience on best practices. We will also promote increasing global participation of developing countries in limiting greenhouse gas emissions (para. 33).

Food, food security and biotechnology

G8 Communiqué, Genoa, 22 July 2001	[A] central objective of our poverty reduction strategy remains access to adequate food supplies and rural development. Support to agriculture is a crucial instrument of ODA. We shall endeavour to develop capacity in poor countries, integrating programmes into national strategies and increasing training in agricultural science (para. 20).	
G8 Communiqué, Genoa, 22 July 2001		Every effort should be undertaken to enhance agricultural productivity. Among other things, the introduction of tried and tested new technology, including biotechnology, in a safe manner and adapted to local conditions has significant potential to substantially increase crop yields in developing countries, while using fewer pesticides and less water than conventional methods. We are committed to study, share and facilitate the responsible use of biotechnology in addressing development needs (para. 20).
G8 Communiqué, Genoa, 22 July 2001	We shall target the most food-insecure regions, particularly Sub-Saharan Africa and South Asia, and continue to encourage South-South co-operation. We will support the crucial role international organisations and NGOs play in relief operations (para. 21).	
G8 Communiqué, Genoa, 22 July 2001		We recognise our responsibility to promote a clear understanding by the public of food safety benefits and risks. We shall strive to provide consumers with relevant information on the safety of food products,

	based on independent scientific advice, sound risk analysis and the latest research developments. We believe an effective framework for risk management, consistent with the science, is a key component in maintaining consumer confidence and in fostering public acceptance (para. 30).
G8 Communiqué, Okinawa, 23 July 2000	Maintenance of effective national food safety systems and public confidence in them assumes critical importance in public policy. We are committed to continued efforts to make systems responsive to the growing public awareness of food safety issues, the potential risks associated with food, the accelerating pace of developments in biotechnology, and the increasing cross-border movement of food and agricultural products

The commitment to a science-based, rule-based approach remains a key principle underlying these endeavours. .... We also support the efforts of the CAC's Committee on General Principles to achieve greater global consensus on how precaution should be applied to food safety in circumstances where available scientific information is incomplete or contradictory.

Policy dialogue, engaging all stakeholders and including both developed and developing countries, must be intensified to advance health protection, facilitate trade, ensure the sound development of biotechnology, and foster consumer confidence and public acceptance (paras. 55–7). |
| *G8 Communiqué, Okinawa, 23 July 2000* | In pursuing this dialogue we will pay particular attention to the needs, opportunities and constraints in developing countries. We will work to strengthen our support for their capacity building to harness the potentials of biotechnology, and encourage research and development as well as data and information sharing in techno- |

logies, including those that address global food security, health, nutritional and environmental challenges and are adapted to specific conditions in these countries.

Open and transparent consultation with and involvement of all stakeholders, including representatives of civil society, supported by shared scientific understanding, is a key component of a credible food and crop safety system. We ... will explore, in consultation with international organisations and interested bodies including scientific academies, the way to integrate the best scientific knowledge available into the global process of consensus building on biotechnology and other aspects of food and crop safety (paras. 58–9).

Because trade is increasingly global, the consequences of developments in biotechnology must be dealt with at the national and international levels in all the appropriate fora. We are committed to a science-based, rules-based approach to addressing these issues (para. 11).

G8 Communiqué, Cologne, 20 June 1999

G8 Communiqué, Cologne, 20 June 1999

In light of the increasing importance of issues concerning food safety we invite the OECD Working Group on Harmonization of Regulatory Oversight of Biotechnology[16] and the OECD Task Force for the Safety of Novel Foods and

Feeds[17] to undertake a study of the implications of biotechnology and other aspects of food safety. We invite OECD experts to discuss their findings with our personal representatives. We ask the latter to report to us by the next Summit on possible ways to improve our approach to these issues through international and other institutions, taking into account the reflections underway in other fora (para. 43).

Health and health systems

G8 Communiqué, Genoa, 22 July 2001

At Okinawa last year, we pledged to make a quantum leap in the fight against infectious diseases and to break the vicious cycle between disease and poverty. To meet that commitment and to respond to the appeal of the UN General Assembly, we have launched with the UN Secretary-General a new Global Fund to fight HIV/AIDS, malaria and tuberculosis. We are determined to make the Fund operational before the end of the year. We

	have committed $1.3 billion. ... We welcome the further commitments already made amounting to some $500 million (para. 15).
G8 Communiqué, Genoa, 22 July 2001	The Fund will promote an integrated approach emphasising prevention in a continuum of treatment and care. It will operate according to principles of proven scientific and medical effectiveness, rapid resource transfer, low transaction costs, and light governance with a strong focus on outcomes (para. 16).
G8 Communiqué, Genoa, 22 July 2001	Strong national health systems will continue to play a key role in the delivery of effective prevention, treatment and care and in improving access to essential health services and commodities without discrimination. ... In the context of the new Global Fund, we will work with the pharmaceutical industry and with affected countries to facilitate the broadest possible provision of drugs in an affordable and medically effective manner. We welcome ongoing discussion in the WTO on the use of relevant provisions in the Trade-Related Intellectual Property Rights (TRIPs) agreement. We recognise the appropriateness of affected countries using the flexibility afforded by that agreement to ensure that drugs are available to their citizens who need them, particularly those who are unable to afford basic medical care. At the same time, we reaffirm our commitment to strong and effective intellectual property rights protection as a necessary incentive for research on and development of life-saving drugs (para. 17).
G8 Communiqué, Okinawa, 23 July 2000	Only through sustained action and coherent international co-operation to fully mobilise new and existing medical, technical and financial resources, can we strengthen health delivery systems and reach beyond traditional approaches to break the vicious cycle of disease and poverty. ... We therefore commit ourselves to working in strengthened partnership with governments, the World Health Organisation (WHO) and other

international organisations, industry (notably pharmaceutical companies), academic institutions, NGOs and other relevant actors in civil society to deliver three critical UN targets:

- Reduce the number of HIV/AIDS-infected young people by 25% by 2010 (UN Secretary-General Report to the General Assembly on 27/3/2000);
- Reduce TB deaths and prevalence of the disease by 50% by 2010 (WHO Stop TB Initiative);
- Reduce the burden of disease associated with malaria by 50% by 2010 (WHO Roll Back Malaria).

In order to achieve this ambitious agenda our partnership must aim to cover:

- Mobilising additional resources ourselves, and calling on the MDBs to expand their own assistance to the maximum extent possible;
- Giving priority to the development of equitable and effective health systems, expanded immunisation, nutrition and micro-nutrients and the prevention and treatment of infectious diseases;
- Promoting political leadership through enhanced high-level dialogue designed to raise public awareness in the affected countries;
- Committing to support innovative partnerships, including with the NGOs, the private sector and multilateral organisations;
- Working to make existing cost-effective interventions, including key drugs, vaccines, treatments and preventive measures more universally available and affordable in developing countries;
- Addressing the complex issue of access to medicines in developing countries, and assessing obstacles being faced by developing countries in that regard;

	• Strengthening co-operation in the area of basic research and development on new drugs, vaccines and other international public health goods (paras. 26, 29–30).	
G8 Communiqué, Okinawa, 23 July 2000	In addition, we will convene a conference in the autumn this year in Japan to deliver agreement on a new strategy to harness our commitments. The conference should look to define the operations of this new partnership, the areas of priority and the timetable for action. Participation of developing country partners and other stakeholders will be essential. We will take stock of progress at the Genoa Summit next year and will also work with the UN to organise a conference in 2001 focusing on strategies to facilitate access to AIDS treatment and care (para. 32).	
G7 Statement, Okinawa, 21 July 2000		We look to the MDBs to play a leadership role in increasing the provision of global public goods, particularly for urgently needed measures against infectious and parasitic diseases including HIV/

Source	Commitment
	AIDS, as well as environmental degradation (para. 11).
G8 Communiqué, Cologne, 20 June 1999	We are concerned at the continuing global spread of AIDS. We reaffirm the need to continue efforts to combat AIDS at the national and international level through a combined strategy of prevention, vaccine development and appropriate therapy (para. 41).
G8 Communiqué, Cologne, 20 June 1999	We also pledge to continue our national and international efforts in the fight against infectious and parasitic diseases, such as malaria, polio and tuberculosis, and their drug-resistant forms. In particular we will continue to support the endeavors of the World Health Organization and its initiatives 'Roll Back Malaria' and 'Stop TB'. We call on governments to adopt these recommended strategies (para. 42).
International finance, tax competition and offshore financial centres	
G8 Communiqué, Genoa, 22 July 2001	We ... will: • implement fully the OECD Bribery Convention • support efforts in the UN to pursue an effective instrument against corruption • Encourage Multilateral Development Banks (MDBs) to help recipient countries strengthen public expenditure and budget management (para. 6).
G7 Statement, Genoa, 20 July 2001	We reaffirm our support for the multilateral effort against abuses of the global financial system and endorse our Finance Ministers' recommendations[18] to address this challenge (para. 14).

G8 Communiqué, Okinawa, 23 July 2000	We hereby declare our commitment to take all necessary national and international action to effectively combat financial crime, in line with international standards (para. 46).		
G8 Communiqué, Okinawa, 23 July 2000	We renew our commitment to combat corruption. We stress the need for transparency in government in this regard, and call for the ratification and effective implementation of the OECD Anti-Bribery Convention by all signatory parties. Working with other countries, we will prepare for the launch of negotiations in the United Nations on a new instrument against corruption, and instruct the Lyon Group to pursue work on this issue (para. 47).		
G7 Statement, Okinawa, 21 July 2000		We will continue to work together with other members of the international community to further strengthen the international financial architecture (para. 7).	
G7 Statement, Okinawa, 21 July 2000			As a universal institution, the IMF must work in partnership with all its members, including the poorest, based on shared interests. In this regard, we attach particular importance to the following measures: **Strengthening IMF surveillance to prevent crises:** A substantial qualitative shift in the nature and scope of the surveillance is needed in light of globalisation and large scale private capital flows (para. 8).

G7 Statement, Okinawa, 21 July 2000	We urge the IMF to conduct quickly assessments of offshore financial centres identified by the FSF [Financial Stability Forum] as a priority (para. 14).	
G7 Statement, Okinawa, 21 July 2000	We welcome and strongly endorse our G7 Finance Ministers' report, published today, on 'Actions Against Abuse of the Global Financial System,'[19] and attach particular importance to the following developments: • **Money laundering:** We welcome the initial work of the Financial Action Task Force on Money Laundering (FATF)[20] .... We are ready to give our advice and provide, where appropriate, our technical assistance to jurisdictions that commit to making improvements to their regimes. We are prepared to act together, when required and appropriate, to implement co-ordinated counter-measures against those NCCTs that do not take steps to reform their systems appropriately, including the possibility to condition or restrict financial transactions with those jurisdictions and to condition or restrict support from IFIs to them. • **Tax havens and other harmful tax practices:** We welcome the OECD Report on Progress on Identifying and Eliminating Harmful Tax Practices,[21] which includes two lists: certain jurisdictions meeting tax haven criteria; and potentially harmful regimes within the OECD member countries. We also welcome the public commitments already made by jurisdictions to eliminate harmful tax practices and we urge all jurisdictions to make such commitments. We encourage the OECD to continue its efforts to counter harmful tax practices and to extend its dialogue with non-member countries. We also reaffirm our support for the OECD's report on	

improving access to bank information for tax purposes and call on all countries to work rapidly towards a position where they can permit access to, and exchange, bank information for all tax purposes.

- **Offshore financial centres:** Regarding offshore financial centres (OFCs) that do not meet international financial standards, we welcome the identification by the Financial Stability Forum (FSF) of priority jurisdictions for assessment. We consider it essential for OFCs to implement all measures recommended by the FSF with a view to improving weak regulatory and supervisory systems, as well as to eliminate harmful tax competition and to adopt anti-money laundering measures. In this regard, we attach priority to the eight areas identified by our Finance Ministers: international co-operation, exchange of information, customer identification, abolition of excessive secrecy, effective vetting of financial institutions, enhanced resources for financial supervision and anti-money laundering compliance, improved legislation on money laundering and elimination of harmful tax practices. We will take steps to encourage jurisdictions to make the necessary changes and provide technical assistance where appropriate. Where jurisdictions fail to meet certain standards and are not committed to enhancing their level of compliance with international standards, we will also take measures to protect the international financial system from the effects of these failures.

- **Role of international financial institutions (IFIs):** We urge IFIs, including the IMF and World Bank, to help countries implement relevant international standards, in the context of financial sector assessments as well as programme design and assistance (para. 26).

G8 Communiqué, Cologne, 20 June 1999	We agreed to intensify our dialogue within the G8 structures on the longer term social, structural and economic reform in Russia. … We agreed to deepen our cooperation on law enforcement, fighting organized crime and money laundering, including as they relate to capital flight (para. 7).	
G7 Statement, Cologne, 18 June 1999	We call upon our Ministers of Finance, in coordination with other Ministers, in particular with Ministers of Justice and the Interior, to coordinate the development and implementation of complementary positions regarding offshore financial centers and the FATF's [Financial Action Task Force's] work on non-cooperative jurisdictions in the various fora where these issues are being addressed (para. 21).	
G7 Statement, Cologne, 18 June 1999	We welcome the establishment of the OECD's Forum on harmful tax competition and the actual start of implementing the guidelines and recommendations adopted by the OECD with respect to the harmful effects of unfair tax practices. We strongly endorse the current work program of the Forum, in particular the efforts to identify tax havens. We also support the Forum's intention to engage in a dialogue with jurisdictions identified through this process. We urge that this work be given a high priority. We also note the ongoing work to implement the code of conduct within the European Union (para. 22).	

	Labour, employment and social policy	
G8 Communiqué, Genoa, 22 July 2001	In the firm belief that economic performance and social inclusion are mutually dependent, we commit to implement policies in line with the recommendations of the G8 Labour Ministers Conference held in Torino last year[22] (para. 32).	
G8 Communiqué, Okinawa, 23 July 2000	We ... welcome the increasing co-operation between the International Labour Organisation (ILO) and the International Financial Institutions (IFIs) in promoting adequate social protection and core labour standards. We urge the IFIs to incorporate these standards into their policy dialogue with member countries. In addition, we stress the importance of effective co-operation between the World Trade Organisation (WTO) and the ILO on the social dimensions of globalisation and trade liberalisation (para. 16).	
G8 Communiqué, Cologne, 20 June 1999		To strengthen the foundations for sustainable growth and job creation, we strongly emphasize a two-tiered approach: 1. promoting structural reforms to enhance the adaptability and competitiveness of our economies and to help the long-term unemployed to return to the labor market;

	2. pursuing macroeconomic policies for stability and growth and to ensure that monetary and fiscal policies are well balanced. The greater the adaptability of our economies, the greater the likelihood that economic growth will result in more employment. We therefore strongly support the elimination of structural rigidities in labor, capital and product markets, the promotion of entrepreneurship and innovation, investment in human capital, reform of the tax/benefit systems to strengthen economic incentives and encourage employment, and development of an innovative and knowledge-based society (paras. 12–13).
G8 Communiqué, Cologne, 20 June 1999	We also endorse the G8 Labor Ministers' conclusions at their conference in Washington last February,[23] namely to provide social safety nets that support employment, to prevent long-term unemployment by early action, to facilitate job search by offering labor market information and employment services, to promote lifelong learning and new forms of work organization, to ensure equal access to the labor market for all workers, including job entrants and older workers, and to take forward the social dialogue (para. 14).
G8 Communiqué, Cologne, 20 June 1999	As the process of globalization has gained momentum, it has brought with it important social and economic progress. At the same time, rapid change and integration has left some individuals and groups feeling unable to keep up and has resulted in some dislocation, particularly in developing countries. We therefore need to take steps to strengthen the institutional and social infrastructure that can give globalization a 'human face' and ensure increasing, widely shared prosperity. Social security policies, including social safety nets, must be strong enough to encourage and enable individuals to embrace global

	change and liberalization and to improve their chances on the labor market, while enhancing social cohesion. We recognize that, faced with financial constraints, it is vital to strike a sustainable balance between social support programs and greater personal responsibility and initiative (paras. 19–20).
G8 Communiqué, Cologne, 20 June 1999	We are convinced that the countries most seriously affected by the recent economic and financial crises will sustain a speedier recovery if they create and improve the necessary social infrastructure. It is therefore particularly important to maintain investment in basic social services during times of crisis. Budgetary priorities and flexibility should enhance the quality of social infrastructure and investment (para. 21).
G8 Communiqué, Cologne, 20 June 1999	We call on the International Financial Institutions (IFIs) to support and monitor the development of sound social policy and infrastructure in developing countries. ... We urge the International Monetary Fund (IMF) to give more attention to this issue in designing its economic programs and to give particular priority to core budgets such as basic health, education and training to the extent possible, even during periods of fiscal consolidation (para. 23).
G8 Communiqué, Cologne, 20 June 1999	We commit ourselves to promote effective implementation of the International Labor Organization's (ILO) Declaration On Fundamental Principles and Rights at Work and its Follow-up. We also welcome the adoption of the ILO Convention on the Elimination of the Worst Forms of Child Labor. We further intend to step up work with developing countries to improve their capacity to meet their obligations. We support the strengthening of the ILO's capacity to assist countries in implementing core labor standards (para. 25).

Macroeconomic policy and poverty reduction		
G8 Communiqué, Genoa, 22 July 2001		Drawing the poorest countries into the global economy is the surest way to address their fundamental aspirations. ... The situation in many developing countries – especially in Africa – calls for decisive global action. The most effective poverty reduction strategy is to maintain a strong, dynamic, open and growing global economy (paras. 3–4).
G8 Communiqué, Genoa, 22 July 2001		To help developing countries improve the climate for private investment, we urge MDBs and other relevant international bodies to support domestic reform efforts, including the establishment of public–private partnerships and investment-related best practices, as well as codes and standards in the field of corporate governance, accounting standards, enhanced competition and transparent tax regimes. We call on the World Bank to provide additional support for programmes that promote private sector development in the poorest countries (para. 13).
G8 Communiqué, Genoa, 22 July 2001		To promote further investments in the knowledge-based economy, we call on the WTO and the World Intellectual Property Rights Organisation, in collaboration with the World Bank, to help the poorest countries comply with international rules on intellectual property rights (para. 13).

G7 Statement, Genoa, 20 July 2001	We pledge to pursue policies that will contribute to global growth by enhancing strong productivity growth in a sound macroeconomic environment, through structural reform, free trade and strengthened international economic co-operation (para. 2).
G8 Communiqué, Okinawa, 23 July 2000	To capitalise on the opportunities before us, we must renew our unwavering commitment to structural change in our own economies, including greater competition and more adaptable labour markets, underpinned by appropriate macro-economic policies (para. 9).
G8 Communiqué, Okinawa, 23 July 2000	[W]e commit ourselves to the agreed international development goals, including the overarching objective of reducing the share of the world's population living in extreme poverty to half its 1990 level by 2015. We welcome the Report on Poverty Reduction by Multilateral Development Banks (MDBs) and the International Monetary Fund (IMF)[24] which we requested in Cologne, and we look forward to receiving an annual poverty report as we review progress each year in reducing poverty across the globe (para. 13).
G8 Communiqué, Okinawa, 23 July 2000	[M]any countries have made significant progress in over-coming poverty in the past quarter century, and their example is a beacon of hope for others. From their success, we have learned that poverty can best be overcome in resilient, peaceful, and democratic societies with freedom and opportunity for all, growing and

	open economies and dynamic private sectors, and strong and accountable leaders and institutions (para. 14).
G8 Communiqué, Okinawa, 23 July 2000	Robust, broad-based and equitable economic growth is needed to fight poverty and rests on expanding people's capabilities and choices. Government must, in co-operation with the private sector and broader civil society, establish economic and social foundations for broad-based, private sector growth. … We will work with developing countries to put in place policies, programmes and institutions that offer people a fair chance to better their lives. We therefore welcome the constructive discussions of the Tenth Meeting of the United Nations Conference on Trade and Development (UNCTAD X) in Bangkok, and will work in the United Nations and other fora to further reduce poverty, especially in the Least Developed Countries (LDCs) (para. 15).
G8 Communiqué, Okinawa, 23 July 2000	Trade and investment are critical to promoting sustainable economic growth and reducing poverty. We commit ourselves to put a higher priority on trade-related capacity-building activities. We are also concerned that certain regions remain marginalised as regards foreign direct investment, and that the 48 LDCs attract less than 1% of total foreign direct investment flows to the developing countries. We urge multilateral development organisations and financial institutions to support developing countries' efforts to create a favourable trade and investment climate, including through the Poverty Reduction Strategy Papers (PRSPs) and the Integrated Framework (IF) (para. 17).
G8 Communiqué, Cologne, 20 June 1999	We welcome the outline agreements recently reached by Russia with the IMF and the World Bank and look forward to their speedy

	implementation as a further important step in Russia's reform program. Once an IMF agreement is in place, we encourage the Paris Club to act expeditiously to negotiate a debt rescheduling agreement with Russia (para. 6).
G8 Communiqué, Cologne, 20 June 1999	We agreed to intensify our dialogue within the G8 structures on the longer term social, structural and economic reform in Russia. To this end, we have instructed our personal representatives to ensure the overall continuity and cohesion of the work among the G8 on this subject. Particular emphasis should be given to concrete areas of cooperation such as small business development, strengthened cooperation with regions, health, [and] the social impact of economic transformation (para. 7).

Technology for development

G8 Communiqué, Genoa, 22 July 2001	We endorse the report of the Digital Opportunity Task Force (dot.force) and its Genoa Plan of Action[25] that successfully fulfilled the Okinawa mandate. ... We will continue to support the process and encourage

	all stakeholders to demonstrate ownership, to mobilise expertise and resources and to build on this successful co-operation (para. 22).
G8 Communiqué, Okinawa, 23 July 2000	IT empowers, benefits and links people the world over, allows global citizens to express themselves and know and respect one another. It also has immense potential for enabling economies to expand further, countries to enhance public welfare and promote stronger social cohesion and thus democracy to flourish. Access to the digital opportunities must, therefore, be open to all. … In support of these goals, we commit ourselves to pursuing the aims and ambitions set out in the Okinawa Charter on the Global Information Society[26] (paras. 10–12).
G8 Communiqué, Okinawa, 23 July 2000	We will set up a Digital Opportunities Task Force (dot. force), which will be asked to report to our next meeting its findings and recommendations on global action to bridge the international information and knowledge divide (para. 12).
Trade and market access	
G8 Communiqué, Genoa, 22 July 2001	Open trade and investment drive global growth and poverty reduction. That is why we have agreed today to support the launch of an ambitious new Round of global trade negotiations with a balanced agenda (para. 10).

		In addition to the policies we are pursuing in our own economies, we agreed today that co-operation on three further elements is important to a strengthened global economy [including] ... the launch of a new trade Round (para. 4).
G8 Communiqué, Genoa, 22 July 2001	We confirm our pledge made at the UN LDC III Conference to work towards duty-free and quota-free access for all products originating in the least developed countries. We support efforts made by LDCs to enter the global trading system and to take advantage of opportunities for trade-based growth (para. 11).	
G8 Communiqué, Genoa, 22 July 2001	[T]o help developing countries benefit from open markets, we will better co-ordinate our trade-related assistance to: • provide bilateral assistance on technical standards, customs systems, legislation needed for World Trade Organisation (WTO) membership, the protection of intellectual property rights, and human resource development • support the work of the Integrated Framework for Trade-Related Technical Assistance • encourage the international financial institutions to help remove obstacles to trade and investment, and establish the institutions and policies essential for trade to flourish • urge countries to mainstream trade expansion by including it in their poverty reduction strategies (para. 12).	
G7 Statement, Genoa, 20 July 2001		

G7 Statement, Genoa, 20 July 2001	Sustained economic growth world-wide requires a renewed commitment to free trade. Opening markets globally and strengthening the World Trade Organisation (WTO) as the bedrock of the multilateral trading system is therefore an economic imperative. It is for this reason that we pledge today to engage personally and jointly in the launch of a new ambitious Round of global trade negotiations at the Fourth WTO Ministerial Conference in Doha, Qatar this November. We are committed to working with developing countries, including the least developed, to ensure that the new Round addresses their priorities through improved market access and sounder, more transparent trade rules. We recognise that there are legitimate concerns in implementing the Uruguay Round Agreements. We welcome the steady progress made so far on implementation issues and are ready to examine ways to make further progress in connection with the launch of a new Round. Capacity building is essential to integrate developing countries into the trading system, and we are intensifying our efforts to assist in this area, including with international institutions. In the interests of all, the new Round should be based on a balanced agenda, while clarifying, strengthening and extending multilateral rules. An improved dispute settlement mechanism is central to this effort. Increased transparency in the WTO itself is also important to strengthen confidence in the global trading system. The WTO should continue to respond to the legitimate expectations of civil society, and ensure that the new Round supports sustainable development (paras. 6–8).
G8 Communiqué, Okinawa, 23 July 2000	Trade and investment are critical to promoting sustainable economic growth and reducing poverty. We commit ourselves to put a higher priority on trade-related capacity-building activities. We are also concerned that certain regions remain marginalised as regards foreign direct investment, and that the 48 LDCs attract less than 1% of total foreign direct investment flows to the developing countries. We urge multilateral development organisations and financial institutions to support developing countries' efforts to create a favourable trade and investment climate, including through the Poverty Reduction Strategy Papers (PRSPs) and the Integrated Framework (IF) (para. 17).
G8 Communiqué, Okinawa, 23 July 2000	We must ensure that the multilateral trading system is strengthened and continues to play its vital role in the world economy. Recognising this responsibility, we are firmly committed to a new round of WTO trade negotiations with an ambitious, balanced and inclusive agenda, reflecting the interests of all WTO

members. We agree that the objective of such negotiations should be to enhance market access, develop and strengthen WTO rules and disciplines, support developing countries in achieving economic growth and integration into the global trading system, and ensure that trade and social policies, and trade and environmental policies are compatible and mutually supportive. We agree to intensify our close and fruitful co-operation in order to try together with other WTO members to launch such a round during the course of this year. We recognise that more comprehensive partnership must be developed to help address the challenges of globalisation. In this regard, international and domestic policy coherence should be enhanced, and co-operation between the international institutions should be improved. We also underline the importance of our engagement with our publics to establish a constructive dialogue on the benefits and challenges of trade liberalisation (paras. 36–7).		
G8 Communiqué, Cologne, 20 June 1999	We pledge to work for a successful ministerial meeting in Seattle in order to launch the new round [of trade negotiations]. We will also seek a more effective way within the WTO for addressing the trade and environment relationship and promoting sustainable development and social and economic welfare worldwide (para. 9).	
G8 Communiqué, Cologne, 20 June 1999	We therefore call on all nations to launch at the WTO Ministerial Conference in Seattle in December 1999 a new round of broad-based and ambitious negotiations with the aim of achieving substantial and manageable results (para. 10).	

| G8 Communiqué, Cologne, 20 June 1999 | We encourage all members to make proposals for progress in areas where developing countries and in particular least developed countries can make solid and substantial gains; all countries should contribute to and benefit from the new round. An effective new round of trade negotiations should help pave the way for the further integration of the developing countries into the world economy. In this context we reaffirm our commitment made in Birmingham last year to the least developed countries on improved market access (para. 10). |
| G8 Communiqué, Cologne, 20 June 1999 | We intend to step up work with developing countries and multilateral institutions to improve developing countries' capacity to exercise their rights and meet their obligations in the global trading system so as to ensure that they derive the full benefits of liberalized trade and thus contribute to global economic growth (para. 27). |

Notes to Appendix 1

[1] E.g. see Stolberg (2002) and Yach and Bettcher (1999).
[2] http://www.worldbank.org/hipc
[3] http://www.g7.utoronto.ca/g7/finance/fm061899.htm
[4] http://www.unctad.org/conference/
[5] http://www.un.org/millennium/declaration/ares552e.htm
[6] http://www.paris21.org/betterworld
[7] http://www1.oecd.org/media/release/dac_recommendation.pdf
[8] http://www.unesco.org/education/efa/ed_for_all/framework.shtml
[9] http://www.g7.utoronto.ca/g7/summit/2001genoa/dotforce1.html
[10] http://www.g7.utoronto.ca/g7/summit/1999koln/charter.htm
[11] http://www.unesco.org/education/efa/ed_for_all/framework.shtml
[12] http://www.un.org/womenwatch/daw/followup/as2310rev1.pdf
[13] http://www.g7.utoronto.ca/g7/summit/1999koln/charter.htm
[14] http://www.renewabletaskforce.org
[15] http://www.g7.utoronto.ca/g7/environment/1999schwerin/communique.htm
[16] http://www1.oecd.org/ehs/PROJECTS.HTM; http://www1.oecd.org/subject/biotech/report_workgroup.pdf
[17] http://www1.oecd.org/ehs/food/
[18] http://www.g7.utoronto.ca/g7/finance/fm010707-b.htm
[19] http://www.g7.utoronto.ca/g7/summit/2000okinawa/abuse.htm
[20] http://www1.oecd.org/fatf
[21] http://www1.oecd.org/daf/fa/harm_tax/Report_En.pdf; for a report on subsequent OECD work on this issue see http://www.oecd.org/pdf/M00021000/M00021182.pdf
[22] http://www.g7.utoronto.ca/g7/labour/labournov2000.htm
[24] http://www.g7.utoronto.ca/g7/labour/labourfeb24.htm
[25] http://www.worldbank.org/html/extdr/extme/G8_poverty2000.pdf
[26] http://www.g7.utoronto.ca/g7/summit/2001genoa/dotforce1.html
[27] http://www.g7.utoronto.ca/g7/summit/2000okinawa/gis.htm

APPENDIX 2

Data Tables

Several of the figures in this book were calculated and plotted using data from multiple sources. Appendix 2 provides the raw numbers for these figures, their sources and some of the calculations we performed to estimate new numbers.

Figure 3.1: Average Annual Key Health Indicators and Health Expenditures in G7, Low-Income Countries and Sub-Saharan African (SSA) Countries

	Public spending as % of GDP, 1995–99 (average)	Private spending as % of GDP, 1995–99 (average)	Spending as % of GDP, 1995–99 (average)	Per capita spending, 1995–99 (average, US$ thousands)	Physicians/ 1 000, 1990–99 (average)	Hospital beds/ 1 000, 1990–99 (average)	Infant mortality rate/ 1 00 live births, 2000	Under 5 mortality/100 live births, 2000
G7	6.4	2.8	9.2	2.4	3.0	7.4	0.5	0.67
Low-income	0.9	2.7	3.8	0.02	0.5	1.3	7.6	11.5
Sub-Saharan Africa	2.0	2.8	4.9	0.04	0.1	1.1	9.1	16.2

Source: World Bank (2002d: Tables 2.15 & 2.20)

Figures 3.2: Trends in Aid to Health as % of Total ODA*

	1990–92 average	1996–98 average	1999	2000	2001
Canada	3	3	1.81	2.63	4.29
France	3	4	4.5	4.4	6
Germany	1	5	4	3.18	3.34
Italy	5	4	7.2	7.7	4.72

Japan	1	2	2.7	2.85	2.83
UK	9	10	6.8	9.63	5.9
US	5	17	4.4	4.11	4.68
G7 average				4.3	4.3

Source: OECD (2001c: Table 2 [1990–92 and 1996–98 data]); OECD (2002b: Tables 14 & 19 [2000 data]); OECD (2003: Tables 13, 15 & 19 [2001 data])

Estimates of 1999, 2000 and 2001 multilateral contributions made by authors.
*Total Official Development Assistance includes bilateral aid (country to country) and multilateral aid (contributions made by donor countries to the European Commission, the World Bank and regional development banks).
Note: Averages for 1990–92 and 1996–98 are for bilateral aid only. Data on country-specific contributions to multilateral health aid could not be obtained or calculated (imputed).

Figure 3.3: % of Total ODA* to Basic Health and Total Health, 2000–01 * *

	Basic health	Total health
Canada 2000	2.1	0.53
Canada 2001	1.9	2.39
France 2000	1.11	3.28
France 2001	1.67	4.33
Germany 2000	1.74	1.44
Germany 2001	2.07	1.27
Italy 2000	3.1	4.6
Italy 2001	1.8	2.92
Japan 2000	0.86	1.99
Japan 2001	1.06	1.77
UK 2000	5.5	4.13
UK 2001	2.15	3.75
US 2000	3.72	0.39

US 2001	4.56	0.12
G7 average 2000	2.4	1.9
G7 average 2001	2.5	1.8

Source: OECD (2002b: Tables 14 & 19); German and Randel (2002); OECD (2003: Tables 13, 15 & 19)

*Estimates of multilateral contributions made by authors.
**Basic health spending is part of total health spending.

Figure 3.4: % of Total ODA* to Basic Health, Population Health and Total Health, 2000–01*

	Basic health	Population health	Total health
Canada 2000	2.1	4.0	0.53
Canada 2001	1.9	3.14	2.39
France 2000	1.11	0.58	3.28
France 2001	1.67	0.86	4.33
Germany 2000	1.74	2.03	1.44
Germany 2001	2.07	1.93	1.27
Italy 2000	3.1	1.3	4.6
Italy 2001	1.8	1.26	2.92
Japan 2000	0.86	0.3	1.99
Japan 2001	1.06	0.27	1.77
UK 2000	5.5	3.2	4.13
UK 2001	2.15	2.7	3.75
US 2000	3.72	7.1	0.39
US 2001	4.56	8.65	0.12
G7 average 2000	2.4	2.7	1.9
G7 average 2001	2.5	3.5	1.8

Sources: OECD (2002b: Tables 14 & 19); Germany and Randel (2002); OECD (2003: Tables 13, 15 & 19)

*Estimates of multilateral contributions made by authors.
**Basic health spending is part of total health spending. Population health is a separate category.

Figure 3.5: Total Health ODA as % of GNI, 2000–01

	2000 as % of GNI	2001 as % of GNI
Canada	0.005	0.0092
France	0.009	0.015
Germany	0.0054	0.0057
Italy	0.0026	0.0038
Japan	0.0056	0.0058
UK	0.0256	0.015
US	0.004	0.0048
G7 average	0.008	0.0079

Sources: OECD (2002b: Tables 14 & 19); German and Randel (2002); OECD (2003: Tables 13, 15 & 19)

*Includes both bilateral and multilateral contributions. Estimates of multilateral contributions made by authors.

Figure 4.1: Trends in Aid to Education as % of Total ODA*

	1990–92 (average)	1993–96 (average)	1999	2000	2001
Canada	8	7	8.7	10.62	9.76
France	25	25	28.5	23.57	25.2
Germany	13	16	18.6	20.58	17.56
Italy	6	5	9.12	5.93	11.6
Japan	6	7	9.35	6.16	7.2
UK	13	11	10.89	8	8.21
US	3	5	3.87	3.05	3.63
G7 average				9.4	9.9

Source: UNESCO (2002b: Table 5.2); OECD (2001c: Tables 13, 15 & 19); OECD (2002b: Tables 13, 15 & 19); OECD (2003: Tables 13, 15 & 19)

Estimates of 1999, 2000 and 2001 multilateral contributions made by authors.
*Total ODA includes bilateral aid (country to country) and multilateral aid (contributions made by donor countries to the European Commission, the World Bank and Regional Development Banks). In 1999, the multilateral contributions for European G7 countries were approximated using EC sector commitments in 2000, as data on EC sector commitments for 1999 are not available.
Note: Averages for 1990–92 and 1993–96 for bilateral aid only.

Figure 4.2: % of Total ODA* to Basic Education and Total Education, 2000–01**

	Basic education	Total education
Canada 2000	1.26	9.36
Canada 2001	3.67	6.09
France 2000	2.31	21.26
France 2001	6.03	19.17
Germany 2000	3.13	17.45
Germany 2001	1.42	16.14
Italy 2000	1.77	4.16
Italy 2001	0.46	11.14
Japan 2000	0.481	5.679
Japan 2001	0.87	6.33
UK 2000	3.49	4.51
UK 2001	2.77	5.44
US 2000	2.04	1.01
US 2001	2.24	1.39
G7 2000 average	1.8	7.6
G7 2001 average	2.2	7.7

Source: OECD (2002b: Table 19); OECD (2003: Table 19)

*Estimates of multilateral contributions made by authors.
**Basic education spending is part of total education spending.

Figure 5.1: Regional Prevalence of Undernourishment, % of Total Population

	1990–92 (average)	1997–99 (average)
Developing World	20	17
Asia and Pacific	20	16
Latin America and Caribbean	13	11
Near East and North Africa	8	9
Sub-Saharan Africa	35	34

Source: UNFAO (2001: Table 1)

Figure 5.2: % of Total ODA to Agriculture Aid, 1979–80, 1999–2001

	1979/80	1999	2000	2001
Canada	12.6	3.46	4.65	3.23
France	6.4	6.96	6.42	10
Germany	10.3	6.05	6.17	6.6
Italy	20.7	6.92	7.1	7.42
Japan	12.9	8.35	6.3	13.3
UK	7.9	10.8	7.67	6.84
US	17.4	3.25	4.13	4.5
G7 average			5.9	8

Source: OECD (2001c: Tables 13, 15 & 19); OECD (2002b: Tables 13, 15, 18 & 19);
OECD (2003: Tables 13, 15 & 19)

Estimates of 1999, 2000 and 2001 multilateral contributions made by authors.
The multilateral contributions for European G7 countries in 1999 were approximated
using EC sector commitments in 2000, as data on EC sector commitments for 1999 are
not available. 1979–80 is bilateral aid only.

Figure 5.3: % of Total ODA to Food Aid, 1999–2001

	1999	2000	2001
Canada	5.2	5.71	7
France	1.67	1.78	2.97
Germany	3.16	3.7	3.34
Italy	9.5	7.21	12.52
Japan	0.4	0.41	0.4
UK	1.62	1.72	1.14
US	19.9	12.1	11.1
G7 average		4.5	5.1

Source: OECD (2001c: Tables 13, 15 & 19); OECD (2002b: Tables 13, 15 & 19); OECD (2003: Tables 13, 15 & 19)

The multilateral contributions for European G7 countries in 1999 were approximated using EC sector commitments in 2000, as data on EC sector commitments for 1999 is not available.

Figure 5.4: US Agricultural and Food Aid, 2001, Compared to Increased Annual Domestic Agricultural Subsidies, 2002–12

	US$ millions
Domestic agricultural subsidies	18 000
Agricultural ODA	514
Food ODA	1 267
Total food and agricultural ODA	1 781

Source: OECD (2003: Tables 13, 15 & 19)

Figure 6.1: Total ODA as % of GNI, 1984–85 (average), 2000–01

	1984–85 (average)	2000	2001
Canada	0.5	0.25	0.22
France	0.62	0.32	0.32
Germany	0.46	0.27	0.27
Italy	0.27	0.13	0.15
Japan	0.31	0.28	0.23
UK	0.33	0.32	0.32
US	0.24	0.1	0.11
G7 average	0.41	0.24	0.23

Source: OECD (2002b: Table 4); OECD (2003, Table 4)

Estimates of 2000 and 2001 multilateral contributions made by authors.

Figure 6.2: Trends in Total ODA, 1993–2001, at 2000 Prices and Exchange Rates (US$ millions)

	1993	1996	1999	2000	2001
Canada	2 321	1 745	1 770	1 744	1 580
France	6 828	5 530	4 916	4 105	4 253
Germany	5 830	5 489	4 752	5 030	5 069
Italy	2 846	1 938	1 595	1 376	1 632
Japan	11 132	9 232	15 869	13 508	11 260
UK	3 495	3 431	3 262	4 501	4 698
US	11 521	10 037	9 353	9 955	11 186
G7 Total	43 973	37 402	41 517	40 219	39 678

Source: OECD (2003: Table 8)

Figure 6.3: % Change in Total ODA, 1993–2001, at 2000 Prices and Exchange Rates

Canada	-32%
France	-38%
Germany	-13%
Italy	-43%
Japan	1%
UK	34%
US	-3%
G7 Total	-10%

Source: OECD (2003: Table 8)

Figure 6.4: % of Bilateral Aid by Tying Status, 1999–2001

	Untied	Partially tied	Tied
Canada 1999	29.6		70.4
Canada 2000	24.9		75.1
Canada 2001	31.7		68.3
France 1999	66.8	23.4	9.8
France 2000	68	25.5	6.6
France 2001	66.6	24.3	9.1
Germany 1999	84.7		15.3
Germany 2000	93.2		6.8
Germany 2001	84.6		15.4
Italy 1999	22.6		77.4
Italy 2000	38.2		61.8
Italy 2001	7.8		92.2
Japan 1999	96.4	2.9	0.7

Japan 2000	86.4	0.5	13.1
Japan 2001	81.1	1.4	17.5
UK 1999	91.8		8.2
UK 2000	91.5		8.5
UK 2001	93.9		6.1

Source: OECD (2001c, 2002b, 2003: Table 23; data on US not provided)

Figure 6.5: Aid from G7 Countries to LDCs as % of Total ODA

	1989–90 (average)	1999	2000	2001
Canada	29	18	17	15
France	29	16	24	25
Germany	28	20	23	22
Italy	39	22	27	27
Japan	20	17	15	18
UK	33	21	31	35
US	17	16	20	15
G7 Average	24.9	17.4	20.4	20.6

Source: OECD (2002b, Tables 4 & 31); OECD (2003, Tables 4 & 31)

Estimates of 2000 and 2001 multilateral contributions made by authors.

Figure 6.6: Aid from G7 Countries to LDCs as % of GNI

	1989–90 (average)	1999	2000	2001
Canada	0.13	0.05	0.04	0.03
France	0.17	0.06	0.08	0.08
Germany	0.12	0.05	0.06	0.06
Italy	0.14	0.03	0.03	0.04

Japan	0.06	0.06	0.04	0.04
UK	0.10	0.05	0.10	0.11
US	0.03	0.02	0.02	0.02
G7 Average	0.07	0.04	0.04	0.04

Source: OECD (2002b, Table 31); OECD (2003, Table 31)

Figure 6.7: Trends in G7 Assistance to Sub-Saharan Africa as % of Total Aid

	1989–90	1994–95	1999–2000	2000–01
Canada	45.3	40.1	35.5	34.2
France	59.1	50.4	44.2	47.1
Germany	40.1	35.7	34.7	34.4
Italy	55.8	33.6	46.7	46.6
Japan	21.0	20.6	12.7	17.9
UK	52.5	45.6	45.7	48.7
US	19.8	29.3	26.2	29.1

Source: OECD (2002b: Table 28); OECD (2003: Table 28)
Estimates of 2000 and 2001 multilateral contributions made by authors.
Reported as fiscal years (e.g. 1989–90) rather than calendar years (e.g. 1990).

Figure 6.8: Number of Sub-Saharan African Countries in Top 10 Recipients of Bilateral Assistance

	1989–90	1999–2000	2000–01
Canada	6	2	1
France	5	5	6
Germany	4	1	1
Italy	6	5	5
Japan	0	0	1
UK	7	7	7
US	1	1	1

Source: OECD (2002b: Table 32); OECD (2003: Table 32)
Reported as fiscal years (e.g. 1989–90) rather than calendar years (e.g. 1990).

Figure 6.9: Trends in Regional Distribution of ODA from All Donors (%)

	1990–91	**1995–96**	**2000–01**
Sub-Saharan Africa	33.8	33	30.4
South and Central Asia	14.1	15.0	17.6
Other Asia and Oceania	16.6	22.1	20.6
Middle East and North Africa	20.9	13.0	10.5
Europe	2.9	4.3	7.8
Latin America and Caribbean	11.7	12.5	13.1

Source: OECD (2003: Table 27)

Reported as fiscal years (e.g. 1990–91) rather than calendar years (e.g. 1991).

Figure 6.10: Trends in G7 Total ODA Disbursements to Sub-Saharan Africa

	1985–86 average	**1990–91 average**	**1998**	**1999**	**2000**	**2001**
Net ODA US$ millions at 2000 prices and exchange rates	16 990	18 885	13 543	12 175	12 702	14 045

Source: OECD (2003: Table 30)

Figure 7.1: Total Tax Revenue as % of GDP in Selected Countries, 2000

	Total tax as % of GDP, 2000
Bangladesh	7.0
China	6.8
India	9.6
Pakistan	12.1
Burundi	16.7

Cameroon	12.8
Congo	6.0
Guinea	11.3
Madagascar	11.3
Sierra Leone	6.8
Sudan	6.8
Uganda	10.3
G7 average	28

Source: World Bank (2002d: Table 5.5)
G7 average excludes France and Japan, for which data were not available.

Figure 8.1: % of Total Aid to Water and Sanitation, 1999–2001

	1999	2000	2001
Canada	2.29	3.56	1.8
France	3.02	4.48	4.14
Germany	6.94	13.06	12.1
Italy	5.27	8.98	4.57
Japan	7.59	14.4	5.96
UK	3.3	2.71	2.76
US	2.66	1.6	5.16
G7 average		8.1	5.7

Source: OECD (2001c: Table 19; 2002b: Table 19; 2003: Table 19)
The multilateral contributions for European G7 countries in 1999 were approximated
using EC sector commitments in 2000, as data on EC sector commitments for 1999 are
not available.

Multilateral ODA Calculations

The OECD Development Assistance Committee report (OECD, 2002b) provides country-specific data for bilateral aid, by key sectors. It does not, however, provide multilateral aid by country for these same key sectors. Comparing sector-specific aid trends without estimating countries' portions of 2000 aid contributed through multilateral agencies would be egregious, to say the least. Instead, we estimate total 2000 ODA (bilateral and multilateral) based on the following calculation: country-specific percentage of total aid contributed through each of the three multilateral agencies (Regional Development Banks, World Bank, European Commission) x the percentage of aid provided to the specific sector by each of the multilateral agencies. The sum of these calculations is added to that country's sector-specific bilateral contribution. While reasonably accurate, there may be small margins of error: the OECD report (2002b) itself cautions that figures for the European Commission are 'approximate.' Total 2001 ODA contributions are based on the same calculations, using provisional data from the OECD (2003). An even greater note of caution is expressed for 1999 multilateral estimates. We applied the same formula as for 2000 and 2001, but the percentage of EC aid contributions by sector is not available for 1999. We used the percentages for 2000 as a rough approximation. For this reason, we do not include 1999 in calculating G7 averages, but rely on years for which data are more reliable (2000, 2001).

% of Total Multilateral and Bilateral Aid Contributions to Specific Sectors, 1999

	Total ODA to health	Total ODA to basic health	Total ODA to population health	Total ODA to agriculture aid	Total ODA to food aid	Total ODA to education	Total ODA to basic education	Total ODA to water and sanitation
Canada	1.81	0.81	0.48	3.46	5.2	8.7	0.9	2.29
France	4.49	0.53	0.13	6.96	1.67	28.48	0.56	3.02
Germany	3.96	2.46	1.02	6.05	3.16	18.6	2.86	6.94
Italy	7.17	2.98	0.5	6.92	9.5	9.12	1.57	5.27
Japan	2.66	0.7	0.11	8.35	0.4	9.35	0.43	7.59
UK	6.77	2.84	3.54	10.8	1.62	10.89	3.84	3.3
US	4.43	3.11	6.09	3.25	19.9	3.87	1.32	2.66

Source: OECD (2001c: Tables 13, 14 & 19); OECD (2002b: Table 19)

% of Total Multilateral and Bilateral Aid Contributions to Specific Sectors, 2000

	Total ODA to health	Total ODA to basic health	Total ODA to population health	Total ODA to agriculture aid	Total ODA to food aid	Total ODA to education	Total ODA to basic education	Total ODA to water and sanitation
Canada	2.63	2.1	3.99	4.65	5.71	10.62	1.26	3.56
France	4.39	1.11	0.58	6.42	1.78	23.57	2.31	4.48
Germany	3.18	1.74	2.03	6.17	3.7	20.58	3.13	13.06
Italy	7.7	3.1	1.3	7.1	7.21	5.93	1.77	8.98
Japan	2.85	0.86	0.29	6.3	0.41	6.16	0.481	14.4
UK	9.63	5.5	3.2	7.67	1.72	8.0	3.49	2.71
US	4.11	3.72	7.09	4.13	12.103	3.05	2.04	1.6

Source: OECD (2002b: Tables 13, 15 & 19)

% of Total Multilateral and Bilateral Aid Contributions to Specific Sectors, 2001

	Total ODA to health	Total ODA to basic health	Total ODA to population health	Total ODA to agriculture aid	Total ODA to food aid	Total ODA to education	Total ODA to basic education	Total ODA to water and sanitation
Canada	4.294	1.9	3.14	3.23	7.0	9.76	3.67	1.8
France	6.0	1.67	0.86	10	2.97	25.2	6.03	4.14
Germany	3.34	2.07	1.93	6.6	3.34	17.56	1.42	12.1
Italy	4.72	1.8	1.26	7.42	12.52	11.6	0.46	4.57
Japan	2.83	1.06	0.27	13.3	0.4	7.2	0.87	5.96
UK	5.9	2.15	2.7	6.84	1.14	8.21	2.77	2.76
US	4.68	4.56	8.65	4.5	11.1	3.63	2.24	5.16

Source: OECD (2003: Tables 13, 15 & 19)

APPENDIX 3

NEPAD's Health Commitments

Introduction

I **Explicit Health Commitments**
General statistics
Child mortality
Maternal mortality
Reproductive health services
Disease control/AIDS, malaria and other communicable diseases
Financial support/affordable drugs
Medical doctors and traditional practitioners
Capacity-building
Sustainable health-care systems
Health as a means to growth and development
The poor as a priority health target

II **Health-Related Commitments Explicitly Recognised**
Poverty
Food and food production
The Environmental and Energy Initiative

III **Health-Related Commitments not Explicitly Recognised**
Safe water and sanitation
People-centered development
Global partnership: Elimination of unequal relations and marginalization
African autonomy and African Renaissance
GDP target for sustainable development
Debt reduction
Development assistance, concessional finance and sustainable development
Structural adjustment programmes
Political domestic reforms

Introduction

Whilst anyone can produce a valid assessment of anyone else, the exercise carries extra weight to the extent that the subject of the assessment agrees with the criteria being used. Health is not NEPAD's primary focus. Development is. Nonetheless, NEPAD does contain health commitments that are explicitly recognized. NEPAD also includes non-health factors that it explicitly acknowledges as having an impact on health.

These acknowledgements are important because they mean that, given the reality of everything being interconnected with everything else, NEPAD is not being assessed in terms of criteria that have been externally imposed on it.

The structure of this Report Card mirrors NEPAD'S own position. This is to say, the Report Card begins with NEPAD's own explicitly acknowledged direct health commitments, which, accordingly, carry the greatest weight. The Report Card follows these commitments with those that NEPAD recognizes as being health-related, even though not in themselves self-evidently health factors. The Report Card ends with NEPAD commitments that are not explicitly recognized as being health related, but which plainly have a right to be included as part of an evaluation of NEPAD's health commitments. These last commitments are not unimportant, even though they might be said to carry less weight than those openly acknowledged by NEPAD as being health-related.

NEPAD's Health Commitments

In the following table, all paragraph references are to the NEPAD document, unless otherwise stated. DRB = Debt Relief and Beyond

#	A. Commitments that can be assessed in quantitative or dichotomous terms (e.g. expenditure figures, agreement reached or not reached)	B. Commitments about which adequate data exist for assessment, but can be assessed only in qualitative or narrative terms	C. Commitments that reflect a basic, but contested, normative vision of the relations among markets, development and health
	Note: Some commitments span columns because they fall into two, or even all three, of the above categories.		
	(i) EXPLICIT HEALTH COMMITMENTS (Health [is] defined by the WHO as a state of complete physical and mental well-being.)		
	GENERAL STATISTICS		
1.	In the health sector, Africa compares very poorly with the rest of the world. In 1997, child and juvenile death rates were 105 and 169 per 1 000, as against 6 and 7 per 1 000 respectively in developed countries. Life expectancy is 48.9 years, as against 77.7 years in developed countries. Only 16 doctors are available per 100 000 inhabitants, as against 253 in industrialised countries (para. 126).		

CHILD MORTALITY		
2.	To reduce infant and child mortality rates by two-thirds between 1990 and 2015 (para. 68).	
MATERNAL MORTALITY		
3.	To reduce maternal mortality ratios by three-quarters between 1990 and 2015 (para. 68).	
REPRODUCTIVE HEALTH SERVICES		
4.	To provide access for all who need reproductive health services by 2015 (para. 68).	
DISEASE CONTROL/AIDS, MALARIA AND OTHER COMMUNICABLE DISEASES		
5.		One of the major impediments facing African development efforts is the widespread incidence of communicable diseases, in particular HIV/AIDS, tuberculosis and malaria. African leaders will therefore take joint responsibility for revitalizing and extending programmes for containing these and other communicable diseases, so that they do not fall short of the scale required in order to reduce the burden of disease. Recognizing the need to sequence and prioritize, the initiating Presidents propose that these programmes be fast-tracked, in collaboration with development partners (paras. 49, 123, 125, 185).

6.		The Declaration emphasizes ... the establishment of conditions for the key challenges of eradicating (or controlling) disease (paras. 46, 92, 123).
	FINANCIAL SUPPORT/AFFORDABLE DRUGS	
7.	In order to mobilize the resources required to build effective disease interventions and a secure health system, Nepad will join forces with other international agencies such as the World Health Organization (WHO) and donors to ensure that support for the continent is increased by at least US $10 billion per annum. Nepad will also encourage African countries to give higher priority to health in their own budgets and to phase in such increases in expenditure to a level to be mutually determined (para. 124).	
8.	To strengthen Africa's participation in processes aimed at procuring affordable drugs, African leaders envisage facilitating the development of a partnership between countries, international pharmaceutical corporations and civil society organisations to urgently secure access to existing drugs for Africans suffering from infectious diseases. Such a partnership would be in keeping with the responsibilities and obligations of those non-African bodies (paras. 124, 185).	

MEDICAL DOCTORS AND TRADITIONAL PRACTITIONERS

9.	Encourage cooperation between medical doctors and traditional practitioners (para. 123).	

CAPACITY BUILDING

10.		To empower the people of Africa to act to improve their own health and to achieve health literacy, Nepad requires the joint mobilization of resources for capacity-building in order to enable all African countries to improve their health infrastructures and management (paras. 123, 124)
11.	The African leaders envisage the translation into concrete commitments of the international strategies adopted in the fields of education and health, as part of the responsibilities and obligations of the developed countries and multilateral institutions (para. 185).	

SUSTAINABLE HEALTH-CARE SYSTEMS

12.	To ensure the necessary support capacity for the sustainable development of an effective health-care delivery system (para. 123).	

	HEALTH AS A MEANS TO GROWTH AND DEVELOPMENT			
13.				The challenge for Africa is to develop the capacity to sustain growth and development at levels required to achieve poverty reduction and sustainable development. This, in turn, depends on other factors such as infrastructure, capital accumulation, human capital, institutions, structural diversification, competitiveness, **health**, and good stewardship of the environment (paras. 64, 94).
	THE POOR AS A PRIORITY HEALTH TARGET			
14.	Nepad is committed to the successful reduction of the burden of disease on the poorest people in Africa (paras. 123, 126).			
	(ii) HEALTH-RELATED COMMITMENTS EXPLICITLY RECOGNIZED			
	POVERTY			
15.				This *New Partnership for Africa's Development* is a pledge by African leaders, based on a common vision and a firm and shared conviction, that they have a pressing duty to eradicate poverty (para. 1).

	What is required ... is bold and imaginative leadership that is genuinely committed to ... the eradication of poverty (para. 6). Poverty, reflected in very low per capita incomes, is one of the major factors limiting the populations' capacity to address their health problems (para. 126).
16.	While globalization has increased the cost of Africa's ability to compete, we hold that the advantages of an effectively managed integration present the best prospects for future economic prosperity and poverty reduction (para. 28). Experience shows that, despite the unparalleled opportunities that globalization has offered to some previously poor countries, there is nothing inherent in the process that automatically reduces poverty and inequality (para. 40).
17.	The new phase of globalization coincided with the reshaping of international relations in the aftermath of the Cold War.

		This is associated with the emergence of new concepts of security and self-interest, which encompass the right to development and the eradication of poverty (para. 43).
18.	The Declaration emphasizes ... the establishment of conditions ... for the key challenges of eradicating poverty and disease (para. 46).	
19.	Although long-term funding is envisaged under this initiative, the projects can be expedited to help eradicate poverty in Africa and place African countries ... on a path of sustainable growth and development and thus halt the marginalization of Africa in the globalization process (para. 62).	
20.		While growth rates are important, they are not by themselves sufficient to enable African countries to achieve the goal of poverty reduction. The challenge for Africa, therefore, is to develop the capacity to sustain growth at levels required to achieve poverty reduction and sustainable development (para. 64).

21.	Long-term objective: To eradicate poverty in Africa and to place African countries ... on a path of sustainable growth and development .... (para. 67). To ensure that the continent achieves the agreed International Development Goals (IDGs) .... To reduce the proportion of people living in extreme poverty by half between 1990 and 2015 (para. 68).			
22.		The strategy has the following expected outcomes: .... - Reduction in poverty and inequality (para. 69).		
23.				The state has a major role to play in promoting economic growth and development and in implementing poverty reduction programmes (para. 86).
24.				The structural gap in infrastructure constitutes a very serious handicap to economic growth and poverty reduction (para. 98).
25.	• To provide focused leadership by prioritising poverty reduction in all the programmes and priorities of the *New Partnership for Africa's Development*, as well as national macroeconomic and sectoral policies;			

	• To give special attention to the reduction of poverty among women; • To ensure empowerment of the poor in poverty reduction strategies; • To support existing poverty reduction initiatives at the multilateral level, such as the Comprehensive Development Framework of the World Bank and the Poverty Reduction Strategy approach linked to the debt relief initiative for Highly Indebted Poor Countries (HIPCs) (para. 115).
26.	• Require that country plans prepared for initiatives in this programme of action assess their poverty reduction impact, both before and after implementation; • Work with the World Bank, the International Monetary Fund (IMF), the African Development Bank, and the United Nations (UN) agencies to accelerate the implementation and adoption of the Comprehensive Development Framework, the Poverty Reduction Strategy and related approaches; • Establish a gender task team to ensure that the specific issues faced

	by poor women are addressed in the poverty reduction strategies of the *New Partnership for Africa's Development* (para. 116).	Improvement in health and nutrition directly contributes to improved well-being as the spread of diseases is controlled, infant mortality rates are reduced and life expectancy is higher. The link with poverty reduction is clearly established (para. 128). It has been demonstrated in other parts of the world that measures taken to achieve a healthy environmental base can contribute greatly to ... reduction of poverty (para. 136).
27.		
	FOOD AND FOOD PRODUCTION	Nutrition is an important ingredient of good health. The average daily intake of calories varies from 2384 in low-income countries to 2846 in middle-income countries, to 3390 in countries of the Organisation for Economic Cooperation and Development (OECD) (para. 127).
28.		

		The urgent need to achieve food security in African countries requires that the problem of inadequate agricultural systems be addressed, so that food production can be increased and nutritional standards raised (para. 130).
29.	Promoting the development of infrastructure, agriculture and its diversification into agro-industries and manufacturing to serve both domestic and export markets (para. 49).	
30.		Productivity improvement in agriculture rests on the removal of a number of structural constraints affecting the sector. A key constraint is climatic uncertainty, which raises the risk factor facing intensive agriculture based on the significant inflow of private investment (para. 132).
31.		There is an urgent need to diversify production and the logical starting point is to harness Africa's natural resource base. Value added in agro-processing ... must be increased (para. 153).

32.	• To ensure food security for all people and increase the access of the poor to adequate food and nutrition; • To integrate the rural poor into the market economy and provide them with better access to export markets; • To develop Africa into a net exporter of agricultural products (para. 154).
33.	• Foster regional, subregional, national and household food security through the development and management of increased production, transport, storage and marketing of food crops, livestock and fisheries. Particular attention must also be given to the needs of the poor, as well as the establishment of early warning systems to monitor droughts and crop production. • Promote access to international markets by improving the quality of African produce and agricultural products, particularly processed products, to meet the standards required by those markets. • Develop new partnership schemes to address donor fatigue for individual, high-profile agricultural projects (para. 155).

34.	• To plan and manage water resources to become a basis for national and regional cooperation and development • To systematically address and sustain ecosystems, biodiversity and wildlife • To cooperate on shared rivers among member states • To effectively address the threat of climate change • To ensure enhanced irrigation and rain-fed agriculture to improve agricultural production and food security (para. 113).		
35.	Accelerate work on multipurpose water resource projects, e.g. the SADC Water Secretariat's investigation of the utilisation of the Congo River, and the Nile Basin Initiative (para. 114).		
36.	Establish a task team to make plans for mitigating the negative impact of climate change in Africa (para. 114).		
37.	• Increase the security of water supply for agriculture by establishing small-scale irrigation facilities, improving local water management, and increasing the exchange of information and technical know-how with the international community; • Improve land tenure security under traditional and modern forms of tenure, and promote the necessary land reform; • Enhance agricultural credit and financing schemes, and improve access to credit by small-scale and women farmers (para. 155).		

| 38. | Expand the ambit and operation of the integrated action plan for land and water management for Africa. The project addresses the maintenance and upgrading of Africa's fragile agricultural natural resources base. Many African governments are already implementing these initiatives as part of this programme. Partners include the Global Environment Facility (GEF), the World Bank, the African Development Bank, the FAO and other bilateral donor agencies (para. 190). Strengthen and refocus the capacity of Africa's agricultural research and extension systems. The project addresses the issue of upgrading the physical and institutional infrastructure that supports Africa's agriculture. Technological innovation and technology diffusion hold enormous potential for accelerating agricultural output and productivity, but the continent lacks the research capacity necessary for major breakthroughs. Major players include the Forum for Agricultural Research in Africa (FARA), the World Bank, the FAO and the Consultative Group on International Agricultural Research (CGIAR) (para. 191). |

THE ENVIRONMENTAL & ENERGY INITIATIVE

| 39. | It has been recognized that a **healthy** and productive environment is a prerequisite for the *New Partnership for Africa's Development.* It is further recognized that the range of issues necessary to nurture this environmental base is vast and complex, and that a systematic combination of initiatives is necessary to develop a coherent environ mental programme (para. 135). |

	It is also recognised that a core objective of the Environment Initiative must be to combat poverty and contribute to socio-economic development in Africa. It has been demonstrated in other parts of the world that measures taken to achieve a healthy environmental base can contribute greatly to employment, social and economic empowerment, and reduction of poverty (para. 136).
40.	It should be mentioned here that Africa will host the World Summit on Sustainable Development in September 2002, and that environmental management forms the basis of the Summit. In this regard, we propose that the event put particular emphasis on the deliberations on this theme in the *New Partnership for Africa's Development* (para. 137).
41.	The Environment Initiative has targeted eight sub-themes for priority interventions: **Combating Desertification.** Initial interventions are envisaged to rehabilitate degraded land and to address the factors that led to such degradation. Many of these steps will need to be labour-intensive, along the lines of "public works programmes", thereby contributing to the

		The Environment Initiative has a distinct advantage in that many of the projects can start within relatively short timeframes, and they also offer exceptionally good returns on investment in terms of creating the social and ecological base on which the *New Partnership for Africa's Development* can thrive (para. 139).
social development needs of the continent. The initial interventions will serve as best practices or prototypes for future interventions in this area; **Wetland Conservation.** This involves the implementation of African best practices on wetland conservation, where social and ecological benefits are derived from private sector investment in this area; **Invasive Alien Species.** Partnerships are sought to prevent and control invasive alien species. These partnerships are critical for both the preservation of the ecosystems and for economic well-being; **Coastal Management.** In protecting and utilizing coastal resources to optimal effect, best practices are again suggested from which a broader programme can be drawn up; **Global Warming.** The initial focus will be on monitoring and regulating the impact of climate change. Labour-intensive work is essential and critical to integrated fire management projects; ... **Environmental Governance.** This relates to securing institutional, legal, planning, training and capacity-building requirements that underpin all the above ... (para. 141).		
42.		

43.	To implement national strategies for sustainable development by 2005, so as to reverse the loss of environmental resources by 2015 (para. 68).
44.	The *New Partnership for Africa's Development* focuses on the provision of essential regional public goods (such as transport, energy, water, ICT, disease eradication, environmental preservation and provision of regional research capacity, as well as the promotion of intra-African trade and investments) (para. 92).
45.	• To increase Africans' access to reliable and affordable commercial energy supply from 10 to 35 per cent or more within 20 years; • To reverse environmental degradation that is associated with the use of traditional fuels in rural areas (para. 109).
46.	Establish a task team to accelerate the development of energy supply to low-income housing.

47.	Broaden the scope of the programme for biomass energy conservation from the Southern African Development Community (SADC) to the rest of the continent (para. 110).	Productivity improvement in agriculture rests on the removal of a number of structural constraints affecting the sector .... The improvement of other rural infrastructure (roads, rural electrification, etc.) is also essential (para. 132).

(iii) HEALTH-RELATED COMMITMENTS NOT EXPLICITLY RECOGNIZED

SAFE WATER & SANITATION

48.		"In Africa ... only 58% of the population have access to safe water" (para. 4).
49.		The *New Partnership for Africa's Development* focuses on the provision of essential regional public goods (such as ... water) (para. 92).
50.	• To ensure sustainable access to safe and adequate clean water supply and sanitation, especially for the poor; • To plan and manage water resources to become a basis for national and regional cooperation and development (para. 113).	

- Collaborate with the Global Environmental Sanitation Initiative (GESI) in promoting sanitary waste disposal methods and projects (para. 114).

51. To improve access to, and affordability and reliability of, infrastructure services for both firms and households (para. 102).

PEOPLE-CENTERED DEVELOPMENT

52. What is required ... is bold and imaginative leadership that is genuinely committed to a sustained human development ... (para. 6).

53. Across the continent, Africans declare that we will no longer allow ourselves to be conditioned by circumstance. ... There are already signs of progress and hope. Democratic regimes that are committed to ... people-centred development ... are on the increase (para. 7).

GLOBAL PARTNERSHIP: ELIMINATION OF UNEQUAL RELATIONS AND MARGINALIZATION

54. The *New Partnership for Africa's Development* calls for the reversal of this abnormal situation by changing the relationship that underpins it.

	Africans are appealing neither for the further entrenchment of dependency through aid, nor for marginal concessions (para. 5).
55.	The *New Partnership for Africa's development* is ... [a] call for a new relationship of partnership between Africa and the international community, especially the highly industrialized countries, to overcome the development chasm that has widened over centuries of unequal relations (para. 8). For centuries, Africa has been integrated into the world economy mainly as a supplier of cheap labour and raw materials. Of necessity, this has meant the draining of Africa's resources rather than their use for the continent's development. The drive in that period to use the minerals and raw materials to develop manufacturing industries and a highly skilled labour force to sustain growth and development was lost. Thus, Africa remains the poorest continent despite being one of the most richly endowed regions of the world

56.	(para. 19). Africans must not be wards of benevolent guardians; rather they must be the architects of their own sustained upliftment (para. 27). Greater integration has also led to the further marginalisation of those countries that are unable to compete effectively. In the absence of fair and just global rules, globalization has increased the ability of the strong to advance their interests to the detriment of the weak, especially in the areas of trade, finance and technology. It has limited the space for developing countries to control their own development, as the system makes no provision for compensating the weak. The conditions of those marginalized in this process have worsened in real terms. A fissure between inclusion and exclusion has emerged within and among nations (para. 33).
57.	In part, Africa's inability to harness the process of globalization is a result of ... unfavourable terms of trade (para. 34).

| 58. | | Global governance ... recognises partnership among all peoples. We hold that it is within the capacity of the international community to create fair and just conditions in which Africa can participate effectively in the global economy and body politic (para. 41).

The United Nations Millennium Declaration, adopted in September 2000, confirms the global community's readiness to support Africa's efforts to address the continent's underdevelopment and marginalization (para. 46). |
| 59. | **AFRICAN AUTONOMY & AFRICAN RENAISSANCE** | The programme is a new framework of interaction with the rest of the world, including the industrialized countries and multilateral organisations.

It is based on the agenda set by African peoples through their own initiatives and of their own volition, to shape their own destiny (para. 48).

The *New Partnership for Africa's Development* will be successful only if it is owned by the African peoples united in their diversity (para. 51). |

60.	This is why our peoples, in spite of the present difficulties, must regain confidence in their genius and their capacity to face obstacles and be involved in the building of the new Africa. The present initiative is an expression of the commitment of Africa's leaders to translate the deep popular will into action (para. 53). However, the struggle they would be waging will be successful only if our peoples are the masters of their own destiny (para. 54).
	The *New Partnership for Africa's Development* is envisaged as a long-term vision of an African-owned and African-led development programme (para. 60).
GDP TARGET FOR SUSTAINABLE DEVELOPMENT	
61.	To achieve and sustain an average gross domestic product (GDP) growth rate of over 7 per cent per annum for the next 15 years (see paras. 109, 68).

62.	Realising that unless something new and radical is done, Africa will not achieve ... the 7 per cent annual GDP growth rate, the African heads of state propose the programme described below (i.e. sustainable development) (para. 70).		
63.		To achieve the estimated 7 per cent annual growth rate needed to meet ... the goal of reducing by half the proportion of Africans living in poverty by the year 2015 – Africa needs to fill an annual resource gap of 12 per cent of its GDP, or US \$64 billion (para. 144).	
DEBT REDUCTION			
64.		Credit has led to the debt deadlock which, from instalments to rescheduling, still exists and hinders the growth of African countries. The limits of this option have been reached (para. 3).	
65.		The Declaration further points to the global community's commitment to enhance resource flows to Africa, by improving ... debt relationships between Africa and the rest of the world ..... It is now important to	

66.	We also recognize that, if infrastructure is to improve in Africa, private foreign finance is essential to complement the two major funding methods, namely credit and aid (para. 100).
67.	To support existing poverty reduction initiatives at the multilateral level, such as the Comprehensive Development Framework of the World Bank and the Poverty Reduction Strategy approach linked to the debt relief initiative for Highly Indebted Poor Countries (HIPCs) (para. 115).
68.	The *New Partnership for Africa's Development* focuses on debt reduction ... as ... external resources required in the short to medium term (para. 144).
69.	The *New Partnership for Africa's Development* seeks the extension of debt relief beyond its current levels (based on debt "sustainability"), which still require debt service payments amounting to a significant portion of the resource gap. The long-term objective of the *New Partnership for Africa's Development* is to

translate these commitments into reality (para. 46).

link debt relief with costed poverty reduction outcomes. In the interim, debt service ceilings should be fixed as a proportion of fiscal revenue, with different ceilings for international development assistance (IDA) and non-IDA countries. To secure the full commitment of concessional resources – debt relief plus ODA – that Africa requires, the leadership of the *New Partnership for Africa's Development* will negotiate these arrangements with creditor governments. Countries would engage with existing debt relief mechanisms – the HIPC and the Paris Club – before seeking recourse through the *New Partnership for Africa's Development*. The Debt Initiative will require agreed poverty reduction strategies, debt strategies and participation in the Economic Governance Initiative to ensure that countries are able to absorb the extra resources. In addition to seeking further debt relief through the interim debt strategy set out above, the leadership of the *New Partnership for Africa's Development* will establish a forum in which African countries will share experience and mobilise for the improvement of debt relief strategies (para. 146).	
70.	The heads of state of the *New Partnership for Africa's Development* will secure an agreement, negotiated with the international community, to provide further debt relief for countries participating in the *New Partnership for Africa's Development*, based on the principles outlined above. The leadership of the *New Partnership for Africa's Development* will establish a forum in which African countries may share experiences and mobilise for the improvement of debt relief strategies. They will exchange ideas that may end the process of reform and qualification in the HIPC process (para. 147). The *New Partnership for Africa's Development* will support a PRSP Learning Group to engage in the PRSP process, together with the IMF and the World Bank (para. 148). Support efforts of the Economic Commission for Africa (ECA) to establish a PRSP Learning Group (para. 149).

71.	Equally important, however, especially in the short to medium term, is the need for additional ... debt reduction. Further debt reduction is also crucial. The enhanced HIPC debt relief initiative still leaves many countries within its scope with very high debt burdens; hence the need to direct more resources towards poverty reduction. In addition, some countries not included in the HIPC initiative also require debt relief to release resources for poverty reduction (para. 152).
72.	The African leaders envisage the following responsibilities and obligations of the developed countries and multilateral institutions: • To accelerate debt reduction for heavily indebted African countries, in conjunction with more effective poverty reduction programmes, of which the Strategic Partnership with Africa and the PRSP initiatives are an important starting point; • To improve debt relief strategies for middle-income countries (para. 185).

DEVELOPMENT ASSISTANCE, CONCESSIONAL FINANCE & SUSTAINABLE DEVELOPMENT

73.	Historically accession to the institutions of the international community, the credit and aid binomial has underlined the logic of

	African development. ... Concerning the other element of the binomial – aid – we can also note the reduction of private aid and the upper limit of public aid, which is below the target set in the 1970s (para. 3).
	The Declaration further points to the global community's commitment to enhance resource flows to Africa, by improving aid .... It is now important to translate these commitments into reality (para. 46).
	The new long-term vision will require massive, heavy investment to bridge existing gaps. The challenge ahead for Africa is to be able to raise the required funding under the best conditions possible.
	We therefore call on our development partners to assist us in this endeavour (para. 66).
	We also recognize that, if infrastructure is to improve in Africa, private foreign finance is essential to complement the two major funding methods, namely credit and aid (para. 100).
74.	

75.	Work with the African Development Bank and other development finance institutions on the continent to mobilize sustainable financing, especially through multilateral processes, institutions and donor governments, with a view to securing grant and concessional finance to mitigate medium-term risks (para. 103).
76.	To achieve the estimated 7 per cent annual growth rate needed to meet the IDGs – particularly, the goal of reducing by half the proportion of Africans living in poverty by the year 2015 – Africa needs to fill an annual resource gap of 12 per cent of its GDP, or US \$64 billion. This will require increased domestic savings, as well as improvements in the public revenue collection systems. However, the bulk of the needed resources will have to be obtained from outside the continent. The *New Partnership for Africa's Development* focuses on debt reduction and overseas development assistance (ODA) as complementary external resources required in the short to medium term, and addresses private capital flows as a longer-term concern (para. 144).

77.	... requesting the developed countries to pledge their Treasury Bills to finance the Plan. In so doing, they would not directly commit their liquid assets. ... We suggest the establishment of Special Drawing Rights for Africa (para. 145). The *New Partnership for Africa's Development* seeks increased ODA flows in the medium term, as well as reform of the ODA delivery system, to ensure that flows are more effectively utilised by recipient African countries (para. 148).
78.	The *New Partnership for Africa's Development* will establish a forum of African countries so as to develop a common African position on ODA reform, and to engage with the Development Assistance Committee (DAC) of the OECD and other donors in developing a charter underpinning the development partnership. This charter will: • Identify the Economic Governance Initiative as a prerequisite for enhancing the capacity of African countries to utilize increased ODA

flows, and will propose a complementary, independent assessment mechanism for monitoring donor performance (para. 148);

- Constitute an ODA forum for developing a common African position on ODA reform, as a counterpart to the OECD/DAC structure;
- Engage, through the ODA forum, with donor agencies to establish a charter for the development partnership, which would embody the principles outlined above; Establish an independent mechanism for assessing donor and recipient country performance (para. 149).

79.	Equally important, however, especially in the short to medium term, is the need for additional ODA .... Additional ODA is required to enable least developed countries to achieve the IDGs, especially in the areas of primary education, health, and poverty eradication (para. 152).
80.	A critical dimension of Africans taking responsibility for the continent's destiny is the need to negotiate a new relationship with their development partners. The manner in which development assistance is delivered in

	itself creates serious problems for developing countries. The need to negotiate with, and account separately to, donors supporting the same sector of programme is both cumbersome and inefficient. Also, the tying of development assistance generates further inefficiencies. The appeal is for a new relationship that takes the country programmes as a point of departure. The new relationship should set out mutually agreed performance targets and standards for both donor and recipient. Many cases clearly show that the failure of projects is not caused only by poor performance of recipients, but also by bad advice given by donors (para. 183).
81.	To reverse the decline in ODA flows to Africa and to meet the target level of ODA flows equivalent to 0.7 per cent of each developed country's gross national product (GNP) within an agreed period (para. 185).

82.			Increased aid flows will be used to complement funds released by debt reduction for accelerating the fight against poverty (para. 185).
	STRUCTURAL ADJUSTMENT PROGRAMMES		
83.		The structural adjustment programmes of the 1980s provided only a partial solution. They promoted reforms that tended to remove serious price distortions, but gave inadequate attention to the provision of social services. Consequently, only a few countries managed to achieve sustainable higher growth under these programmes (para. 24).	
	POLITICAL DOMESTIC REFORMS		
84.		Democracy and state legitimacy have been redefined to include accountable government, a culture of human rights and popular participation as central elements (para. 43).	

85.	Across the continent, democracy is spreading, backed by the African Union (AU), which has shown a new resolve to deal with conflicts and censure deviation from the norm (para. 45).
86.	To achieve these objectives, African leaders will take joint responsibility for the following: • Strengthening mechanisms for conflict prevention, management and resolution at the subregional and continental levels, and to ensure that these mechanisms are used to restore and maintain peace; • Promoting and protecting democracy and human rights in their respective countries and regions, by developing clear standards of accountability, transparency and participatory governance at the national and subnational levels (para. 49).
87.	Efforts to build Africa's capacity to manage all aspects of conflict must focus on the means necessary to strengthen existing regional and sub-regional institutions, especially in four key areas: Prevention, management and resolution of conflict; Peacemaking, peacekeeping and peace enforcement; Post-conflict reconciliation, rehabilitation and reconstruction; [and] Combating the illicit proliferation of small arms, light weapons and landmines (para. 74).

		At the Lusaka Summit, the AU decided to take drastic measures in reviving the organs responsible for conflict prevention and resolution (para. 78).	
88.	The leadership of the *New Partnership for Africa's Development* will consider, within six months of its establishment, setting out detailed and costed measures required in each of the four areas above (para. 74). The exercise will also include the actions required of partners, and the nature and sources of financing such activities (para. 75).		
89.			
90.	It is generally acknowledged that development is impossible in the absence of true democracy, respect for human rights, peace and good governance. With the *New Partnership for Africa's Development,* Africa undertakes to respect the global standards of democracy, the core components of which include political pluralism, allowing for the existence of several political parties and workers'		

unions, and fair, open and democratic elections periodically organized to enable people to choose their leaders freely (para. 79).

Within six months of its institution-alization, the leadership of the *New Partnership for Africa's Development* will identify recommendations on appropriate diagnostic and assessment tools, in support of compliance with the shared goals of good governance, as well as identify institutional weaknesses and seek resources and expertise for addressing these weaknesses (para. 82).

91. The Heads of State Forum on the *New Partnership for Africa's Development* will serve as a mechanism through which the leadership of the *New Partnership for Africa's Development* will periodically monitor and assess the progress made by African countries in meeting their commitment towards achieving good governance and social reforms.

The Forum will also provide a platform for countries to share experiences with a view to fostering good governance and democratic practices (para. 85).		
92.		A basic principle of the Capital Flows Initiative is that improved governance is a necessary requirement for increased capital flows, so that participation in the Economic and Political Governance Initiatives is a prerequisite for participation in the Capital Flows Initiative (para. 144).
93.		To counter Africa's negative image through conflict resolution and marketing [and thus promote African exports] (para. 165).
94.		The African leaders envisage the ... responsibili[ty] and obliga[tion] of the developed countries and multilateral institutions ... to materially support mechanisms for and processes of conflict prevention, management and resolution in Africa, as well as peacekeeping initiatives (para. 185).

INDEX